Still There!

Dave Burnley

Still There!

Once again, as in Part One this tribute is...

To all devoted football fans anywhere in the world, but particularly to those supporters whose loyalty remains strong when their team becomes weak, for to stand the test of time is to stand the test of faith.

And especially for Clarette, a wonderful daughter, named in honour of the Clarets.

Keep The Faith!

Dave Burnley

Remember This!

Choosing to support your football team is like adopting a child. You love, cherish and invest in it as part of your extended family. When hard times hit, you feel their pain, but when success is achieved your pride knows no bounds.

This book is written for all the fans under the age of 50 who will remember it, and all the fans over the age of 50 who now might just need reminding of it!

Footballing 'Brothers In Arms'

Photo by Adrian Ashworth

Myself and 'Tricky' Trev Slack in exuberant celebratory mode after another crucial win at 'The Turf'.

I'm indebted to many Burnley fans who over the last fifty years have helped me with obtaining matchday tickets, transportation to games, and accommodation when stranded, but one man more than any other has always gone that extra mile on my behalf.

Dedicated to Trevor Slack. A loyal supporter, true friend, drinking partner, chauffeur, loan provider and much much more, now spanning six decades and counting.

Cheers pal.

Missed Part One 'GOT TO BE THERE!' 1964-1987

I am pleased to announce due to demand an additional reprint has been produced for the book that will never age.

For signed copies with a message of your choice please email the author with your request at dburnleyextreme@gmail.com to place an order. Prices are £10 per book or £22 for both paperback additions plus £3 per book P&P to mainland Britain & £5 overseas.

C Dave Burnley 2017

Published by Ralphyburl Publishing

ISBN 978-0-9996810-0-8 (Paperback)

A catalogue record for this book is available from the British Library.

Cover photo: Premier League promotion on home 'Turf'. Ecstatic Burnley fans including the author (circled) invade the pitch after the 2-0 defeat of Wigan Athletic April 21st, 2014.

Cover prepared by Clare Brayshaw

Prepared and printed by:

York Publishing Services Ltd
64 Hallfield Road
Layerthorpe
York YO31 7ZQ
Tel: 01904 431213

Website: www.yps-publishing.co.uk

Contents

Acknowledgements

First and foremost, to the major sponsors of this second edition whose backing has made this publication possible. So, a big thank you to:

JOHN BANASZKIEWICZ	London
MIKE GARLICK	Hertfordshire
ALASTAIR CAMPBELL	London
MARK SUTCLIFFE	Kowloon, Hong Kong
SSGT. LIAM WALSH	Kathmandu, Nepal
TREVOR SLACK	Heald Green, Stockport, Gt. Man.
NIGEL STANDIGE	Burnley, Lancs.
MARK GRIFFITHS	Winsford, Cheshire
BRIAN SPEAK	Maidstone, Kent
GRAHAM & GINA EXTON	Duddon, Cheshire
IAN & MRS A HOLDSWORTH	Burnley, Lancs
DR. STEPHEN HODGSON	Chorley, Lancs
DEREK WILSON	–
PETE TONER	Fulwood, Preston, Lancs.
DR. PHIL RATCLIFFE	Highfield, Southampton, Hants
JOHN SMITH	Haslingden, Accrington, Lancs.
KEITH RILEY	Adswood, Stockport, Gt. Man.

BRYAN WYLD	Nantwich, Cheshire
DERMOTT O'NEILL	London
ANDREW & DAVID SMITH	Waterfoot, Rawtenstall, Lancs.

And of course, all the other contributors who have supported this project.

Thanks also to Sarah Bonam and Anne Kinnaird at 'Letting in the light' for their computer technology input and help with social media, and Val Bargewell for her valuable production assistance.

The Bombay Sapphire Spirits company whose vapour infused London Dry Gin has helped to ease the efforts of writer's block on many a long night.

And of course, last but certainly not least, once again, Reggie Bradshaw, for helping me determine my chosen team.

Foreword

'J.B.' and current manager Sean Dyche face the cameras.

I am genuinely honoured to write this foreword for the latest edition of Dave's history of following Burnley Football Club.

Every team has its extreme fans or fanatical supporters; Dave is the epitome of that for our club, known to one and all from top to bottom.

He never misses a match and is a fantastic ambassador for our club. Well known for his predictions and post-match analysis through his newspaper column.

I first met Dave in Singapore in July 2010. At the time I was trying to promote Burnley overseas, organising fixtures against local teams in the Asian Challenge Cup that I had sponsored by my company.

Intermittently, I kept bumping into this character with a strange haircut who wasn't letting the 95 degree heat stop him shouting on the team at every opportunity.

After our final game in the Jalan Besar stadium I asked the travelling supporters to come for a drink with the squad at the exclusive Swisshôtel. It was there that I got to know him properly and heard his crazy tale of getting to Singapore via Bombay, India where he slept overnight in a waiting room before making his base in Malaysia to save on extortionate beer prices in the city.

Since then we have become great friends, and we should be grateful that his devotion to the club has never wavered. This book being a permanent reminder of that astonishing commitment. Well done Dave, we salute you.

John Banaszkiewicz
Formerly Burnley co-chairman and now club director.
August 2017.

My forty year attendance milestone reached 2014

The build up to 40 years without missing any competitive fixture supporting Burnley F.C. anywhere in the world. As always, the event is commemorated by donning my 'thirty three piece' suit (circa 1968) with accompanying claret beret to the very first away game after the date of that last match not attended at St. James's Park, Newcastle on Wednesday April 10th 1974.

Hull City 2010.

Notts Forest 2011.

Doncaster Rovers 2012   *Blackpool 2013*

Blackpool 2014.

My forty year attendance milestone reached 2014.

Still There! 1987-2017

After attending all Burnley F.C. matches throughout each of the four divisions for the full duration of this second book I gained a comprehensive insight into the dramatic wholesale transformations that would revolutionize English football irrespective of which team you supported.

It's fair to say that following your chosen club from this bygone era to the present day has seen a transfiguration that no one could have envisaged, and the match day experience would never be the same again.

But this book is not just about going to the game. Its about getting there and back with everything in between.

Introduction

Outside Everton F.C. 15th April 2017 with 'Speedo Mick' Cullen charity fundraiser in swimming trunks and goggles.

As a written narrative that naturally progresses from Part One, my quite logical, but admittedly unusual running order begins at Chapter 21 to ensure a smooth continuity from the first book to the second. The entries running in chronological order picking up from where part one finished on Saturday May 9th 1987 right up until the present year 2017 which also happens to commemorate thirty years since that future defining 'Orient game'.

What hasn't changed is my introductory abridgement to each chapter comprising a condensed essence of the tales to follow, which will hopefully sufficiently inform the reader of what to expect from thereupon in.

Besides this, there are two constants that will become recurring themes.

As well as updating the lives of the primary characters from the first book, with the passage of time naturally a raft of new personalities have emerged in the storylines.

Finally, it is a sad fact of our existence that we are all mere mortals on this earth, each awaiting that unknown date that will determine our ultimate fate. That stark reality is further compounded when some fellow human beings, fail even to reach what should be a standard life expectancy of three score years and ten.

This is why my grey shaded 'In Memoriam' boxes located at the end of a number of relevant chapters which featured in my initial memoirs, continue to be my personal tribute to the memory of the people I have known and been associated with in this volume, the previous one, or indeed both, for which I make absolutely no apologies.

Accordingly, I cannot think of a more fittingly appropriate way to open Part Two than presenting my own eulogy to the player who scored that winning goal on the very day Part One ended – Mr Ian Britton.

In Memoriam

IAN BRITTON 1954-2016
The man who saved me from jail, triumphantly hoisted aloft after
the 'Orient' game.
Photograph courtesy of Burnley Football Club.

I was setting off for a weekend away in Eastbourne ahead of
Burnley's crucial championship match at Brighton & Hove
Albion when my mobile phone rang.

'Tricky' Trev's name immediately flashed up on the screen, which was unusual in itself as he rarely phoned from work on the building site.

However, it was no ordinary day of the calendar, but Friday April 1st 2016 or 'All Fools Day' to give its more formal title. Probably the most light-hearted date of the year when all sorts of customary pranks, japes and hoaxes are made to catch out the unprepared.

The difference being, I was readied for any such practical joke as having suffered previously well documented annual exchanges throughout the years with my mother it had put me on my guard each time it came around.

With that in mind, and knowing 'Tricky' to be partial to winding folk up I pressed the accept icon to engage him, suitably poised to call his bluff.

That notion disintegrated within seconds as Trev informed me of some grave news in a deadly serious tone.

"Hi mate, have you heard?"

Without giving me time to reply Trev carried on his announcement,

"Ian Britton died yesterday".

This statement stopped me in my tracks and I took a short pause to compose myself with a sharp intake of breath, before instinctively sighing down my 'moby'

"Oh no! Nooooo! That really is so sad Trev". After a short chat I thanked him for letting me know before sheltering in a shop doorway to fully take in the gravity of the tragic news.

My eyes welled up, but I managed to stop an actual tear trickling down my cheeks, although there would have been absolutely nothing wrong with that if I hadn't. I carried on walking, but considerably slower as my mind tried to take it all in.

Ian was initially diagnosed with prostate cancer in 2013, the disease was found to have progressed to his bones, and he died after a spell at Pendleside Hospice with his friends and family at his side. He was only 61 years old.

Immediately all those memories of the 'Orient Game' flashed through my head.

For it was Ian Britton, just five feet, five inches tall and weighing less than ten stone wet through, who achieved sainthood amongst Burnley fans. When at thirteen minutes past four o' clock, in the forty eighth minute of the delayed kick-off on Saturday May 9th 1987 he headed in a cross from the other hero of the day, and scorer of the first goal Neil Grewcock, to make it 2-1 at the final whistle.

Even with a win, other results had to go our way, and of course now we know they did with Lincoln City the unfortunate club slipping through the trap door to the Conference League after their defeat to Swansea.

But what has this got to do with the sub-title 'the man who saved me from jail' you may well ask?

Well, readers of Part One of my autobiography 'Got To Be There!' will know the answer to that question. The last chapter of which is dramatically, but totally aptly named 'The Apocalypse Cometh?'.

My intent was to force a postponement of the game if it was going against us by securing myself to the goalpost with a heavy duty bicycle lock that was wrapped around my jeans like a belt.

It may or may not have had the desired effect, but one thing is for sure I would have certainly been banged up for attempting to disrupt a football match. Because of one man it thankfully didn't come to that.

Of course it goes without saying that if any member, past or present employee of the Lancashire constabulary are reading this I will completely retract this statement of intent and admit to being the complete fantasist that I am!

But all joking apart I was delighted to have been introduced to the wee man with a big heart who never dined out on his new found status as a demi-god.

Ian much preferred to be seen as one of the boys. Although still turning out to play in celebrity matches until his illness, and retaining links with many past and present professional and amateur footballers, he was equally at home partaking of a few pints with friends down at his local pubs.

One such friend was a devout Burnley fan who I affectionately term 'Plain John Smith' solely because of his common combination of Christian and surname. Smithy's treatment towards his pal 'Britts' as he generally termed him was far from plain however. Offering not just regular companionship throughout the full period of him being ill, but travelling the length and breadth of the British Isles to accompany him on business, medical and social trips, and even being by his side at his passing.

It was Smithy who first introduced me to this ebullient character who always seemed to have a broad smile on his face. Although I was only a passing acquaintance by comparison Ian treated me in the same way as his best pals for which I respect him even more.

His career began with Chelsea in 1972 where he played more than 250 games for the Blues. He returned to his home town to join Dundee United in 1982, then had a spell at Abroath before joining Blackpool in 1983 and then Burnley in 1986.

Ian leaves his wife Eileen and four children.

R.I.P. 'little man'. You meant so much to so many.

21 This is the Modern World

Still game for a laugh! My irrespressible ma, now 87 years young.

As a lot can happen in thirty years, allow me to present
you with a brief résumé of my frequently dysfunctional
home life that will help to set the scene for the content
of the following twenty six chapters.

How's the family ...?

Okay, since you asked, I'll start with myself. On Friday October 13th 2017 I will have celebrated being a resident of planet earth for sixty four years.

I know everyone asks the same question, but really – "Where did all those years go?"

Well, up to press fifty three of them have been spent avidly following the fortunes of Burnley Football Club, the last forty three of which having seen me attend any and every category of competitive first team game both home and away throughout Britain and abroad.

Indeed, it remains a fact that there is just the one well documented match that I didn't travel to in the past forty eight years. It is a statistic that has gained me the title of 'extreme supporter' acquired from numerous quoted sources, amongst several less polite descriptions. Yet I embrace them all, as each has probably some merit attached to it given some of the lengths I have had to go in order to devoutly attend all fixtures involving my club.

But enough of the stats., what about my personal life in relation to what is now over three decades ago.

Yes, you've guessed it, I'm still living at the same humble council house that we first occupied in 1962. A semi-detached residence set right alongside the large pool which is home to a variety of wildfowl but predominantly Canadian geese, located in the picturesque village of Madeley, near Newcastle-Under-Lyme, Staffordshire.

Since 1987, although I have had a number of girlfriends including the mother of my daughter Clarette of course, my status of having never been married or even engaged has been effortlessly retained.

That could just have something to do with the pledge I made to a national newspaper in 1974 stating that I wouldn't tie the knot until Burnley won the title in the top tier of English football.

A safe bet you may think. Well, we came up with Leicester City in 2014 and just look what happened to them two seasons later.

Even so, before any of my relationships reach the serious stage I'm always completely up front about my consistent, chosen lifestyle as a football fanatic, regular drinker and a seasoned traveller.

That way the one accusation they cannot level at me when we do part is 'You've changed!'

The other two human occupants of the premises are my brother Shaun who hit the big Six-O back in April 2015 and my elderly mother Herta Maria who is now an eighty seven year old as of New Years Day 2017.

My father Percy died in 2002, within a week of his seventy eighth birthday.

Times are hard for Britain's low earners, in fact I would say given the cost of living today, combined with the current raft of austerity costs implemented, it probably constitutes the hardest of economic times since the early 1980's under dictatorial Thatcher rule.

Back then my career stock turned turtle, plummeting from being a respected invoice clerk to a downtrodden dustbinman all within a few short months. That rich and poor divide continuing to this day as due to the progressive ill health of my mother I have now volunteered to take on the role of her chief carer. The non-negotiable alternative would be to admit her to a residential home which understandably she is completely and utterly against, commenting somewhat truthfully that,

"Once you go in there you never come out!"

Currently immobile she now relies on all the family to help her with everyday chores from cooking to cleaning, and even washing herself.

Shaun meanwhile continues in his physically demanding role of a labourer on the production line of a pie-making factory. I too had a Christmas stint there when my night shift was of eight hours duration as opposed to my brother's laborious, mind numbing twelve hour day, on a four on, four off continental shift basis.

So for the moment my continuous task of taking on a myriad of occupations amounting to literally scores of short term contracts over the years to simply fund, what seems the ever escalating cost of following a football team wherever they perform has come to an abrupt halt, although thankfully that hasn't affected my 100% attendance record. My eldest sister Susan is also now 60 and retains part-time employment as a volunteer advisor for 'disability solutions' bodies.

The runt of the litter is youngest sister Rosemarie who attained her personal milestone of fifty years of age in 2013.

Rosie, it would be fair to say, has comfortably surpassed us all in career progression and is currently a team manager for an organisation assisting young people with rehabilitation for their drug and alcohol problems. As such she effortlessly maintains the designated title I bestowed upon her as the 'black sheep of the family'.

Both these sisters are parents, each having three grown up children. I always make sure I get on extra well with my siblings as you just never know when you might need a kidney donated.

Then there's my mum.

As stated my mother isn't the active 57 year old that she was at the closure of Part One in 1987. In fact, with the passage of time she has found it very hard to even get around the house at all these days as arthritic problems affect her mobility acutely as do a series of mini-strokes.

The turning point on this issue coming when she fell out of her upstairs bed late one morning while Shaun and I were at work. There she lay for four hours, unable to move because of her resultant injuries, until her cries for help were heard by our next door neighbour's son Simon. He managed to gain access to the house and after numerous attempts, succeeded in hoisting her considerable bulk onto the bed.

After that incident we both decided to relocate her to the ground floor lounge in a bed complete with pressure pads and nearby panic alarms to monitor her movement and provide a form of emergency communication. Besides these measures, a series of support rails are now fitted to the walls in each room to help her get around, as well as a metal walking frame which she amusingly terms 'the iron bar'.

All five kittens from the Eighties household with their simplistic names based upon either the colour or pattern of their fur have of course passed onto the great cat basket in the sky.

In their place, a much more low maintenance pet had emerged. It was a chirpy budgerigar which she just called …you've got it…..Joey!

This bird must have had the most congested cage in the area. Besides its standard requirements of a water tube and four rounded horizontally placed wooden supports to perch upon, there were additional accoutrements of an abrasive slate to file down its beak, two feeding trays, a swing to play on, plastic balls, figures to prod, bells to chime, ladders to climb and an assortment of colourfully framed mirrors to preen itself in. A life size, intermittently cheeping plastic budgie being added for company.

Unfortunately that was not its only companion from the bird world, as inexplicably my ma thought that it would make Joey feel even more at home if she installed a cuckoo clock!

This she had done, affixing it directly above her own bed nearby. Predictably after the passing of each sixty minute period the fearsome sounding wooden version flashes out on its extended rod, through its double doors, loudly cuckooing to signal the start of each new hour.

Instead of my mother's preconceived desired effect of the two exchanging tweets, her feathered friend beats its wings furiously, perhaps fearing a predatory strike. And once the clock struck midnight, the poor thing went into budgerigar meltdown under its protective night blanket set over the cage, probably wishing to itself that it had stayed in Australia where it originated.

I would guess that in the majority of households which have a fledgling bird as a pet, a small towel or the like would be placed over its cage as an indicator that it was time to rest up, yet their sleeping habits remain a complete mystery.

Just how this species achieves any kind of recuperation constantly standing on legs the width of pipe cleaners with no cosy nest to curl up into, I don't know. Add to that Joey had to contend with an ear-splitting reveille on the hour, every hour throughout the night which must have left his nerves shot to bits!

Joey drops off his perch....

This could have been the case one early Monday morning in late November 2014. That day I was about to perform the ceremonial unveiling of the bird as usual in the living room where my mum now permanently resides. But there wasn't the customary apprehension generally denoted by flapping feathers and a nervy series of chirps, in fact there was no noise at all.

As the cover was pulled back the reason it was so silent was there for all to see.

Joey had fell off his perch for the very last time and lay rigid on the floor of his restrictive residence, stone cold dead.

Now I had to break the news to my already awakened and

alert mother who was looking to greet her pet with her usual extravagantly cheery 'Good morning' welcome.

"Hello…Joey, Joey Joey," formed her opening line, followed by a dining request.

"You want some breakfast Joey? Yes you do", she answered for it in her well-practiced manner.

I had to quickly intervene, even though I knew she would take it badly.

I tried to put Joey's demise as subtly as I could, given the circumstances, because I knew she doted on the bird and would freak out.

"Joey won't be having any more breakfasts mother".

I paused for a moment so she could gather herself then added, "He's dead."

"Stop it David, stop it!" she fired back, as an uneasy frown spread across her forehead.

"Don't you ever say that again!"

Up until then I had been as sensitive as I could about the poor creature's passing, but now indignation set in at the thought that I would ever joke about something that I realised meant so much to her.

"Don't be chupitch (stupid), it must still be sleeping" added my mother, "He's not dead. He can't be!"

Suitably annoyed about her doubting my credibility of the situation I then found myself slipping into 'Monty Python' mode partly replicating their 'Dead Parrot' sketch.

"Well he's not resting!" I replied sarcastically, picking up the poor creatures lifeless body before waving it slowly to and fro in order to categorically confirm its sad end.

I carried on pushing the point in my, by now irreversible comic mode.

"No mother, I'm sorry, but it's definitely died. He's deceased I tell ya, brown bread, popped it's clogs, expired – dead! This is now an ex-budgie!"

Of course my Pythonesque satirical references were totally lost on my mother and all it seemed to do was to trigger a spontaneous outpouring of grief normally reserved for the passing of a North Korean leader.

There was uncontrollable wailing, considerable gnashing of false teeth with a fair degree of gratuitous hair pulling as the distressing reality of losing a loved one set in.

Feeling for her, I gave mum a minute to grieve before offering to dispose of its tiny body by burying the corpse in our back garden. That only served to agitate things even more so I left the living room and went into the kitchen to make her a soothing cup of tea while she got over the loss, returning Joey to the bottom of his cage for the time being.

But on re-entering the front room with a brew, I was mortified to see her clasping both hands over the prostrate carcass of the budgerigar in prayer-like fashion from the airmchair. She had taken it from the cage and placed it on the tiled hearth in front of the fireplace.

Worried that she may spread germs through handling the bird I insisted on taking it away, only for mum to place her substantial frame between me and the pet preventing me from doing so, whilst at the same time accusing me of its death.

"You've killed it! He was O.K. last night, you've poisoned it you swine!"

I just stood there aghast. Although I knew that this passing the blame was her form of a coping mechanism, never before had I been castigated as a 'budgie murderer'.

Still crying over – emotionally I decided it might be best to compromise, maybe by fetching a shoe box lid and placing the bird within. And there it lay, in state like a latter day Lenin or Mao Zedong until her good neighbour Margaret Salmon paid her a visit later that afternoon to perform a formal burial under my mum's front garden bench as requested.

Herta continued to mourn Joey's abrupt end over the next few days, but within a month we welcomed a new resident as a larger cage was drafted in to accommodate a particularly aggressive crested cockatiel that my mother claimed could talk. However, in real life, as soon as its cage cover came off it just seemed to persistently let out a shrill series of whistles.

After being encouraged to perhaps be a little more imaginative when naming her new acquisition, a short pause preceded the title she was going to bestow upon it.

"Jethro! Dat's what I'll call him", already presuming that it was of the male gender, although in truth she didn't have a clue.

"Well at least that's a bit more original mother. Where did you get that name from then?", I wondered.

It transpired that it was a derivation of her personal genial taxi driver and fellow villager Geoff Lafford

My Ma's new bird on the block.
The irascible 'Jethro' her replacement for
'Joey' who tragically fell off his perch.

who transports both my mother and sister Susan to the town of Newcastle-Under-Lyme every Wednesday to do the weekly shop.

While it may not be the same as having a road or building named after you, in my mum's eyes there could be no higher honour!

My dad Percy ...

As earlier mentioned, my father Percy passed away on the 18th November 2002, aged 78.

In his later years he had suffered with his health succumbing to debilitating chest problems symptomatic of two contributory lifestyle factors.

Dad smoked a packet of twenty cigarettes a day for the majority of his adult years, only completely abstaining in his late sixties on doctor's advice.

Additionally a near on thirty year stint of employment at our local brickworks where he worked a rotating three shift system must have impacted on his overall wellbeing. There, his job was to fire the clay tiles through an extremely hot kiln oven for hardening. Fire brick dust permeating the surrounding air where he stood, with protecting face masks not being a mandatory requirement for the task in those days. The accumulative effect of regular exposure to inhaling such minute particles almost certainly damaged his lung capacity, thus later necessitating the use of an oxygen tank apparatus, ironically in conjunction with a breathing mask.

I was upstairs in my room when a piercing scream from my mother sent me hurrying to the front lounge where my father lay slumped in his armchair by the coal fuelled fireplace.

"David, David, help-help!" she cried.

After finding no sign of a pulse I loosened his shirt before lifting him to the floor which was directly in front of the roaring fire that was always topped up with logs to maximise the heat. I also had to phone for an ambulance as my mum was sobbing and shouting hysterically.

As I attempted the kiss of life a truly weird dialogue was blasting out from the television screen, which because of his deafness, he insisted having on full volume.

For whatever reason my dad liked to watch those American cartoon characters 'The Simpsons' around tea time. After having no response to my mouth to mouth resuscitation I proceeded to administer cardiopulmonary resuscitation, more commonly known by its abridged initials of C.P.R.

Myself, and my brother Shaun had moved my dad's bed downstairs, as due to his illness he found stairs too difficult to ascend. It meant that because of the restricted space in our already small, cluttered living room I could only lower his torso upon to a small area between the long coffee table and the blazing flames of the fireplace.

Crossing my hand, one on top of the other, I applied the required vigorous pressure to his breast bone at short sharp intervals.

As I frantically carried out the procedure sweat dripped down my face due to the close proximity of what now felt like an inferno just one yard in front of me.

It didn't matter, I knew I had to try everything until help arrived and all the time the relentless din of an American drawl supplied by the animated characters loudly resonated in the background from the TV that I simply had no time to turn down because of the critical life-threatening circumstances my dad was in. Then after around two minutes into my course of action with my mother still crying relentlessly, an even louder shriek jumped out of the television which up until now I had made myself oblivious to. But this was far more poignant, yet totally bizarre.

Simultaneously, it seemed that a similar scenario was being re-enacted from this particular episode of the Simpsons.

"I think he's dying Homer!" shouted one of the cartoon cast.

"Homer! Homer! He's dying. What shall we do?" asked another.

"Try .C.P.R", advised Homer.

I couldn't believe my ears. Here I was furiously pumping my father's chest for dear life and they were conducting a comparable manoeuvre in their own cartoon land.

After ten minutes without any response, the paramedics came through the door. As I cast an inquisitive first glance towards the still blaring television, it pictured its star personality Homer Simpson standing over a laid out body with his friends, one of which yelled out,

"Homer! He's dead. He's dead Homer!"

The medics attached electrodes to my dad's chest in a last ditch attempt to jump start his heart. Three times they tried before stretchering him off to the waiting ambulance, but it was too late.

Just like Homer's friend on the box, my dad had died too.

Unlikely as it may seem that uncanny incident did actually take place. With fantasy and fiction running in tandem with a much harsher reality, I ask you, what are the chances of that happening?

In Memoriam

I'd be lying if I said that my father and I always saw eye to eye. We simply didn't. In fact my devotion to the Burnley cause was more likely to see us go toe to toe given the many sacrifices I had to make.

His tough upbringing amongst siblings that reached double figures moulding the way, he thought, everyone should live their life.

Nevertheless, he did bring me into this world and without him I wouldn't be writing this book. So thanks, and R.I.P. dad.

Clarette...

My only daughter Clarette is now 28 years of age, and after five tough expensive years both at the University of Birmingham and the more local Keele University, she finally passed all her teaching exams securing a full time post at a comprehensive school just six miles from our village location. Here by choice Clarette educated senior pupils in English Language and English Literature.

That busy schedule also included additional part-time work greatly restricting attendance at Burnley games to just the odd few a season.

Then in August 2014 after being disillusioned with the overbearingly heavy workload now expected from the majority in the teaching profession which included marking homework regularly up until midnight, and that after dealing with the many detentions she was forced to dish out for disciplinary procedures which all had to be supervised by herself after lessons, Clarette decided to begin a new life in Dubai.

Having been successful in the final round of interviews that were held in London for the prestigious posting to the United Arab Emirates where she taught the same subjects at a new-build education establishment of 4,000 plus pupils, Clarette seemed blissfully happy.

Wishing her well in her exciting venture, I gave her my blessing, encouraging her to try and stick it out until at least 2022. That of course was nothing to do with the possibility that I might need accommodation for the world cup tournament designated to take place in neighbouring Quatar that particular year.

That is if indeed this country remains the unlikely chosen host nation. Because besides players and fans having to deal with the oppressively hot temperatures, the independency still has to come through an on-going inquiry into bribery and corruption accusations that have been levelled at the controversial bidding process for the rights to hosting the tournament.

Whatever the outcome her Middle East residence will not now be my staging post as Clarette returned to work in England during January 2016 at our local High School in the village citing the extortionately high cost of living over there as the main reason to come back.

Although my daughter has now blossomed into a self-assured, confident woman that certainly wasn't always the case.

As a Primary School pupil I was informed by the dinner-time supervisor that she would persistently refuse to eat her meals within the constantly noisy environment of the food hall, and became very withdrawn when present in a crowded playground situation. Additionally my contact added that if anything accidentally brushed her hair or face Clarette would go into a panic attack.

Naturally, like any father I was perturbed to hear of these timid behavioural traits, so one day I asked her if they had been brought about because she was living at her mother's house and missing me.

Clarette turned all emotional as if confirming my suspicions before blurting out a protracted statement after taking a large deep breath.

"No dad, it goes back to when you used to take me to those loud karaoke pubs, and when that herd of mad cows surrounded us in the corner of the field when we went on one of your adventure picnics. As well as when you made that home-made revolving mobile from all those cut out shapes and stuck it on the ceiling above where I was sleeping, and it fell off landing right on my head in the middle of the night scaring me to death! It's made me feel nervous and worried in certain situations."

The poor deluded little girl. That is all part of growing up as every parent knows.

The birds and the bees...

There comes a time in life, when as the old idiom goes "A man's gotta do, what a man's gotta do", and follow the dictates of his conscience, no matter how difficult the situation, or in this case how sensitive the subject.

You know how it is when you're a parent striving to guide and protect your child from all the trials and tribulations of growing up. There's the fundamental stuff like getting them to eat a healthy diet, always being compromised by the far more appetizing attraction of getting stuck into a calorific combination of sweets, chocolate, crisps and ice cream. Most kids are the same, as naturally their junior taste buds are far more appreciative of confectionery goods than savoury offerings. Given a choice of a Cadbury's creme egg or a boiled sprout you would have no takers for the latter in the under five's category for sure.

That of course is why, as guardians of their welfare we sometimes have to tell a few 'white lies' to maintain good health. Such as the well-practiced claim that once they hear the sound of those loud rhythmic chimes emanating from the ice cream van it means they've sold out all their stock. Or insisting that the more vegetables they consume the more presents Santa Claus will leave them at Christmas are allowable falsifications given that they are designed to safeguard their well being into adulthood when a more measured individual decision can be made.

But probably the first real test of trust between parent and child takes place when they are summoned for their immunization programme.

There's the 5-in-1 vaccine protecting against such nasties as diphtheria, tetanus, whooping cough, polio and influenza dispensed at eight, twelve and sixteen weeks accordingly. Now as frightening as they may be to your tot with floods of tears accompanying the procedure, by the next day it just feels like a bad dream with little or no recollection of the terrifying episode. Yet when they are required to take their 4-in-1 pre-school booster at around three years and four months of age, not only has the infant's awareness grown, so has its power of memory!

Although Clarette's mother had taken her for the preliminary jabs it was deemed my duty to convey her to the secondary innoculations. This I did with no hesitation, but with a serious amount of trepidation given my daughter's disposition.

It is fair to say that Clarette's best friend was her dummy teat right up to five years old. It did what its American alternative name suggested and pacified the child.

Clarette was very conscious of visiting such places and as I entered our local village hall centre for our appointment I was very mindful of her reaction.

I tried my absolute best reassurance technique by informing her that although it might hurt a little, the pain would be worth it to prevent any illnesses in the future.

She sucked harder and more hurriedly on her plastic mouth insert as her arms wrapped around my head gripping me ever more tightly. Her big brown eyes gazing into mine almost pleading for salvation from the forthcoming ordeal. Then came the inevitable waterworks and the look of sheer fear that a father never forgets.

Even after my comforting words Clarette's last tortured look in my direction as the nurse produced what to a child resembled a terminal weapon had 'traitor' written all over it. Then the syringe was applied amid disturbing shrieks of horror, and that was just me!

Many hugs, kisses and special treats later Clarette's forgiving temperament was renewed cementing our father and daughter bond stronger than ever.

Of course children soon grow up, and ever more quickly it would seem. As they approach adolescence they begin to become increasingly more aware of the opposite gender around about the time that quantum leap is made from junior to senior school.

Of course nowadays sex education is part and parcel of most scholastic establishments as an important element of the curriculum, yet it didn't stop me reminiscing back to my rudimentary indoctrination of the subject that took place in just one Biology lesson back in the 1960s.

Then, an embarrassed teacher would quickly flick through an anatomical slide show pointing a stick at both male and female reproductive organs amidst awkward pauses and giggling fits from the assembled class of lads that would ascend into raucous laugh out loud hilarity and juvenile sexual innuendo. The essential communiqué being completely lost in a hurried translation.

So like any accountable parent I decided that it was my resolute duty to inform my only child Clarette about the 'Birds and the bees'.

I, as most lads our age did, found our natural instincts through a combination of chat and quick fumbles behind the bike sheds, or whatever convenient shelter was available whenever we met a fanciable girl.

However such ill-thought liaisons are not without risk particularly to the female as one thing can lead to another, and before you know it, well in nine months anyway, you're a grandad!

It's every dad's fear, but just at what age would a responsible parent take their child to one side for that little chat. Not until they are teenagers surely?

But no, I decided that the step up to secondary school was just about the right watershed moment to inform her of this essential carnal knowledge.

I chose my execution of the tricky task perfectly as Clarette was taking a break from leaping around the 'Wacky Warehouse' kids playing area, an extension of a local pub where I took her on my access days.

With a fresh glass of coke and a full bag of cheese and onion crisps placed in front of her, I called Clarette over for our little 'chat'.

Not wanting to embarrass my girl I assured her that my short talk wouldn't last longer than just one minute , and then I began.

"Right Clarette, as your dad I feel it's my duty to prepare you for when you start to go out with boys which you probably will soon".

Clarette looked a bit bewildered by my opening gambit, her eyes glancing everywhere but into mine.

"I'm here to tell you what people call the 'birds and the bees'. Have you heard of that term?".

"Yes dad I have", Clarette replied quickly.

Although I wasn't expecting such an affirmative answer Clarette continued to look uncomfortable with the situation taking a loud slurp of Coca-Cola through her straw in defiance.

I took a deep breath before making my condensed announcement.

O.K. 'Tubs', using my pet name for her, here we go.

"A boy has a willie and a girl has a fairy, and when that boy puts his willie into a girls fairy it can squirt out 'baby gravy' which are like thousands of little fishes that are swimming around inside to try and fertilize an egg in what they call the womb which after nine months will create a living child. That's it!"

Clarette chomped on a handful of crisps now looking me straight in the eye but with a much more serious look on her face.

I took that as a sign of her innocence and I waited with a degree of apprehension for a response which was soon forthcoming.

"I know that 'Daddy Waddy' because we have had sex education classes last term where we learnt all about your 'birds and the bees'.

"What! They've no right to tell you about such things so early. Who's your teacher? I'll be having a few words with him or her. Anyway drink up ya coke the attendant's just whistled for the orange wrist bands to come out. I'll just have a last quick pint."

While finishing the beer I contemplated my delivery of abridged sexual guidance. Was it enough or any use at all? Whichever the answer I'm pretty sure my short speech remained in Clarette's head for quite some time.

I had at least attempted to do my 'dad's duty' of pre-warning my daughter of the possible consequences of a sexual liaison. My only worry now was, that she might just decide to relay her new found information to her form teacher!

So now I've brought you bang up to date with my immediate family members, it's time to turn the clock back over thirty years to where I left off.

22 The Beginning of the Second Half: 1987

My personal 'team' rebuilding sabbatical ends in ruins

After what for any avid fan constituted a near death experience in football terms, I needed to take a step back to reassess life. To reflect on the past, take stock of the present and restore hope in the future for my club. In other words I needed to take a long break away from it all to gather my thoughts.

A horrendous year ......

Part one of my autobiographical account ended when I pressed the metaphorical pause button documenting my own in depth analysis of that momentous day in May 1987 when Burnley defeated Orient F.C. in the last game of the season to preserve their near century of league status by the skin of their teeth!

Thankfully, we had averted a disaster, but for many citizens of the United Kingdom nineteen eighty seven would have far more devastating consequences on their lives than my team surviving expulsion.

So just what was going on back then?

Although unemployment had fallen to 3 million, 107 thousand, 1 hundred and 28 when the monthly figures were announced on the 14th May, they were still far too high bringing abject misery to many out of work families throughout the country.

Worse was to follow for the beleaguered working class as Margaret Thatcher, the Prime Minister overseeing those shocking statistics, was re-elected for a third consecutive term of office in June of that year thus extinguishing all hope and aspirations for their future.

It would also go down as one of the most tragic years on record for home based grief and tragedy.

At the turn of the year Terry Waite, the Archbishop of Canterbury's envoy was kidnapped whilst on a peace mission in Beirut, Lebannon , where he would remain hostage until 1991.

On the 6th March the Townsend Thorensen car ferry, the Herald of Free Enterprise left its berth at Zeebrugge, Belgium with her bow doors still open, leading to the ship capsizing within ninety seconds of leaving the harbour as sea water rushed in to the vessel. 193 passengers and crew losing their lives as a consequence.

On the 19th August firearm obsessed Michael Ryan aged just 27, ran amok around a Berkshire town brandishing a semi-automatic rifle and a hand grenade.

There were 17 killed including the perpetrator in what would become known as the Hungerford massacre.

In the middle of October the British weather led to apocalyptic scenes in southern England as violent, extratropical cyclonic hurricane force winds uprooted a staggering fifteen million trees and caused over one billion pounds worth of damage.

The 'Great Storm' as it was termed, turned out to be the worst since 1703 and claimed twenty three lives.

Only hours previous in a lunchtime broadcast, television meteorogical forecaster Michael Fish finished his round up by commenting,

"Earlier on today, apparently a woman rang the B.B.C. and said that she had heard that there was a hurricane on the way. Well, if you are watching, don't worry, there isn't".

It was a quote that infamously came back to haunt him time and time again.

In fact, because of the total inaccuracy of that prophecy it led to the Met. Office conducting an internal enquiry in an attempt to establish how they could get it so wrong.

Then in November the horror of the Kings Cross destructive tube fire was reported on extended news bulletins across the country.

The flames having originated in a machine room under a wooden escalator connecting St Pancras to the Piccadilly line.

31 people perished in horrific circumstances as the flames were bellowed by the underground waft of air emanating from the series of tunnels.

Although no one was personally held responsible for the catastrophe it was concluded that the fire was probably started by a discarded match.

Ironically smoking on the tube had been banned after burning broke out at Oxford Circus station in July 1984. However so lax were the regulations that once clear of the train, smokers would often light up on escalators as they made their way out.

In other news, the first criminal convicted using D.N.A. identification was made, and work started on the Channel Tunnel.

Bangle watches and buckle boots were all the fashion rage for women, with denim shirts and tassle loathers being seen as de rigueur for men. The karate kid action figures turning out to be the top toy for boys.

If you visited the cinema you would be watching Dirty Dancing, Fatal Attraction, Robocop or Good Morning Vietnam. And the top tunes of the day would have you tapping your fingers and maybe your toes to the likes of 'Faith' by George Michael, 'Bad' by Michael Jackson and the either irritating or catchy, depending on your personal musical tastes, 'La Bamba' by the Los Lobos band. 'Always on my mind' by who I refer to as 'The Chip Shop Boys' was the Christmas number one.

To enjoy them all that little bit more, a pint of beer would set you back around 93 pence!

Everything considered, you could say that 1987 Anno Domini was already turning into what the queen would later term as an 'Annus horribilis ' in her Christmas Day speech of 1992. But back to the football, or rather the effect football had on me.

Time to go....

Given the nerve jangling traumatic stress of the past nine months I knew I needed to get away – far away. My batteries needed recharging during a period of convalescence following the most torturous period of my Burnley supporting life!

After much deliberation I plumped for a trip that I had always wanted to make. Greek island hopping. If only I had known then what was in store for me on my adventure voyage.

Trawling the travel agents I settled for the cheapest deal I came across which cost me a straight ton. My £100 Monarch Airlines ticket being valid for one month entitling myself to a return flight from Manchester to Athens. Taking only double that amount for my spending money I knew it would be another frugal break.

In those days to comply with the regulations of the Civil Aviation Authorities governing inclusive tours some minimal accommodation had to be included. This of course was just a ploy to get around the conditions of sale. That is why my designated base gave the address of Petsas camping site, Marathon, Athens, courtesy of Intasun Skyworld booking company.

As my good pal 'Tricky Trev' lives just a mile from Ringway airport I always invite him out for a farewell drink when I fly from there to begin the holiday in style.

Halebarns fitted the bill and so we took in a few pubs in this salubrious neck of the woods, home to the rich and famous, most of which were footballers.

I'd hitchhiked up the A34 road to meet Trev, so with that, and a fair intake of beer I slept on the 3½ hour flight all the way to Athens arriving at 5am.

The airport bus dropping me off an hour later in the city.

Scouring the maze of streets I eventually located the main youth hostel where I paid 400 drachmas, about two quid, for a bunk bed in a large dormitory.

For a night out I headed to Omonia Square, a bustling rendezvous point on the edge of the northern quarter near the so called downtown district.

There I supped a few bottles of Henninger beer before setting out for a stroll to acquaint myself with the surroundings.

That's when I inadvertently strayed into the region's red light location. Within minutes I had been approached by a dog-rough looking heavyweight hooker that had a passing resemblance to Demis Roussos in a tight black leather skirt. Ugh!

Decided instead to take in a Woody Allen movie titled 'Hannah & her sisters,' that was being screened in an open air cinema. It was little more than mildly amusing which always seems the case when I watch this particular American actor.

A sweaty night's sleep followed even after going for a cold shower beforehand.

As a consequence I rose soon after dawn broke, and made my way to the port of Pireas in readiness to set sail to the islands in the next couple of days after seeing the sights.

The best deal that I could spot was a 15 day pass at a cost of approximately £22 that would give me a good choice of islands to visit with this particular shipping company. 'The Kyclades' was the name of the vessel that traversed the Southern Sporades strait of the Aegean Sea and this would be my transportation for the next fortnight – or so I thought.

My longer term plan was to finish my seafaring journey at the furthermost northern greek port of Kavala after dropping off to explore around half-a-dozen islets along the way. From there , my idea was to hitch a ride into neighbouring Turkey for a few days before travelling back down to my departure airport by the same method.

Great expectations lay ahead, yet neither of these objectives would be fully fulfilled due to completely unforeseen circumstances beyond my control.

YESTERDAY,MIDDAY:c,cloud;f,fair;fg,fog;r,rain;sn,snow;s,sunny

	C	F			C	F			C	F			C	F
Aberdeen	c	15 59	Carlisle	c	20 68	Kingston *	s	32 90	Peking	f	33 91
Aberdovey	c	17 63	Casablanca	c	25 77	Kuala Lumpur	r	31 88	Perth	c	16 61
Accra *	c	31 88	Chicago	r	23 74	Las Palmas	s	25 77	Plymouth	c	19 66
Algiers	s	31 88	Christchurch	r	8 46	Lerwick	c	13 55	Port-au-Prince*	s	34 93
Amsterdam	f	20 68	Cologne	s	24 75	Lima	c	21 70	Port Stanley *	sn	-4 25
Ajaccio	s	28 82	Copenhagen	f	19 66	Lisbon	f	28 82	Prague	s	20 68
Akrotiri	s	27 81	Corfu	s	32 90	Liverpool	r	17 63	Reykjavik	c	13 55
Alexandria	s	27 81	Dakar	f	29 84	Lizard	c	15 59	Rhodes	s	28 82
Anchorage *	c	11 52	Darwin	s	20 68	Locarno	f	28 82	Rio de Janeiro	c	34 93
Anglesey	f	18 64	Denpasar	c	30 86	London	c	25 77	Riyadh	s	44 111
Athens	f	35 95	Dover	s	21 70	Los Angeles	f	28 82	Rome	f	33 91
Ayr	c	20 68	Dublin	c	18 64	Luxembury	s	24 75	Ronaldsway	f	16 61
Bahrain	f	38 100	Dubrovnik	s	30 86	Madrid	c	29 84	Salzburg	s	26 79
Bangkok	f	33 91	Edinburgh	c	21 70	Majorca	s	32 90	San Francisco	c	20 68
Barbados	c	30 86	Faro	s	29 84	Malaga	f	28 82	Santiago	r	13 55
Barcelona	s	28 82	Florence	s	29 84	Malta	s	31 88	Sao Paulo *	c	24 75
Beirut	c	22 72	Frankfurt	f	23 73	Manchester	r	17 63	Seoul	c	25 77
Belfast	f	20 68	Funchal	s	23 73	Manila	r	31 88	Singapore	r	28 82
Belgrade	s	33 91	Geneva	f	30 86	Melbourne	f	10 50	Southampton	r	21 70
Belize *	r	29 84	Gibraltar	f	25 77	Mexico City *	c	26 79	Southend	f	23 73
Berlin	c	23 73	Glasgow	c	21 70	Miami	c	32 90	Strasbourg	s	25 77

Killer heat hits Greece....

My last day on the mainland was spent sightseeing in what was now a regular 95 degree heat.

Few tourists braved the intense temperatures, and even less locals given that an estimated 64 nationals had already died from the oppressive conditions.

A glance at a discarded 'Independent' English newspaper confirmed my location as currently the third hottest place in the world, surpassed only by Bahrain, Islamabad and New Delhi with recorded readings at 100 and 102 degrees Fahrenheit respectively.

I'm fairly resistant to the sun's rays due to my olive skin colouring and it was an eerie sight to wander virtually alone through the centre of such a metropolis in the middle of the afternoon. The Acropolis ancient ruins attracted significantly more visitors, but was hardly packed for such a major place of interest.

On the following Tuesday afternoon I embarked on my island hopping adventure catching the 5p.m. ferry to Kos. It was a blowy crossing all through the night arriving in the dock at 2p.m. on the Wednesday.

Walking two miles to my proposed camp site of ready erected tents with my holdall in the blazing sun was bad enough, but actually sleeping under one of the single berth canvas shelters was o.k. until the sun rose around 6.30a.m. As from then on it would adopt the rate of an increasingly hot incubation unit, and by 8a.m. condensation droplets would be dripping down incessantly from its interior roof, ensuring an early rise whether you wanted one or not.

Over a morning coffee at the breakfast bar I was reliably informed by the locals that because of the ongoing bad feeling between the two countries, if I entered Turkey I would lose the right to fly back home from Athens on my charter flight ticket.

That was a real body blow as now I was restricted to spending all my time in just one nation. But at least with plan A scuppered I would get to see a few more of the Greek Isles adopting my plan B, or would I?

Hiring a bicycle for three days I explored the other two main beach resorts of Kardamena on the east coast and Kefalos down south which were approximately a forty and sixty mile round trip alternately from my base near to Kos Town. Then it was time to go to a traditional greek dance night which is surely always a prerequisite for most visitors to any part of Greece. This was the first time I'd witnessed an event live, although I had seen it performed many times on T.V.

It's quite a spectacle to watch the male participants hold each others hands in a camp manner as they dance in a circular motion at high speed traditionally smashing dozens of pottery plates as a grand finali with audience participation eagerly anticipated and encouraged.

As an amusing sight to behold it is only second to the Euzone presidential guards protecting the tomb of the unknown soldier in the capital. Where, wearing their full Pontic uniform of white tights with a black knee garter, a white kilt of 400 pleats to represent 400 years under Ottoman rule, a claret coloured beret type hat with a 2ft long black side pleat and red clogs that weigh over seven pounds, they are expected to raise their legs to shoulder height as they march, reminiscent of 'The ministry of silly walks' Monty Python sketch.

Add to this their requirements to stand motionless for over 100 hours a month and you get some idea of the surprisingly stressful life they must lead under extreme temperatures and occasional teasing from children and tourists alike.

Yet these elite protectors still regard their position as one of the highest honours to hold given their rigourous training to carry out their tasks.

But it was time to leave Kos and head for my next destination of Chios.

Arriving at the port next day I got the devastating news that the Kyclades ship which had transported me from the mainland was out of service for up to a fortnight due to a serious technical fault.

What! Where did that leave me after I had recently booked a 15 day rover ticket with that company?

My angry protestations came to nothing as all I got for answers were a cursory shrug of the shoulders from the less than helpful officialdom who eventually passed me on to a senior member who informed me that I would have to take it up with the booking agent at Pireus where I had purchased my docket. It left me with no choice but to stay on the island another night before reassessing my next move.

Now, after only five days into a 28 day holiday both plan A and plan B had been blown apart!

That could only leave plan C which would be to finance my own boat passage with the hope of reclaiming it on my return. Kos was only a few miles from Turkey by sea, but that would be as close as I would get to it this year.

So I pencilled in Leros as opposed to my original choice of Chios in order to progressively make my way back from whence I came. Paying fares again for what should have been complimentary excursions were also eating away into my meagre resources.

During the next few days I slept rough on windswept Samos and Patmos, before taking in Paros as my last island stop on my return to the port of Pireus where I hoped to get a refund for my total inconvenience.

Arriving there after two weeks away, my watch said 9.30 a.m. as I entered the shipping office where I had bought my island pass. There, they referred me to their International office after I had stated my case for some form of monetary recompense, so I walked round the corner to it.

However , after asking politely to see the manager an off-hand middle aged bloke directed me on to their head office another few hundred yards away.

By now I was sweating quite profusely after being passed from pillar to post. The so called officer in charge somehow reasoned that I had had my money's worth even though it was clearly only possible to have caught the single ferry to Kos as stipulated by the official ink verification stamp on my pass.

In protest I took my tee shirt off, sat on his desk in full view of the open office workers and refused to leave until I had received some form of compensation. Now I was absolutely livid!

Getting ever more agitated and embarrassed by my demonstration in front of many work colleagues his threat to phone the police proved impotent as I called his bluff to do so. He was joined by another high ranking employee of the company who, after hearing that the aim of the trip was to catch their ferry up to Kavala dropping off at individual islands along the way through the Aegean Sea from which I was prevented from doing so by the withdrawal of the stated ship's service, seemed to show some consideration.

Both then indulged in a ten minute long conversation, but it was all greek to me as that was the language they were conversing in.

Then it seemed some progress was being made as a replacement voucher was produced and given to me.

It confirmed my hope as it was placed in my hand. There in large lettering I saw the words Pireus to Kavala. I thanked the man and trotted off contentedly.

Bingo! My efforts had all been worthwhile. Now I had a second authorization to travel the high seas and take in a few more islands on my journey north to Kavala – or so I thought.

Now fast running out of cash as I had not received the equivalent drachma reimbursement for my ticket that I had hoped, I knew I had to raise some money to get me through my last ten days.

'Just calling.'
The 'ship's cat' bids farewell to yet another island from his improvised sleeping accommodation.

The ship's cat....

My ship to Kavala departed at 5p.m. the next day which meant another night in the Athens youth hostel. I put an advert on their noticeboard asking for the equivalent of twenty pounds for my relatively new camera.

After drinking a half bottle of Metaxa brandy I rose next day with a thumping headache, a price I always pay when consuming neat spirits, yet it was one of the cheaper options for a night out, and maybe someone had shown an interest in my camera.

But no, the receptionist said nobody had enquired about it. That left me with just £20 to last ten days. In desperation I used most of the day to try and find the local blood bank where I knew that they paid you a small amount for an extraction of the liquid. However, after walking for hours I finally located the relevant building which to my dismay was boarded up and out of use.

With no alternative I boarded my designated ferry which would at least give me an overnight shelter before I docked at my first destination of Rhodes in the early evening of the following day.

Sure enough we arrived there, albeit two hours late at 8p.m. which was an added inconvenience to looking for a place to sleep out. I made my way down the gangway linking me to the shore where passage tickets were being checked.

The official looked at my docket stamped with the destination city of Kavala then began to shake his head before putting an outstretched arm between me and the hand rail.

"What the bloody hell was going on?", I asked myself.

After calling for an English speaking assistant I was hit with even more bad news. According to the translator my new ticket was valid from the port of Pireas to Kavala alright, but a scribbled message in greek underneath apparently stated 'by direct journey only.'

In other words, although the issuing officer had authorized ferry transportation to my required destination it didn't permit me to get off at ANY of the intermediate islands on the way! If I did, then I would forfeit my right to board another ferry. I had been stitched up big style after my vehement protestations in Athens.

Which all meant that I would be at sea for over four flaming days! There was just no other option available to me now so I resigned myself to the fact that at least I had a safe place to sleep. That was little more than an uncomfortable orange and white painted plastic bench with slats in it on the middle deck which at least offered some degree of shelter.

I got by through selling my sunglasses, sun tan lotion and a 'Rough guide to Greece' which covered a few cold beers and a couple of basic pizzas.

As each night progressed the ship's crew would always walk by and eye me with suspicion as I settled down in my sleeping bag on my hard bed.

The route took in the islands of Kithnos, Sifnos, Thira, Crete, Karpathos, Rhodes again, Naxos, Mykonos, Tinos, Siros, Paros then Rhodes again before eventually making headway to Northern Greece.

After 101 hours I felt like the 'ship's cat', given the length of time I been confined to its quarters, as at long last we reached our destination of Kavala at 1.30.a.m. on Saturday morning.

Even the captain turned out to see me off probably more in relief, as each time he sighted me his glare of disdain gave me the distinct impression that he thought I was going to try and take over his ship.

So tired was I that a town centre metal bench comparable to the one I'd been sleeping on as I circumnavigated the Aegean Sea became by bed for the night.

Survival doesn't go without a hitch...

Later that morning I assessed the gravity of the situation. I was around 600 miles from my departure airport of Athens with four days to get there. I retained the equivalent of about a fivers worth of drachmas with little food to eat and currently no fixed abode.

There was one plus point though, I had a teak coloured skin which let's face it would have cost an absolute fortune to attain at a tanning salon!

But the bottom line was I now needed to scavenge for food. Some discarded tomatoes and a baby melon still looked edible which I gathered from the harbourside. With the purchase of a small chunk of cheese and some fresh bread I was set up for the day ahead.

Considering that I had little spare cash I came to the decision that my best bet of making sure that I got that plane home was to set off now, even though it had taken me an age to get up to here. So without seeing much of what should have been my main destination I was off.

Locating the main E90 road out of the town I held aloft my only lettered sign which read ATHENS knowing that it was very unlikely that any vehicle would be going the full distance.

An hour passed before a car stopped. It was a greek teacher called Tassos providing the lift. After enquiring of my circumstances, without telling him I was destitute, he not only insisted on buying me a couple of very welcome beers half-way through the journey but offered to put me up at one of his beach houses for the night. Of course, a degree of caution has to be maintained with such a request from a stranger you've just met, but generally I think you can gauge a person's character within a relatively short period of time, and besides he was a good thirty years older than me if push came to shove and I had to defend myself.

As it happened Tassos was such a genuine bloke he insisted on cooking me a local speciality of mussels with an egg and tomato salad. Bad mistake! Seafood, particularly molluscs, just do not agree with me, and although I felt obliged to consume the lavish meal I saw it again within around ten minutes as I dashed to the bathroom to churn my heart out! Thankfully Tassos was oblivious to the after-effects of his prized dish and we chatted over a few beers on the balcony till midnight.

His alarm woke me up in the neighbouring room and after a bread and marmalade breakfast he obligingly dropped me off at an auto-stop junction in order to carry on my journey south. I gave him a Burnley F.C. silk scarf as a small momento which he seemed genuinely pleased with as he kissed me farewell on both cheeks. Hmmm! Maybe he wasn't as straight as I had portrayed him.

A couple of quick lifts took me to the outskirts of Thessalonika, where after selling an England tee shirt to one of the residents I booked a night at the youth hostel.

I was still 350 miles from my destination and needed to crack on so made the following day a full-on hitch which got me to a town called Larissa for midnight. Had a beer and a souvlaki with meat and vegetables grilled on a skewer with a pitta wrap, before getting my head down on the grass outside the railway station until boarding passengers woke me around 6a.m.

Washed at the station then walked a mile to the auto-stop route to Athens. Eventually got a ride off a long haired character who sold top of the range cars internationally for a living. Driving at speeds up to 100m.p.h he got me to the capital for 11p.m. Sold my mosquito spray for 500 Drachmas to Fiona who just happened to come from Stoke, which enabled me to spend my last night at the same youth hostel from where my unwanted adventure began. A repeat beer and souvlaki tea followed before getting the late bus to the airport with my last change and the 3.45a.m flight to Manchester. I'd survived on £2 a day from my allowance with the help of a few sales of possessions along the way, and the immense kindness of a number of people from all walks of life.

I had intended to go on a voyage of discovery in the hope of returning suitably refreshed, revitalized and raring to go again for the new season.

Instead, I was taken on a voyage of sheer purgatory, coming home absolutely shattered through sleep deprivation, penniless due to circumstantial factors that I couldn't influence and a good stone lighter on account of affording little to eat.

Yet, although there was no question that my island hopping sojourn had been more ordeal than ideal, the realization that Burnley still remained fully paid up members of the Football League after the trauma of the last campaign more than compensated for my castaway experience.

Stuff the supposedly idyllic locations of the northern and southern Sporades, I was now more than happy to relish the prospect of exploring the hidden delights of Hartlepool, Halifax, Scunthorpe and Newport County in the upcoming 1987-88 season. At this moment in time those were the venues of true paradise.

Sherpa tensing...

If 1987 were regarded as the salvation of the football club, 1988 would be those first baby steps to its re-establishment.

Although Burnley still languished in the Fourth Division finishing in tenth position they had earned a trip to Wembley Stadium for the much-maligned Sherpa Van Trophy Final. Wolverhampton Wanderers had won the same league and they would be our opponents.

It had all started at Tranmere Rovers way back in October with only around 1,800 fans in attendance, but would finish beneath the twin towers with a crowd of over 80,000 inside. It beat the Coventry versus Tottenham and England versus Scotland attendees that had been contested in the previous weeks, and remains the highest turnout ever for two Fourth Division clubs.

In the two-legged Northern final Burnley's first leg opponents were Third Division rivals Preston North End at Turf Moor. 'The Lilywhites' coming away with a favourable 0-0 result.

They thought is was all over, but the mass exodus of Burnley fans making the short 20 mile trip did not.

George Oghani drew first blood for the Clarets but Brazil sent a high octane clash into extra time with an equalizer.

Three minutes into the first period, Ashley Hoskin scored for Burnley with firm favourites Preston becoming ever more desperate. Paul Comstive eventually putting them out of their misery with a goal three minutes from the end to settle it 3-1. The terraces shuddered with the weight of thousands of bouncing bodies.

For Burnley fans it was sheer unconfined delight as many realized their dream of seeing their team walk out at the home of football, the magnificent Wembley Stadium to play Wolverhampton Wanderers.

As comparisons go the stark cataclysmic change that transformed the fortunes of these once famous clubs at that moment in time was strikingly similar.

For both had now hit rock bottom in their past illustrious histories of over a hundred years standing, after being at their football height little over a quarter of a century ago.

Back then in the 1959-60 season, it was small town Burnley who had claimed the champions of England title by winning Division One, whilst Wanderers had lifted the F.A. Cup by overcoming Blackburn Rovers 3-0 at Wembley.

That's a League and cup double for a pair of teams now completely down on their footballing luck.

So much so that in the 1986-87 campaign both languished in the Fourth Division doldrums with Wolves freshly relegated from the third tier and ourselves on a second term.

There was further humiliation as both Burnley and Wolves bowed out of that year's F.A. Cup in the very first round each by the same 3-0 score line to the might of non-league Telford United and Chorley F.C. respectively.

It would be a watershed for both clubs with Burnley calling the following season a 're-birth', and the Black Country Men 'Wolves A.C.', which stood for Wolves after Chorley.

Both founder League members would face each other in what many termed the 'Mickey Mouse Cup', but over 80,000 would travel down for that Sherpa Van sponsored trophy final at Wembley Stadium to signal the dawn of a new era for two loyal and proud sets of supporters and their team.

Finances once again dictated that I could not cover both a ticket for the big match as well as a room so I set off the day before hitching down the M6 to meet up with a coach load that had booked into a hotel in the Barbican region of the capital.

I need not have worried as the hotel's bar manager announced that they would carry on serving until the last one left the premises. Most of us stayed up until around 6 a.m. before I crashed out on a floor of one of the lads bedrooms.

To the match, and a workingmen's club had been booked by a number of Burnley coaches not too far from the stadium. There were a lone party of around only ten Wolves fans already there, and although we made them welcome they decided to sup up and leave quickly.

The game itself went to worthy winners and fellow founder members Wolves which was quite appropriate as the Football League celebrated its centenary year.

We may have lost that particular battle 2-0 but Burnley would ever so slowly win the war of attrition that had ground them down so mercilessly over the last decade.

Burnley weren't back just yet, but those first baby steps had now got them walking tall once more, and unbeknown to me then, my first trip to Wembley with Burnley would certainly not be my last.

23 Large Golden Pies and Little 'White Lies': 1988-89

Fundamental footie fodder – pie & peas

As a toddler needs his rusk, so a footie fan needs his pie. And none more so than Burnley supporters who once held the record for the highest rate of pie-eating per head in the Football League when they munched their way through more than 102,000 of the Holland's company delicacies in one season! But what happens when these delicious savouries run out prematurely? Read on for the shocking truth.

Mutiny at the pie stall...

On the face of it, there was precious little to look forward to during the Eighties when our team was stagnating in Division Four.

A combination of the inevitable poorer standard of play, reduced crowds generating less atmosphere and antiquated grounds with abject toilet facilities all made the attending experience less palatable.

For the already downcast fan, it may have been of little consolation, but at least there was one redeeming advantage of basement league football. That was the fact that the smaller crowds gave you a much easier passage to, and therefore a speedier service at, the regulation in-house refreshment point which generally took the form of a humble tea hut. This was also of course the base for the distribution of that match day treat – the hot pie.

Footie fans have been brought up on this staple convenience food for years and although a slightly more diverse menu is now served, the joy of the traditional pie at the game will never be surpassed. Indeed, with a quick turnover of service paramount given the limited constrictions of the half-time break, it has become a necessary ritual which must be observed with strategic planning.

I have found that the quality of these savouries tends to be better the further down the pecking order we travel.

Take Wigan for instance, who were long time lower divisions' material until the late Nineteen Nineties. Not only the followers of their rugby league and football teams are known as 'pie-eaters,' but the whole community revels in the nickname. The term is said to originate from Winston Churchill's one time vow to send in the troops to defeat the town's striking miners and make them eat 'humble pie,' but it is an appropriate one for this pastry loving populace.

Then there's Hartlepool United, for many years residents of the old Division Four until their shock demotion from the Football League in 2017. Yet at the dawn of the new millennium, they secured what many would class as one of the club's highest honours to date.

The 'Pools' topped the National Pie League thanks to their consummate version of a giant 'Desperate Dan' sized 'growler.' Having tasted it myself, I'd have to pretty much agree, though if the competition extended to Scotland, my clear winner would be the 'Killie Pie' available at Kilmarnock. I sampled one during our visit for a pre-season friendly and concluded that the superb creation of light pastry and juicy minced meat actually does live up to the statement 'melts in the mouth.'

Burnley themselves regularly maintain a very creditable top six position in this nationwide league, and as stated on occasion have actually topped it.

Commendably, many seasons of dedicated weekly workouts in all weathers by the club's fans, involving ravenous devouring by the pie predators in the ranks, have taken place all over the country. It has been at the expense of both the health and wealth of each individual but has nevertheless propelled Burnley fans into the elite pie-eating strata.

Although this fact must have escaped the catering operations manager and meat pie surveillance team at Rochdale Football Club one Tuesday evening back in August, 1988.

This was hardly a compelling fixture. The first round of the League Cup in its various guises has always been treated with apathetic disdain, particularly when, as was the case with this game, the tie was decided over two legs.

However, this first leg clash came just weeks after Burnley's Wembley appearance the previous May in the Sherpa Van Trophy Final, which they lost 2-0 to Division Four champions Wolves.

With that memorable day fresh in the mind of the Clarets hordes, perhaps a little more enthusiasm than normal had been generated for the tie at Rochdale.

Or was there another attraction that night? The final score was 3-3, but that was of little consequence in comparison to the unprecedented chain of events off the field that preceded this result.

More than 2,000 Clarets had descended on Dale's home ground 'Spotland' for the game, a fine following which amounted to more than the total attendance when the two sides clashed in the same competition two years previously.

Because of this unexpected influx of bodies, the mobile tea bar at the Sandy Lane End of the ground was doing a roaring trade as it endeavoured to keep everyone fed and watered. In fact, according to eye witness reports, a continuous snake of a queue had formed a good half hour before the kick off.

There was a very good reason too, for the 'Dale' produced a particularly tasty line in pie and peas, a favourite nosh of Lancastrians. Served in a polystyrene tray, the meat pie would be barely visible as it was submerged beneath a mound of perfectly rounded, fluorescent green processed peas. And despite the stark, bright green, radioactive appearance of these vegetables, to a seasoned pie disposal team of visiting supporters, this dish was the Egon Ronay pinnacle of footie ground grub.

Right up to the moment the referee blew his whistle to signal the start of the game at 7.30pm, eager customers had patiently filtered their way down the line, and even after that, they continued to queue, as with the refreshment caravan being adjacent to the touchline, they were still able to follow events on the pitch. Perhaps it was this rarely found convenience that encouraged more than the usual number of punters to indulge themselves in meat 'pize,' as the colloquial plural pronunciation sounded.

Wot! No pize?...

IT was five minutes into the match and up to this point, the away support had been nothing more than boisterous, even giving the impression that they had once again come to terms with the inadequacy of another example of rustic terraced surroundings.

Additionally, ever increasing numbers reluctantly resigned themselves to a long stay in the pie queue as they joined the human train of waiting fans. It was part of their regular refuelling regime, the superb tray of pie and peas a fine compensation for their prolonged patience.

Then suddenly, for a brief moment, the babble of a thousand tongues stopped. There seemed to be a disturbance at the front of the queue. Heads were turning, fingers were being wagged and voices were raised.

"It'll be some knobhead trying to push in, I bet," offered one derogatory objector.

But no, it was much worse than that as word was passed down the line to confirm the situation.

"There's no pize. They've got no more pize," whispered someone.

"What! No pize?," shouted another.

"No bloody pize!," queried a third, followed by a cacophony of various versions of the same cry using different words, mostly obscene.

All relayed the same sorry message. There were no pize left!

"It's the only reason we've bloody come and you've got no pize!" bellowed a pensioner in a flat cap, inciting others around him to show their disapproval.

"Absolutely scandalous. How many did you think were coming? It's Burnley, not Bury, you plonkers," bawled another of the deprived as he moved aggressively towards the white-coated vendor.

The main bulk of the queue began to melt away in disgust but this particular renegade began thumping his fist on the counter demanding an answer.

"Where's my bloody pie? Eh? Where is it?"

"Sorry, we're sold out, they've all gone," came the nervously apologetic reply.

Then a breakaway group of about a dozen fans of all ages from 16 to 60 mounted a despairing surge towards the caravan to vent their anger. Rocking it from side to side, a frenzied shout of "Pize, pize. We want pize!," rang out from the mob.

Plastic cutlery, cardboard containers and cooking equipment rained down on the occupants as they finally succeeded in pulling down the metal shutters to seal themselves off from the aggressors, but not before the squeezy plastic sauce dispensers had been utilised by the mob who squirted the two man team, covering them head to foot, one in red sauce and the other in brown.

The near riot was eventually quelled when a posse of police fought their way through the crowd to apprehend the perpetrators. The tea bar was closed on the spot as the remaining rebels dispersed.

It was hard to believe and amazing to think that I had witnessed a revolution, the principle element of which was a savoury pastry. A pie uprising, or more accurately a 'lack of pie' uprising had sparked this major uproar.

Yet there was a lesson to be learnt here. This 'peasants' revolt' style of protest couldn't simply be dismissed as football yob behaviour. No, it was much deeper than that. It clearly underlined the importance to the ordinary working class man of the small but significant luxury of a simple match day pie.

In a subsequent statement to the police to explain the disorder, the refreshment stall proprietor claimed that he had purposely ordered three times the normal quota of pies to cater for the insatiable appetites of the Burnley fans.

"It just wasn't enough," he apologised lamentably.

The following year, we played Rochdale away in our opening Division Four fixture of the season.

There was no sign of the apologist but as we lost 2-1 in front of an even larger away following than that fateful evening, it was not surprising to note that there were pies aplenty.

Maybe he had gone back to school to study the theory of Pi squared. Not so much the ratio of a circle's circumference to its diameter but the ratio of a supporter's circumference to their diaphragm!

The whole noodle & caboodle ....

But if 'The Dale' topped the tasty league for their match day fayre there was no question in my mind who were bottom of the catering pile.

The excuse for sustenance that I received at Bloomfield Road home of Blackpool F.C. has left an indelible stain in the memory segment of my brain.

During the same era Burnley had not played the Tangerines in a league fixture as they swapped divisions during the eighties only to find themselves drawn away in the 3rd round of the F.A. Cup in 1990.

I was in the side terrace along with a good following of Burnley fans on a bitterly cold Saturday in January.

Queueing for some much needed half-time refreshment to warm up I noticed the unusual addition of a Pot Noodle to a very limited menu board in the tiny one-man wooden hut.

That seemed a far more appetizing alternative to the appeal of an omnipresent boring Bovril so I ordered a chicken and mushroom version which for me is the only decent variety anyway. At one round pound it was grossly overpriced as you could get a set of four from the supermarket in those days for the same cost.

As the young server added what I presumed to be some boiling hot water from the baby Burco metal container I waited for the liquid to dissolve the thin strips of pasta into some form of digestible matter. Upon prodding my spoon into the congealed mass the plastic shattered on impact after giving it the statutory two-minute stand.

I tried to swirl the water around hoping to agitate the dried noodles, but there was no further breakdown of the substance.

It was therefore quite obvious that the boiler hadn't dispensed anything like a hot enough fluid to reconstitute said ingredients. It resembled a ball of rubber bands.

I was left fuming at that. Not only had I been ripped-off I couldn't take it back either as the queue had grown far too long.

So there I stood, still freezing my balls off with an aberration of a Pot Noodle clutched in my hand like some kind of match memento.

That didn't stop me from glancing down at it to see if the mound had eased from its solidified state at all.

It hadn't, so I went without and worse was to follow. The home side scored with twelve minutes to go which would turn out to be the only goal of the game.

I flicked my pasta disaster out of its tub on to the side of the pitch in disgust and there it lay like some miniature tumbleweed.

Within minutes of going one down the ball was played out to the touchline on our side as Blackpool mounted another attack. Then just as their winger steadied himself to cross it first time the ball bobbled over my discarded filling leaving it to roll out harmlessly for a throw-in. The forward being ridiculed mercilessly from our travelling support for taking an air-kick after the ball's trajectory had been completely changed.

And would you believe it my noodle snack remained intact!

Serves you right I thought, and at least I'd had the last laugh.

I'll be supporting someone else next season: 1989

And this is who?
Daughter Clarette attends her first Burnley match aged just coming up to six months. A rather uninspiring 0-0 draw at Turf Moor, Division Four. February 24th 1990 v Lincoln City.

In most fans' eyes, a less frequent attendance at your chosen club's games, for whatever reason, is deemed acceptable. This is as long as the individual concerned still remains a follower of the club's fortunes. However, intimating to fellow committed supporters that you may be defecting to another team and breaking your allegiance when the going has got tough is the football equivalent of abandoning your own child!

A positive result – before the match...

"I'll be supporting someone else next season."

Little did I realise the ongoing implications of those few choice words, voiced during the 1888-89 campaign, or the consternation they would create. For what started out as a practical joke among a few friends was destined to spread with the speed of a forest fire into a defamatory scandal of sizeable proportions. Allow me to explain.

Ever since Burnley had been relegated to the old Division Four in May, 1985, I had teasingly claimed I was only prepared to give them a generous four years of my total support, both home and away, in order to allow them the chance to resurrect themselves from the basement league.

After this period, I stated that I would then reassess the situation to decide if it was worth fully supporting the team at this level. Of course, this was only a fit of pique, my way of protesting forcefully about the fact that the club I loved had sunk into the lowest division in which they had ever played. In reality, I would watch them in any division in any league, anywhere in the world, in the firm belief that it was my life's destiny.

Now, promotion from Division Four was surely hardly a tall order for a club of Burnley's standing? With this in mind, I relayed my 'pledge' to a number of regular supporters, safe in the knowledge that I was convinced it would never take as long as four years to get out of the lower depths of the Football League.

After all, we commanded the best support at that level and the finest stadium which was in keeping with a club of our stature, and we also had the best post-war league and cup record of any team outside the top division. Promotion was surely easily attainable, and our relegation viewed as merely a temporary distraction, with the bonus of enabling me to see Burnley play at all 92 grounds of the Football League.

But as things turned out, it took us SEVEN desperately long seasons to claw our way out, one of those seasons seeing us pull back from the very brink of obscurity.

Back to the plot, for which Friday, February 10, 1989 was a truly significant date. That night, we played at Layer Road, Colchester, scraping a 2-2 draw. My mode of transport to the game was a Volvo 305, driven by my then girlfriend, the unfortunately titled Miss Sue Goodhead. That was her real name but from here on she would be alternatively known by me as 'Miss Badhead' in view of what I would soon perceive as an immediate erratic temperament change, combined with sometimes raging mood swings of bipolar dimensions. In effect, she became pretty much a female version of Victor Meldrew, though this one wasn't acting.

We had set off especially early to catch a drink at what according to the Guinness Book of Records was one of the smallest pubs in the country, the aptly named Nutshell in Bury St Edmunds, Suffolk, This was a prelude to sampling the various ales of Ipswich, which neighboured our destination county of Essex. While I was participating in my hobby of pub-copping, which involves me partaking of a pint of bitter in as many different boozers as is comfortable, Miss Badhead decided to go shopping.

But one of the purchases with which she later returned would dramatically change my life. It was a home pregnancy test pack, consisting of three chemically treated applicators, which claimed to provide accuracy in 99.9 per cent of cases.

On the long drive down, Miss Badhead had repeatedly stated that her monthly period was overdue by some two weeks, though this was not the first time such a thing had happened in the many years I had known her. As a matter of fact, I recalled a similar occurrence during our first courtship when she was just 17, more than 14 years previously. On that occasion, she had knitted the first pair of baby bootees before a false alarm was diagnosed. In any case, this time she was taking the contraceptive pill, which made a pregnancy highly unlikely.

Therefore, there was a considerable spluttering into my beer when she returned from the ladies after a simple urine test to exclaim: "It's turned blue!"

"It's probably the cold weather. I told you not to hang around," I replied flippantly.

"No, I mean the applicator. It's given a positive reading," she retorted.

"What a waste of eight quid," I chuckled. "It can't be right, can it? And it's supposed to give a near 100 per cent success rate. What a rip-off!"

I detected an apparent lack of acceptance to my conclusion, so I assured my girlfriend that because she was taking the pill on a daily basis, the likelihood of her being pregnant was at best negligible.

"You, er, are remembering to take the tablets?" I inquired undiplomatically.

"Ye-ess," she replied, without a great deal of conviction.

"We'd better do another test then," I said taking her glass and buying her another half of lager.

Anyway, it came to pass, literally, that the second test also gave a positive result, the pregnancy subsequently being confirmed by Miss Badhead's local GP on our return after an overnight bed and breakfast stay at Clacton-on-Sea.

Susan knew I wouldn't change my long held view on parenting, that a child needed two people in a stable co-habiting relationship to have an ideal upbringing. She must also have deduced that my pledge to only ever get married if Burnley won the old Division One title was nothing more than an empty promise because it was based on a pipe dream. So with her biological clock ticking down, she had resorted to what was in effect emotional blackmail.

Suffice to say, the calculating Miss Badhead had been more than a little economical with the truth when she claimed she was religiously taking her preventative measures, as I discovered later when unearthing the incriminating evidence in the form of three months of 'smarties' lying unconsumed in the bottom drawer of her bedroom cabinet. She simply had not been using her contraceptives.

However, there was no getting away from it now. I had been tricked into creating a new life, and to quote a topical phrase "Entrapment had won!"

Yet although it was a deliberately premeditated conception of which until now I had no inkling, I was willing to stand up and be counted as a father. But how did I break it to the lads?

Now, before all you liberated females put down this book in favour of 'The Female Eunuch', let me state at this point, my own individual case for the defence.

There I was, a happy-go-lucky, contented 36-year-old, with no real career and little money, yet few responsibilities but my own. I lived at home with my ma and pa and brother Shaun. I went out with my mates into town for the traditional Friday night session each week, before going to the game on the Saturday or midweek, and played amateur football for our local pub, the Offley Arms, on a Sunday morning.

On my footy watching trips of course, as stated, I would continue my most enjoyable hobby of pub-copping, a personal crusade which had started on January 1, 1976. This involved visiting pubs in every county in England and also the Isle of Man and the Channel Islands, and has now amassed a figure of 19,000-plus hostelry visits, each involving the consumption of a full draught pint of beer.

Dating was confined to the occasional evening, while casual relationships nationwide helped to keep the accommodation costs down during long trips to far flung destinations for night games. I had a collection of more than

100 home-made place name signs, enabling me to hitchhike with ease all over the country following Burnley.

All in all, I was a self-sufficient bloke whose intentions were clear and whose life was pre-planned, as it had been for years. I was as free as a bird and in charge of my own destiny... until now! From next season, besides a football team, I also had a child to support whether I liked it or not.

I decided that the best way to inform my regular Friday night drinking pals was to gather them in a circle to make a public announcement in the pub. The abject look of shock on all their faces testified to the impact from my statement of imminent fatherhood.

So if that was the local reaction, imagine how the Burnley fans would take it, especially given my proposed added twist to the tale!

Breaking the news....

AT this point, I recalled my contrived pledge way back in 1985 to give Burnley four years to get out of the old Fourth Division. The 1988-89 season was scheduled to be the final chance, and they had blown it by Christmas, so I decided to get some mileage out of my forthcoming paternal role and have a bit of fun with some close friends at the same time.

My first task was to recruit a confidant, and who better than my regular pub and match chauffeur 'Tricky' Trev Slack from the village of Heald Green near Stockport.

So on the following Saturday's journey to Turf Moor, after being picked up by Trev at Handforth station and exchanging the usual greetings, I purposely picked my moment when he was driving along a straight stretch of road.

"I've got a surprise for you Trev," I said.

His head turned towards me, his eyes open and alert with expectancy.

"Well, it's more of a surprise announcement, really."

He looked at me again, but this time more intently, knowing from my stage managed tone that it was big news. I could almost see the cogs in his head engage poste haste.

There was a short delay before Trev blurted it out.

"Miss Badhead's preggers, isn't she?," he guessed.

I didn't answer straight away, a bit peeved that I hadn't kept him in suspense a little longer. But then again, I suppose my dialogue, delivery and serious demeanour had blown my cover.

"Isn't she?," he asked again in a louder, more inquiring voice, frantically flicking his vision from me to the road as he waited in anticipation of an affirmative answer. I maintained the hesitation a little more before my shock proclamation.

"You've got it in one, Trev," I finally admitted, putting him out of his misery.

"Bloody hell, I never thought I'd see the day!," was his amplified reply as he regained control of the vehicle after momentarily mounting the kerb in shock. A grin of Cheshire Cat proportions then spread across his face.

"Anyway, why should you be so happy?," quipped Trev, who was a father already. "Come and join the rest of us miserable buggers."

This was obviously a reference to the forthcoming sleepless nights, rounds of nappy changing and the costly upbringing of any new born child. I dismissed it with the contempt it deserved and moved on to inform him of my plot. From his reaction alone, I could gauge the degree of astonishment my 'revelation' would provoke, so I knew then my ruse would be a success.

However, to fully understand why emotions would run so high as my plan unfolded, there is a need to comprehend the brotherhood of the football fanatic. In the majority of cases, the loyalty of supporters to their club is for life, while players as well as managers are regarded as mere transient believers in their quest for personal ambitious success.

Perfect timing...

Burnley F.C. gave the impression that they too wanted to join in with this caper, their contribution being a 10 match run without a victory. By the end of March, they were destined for the lower half of the table, giving the perfect mood of depression among the fans for which to fuel my rumour.

After yet another home defeat, I embarked on my mission by entering the Wellington pub near Turf Moor, a then stronghold of Clarets fans which has now sadly been converted to a Turkish restaurant.

I walked in with a face like thunder, which was relatively easy after such a dismal performance. All eyes turned to me as I entered through the main door.

"That's it. I've had enough!," I bellowed across the massed ranks of supporters. "I'll be supporting someone else next season."

"You know you won't be, Dave," came a hasty reply from one of the throng.

"Would anyone like to bet me?," I offered, holding out my open hand in all seriousness.

Well, there's always one, and this time it was Cronny, a six foot, seven and a half inch giant and dedicated Claret.

"There's no way you're going to give up Burnley and support someone else."

I reiterated my vow with added emphasis.

"I'm definitely going to be supporting someone else next season."

A 'Cronny stand-off' developed, and his initial £100 wager offer was, after a rethink, quickly decreased to a fiver, while Trev put on his best solemn face and nodded to the inquirers accordingly. Remember, I'd only missed one competitive first team match home and away in the last 20 years, so this was something of a bombshell. I liked to think I was considered a man of my word by my fellow supporters, but this time I was banking on it.

After casting guarded glances around the congregated drinkers, I knew they'd taken it in. There were no more than half a dozen regular home and away fans among them, but their drawn faces and overheard comments let me know I'd tugged a few heartstrings. I covertly eavesdropped on the surrounding conversations to gauge further reaction, while after initially being encircled by the mob, I watched as each one filtered off as personal harbingers of doom.

"Have you heard? Dave Burnley's supporting someone else next season. He's had enough."

The widespread reaction was one of disbelief and resigned sadness, and I was now under scrutiny for my act of treason.

"Is it true, Dave? Are you watching someone else next season?," was one of the more awkwardly worded questions. I had to be careful with this reply, phrasing it so my words remained true to the facts.

"Yes, it's true, I'm supporting someone else next season," I guiltily countered, switching a few words to maintain the element of truth.

"Well, I don't blame him," remarked a sympathiser. "All that money he's spent in the last 20 years, coming from Stoke to watch that rubbish."

This triggered a confrontation with an unimpressed fan, who argued: "Even so, I could never support another team. Once a Claret, always a Claret."

Of course, this last contributor was absolutely right. Only the easily led species of football follower, the 'lesser scrupled glory hunter,' would even consider changing allegiance and divorcing an adopted love that was showing signs of terminal illness in favour of a healthy member from the elite aristocracy of the top flight, or any other big name club for that matter.

As Trev and myself left the pub, the controversy and arguments continued, and we knew what a hornet's nest had been stirred up by my revelations. When we got outside, handshakes were exchanged.

"You've done it, they've bitten," said Trev, curtseying with excitement.

"I think we have," I agreed.

"Calling Cronny's bluff when he tried to bet against you tilted it in your favour. It'll be all around Burnley next week Dave. You know what Cronny's like. He'll put the word out."

Trev was right, and it was common knowledge throughout town from that day on.

The desperately disappointing 1988-89 campaign culminated in a gloomy 1-0 home defeat at the hands of 'mighty' Scarborough, which ensured Burnley finished a lowly 16th in Division Four. The traditional end of season pub get-together took place after the game and the concluding analysis of the campaign was unanimous, ie. yet another promotion effort aborted at a very early stage. Farewells were then exchanged, distinctly sadder than normal in view of my insinuated departure.

"I'll probably go to a couple of pre-season friendlies, lads, just to keep in touch," was my closing line. This was said to explain my presence before the impending birth date, which was due to be some time in late August.

It almost shames me now to remember the stricken responses as I left the Wellington on the Brunshaw Road corner of Turf Moor. In the preceding weeks, the tongue in cheek quote to a selective few had gone from a mere rumour to a topical subject of discussion. As a result, the inevitable hundreds of Clarets fans I had met week in-week out, season after season, had got wind of the tale and were seemingly demoralised by my proposals.

My emotions changed. I thought: "You bastard, Burnley! How could you deceive so many people who obviously think so much of you?"

People who had been inspired by my loyalty over many years were now disheartened by my disloyalty. After all, this was the bloke who, in 1976, had changed his name to that of the club he supposedly loved. The bloke who had only missed going to one game since January 18, 1969, and who cycled 10 miles back to his village outpost in the early hours after each game. I think I would also view such a deserting supporter with disdain.

But then again, after going through such trials and tribulations, did they really expect me to leave now? Although I was having doubts about my deception, I was equally affronted by their lack of belief in my very own faith.

To add to my unease, I recalled the only other occasion I had performed a trick of similar duplicity, and how acrimoniously it had all ended.

It was at my place of work, Castle House, headquarters of our local Co-operative Society. Myself, fellow clerical worker Rob Cocker, then a never-miss Stoke fan, and Lily Slack, the managing director's wife and a Liverpool season ticket holder, were all involved. Indeed, it was Lily's participation that gave our prank the required credibility.

I was due to be relocated to the nearby Silverdale Colliery offices for a two week period to cover holidays, but for our purposes, the impression was given that I was leaving the Co-op for good. There's always an office gossip, and our trio made sure she heard the supposedly private discussion of my 'supposedly' impending departure. Again, news travelled fast and before you could say: "Let's have a whip round," there was one, organised for all eight departments in the four storeys of the building as well as the fashionable clothes emporium subsidiary 100 yards down the road. Money was collected and cards written.

The problem that occurs when performing such deceit is that once you have made the first declaration of intent, it's like stepping on to quicksand. The longer it goes on, the deeper you sink until you come to a point where you simply can't get out of it. Scores of fellow employees from our base and its 12 Co-op branches all offered me their sincere best wishes each time we met, to which I appeared suitably nonplussed.

The day of the presentation came around, and I discreetly went to the gents to allow the office girls to surprise me on my return. I duly obliged with a look of astonishment on my re-entry to the office. Lily Slack acted as spokesperson with a short speech and wished me all the best with my future employment.

But then came the sting as I received my deluxe battery shaver farewell present.

"Well thanks girls," I grinned. "I didn't expect such a generous gesture for a two week holiday cover departure. Then again, I should have realised how lucky I am to be working with such thoughtful friends. Thanks again, and I'll see you in a fortnight."

Eyes widened, chins dropped and I left amid the chaotic interrogation of the office gossip.

Upon my return two weeks later, it's fair to say I wasn't exactly flavour of the month, but then again, was it my fault that the works eavesdropper had misinterpreted our 'private' conversation? I kept the shaver, as it would have been impossible to return the donations. Perhaps a kind of retribution occurred as the appliance was stolen when I was on holiday in Lisbon the following year, and upon my actual final departure from the Co-op in 1978, my leaving collection was, not surprisingly severely depleted.

Back to 1989, and as I walked on towards Burnley Central railway station with 'Steve the Veg,' a loyal Wolverhampton based Burnley fan and strict vegan, the Co-op prank was increasingly coming to mind as it became apparent some of my mates had taken my statement more to heart than was intended.

The situation was getting to me now. I grew progressively more angry as the deceit accelerated, and became deeply ambiguous about the whole thing. I could either take it as a compliment that that my fellow fans considered me to be a truthful person and respected my decision to the extent that no real animosity had been demonstrated against me in my presence. Or, I could interpret it as a wounding insult that after so many physical, emotional and financial sacrifices for this most heartbreaking of football clubs, anyone would believe I was about to abandon them. It made me realise that even ultimate commitment hadn't convinced the 'Doubting Thomas's' of my faith.

Nearing the station, I turned towards a very forlorn looking Veggy.

"Stevie boy, I've decided to tell you who I'll be supporting next season."

'The Veg' sheepishly turned his head towards me, now with a look of complete resignation on his face as he awaited my announcement of intent.

"Gow on then Dayve, surprise moy. I bet it's the Veella, ain't it?," he speculated in his ever-depressive Black Country twang.

It was time for my revelation now as his watery eyes were welling up and 'traitor' signs seemed to be flashing from every quickening blink.

"I'm not supporting another footy team next season, you fool. But I will be supporting someone else. I'll be supporting a child. Miss Badhead's pregnant."

"Who's is it?," was Veggy's frankly insolent reply, jokingly delivered in his trademark defensive manner in an attempt to disguise his instant deep relief at the news. But the permanent wide smile for the next five minutes was an animated testimony to the reassurance I had just given him.

There was a sense of solace on both sides from this clearing of my conscience as we began to ascend the stairs up to the station platform with an added spring in our step.

But that feeling was brought to an abrupt end halfway up the concourse when we sighted two female Clarets sitting forlornly on a bench. It was Jo-Ann from Wolverhampton and Jan from Runcorn, their miserable looking faces the legacy of regular attendance at Burnley games that season. We exchanged greetings, then came their questioning about my defection from the Claret faith, which even prompted tears from Jan. Once again, I felt compelled to come clean, this time as a precautionary measure to avoid flooding the station. I confessed my plot, but swore them to secrecy until the following August.

And so the close season arrived and with it came the general chit-chat over the phone with many of my fellow fans about Burnley's prospects for the forthcoming nine months. The hopes of our supporters seemed to be presented with more than the usual level of enthusiasm and optimism in a bid to convince me that better times lay immediately ahead. New signings were enthused over, despite none of them having any sound pedigree, and there was genuine belief that we couldn't do worse than last season's wretched 16th spot. As things turned out, they were quite right. We didn't do worse. We again made 16th position our own.

Full steam ahead...

Pre-season friendlies at Gloucester and Worcester had been arranged for early August, by which time Miss Badhead still had almost a month to wait before giving birth. So how was I going to explain away my presence at these games?

It was 'Steamy Windows,' aka Pete Toner from Preston, who provided the solution to this problem.

Steamy's nickname derived from the National Health Service jam jar specs he wore. And despite being diminutive in stature and wearing a natural hairstyle of boyish tight brown curls, he had a wickedly acidic tongue in an argument and was more than capable of destroying an opponent's point of view with one of his vitriolic comments delivered like a scorpion's sting! In fact, this was so much the case that when he cranked himself up to full machine gun rapidity, his glasses would actually steam up with condensation from the rise in facial temperature. Steamy suffered further in the coming years when Tina Turner brought out a hit single with the same title as his moniker, but he was and still remains one of Burnley's most ardent fans.

Steamy was one of those who gave me a call that close season.

"Eyup, yoof," he greeted me, mimicking my Potteries vernacular. "Have you heard? Burnley are playing friendlies at Gloucester and Worcester. Do you fancy going down to cop a few pubs?"

Now in previous years, he would have rightly taken for granted that I was going down, and would have just asked how I was getting there. But now he almost implored me to go, as if it was a final farewell.

"I won't charge you for petrol," he continued, providing an added incentive.

I refused his generous offer of a free trip, but did agree to travel with him as a friendly gesture and thus, thanks to Steamy's invitation, my presence would be vindicated.

After doing the compulsory pub-copping, on we journeyed to the first game against Gloucester City, who turned out to be a workmanlike side from a very lowly division but nevertheless played to win. In contrast, our 'heroes' seemed to have reasoned that by slowing the pace to an almost pedestrian level, the home side would be overawed by their apparent composure. Instead, Gloucester won the game 3-1 at a stroll, with the Burnley side being accused of not even trying by the hundred or so Clarets' faithful.

In his own mind, I think Steamy was banking on a convincing performance in the hope that it might yet win over my affections. But because of the progressively worsening situation, he could see the plan evaporating before his eyes. His mood was becoming steadily darker as the players' ineptitude increased.

During the game, Steamy had been directing his anger at this lacklustre show in the direction of any Burnley player who ventured within 50 yards of his position behind the Burnley dugout, and for a little chap, he had an enormous booming voice.

Most of the insults were in the form of sarcasm, with comments such as: "You should have shot from there," to one of our attackers who had just ballooned his effort high and wide.

However, one player was being singled out more than any other. Joe Jakub, a pocket sized midfielder who had only rejoined the club for a second spell in the summer. But it was he who became the chosen scapegoat.

Steamy's comments were getting more and more personal and in such a tight little ground with few spectators present, his words were clearly audible, so much so that the Gloucester City players were visibly consoling our lads by placing comforting arms around their shoulders in a show of sympathy. It was a sorry sight.

Matters came to a head when the ball went out for a throw-in right in front of the dugout behind which Steamy was standing. Sure enough, it was Joe Jakub who walked over to retrieve it. I could see Steamy's bottom lip literally quivering with pent up rage, like a hair-trigger ready to be activated. I envisaged that there was going to be a confrontation. Sure enough, as Jakub gathered the ball, Steamy vented his frustration by fiercely letting rip with a concerted verbal barrage that didn't hide his feelings, finishing off with a particularly pointed reference to myself.

"It's no wonder Dave Burnley's giving up supporting this club when we have wankers like you Jakub," Steamy blurted out with his finger wagging furiously.

He didn't hold back as his barely controlled tirade made his face turn progressively more purple as it contorted almost as if he was gurning. His blood pressure had risen to such an extent that the trademark condensation which had given him his nickname completely obscured the view through his NHS bi-focal specs, and you could quite easily have fried an egg on his vaporous forehead. Even the locals gathered around us gasped open-mouthed at this raging riposte which had been dispatched with such blatant venom.

But that was not the end of it. Soon afterwards, the referee blew the half-time whistle, which was the cue for the now completely humiliated Jakub to make a direct beeline to the cause of his grief. The weapon of words had obviously caused a deep wound and reaching over the perimeter wall, he grabbed Steamy with both hands so forcibly that he lifted him almost completely off the terracing in the process. He was clearly aggrieved and delivered a thinly veiled threat of decapitation in his broad Scottish brogue which left Steamy under no illusions.

"If any more of your f***ing poisonous comments come my way, I'll rip your f***ing head off. Understand?," Jakub thundered, before releasing his grip and sloping off angrily towards the dressing rooms.

Steamy was visibly rattled by the confrontation but defiant as ever, he continued his criticism in a more subdued fashion, and at least he knew he had made his point and sparked a reaction, though probably not the one he was expecting.

Joe Jakub certainly wasn't the worst player that night, and he went on to become an established lower division footballer. But perhaps as a consequence of this ugly set to, he didn't appear for the second half, during which the refrain "Teasdale out" echoed around the ground, this chant being directed at our club chairman who was held primarily responsible for Burnley's demise.

As a result of the hostile events on that night, future announcements of friendly matches weren't made available to the fans quite so publicly after that. This resulted in a missed midweek game at Ryde Sports on the Isle of Wight going unannounced later in the season with no Burnley supporters at all in attendance.

The following Wednesday, we went on to play Worcester City, then champions of the Midland League. Another dire performance accompanied a 3-0 defeat. The manager Frank Casper, after once again condemning the behaviour of the travelling faithful, was quoted as saying that he didn't take these games seriously and neither should the fans. I, as well as most others, took a different view. Although understandably not expecting a full 100 per cent effort in warm up fixtures, any professional's pride would be dented losing in such a way to lowly opposition. To me, the bottom line was that we were simply not good enough, a view that would be endorsed by the end of the coming season.

Because of Steamy's passionate but anguished outburst, which was obviously on my behalf, by the time we played Bolton at home in the Lancashire Manx Cup preliminaries, I knew I had taken my joke far enough.

So in the same Wellington public house in which my plot had been hatched, I announced my revelation to the gathered crowd who were awaiting what was fast becoming an overdue answer.

There was a tangible degree of apprehension in the air as I delivered my admission to a captive audience.

"Yes, I will be supporting someone else this coming season...." I paused intentionally, increasing the sense of foreboding, whilst still retaining a doleful demeanour. "But it most certainly won't be another football team!," I emphasised with added gusto.

Bewildered expressions gazed back at me, suitably confused by that latest statement. I let them stew for a while over a longer premeditated hiatus as they hung on every word, before I answered their enquiring cross-examination with a loud, proud declaration.

"But it will be a child! Due to be born at the end of this very month!" I added hurriedly.

The prank had run its course and I'm pleased to say that cheers rang out, congratulations were offered and hands shaken, as smiles were reinstated back onto the gathered faces with one notable exception.

'Cronny,' the six and a half foot plus colossus, was never going to openly admit to being 'done up like a kipper,' so he just shook his head vigorously before fixing me with one of his fearsome, bulging eye stares that he most probably administers to any misbehaving primary age pupil at the school where he teaches.

"I knew you'd be lying," he accused me wrongly.

"You'd never leave Burnley, ... Beeston," he continued, addressing me by my birth surname as is his mildly amusing recurrent whim.

"Well, Cronny, you were half-right," I replied. "Though I wasn't lying, was I? It was everyone else's misinterpretation of my quote. But you are correct about the last bit. I would never leave Burnley, Cronshaw," I added, addressing him in turn by his full surname.

Cronny uttered his trademark tut-tutting of disapproval whilst still retaining a wide grin as he turned to leave the premises which told me that he, perhaps more than anybody else, was mightily relieved at the eventual outcome, but evidently didn't want to show it.

Clarette Annalisa Burnley was duly born on the 27th of August, 1989, weighing in at a mighty nine pounds, twelve ounces.

After exactly three acrimonious years myself and Susan decided to split by mutual consent.

In Memoriam

Lily Slack, wife of the Managing Director of the Co-op's Castle House headquarters Tom Slack, was laid to rest in September 2014 aged 82 years. Now reunited with Tom who passed away in 2009 aged 77. Lil's mischievous sense of humour was at the forefront of my work's leaving prank that was executed so convincingly in the late Nineteen Seventies.

24 Italia 90: 1990

So close to glory.
Semi-final ticket England v West Germany

Following the English national team was, due to the demands of supporting Burnley, a summer occupation that invariably ended in disappointment But there was one glorious night in 1990 when England came so close to reaching a second World Cup final, and I was there! It brought the whole country together at a time of revolutionary disorder.

The 'Nasty Nineties'....

My terminology describing this decade as the 'Nasty Nineties' was graphically illustrated within the first few months of the year when social inadequacies deteriorated into full scale anarchy.

The whole country needed a pick-me-up, after some of the worst unrest ever witnessed in London had taken place on the last day of March 1990.

The cause of this discontent was one of then Prime Minister Margaret Thatcher's biggest ever mistakes – the implementation of the despised poll tax.

Officially the Community Charge, it was based on people, not property. Every adult had to pay the same charge, which in effect meant that two people living in a council flat would pay an identical rate to a pair residing in a country mansion.

It earned its nickname from the equally hated 13th century poll tax, a major cause of the Peasants' Revolt.

A grossly unfair levy that signalled the final straw for voters already increasingly disillusioned with the Conservative leadership, the more civilised members of society showing their indignation with a large anti-government protest in both local and by-elections.

But that wasn't enough for a rebellious hardcore who displayed their antipathy of the new duty by rioting in their thousands in the capital's Trafalgar Square and beyond, on the back of an organised demonstration against the poll tax. Scenes shown on extensive television coverage depicted bloody hand to hand combat with the beleaguered police units feeling the full force of the aggressors' angst.

Comparisons with the confrontational clashes of the early 1980s miners' strikes were an accurate portrayal, as once again the might of the English constabularies had been coerced into protecting Thatcher's absolute rule.

I was as angry as the next man over the unjust application of the tariffs, with my irascibility coming to a head when a final demand for a payment of £102 and 48 pence for the governmental tax dropped through the letterbox addressed to my pensioner parents. With no regard given to its recipients, it was just about as insensitive as it could be.

They were asked for money that they simply didn't have, even after working all their lives. So they were both naturally perturbed that a threat of court action was being made against them. I was absolutely livid!

After reassuring them that I would pay the outstanding amount myself, next day I planned my own personal protest which didn't involve violence, just sheer, bloody-minded insubordination.

I had collected loose change for the last three years in an empty gallon bottle of Teacher's Highland Cream scotch whisky for a rainy day. That 'rainy day' had arrived.

Laboriously counting out the required figure, I placed the mixed coinage into a strong carrier bag which in turn was put into my sturdier shoulder bag.

Our village came under the jurisdiction of the borough of Newcastle-under-Lyme, where I entered their civic offices and although aggrieved, patiently waited in line at the payment counter. There were six tellers for the increasingly long queue as the tills rang out like a New Year sale in a department store, such was their frequency of use. That angered me even more. It amounted to nothing more than the forced implementation of a giant money cow for the treasury.

My ticket number eventually flashed up on screen and I approached the desk clerk as appointed.

Lifting up my heavy bag, I deposited its full contents along with the bill on to the stainless steel holding tray. The room fell silent after a few "Oooohs!" greeted my unorthodox settlement of rattling currency.

Twenty, ten, five, two and one pence coin denominations had cascaded down forming an arcade-style machine mound of alloyed metal.

"I think you'll find that's right," I assured the chap.

The hitherto polite, mature of years administrative assistant gazed down disconsolately at the task now facing him with his left hand now supporting his chin.

I attempted to put him at ease as the waiting crowd looked on.

"This isn't a personal attack on yourself by any means, mate. It's just a way of registering my disgust at the powers that be who consider it acceptable to send out an intimidatory letter to my elderly parents for an overdue collection of the despicable poll tax!"

To my utter surprise, some, not all, broke out into a spontaneous round of applause with a few also nodding their heads in agreement.

The by now agitated employee may have been slightly swayed by this apparent show of support and seemed to choose his words carefully whilst at the same time administering a tame reprimand that I am sure he had recited many times.

"We don't make the laws of the land, we are only here to carry out our duties of work. By rights, I do not have to accept a collection of coins over a certain limit, and I could ask you to take them back. However, in this case I will make an exception due to the mitigating circumstances" he said.

With that, he swiftly began to tot up the silver and copper coins and deposit them into their relevant plastic money bags. As efficient as he was at his job it still took exactly 24 minutes, 33 seconds according to my stop watch to fully count up the hoard. I'd purposely timed the reckoning up to see just how long I had delayed normal proceedings.

"Don't tell me I'm a penny short," I joked flippantly.

"No sir, that's as you said, 'dead on' thank you. Here's your receipt," he added in a dignified but vexed tone.

Protest over, I was gone. A few months later, thankfully, so was the poll tax!

The usual organised chaos denotes our first game...

We rarely do preliminary stages of World Cup finals, reasoning that England should be good enough to qualify for the latter stages of such competitions. Generally, but not always I might add, we are proved right, thus saving our money for the business end of the contest.

This particular year, they had been their usual lethargic selves and had just managed to scrape through to the knockout stages in far from impressive fashion.

But I and thousands of others were ready to give them our wholehearted support in the vain hope that this could at last be our year.

My daughter Clarette was only 10 months old, and although my relationship with her mother Susan was more than a little fractious at this stage, I was determined to go in the hope that maybe absence might just make her heart grow a little fonder.

In fairness, she did bring Clarette to see me off which I wholly appreciated. Then it was time to go.

Five of us set off for Italia '90. Besides myself, the party consisted of my brother Shaun, Weedy and Steve 'Sten' Woolley, all from our village, along with Burnley fan Ant Dawber from Chorley or "Charlie from Chorley" as my mother regularly misinterprets it on the telephone.

We all met up at The Albion pub in Hanley, Stoke-on-Trent's biggest town of the six that make up the city. It was also the closest to the bus station where we were due to catch our National Express coach down to Luton Airport and our booked flight to Bologna for England's next game.

The lounge bar's jukebox belted out New Order's seminal World Cup song 'World in Motion,' ironically with John Barnes, easily England's worst performing player in the previous European Championships of 1988 held in Germany, having the gall to play a rap medley on the single.

From all accounts, Paul Gascoigne was first choice to take the microphone originally, as it was decided that he had the most rhythm. This proved to be a non-starter as no one could understand his broad Geordie accent.

After arriving at our departure airfield on the Sunday night we were met with the news that a catering van had collided with our scheduled plane and the flight cancelled. Another coach ride to Gatwick was organised where we boarded a later plane which astonishingly only carried 13 passengers on a 300 seater aircraft!

Landing mid-morning, we caught the train to Réggio nell'Emelia, a small town about 30 miles from Bologna, knowing full well that accommodation prices would be hiked up accordingly in the host city. Consequently we secured humble two star lodgings for just under a tenner apiece.

That night the home nation beat Uruguay 2-0 triggering an outpouring of joy upon the streets. Thousands of them took to their cars to celebrate in their traditional style. Both drivers and passengers set out to create a totally uncoordinated barrage of noise that would be repeated in countless towns and cities across the country. By loudly peeping their horns whilst singing and waving flags along the main thoroughfare, the tedious racket would persist until way past midnight. If you value peace and quiet it is the single biggest reason not to visit Italy when an important football tournament takes place.

Next day, Tuesday, we all caught the train to Bologna picking up many England fans along the way, only to be greeted with the half-expected Italian welcome.

The local Carabinieri were herding anyone resembling an England supporter into a designated corner. There, they had to queue in order to get their bags checked for potential weapons, a deliberate processing that took over an hour to clear. As it happened, we had arranged to meet a couple of friends from the Stoke area soon after who were arriving by hire car. Gary Tunstall, alias 'Snoz' later to metamorphose into 'Zippy' and his partner Jane Brownridge colloquially known as Ziggy' because of her fondness for David Bowie's 'Ziggy Stardust' alter ego persona, turned up an hour later.

We then all caught a bus to where we heard remaining match tickets were being officially sold. This is where you couldn't really make it up.

Due to the usual excessively stringent method of distribution by the English F.A., literally thousands of Three Lions fans had turned up without tickets. Of course with so many ticketless supporters, there was a very real threat of disorder due to the hierarchy's complete incompetence.

To offset this, through the England Supporters' Club official body they had organised a lone caravan selling point in a random field approaching the Bologna stadium where for the price of £10 membership a ticket could be purchased.

However, all the cheaper category options had been sold making it too much of an outlay for us to splash out.

We left the long snaking queue of bare-chested rag-tag hopefuls and went to convene under a nearby tree to shade ourselves from the 90 degree heat of the afternoon.

With the kick off not arranged until 9pm local time, we had plenty of scope to plan an alternative strategy which wouldn't break the bank.

It was decided to check out how the opposition were selling their allocation on the day. The answer was much more efficiently. An office building was handling the issuing of the dockets requesting proof of identification from any of the Low Countries of Belgium or Holland to secure admittance.

The rest was relatively simple. With an offer of a 5,000 lira tip (about a fiver) we secured five £10 category 4 tickets in the Belgium end courtesy of an obliging 'Cloggy' from Rotterdam.

By the time we entered the ground it was evident hundreds of fellow patriots had done the same, who like ourselves were solely concerned with gaining access to the game. No segregation was deployed and besides the odd half-time scuffle over a minor incident it wasn't needed, the Belgians being a generally compliant race of people.

England produced a good first half in front of around 10,000 followers, but the second half was flat and the score remained 0-0 after 90 minutes with Belgium finishing much the stronger.

They looked the more likely to win the game in extra time too as the ball cannoned off our woodwork for the second time from Enzo Scifo during the match.

Then one flash of genius stole victory from the battling Belgians. Paul Gascoigne stepped up to take a late free-kick in the very last minute of the second period of additional time, David Platt spun a 180 degree turn to volley in one of the most spectacular England goals I've ever witnessed live or on TV. It was a sensational finish at the opposite end to where we were stood, and the England contingent just erupted with glee all around us. We prepared to celebrate the win throughout the night in town but the Italian police had other ideas.

When the gates to the ground were finally opened at 11.30pm, England fans were rounded up and herded onto a convoy of waiting buses where we sweated until setting off an hour later. A massive security operation followed with us all being ferried back to the railway station where we were forced to stay until our first train out to Rimini at 5 in the morning.

There, we were met by scores of residents touting for hotel and guest house business. After checking out a few deals, we settled for a family run place owned by an old couple for about the equivalent of £7.50 per person each night, and booked in for two.

All of us caught up on some much needed sleep before heading off on the strip of bars that they call the 'Rimini Mile.' We were back down to five now as Snoz and Zig had set off by car to the venue for England's next game at Naples.

Our belated victory celebration finished at the Rose & Crown, a plaque commemorating it as the first English pub to open in Italy in 1964. This site also marked where what the press referred to as 'The Battle of Rimini' broke out when England supporters took exception to Italians excessively celebrating their country's win against Uruguay on the Monday night by driving around in a cavalcade of horn-tooting vehicles for many hours. As a result, more than 300 England fans were immediately deported by special plane after the large scale disturbance without any possessions including famously, one bloke who had nipped out of his apartment just to buy a packet of fags from the local store. Apparently his missus, frantic with worry after his non-return from the nearby shop, phoned the police to report a missing person. Not until he phoned her upon touchdown in London did she realise how far he had been forced to travel in his quest for a simple box of cigarettes on the Adriatic coast.

Ant's sandwiches nicked by the Camerooners!

Next day, we took in the principality of San Marino to stock up on duty free booze before catching the train south to a town called Terni, about halfway towards our next match which had been confirmed as Cameroon in the city of Naples.

We were staying out tonight so we deposited our bags at the left luggage department of the station, just taking our sleeping bags for protection. It was an eerily quiet place but we made the most of the local bars and even got chatting with a group of the local team's fans who had termed themselves 'The Freak Brothers' as a title for their more fanatical followers.

Ant swapped a Burnley scarf for one of theirs and they showed us to a park where we got our heads down on large cardboard boxes that we'd flattened out.

The usual night of interrupted sleep followed with prowling dogs, passing traffic and even seeds falling from the trees preventing any quality kip.

Even so, it did give us a required early start to Cassino, our next stopping off point 80 miles south of the teeming metropolis that is the capital Rome.

Scene of the Battle of Monte Cassino during World War Two, it was a place my father Percy had fought at in the British Army's offensive against the German occupation. The rebuilt abbey fortification high on the overlooking hill being a strategically located military position that was greatly prized.

History lesson over, we carried on our journey to Naples where as planned we caught up with Snoz and Zig who had suffered navigational problems attempting to locate the architectural city-state gem that is Florence.

"We were driving around for hours," sighed a forlorn Snoz, "but all we kept seeing were road signs for Firenze."

"You sloppy bastard!," I countered curtly to the usually self-assured Snoz. "Are you sure you went to our grammar school? Firenze is the Italian pronunciation of the self-same place, you muppet!"

By now, he was doing a fair impersonation of 'Stavros the Kebab Seller,' a character in the 'Harry Enfield and Chums' comedy television sketches. Dressed in flip-flops, a touch tight pair of denim shorts and a garish canary yellow vest, his mullet haircut and thick black slug of a moustache gave him a look that was more Monty Python than Monte Carlo.

"Well, how were we supposed to know that?," he spluttered, waving his arms around manically in embarrassment almost insinuating it was our fault for not informing him sooner.

Point made we got on with the job in hand, finding both accommodation and tickets for the game. As it turned out, each were cheap. This being our second visit to Naples after watching England play here in the European Championships in 1980, myself and Weedy knew that Southern Italy was vastly poorer than the richer north of the country. Ticket prices were also down as Cameroon attracted little interest in this region, and so the touts got a real spanking! We managed to haggle the category '2' £50 equivalents down to a mere £15 exchange rate.

As in Bologna, an alcohol ban was in operation but there were always a couple of back street outlets willing to make a few thousand lira and we sussed them out.

A traditional photo was taken with a rare group of 'Came200ners,' as we had christened them, showing us all flying our flags in a location near to the ground.

Unfortunately, whilst we mingled with the half-dozen or so visiting African supporters, one of their 'tea-leaves' nicked Ant's plastic carrier bag never to be seen again.

Ant lost his Union Jack flag and some sandwiches he had made up, and although the value of the theft wasn't a great deal, he was fuming, and meted out a harsh verbal reposte.

"Bloody Came200ners!," he blustered. "That's the last time I give to Band Aid!"

After I offered him one of my sandwiches, Ant calmed down and we walked to the Stadio San Paulo.

Me and Sten got stopped outside the ground by security as we both had Union Jacks draped over our shoulders as we entered the end designated for Cameroon fans. But it didn't turn out to be a problem as no more than a few hundred had made the long journey from their homeland.

So the match kicked off in one of the most subdued atmospheres ever experienced at an England international and this was the quarter-final of the World Cup!

In a topsy-turvy 90 minutes, England took the lead, then astonishingly Cameroon came back to score twice. With 10 minutes to go, I will always remember the sight of dozens of cameras and arc lights being set up around about 50 all-singing, all-dancing 'Rooners' banging away on their drums in anticipated celebration directly in front of us.

Then with seven minutes left England won a penalty that was despatched into the back of the net by Gary Lineker, a player who would in later life make it big by advertising a brand of crisps amongst other things in what would prove to be a lucrative career on the television.

That took us into extra time once more as the camera crews that were fighting for space to capture the Africans rejoicing began to dismantle their equipment and viewing platforms before our eyes.

The dependable Lineker made it 3-2 from another penalty kick and England had nicked another game with the prize a semi-final against old adversaries West Germany in Turin. So that was where we were heading next.

Caught out singing in the rain...

In the morning, first stop was Rome for a day trip as Shaun and Sten hadn't visited the 'Eternal City' before.

As we waited at the station to get our bearings, a large jovial Italian approached our motley crew. He first spotted my brother Shaun, whose multi-tattooed upper torso resembled a roll of flock wallpaper. Combined with his broad build, skinhead haircut and dark glasses, it made him look pretty fearsome. The Italian bloke asked his occupation.

"Ballet dancer," I replied mockingly. He looked on in amazement, declining Shaun's offer to demonstrate 'The

Nutcracker Suite.' Asking where we'd been, we rightfully informed him of last night's match.

He then turned his attention to Sten, the palest member of our party whose complexion was more snooker hall white than Rimini tan. His slender white legs poking out from baggy black shorts made him look like a two-pronged plug.

"And him?," enquired the same Italian, eyeing Sten's multicoloured shirt. "Is he from Cameroon?"

We just rucked up in laughter to Sten's utter consternation. The look on his snow-white face was absolutely priceless as he made a contemptuous reply.

"No, I'm bloody not!," he said before returning to study his two day old Daily Mirror, suitably disgruntled.

St Peter's Basilica, the Sistine Chapel and the Spanish Steps tourist sites were taken in before we caught the overnight train to Florence, or 'Firenze' as we all knew it after Snoz's translation failure.

By now, we were all running low on funds and we still had what could be a very costly semi-final ticket to pay for. We'd met loads of England fans along the way who claimed they had never paid to travel on the Italian rail network.

"We just keep singing England songs and they just move on to avoid any hassle," was one of the typical blasé statements made by the many fare dodgers we had come across.

It was decided that if we had any hope of attending the forthcoming big game then this was a case of 'needs must' and we would also have to employ similar distraction tactics to save much needed lira. A plan was duly hatched.

First, we would have to get in stereotypical England fan character mode and get progressively drunk. That wouldn't be a problem as we all had leftover duty free booze from our trip to the Republic of San Marino. Then the intention was to burst into a suitably raucous rendition of song to deter a ticket examination. As a further deterrent we were going to pull down the blinds and tie off the sliding door to discourage entry.

Putting our scheme into action, we commandeered a compartmental carriage on our scheduled train and continued to drink from our passed around spirit bottles throughout the night, taking it in turn to act as a lookout for the imminent ticket inspector. Once alerted we would all sing our hearts out to discourage any scrutiny. Our choice was to be one of the adopted versions from the 'Burl' repertoire that we sing on our annual 'jolly boys' outings. A stirring presentation of that age-old favourite 'Singing in the Rain' that involves extended audience participation to the chorus which considerably prolongs the ditty.

"Here comes the clippie!," exclaimed Shaun who was on third watch.

"Right. Let's go lads," I beckoned, and started the introductory line, flicking my fingers in a downward motion from above my head.

"I'm siiinging...in the rain,
Just siiinging ...in the rain,
Oh what a glorious feeling,
I'm hap...hap...happy again!"

Just then there was a loud thump on the front of the compartment door.

"Thwack! Thwack! Thwack!"

"Carry on singing!," I shouted. "But louder!"

I boomed out the chorus in its full entirety which involved me shouting out instructions that the others repeated as they copied my actions 'Simple Simon' style.

"Wrists together!...Wrists together!
Arms out!...Arms out!
Arms together!...Arms together!..." and so on until we'd exhausted all body part names during the 10 minute performance.

It was to no avail. The door slid open and a shadowy female ticket inspector popped her head in. With her pencil thin eyebrows now halfway up her forehead and rubbing her fist vigorously from her continuous banging on the glass barrier she demanded: "Biglietto! Biglietto!"

We knew what she wanted but we carried on singing even louder, ignoring her cries.

She then shouted out something completely unintelligible in Italian and stormed off.

Loud cheers of "Eng-er-land...Eng-er-land...Eng-er-land," rang around the carriage in recognition of what looked like mission accomplished.

But no, this one wasn't in the mood to give up quite so easily. She returned with an English speaking male colleague who spelt out an ultimatum.

"You must pay full price for your journey, plus a penalty charge for not purchasing a ticket in advance or we will ask the police to arrest you at the next station. Your choice," he threatened confidently

Bollocks! It was 2.15am and being thrown off a train to try and plead any kind of case to the cops would be a non-starter. So we all had to reluctantly bite the bullet and pay our rightful dues.

That was the last straw for Ant. Paying the excess fare had hammered his budget, so he considered cutting his losses and catching a train to Paris for his journey home.

'The Beast of Firenze'...

We arrived in Florence at the unearthly hour of just before 4 a.m. It left us no choice but to prepare our sleeping bags in readiness for the twilight hours before sunrise.

Of the hundreds of thousands from around the world who flock to the city that is regarded as the centre of the Italian

Renaissance for art and sculpture, not surprisingly few sleep rough like we had planned to do.

There was a very good reason for this and he was called 'The Beast of Firenze'

As we settled down under a covered entrance to one of the many centrally located art galleries, I began to read out loud a passage detailing the man's notorious exploits from the most recent edition of the 'Lonely Planet' travel guide that I had brought along.

It was in a framed section at the bottom of the page, at the very end of the chapter on the city's highlights and simply titled WARNING! in large black lettering. The following text sending a chill down anybodies spine.

"Under no circumstances, repeat- no circumstances consider sleeping out in Florence no matter how romantic the notion may seem.

For the last five years or so a deranged serial murderer has been at large. Harbouring a particular resentment towards students, to date he has killed eight tourists by either stabbing or strangling them to death-or both!

Local police have termed him 'The Beast of Firenze' on account of this gruesome way he slaughters his victims. Despite extensive police enquiries he remains at liberty".

Although our party were still a bit bleary-eyed, a casting glance told me they were all taking it in, one more than any other.

'Sten' was still staring at me, as he had been throughout my oratory, his eyes wide open with incredulity as they bulged out of their sockets.

"You're kidding aren't ya Ralphy?" asked Sten portraying an edgy smile.

'Sten, I wouldn't joke about something like that would I?" passing the book to him for his own perusal.

His facial beam physically withering as he read the confirmation to exclaim,

"Well, what the bloody hell are we doing out here then Ralphy?"

I tried to make light of his concerns.

"Don't worry Stenna he's only after students, so we're o.k."

Before he could utter a reply, right on cue the local Carabinieri turned up in one of their patrol cars.

We'd hardly been there ten minutes, but perhaps in view of what we had just been reading this was their preventative response.

Once again we were forced to uproot leaving us no choice but to tread the streets searching for shelter. After inspecting various nooks and crannies that we considered unsuitable the mainstay of the railway station was returned to.

After no more than a conservative 'twenty winks', security kicked us back out at their clocking on time of 6a.m.

All that upheaval had left us all feeling absolutely knackered so a decision was made to hire a room for the night in our next destination of Genoa.

All except for Ant that is. 'Charlie from Chorley' had calculated that he now had neither the funds nor probably the sandwiches to see him through to the semi-final.

With that, Ant exchanged goodbyes' before booking a single to Paris for the equivalent of around fifty quid.

Which left our remaining 'culture vultures' to take in some of the primary sights of this beautiful city.

We figured the best way to do that would be to climb the steep hill for a mile to reach Michelangelo Square. Weary as we were our now diminished party reached the summit to be rewarded with a panoramic vista.

Now they say that no trip to Florence is complete without viewing Michelangelo's 'David' in the flesh. This marble statue carved around the turn of the sixteenth century being the biggest draw for the creative classes.

Well feel free to call me a pleb, but after seeing a photograph of the effigy and others like it I always ask myself the same base level question.

"Why do the artists always give their graven images such little todgers?"

Aren't effigies allowed to have a standard sized penis, and wouldn't it be refreshing to see 'Dave' cast with a budget busting Errol Flynn appendage instead of the button mushroom, last in the queue afterthought , that they bestowed upon him. That would give those ostantatious art luvvies something really interesting to evaluate and discuss the merits of, wouldn't it?

After a full day in Florence we progressed to Genoa by train once again. Once again we didn't buy tickets and once again we got fined.

'Those England Fans mouthing off about jumping the trains were talking bullshit!', Weedy concluded.

It was hard to disagree. We were copping more penalties than the England football team, and so decided to call it a lesson learnt and pay our way in future.

That night we went to the main square as the host nation were playing Argentina for a coveted place in the World Cup Final.

Italy took the lead but the 'Argies' equalised forcing extra-time and then penalties after neither team could settle the issue.

The whole country held its breath, but it was the South Americans who held their nerve to triumph 5-3. With the giant wellington boot of Europe leaking too many goals the nation fell silent – which was great news for us as it meant no more bloody peeping horns keeping us awake all night!

Only tears for souvenirs …

Next day we caught the train to Turin as legitimate full fare paying passengers and made our way to the new stadium by tram to assess the availability of tickets. At the make-do camp ground selling point, only the higher priced category was available at £35 plus. A crucial match it may have been, but over a quarter of a century ago that was big bucks.

All four of us carried on walking to find a few bars that were serving. As we did we heard how thousands of German supporters had come over on the day and were having no problem obtaining their dockets for the game as their football federation was properly organised.

It was infuriating, so much so that when a roaming German television crew asked my views on the subject I berated all those responsible for the England allocation and distribution.

At the V.I.P. entrance a harangued Ted Croker the former long standing secretary of the Football Association was also running the gauntlet of ticketless England Fans. Then we spotted the distinctive figure of Garth Crookes. The chunky black player was born in Stoke, appearing for them between 1976 and 1980 before moving to Tottenham Hotspur, Manchester United, West Bromwich Albion and Charlton Athletic.

Elected as chairman of the professional footballer's association he gained an O.B.E., for me in the form of an 'Obliging Bogus Entry!'

I gave it a try hoping that he may still have some affiliation with folk from his birthplace.

"How ya doing Garth? All the way from Stoke. D'ya happen to have any spare tickets for tonight mate?" I asked grovelingly.

'I've only just managed to get one myself', was his ominous reply as he carried on walking apace.

It looked like they were going to be as rare as moon rock, and on that basis when Shaun and Sten were offered £100 tickets for £25 each they snapped them up.

But me and Weedy were reasoning that a lot of Italians would have them on their hands for the German end figuring that their country would still be there at this stage.

And so it proved, supply still outstripped demand as scores of locals tried to get a big return on their outlay and most of the Germanic following had also pre-booked their places, more confident than most that their optimism would be rewarded.

That meant with time fast ticking away towards kick-off it was progressively becoming a buyers' not sellers' market as we had observed. Which of course meant that the longer we held our nerve the more prices would drop.

It was me and Weedy's turn to call the touts bluff, so we slowly circled the ground nonchantly sipping from the bottles of white wine we had purchased for our refreshment, all the time clocking their desperation for a sale.

£83 tickets in the German enclosure were now down to £20 with fifteen minutes to go before the game started. We hung on as most people were now in the ground and we knew they would have to tumble even further.

With just five minutes to go we negotiated two for £25 as the disgruntled sellers baled out. We were in!

'Deutschland! Deutschland!' was the chant from our corner but we still draped our England flag over a barrier in isolated defiance of the overwhelming majority.

What a game we saw at last as Brazilian referee Jose Ramiz Wright blew his whistle just after we had claimed our place in what wasn't a full section by any means in an attendance of 62,628.

The respected manager Bobby Robson pitted his wits against the equally revered Franz Beckenbauer and perhaps it was appropriate that a goal from Gary Lineker had cancelled out an Andreas Brehme free-kick unluckily deflected over Peter Shilton by the out-rushing Paul Parker. The woodwork denied both teams in an extra-time period that will always be remembered for Paul Gascoigne's tears after he received a yellow card that would have ruled him out of the final. But the tears really flowed when Stuart Pearce and Chris Waddle missed in the resulting penalty shoot-out and England were going to Bari for the 3rd place play-off against Italy which they duly lost as well.

Gazza himself described that booking against the then still independent nation of West Germany as, 'The Darkest moment of my life."

And there's the clue – my life. It was all about him. The 'me, me me' self-pitying syndrome that was conceived on that famous night and has grown up with him ever since.

'Gazzamania' was born! The following days after England's exit from the world cup it seemed like the maternal instincts of all the women in the country had come out to comfort him amidst their casual conversations

"Did you see the England match last night? Poor Gazza was crying his eyes out after getting booked. Oh! I felt like hugging him, he was so upset."

A female companion would then join in.

"Oh yes! I saw that too. I don't usually watch football, but my husband said we had to, and when he burst into tears I thought I was going to cry too. Poor little lamb."

That would start a gaggle of inane comments from the rest of the gathering which would always end with, "Wasn't it a shame for him?"

Well no it wasn't! It could easily have been a shame for the England team and the nation as a whole because it jeopardised their chances of at least winning some silverware. Beckham's impulsive and petulant back flick at Argentinian

Diego Simeone whilst on the ground during the 1998 World Cup leading to his sending off and a consequent defeat fall into the same category of a lack of self-discipline.

But Gazza's boyish enthusiasm and those enduring images also did more to attract the fairer sex to football than any advertisement could. They were scenes that captured the imagination of the English public, and for that alone, however inadvertently and unintentional, we do owe Paul Gascoigne a debt of gratitude for putting the game of football firmly in the spotlight.

25 Births, Marriages And Deaths

Clarette's Christening just a few weeks after her birth

In order to devoutly follow your football team to each and every game many day to day obstacles have to be overcome.

All work, family and social arrangements need to be factored into the attendance equation, as do the less predictable aspects of our lives, not withstanding the constants of traffic delays and Britain's unpredictable climate.

Births…

So let us start in chronological order with births. Personally, having only attended the one, I have no inclination to become a voyeur of the amazing life-giving procedure given the amount of traumatic pain and trepidation that has to be endured. And it can't be much fun for the woman either!

That once, was of course the day my daughter Clarette announced herself to the world on the date of August 27th 1989.

On the Friday going into the Bank Holiday weekend her mother Susan was already overdue by a couple of days, and it has to be said that her belly did look ready to burst.

Susan had already been complaining of lower back pain and cramping, along with strong and regular contractions which I put down to her pregnancy urge to dip her Cheesy Wotsits into a tub of whipped cream. "I've got a feeling it will be tomorrow", she reasoned.

But if she thought she had problems so did Burnley. They had started their fifth consecutive season in the Fourth Division of the Football League with a 2-1 away defeat at near neighbours Rochdale. 'The Dale' had finished in 18th position last year, and next up at home were our newly acclaimed rivals Stockport County who could only cement a lowly 20th spot at the end of the same campaign.

We needed to shape up and fast, but first I had to reassure Susan that she would be in my thoughts as I travelled up to our fixture the following day.

"I'll ring you straight after the match then come rushing back, forfeiting my usual gallon of beer in Preston town centre where I change trains."

Susan gave me that sulky, not amused look which I immediately recognized as 'baby blues' syndrome that I'd read about at paternal classes.

So off I set feeling like I had the weight of the world on my shoulders knowing that we desperately needed a win against County to prevent a further slide down the table.

It didn't happen, in a dull affair after ninety minutes the score remained as it had started at 0-0.

I'd made my way round to the Bee Hole End open terrace for a quick getaway. There were no telephone kiosks available until I got into the town centre. Susan's phone wasn't being answered which I found slightly ominous so I rang home.

My dad answered without a greeting, "You'd better get yourself over to the hospital. Susan got taken in by ambulance this morning about eleven o'clock".

"Bloody hell! Right, I'm on my way", I spluttered down the receiver. Susan's hunch had been right.

As I exited the red booth I bumped into good friend and fellow Clarets fan Keith Riley who lived near Stockport.

After relaying the situation to Keith, he kindly offered to whisk me to Stockport station in order to catch an earlier train back to Stoke-On-Trent.

This he did, and my immediately departing homebound carriage got me there the earliest I had ever been at just gone 6.40p.m. A taxi getting me to the maternity block for 7p.m.

Had I missed the birth of my child? Had everything gone well? Is it a girl or a boy?

I was about to find out.

"Where'vyabin?", asked Susan tersely, without even asking how Burnley had got on.

"Where'vIbin?, I've flown down faster than Superman. Never mind that, how are ya doing?"

It transpired that Susan's waters had broke soon after I had left for the game and she'd been in labour from thereon in, around seven hours and counting.

I had dashed back for nothing, but of course I wasn't to know that, and it seemed churlish to ask her to go halves on my cab fare given her troubled predicament.

Susan was having a hard time, and it became clear baby didn't want to be born on the day we couldn't beat Stockport County, as the clock ticked past midnight into Sunday.

After much wailing and alternate masks of gas and air being administered the baby's head made an appearance around 5 a.m.

"One big push!", advised the nurse as Susan asked me for more gas but it was to no avail, baby wasn't budging.

Eventually a doctor was called and one of those rubber headed plunger utensils was affixed to the skull and out popped a baby girl as her mother rather uncharitably yelled ,

"Get the bloody thing out of me!"

Charming I thought, as I cradled my daughter ever more lovingly after the clean up.

All had turned out well, so a few hours later I returned home to catch up on some much needed sleep. It had been a tough twenty four hours.

The following Monday being a non-opening day in town I just about managed to get the last bunch of sorry looking flowers from the market stall as they were about to close. Getting them for half-price couldn't compensate for how limp they looked with almost apologetic wilted heads nodding towards me.

Of course when I arrived at Susan's bedside it was adorned with a mass of professionally arranged bouquets of blooms from her parents and relations. All probably personally delivered through 'Interflora', a high-end of the market transportation service that was certainly out of my financial reach even if I had thought about them – which I hadn't as it was a Bank Holiday.

Strewth! Even my local bus only ran once every two hours to get me to town, before the good mile walk to the hospital.

But was there any degree of appreciation shown after my troublesome trek as I handed Susan my humble posy of congratulations?

Not a bit of it! A face that looked like it had just chewed on half a lemon looked scornfully into my eyes with the exclamation,

"They look like they've come out of the ruddy cemetery litter-bin!" fired back at me accusingly.

I'm not a doctor, but I am a betting man, and I would like to wager that my instant diagnosis of the onset of post-natal depression began with this irrational reprehensible reprimand.

Because, believe me, from that day on, things would just never be the same between myself and Susan.

In retrospect, perhaps I should have gone to 'Interflora' – or maybe applied that gas mask considerably longer after the birth!

Marriages...

My youngest sister Rosie decided to tie the knot and get married to her partner Paul during the football season which of course is their prerogative.

However, for some inexplicable reason, without even considering checking the fixture list they chose to get spliced on Saturday 11th of October 1986.

So what? I hear you say. Well, it was 'Sod's law' that for me personally she couldn't have picked a worse day!

Rosie informed me of her decision all upbeat and cheery as any upcoming bride would, awaiting a compliant unequivocal acceptance of her invitation to first join them at our local All Saints village church, followed by a traditional evening reception at The Black Horse public house located in the settlement of Betley where we were originally raised.

She didn't get the response that she had hoped and expected.

"You've got to be joking! The 11th of October. Why ever have you selected that date?", I retorted quite unreasonably.

"Why? Because that just happens to be the particular day we both wanted to exchange our vows" replied Rosemarie totally reasonably.

Clearly taken aback by my unsettling riposte I went on to inform her firmly that I couldn't make it on that specific date.

"Don't tell me!", she second guessed,

"You're putting football before my wedding day. Well thank you very much. I am your sister you know!" exclaimed my sister angrily.

I took a step back and let her settle down a little to prevent the imminent tears that always accompany such a personal spat. Of course it is a dilemma that every dedicated football fan has to face some time in their life if they have brothers or sisters.

Just like funerals of family or close relatives, or indeed your intermediate friends their passing away is obviously something that you just cannot legislate for. But come on, this wasn't anything like a case of life or death was it? It was a celebration to be enjoyed by the bride and groom whether I was present or not.

Consequently, I've always found that the best way to deal with such highly sensitive issues is to make your case and go on the offensive , which is exactly what I did.

"Rosie, you know that I go to each and every Burnley game. That's why I missed Susan's (My eldest sister) wedding to Mark in 1980 because I was away from home".

That combination of the realization that a precedent had already been set for my absence, along with my thinly veiled insinuation in relation to her lack of thorough planning seemed to placate her.

"Yehhh, I'm sorry David. I've had so much on, that I didn't give it a second thought. I foolishly overlooked the fact of how serious you take your football".

"Don't worry about it. I'll still get you a present", I assured her flippantly.

"Well at least you can still make the reception at the Black Horse can't you?" Rosie asked assuredly.

"I'll try my best, but you could hardly have picked a worse fixture for that weekend."

"Why? Where are they playing – Timbuktu?" asked my sis. indignantly.

"No, not quite that bad, but we are at Aldershot, Hampshire, which allowing for me to catch the last bus back will mean I probably won't get there until just before midnight."

As it happened that forecast was exactly as events turned out, clocking in at my sister's reception party for the last dance, last orders at the bar and the very last mushroom vol-au-vent!

My eldest sister Susan decided to have a second plug at marriage, yet there was not one single offer of recompense for the hardly inexpensive toast rack and tea set I donated the first time around! Gratitude eh?

Although, I was willing to overlook such an oversight given the solemnity of the forthcoming occasion. However her choice of date for their big day was less pardonable.

There was an estimated generous two in three chance that Burnley could be playing either at home or an away game within a fifty mile radius that season so surely this time I would be accommodated.

But no, my sibling had chosen to retie the knot when we were down in London to play Tottenham in a Premier League clash, on the 26th September 2009.

Does anybody consider to check where I'll be travelling before making such plans? No, I guess not, and unquestionably it is their right, but woe betide anyone who dares to have a go at me for my non-attendance when even a cursory glance at the fixture list would tell them I would be back late, if at all!

It all meant that I of course missed all the wedding speeches and just got back to sample a saved paper plate of curled up sandwiches, a flaky sausage roll, an exposed half of pork pie, some crunchless sprinkling of potato crisps and a couple of mandatory mushroom vol-au-vents that I always request for my wedding reception hospitality rider.

So I'd now missed both of her ceremonies, and after forfeiting the entire day for marriage number one, besides the aforementioned buffet remains from this event, all I had for memories of the day in exchange for a deluxe his and her bath towel set was a 5-0 thrashing at White Hart Lane and a couple of hours of D.J. party tunes from the seventies and eighties!

Deaths…

It was Benjamin Franklin's quote in 1789 that stated "The only certainties in life are death and taxes".

You may be able to add a few more to that, but of course the first mentioned is inevitable.

To quote a soliloquy from Shakespeare's 'Hamlet', 'No one knows with any accuracy when they shall 'shuffle off this mortal coil'. And for sure, the final day of being laid to rest cannot be compromised if the team you follow just happen to be playing their fixture at the same time.

So far I have been fortunate in that respect with the only family bereavement being my father Percy who died during the week on a non-match day in November 2002, with his funeral taking place on our joint specifically chosen date to avoid any clash.

That entitlement can be duly negotiated if it is your own flesh and blood to purposely ensure that there is no conflict of interest. However there is no such bargaining procedure when arrangements are out of your jurisdiction, when for instance a friend or close relative pass away. No, I'm afraid saying that you can't attend because your club are playing a couple of hundred miles away on a Tuesday night doesn't really go down well with the congregation, yet I have to remain resolute.

Because of that I have been forced to miss a handful of interment and cremation ceremonies that I would normally have witnessed . But whenever I can be present at both the committal and the game I always endeavour to do so.

Indeed, I have previously re-booked advance rail tickets at extra cost to facilitate an appearance at each, on the same day.

Which brings me to my very own inescapable fate, and some would believe 'day of reckoning'.

Well, if indeed I am brought to account for my actions in this life I will claim to have tried to live life to the full in every respect, whilst showing a devout loyalty to my football club.

To such an extent that I have already made tentative enquiries to senior personnel at Burnley requesting one final visit to my beloved Turf Moor AFTER my demise.

It goes without saying that I would first be injected with embalming fluids to preserve my appearance before hopefully a couple of my fellow supporters will carry me over their shoulders to the very front of the upper Longside to the seat that I have occupied since its opening. There I will remain for the ninety minutes plus added on time as a homage to the team I adopted in 1964.

It's fair to say the replies I received weren't favourable with amongst others media manager Darren Bentley quite reasonably claiming that it would create a number of health and safety issues.

Not for me it wouldn't Darren, given the circumstances!

Ah well, I live – or die, in hope.

Keep right on to the end of the road...

Tuesday November 19th 1996.

Bristol Rovers (away) Division Two (old Three)

It was a typically cold winter's morn as I clocked on for the start of my early shift around 6.50 a.m. at the Mr Kipling cake factory. The pavements were icy and a smattering of light snow was beginning to fall.

More worryingly, the forecast was for a heavier snowfall as the day progressed. I was knocking off at two o'clock to pick up my lift which would take me to our league game down at Bristol Rovers.

The 'Gasheads' as they are known due to the close proximity of giant gas storage containers near to their old ground at Eastville, had recently moved from their rented ground at Twerton Park Bath which they had shared with Bath City F.C. Their new residence at the 'Memorial Ground' in the suburb of Horfield was also a dual occupancy, with Bristol Rugby Union Club as their bedfellows.

But as had been predicted the bad weather started to sweep in from midday onwards to such an extent that roads outside were now caked in packed snow.

I summoned Phil Law, or 'Bungle' as I had termed him when he gets on my nerves, to religiously keep me informed about any developments broadcast on the radio regarding ongoing traffic flashes and possible match postponements on the hour every hour, as we weren't allowed to have any form of distractions in the mixing bay where I worked.

This he did, but each bulletin brought with it reports of horrendous traffic delays on the nearby M6 motorway upon which I was travelling.

Steve and Bev. Todd were due to pick me up outside my works at 2p.m. in the mini-bus they had hired for Rossendale Clarets Supporters Club.

Come 3p.m. there was still no sign of them, and by now I was starting to get more than a little bit twitchy. Bristol would be a good three hours away in these conditions with no hold ups, and that's if they made it through at all.

I waited for the traffic and sports report once again on my portable pocket transistor that I'd brought to keep myself informed. The news wasn't good, in fact it was dreadful.

Due to the adverse weather conditions a number of roads had become impassable and the M6 motorway was down to crawling pace in and around junction 15 for the Stoke turn off. I was in big trouble.

There had been other postponements that night but our match down in the more sheltered west country wasn't one of them.

So my situation was rapidly worsening. None of our travellers including myself possessed a mobile phone in those days as they hadn't yet become mainstream or even readily available, which made both parties completely uncontactable.

The M6 motorway was gridlocked meaning I couldn't even hope to hitch a lift down. But anxiously clenching both fists and buttocks in unison I knew I would have to try and get there somehow as time was ticking away.

Just then Gaz Tunstall came off site after finishing his shift as a fitter.

"Zippy! Come here. I need a lift", I shouted him over gesturing him towards me with my arms.

"My transport hasn't got through so i've got to try and thumb a lift. Can you drop me off at junction 15?"

Normally Zippy would reply with a curt, "You can fuck yerself off!", but he must have had a good day doing little at work, as he agreed.

After all it was only two miles distance, and he could tell by the desperation in my voice that I was fast running out of options.

Although it was only a five minute ride away during that short space of time I found despairingly evil plans creeping into my head.

I knew for sure that it was a pointless exercise offering 'Snoz', his colloquial name by the way, any amount of money to drive me the full 130 miles, as he simply wouldn't. But if I forced him to take me, then he would have no choice in the matter would he?

In my plastic sandwich box which had previously housed my cheese butties was a six inch serrated kitchen knife to slice up my tomatoes at dinner time.

I now had the weapon capable of staging a kidnap making him transport me to Bristol!

It was only a fleeting dark thought however. After radically thinking it through, the bottom line would be that I might get to this match, but after that I'd probably be banged up inside for the following five seasons.

He wished me luck and added scornfully, "You're going to fucking need it!" as I made my way to the slip road hitching point.

The time was now 3.15p.m.

When I got to the turning heading south my heart sank even more. It was just one snake of gridlocked cars, vans and lorries across all three lanes.

In keeping with my lifetime motto of, "Always expect the unexpected!" I pulled out one of my cardboard destination signs with M5 lettered upon it in the forlorn hope that the road would clear.

It didn't for half-an-hour, then ever so slowly started to move forward.

Four o'clock passed and the radio broadcaster was recommending motorists not to travel for their own safety unless it was absolutely necessary on police advice.

Of course from my perspective it was completely necessary, but as I looked forlornly down on the main artery, vehicles were still only creeping along at a conservative 10 miles an hour.

It was bitterly cold in the blizzard now, and I had been exposed to the elements for over two hours solid, but although the traffic was hardly moving neither was I.

Step on the gas to the Gasheads!....

I cursed the air loudly for putting myself in a position where I was completely reliant upon other people to get me there. And even though it had been freak weather conditions at the root of the problem I was regretting not taking a day off work in order to be sure of arriving in Bristol. It now looked like I was going to miss my first game in 22 years!

The situation really did look hopeless. I couldn't phone a taxi, as besides being in the middle of nowhere, the motorway wasn't easing sufficiently for transportation. No trains would get me to Bristol , if indeed they were running. I was stuck up the creek without a paddle, and yet refused to move hoping some kind of miracle might happen.

I concluded Steve and Bev's mini-bus must have been forced to turn back as it was now approaching 4.30p.m., two and a half hours after they should have picked me up.

Then that miracle happened. A horn peeped loudly on the other side of the exit slip road and main beam lights flashed on and off in my direction immediately opposite. Dusk was falling so I found it hard to distinguish from which vehicle it was coming from until a lone voice called across like a guardian angel from the heavens.

"Derv, its Steve from Accy.Clarets"

My heart rate almost doubled on the spot as I pointed him to the roundabout a hundred yards down the road.

I flagged Steve down before he committed his bus to the one way entry back on to the motorway.

"You will never know how bloody happy I am to see you lot!" I greeted the passengers as the door slid open, and I quickly jumped in.

"But there's no point going on the M6 here as its barely moving. I'll take you along the A34 to Wolverhampton to pick Steve The Veg. up."

With that we were away but because of their severe delay, time was against us.

A much clearer run took us to the junction we were due to meet Steve, but he wasn't there. It later transpired quite logically that he had given up on his proposed lift and with no way of contacting anyone they couldn't inform either him or me that the bus was still coming.

Conditions were awful for the first hundred miles but as we approached Bristol it had eased considerably.

At 7.36p.m. We joined a few hundred other hardy souls who had managed to get down on the small open corner away terrace next to the Centenary Stand of a typically antiquated rugby ground.

It was one of the few venues that had a 7.30p.m evening kick off so we missed the first six minutes but no goals, as Burnley went on to win the game 2-1 with Paul Barnes netting a brace to partly compensate the followers for what was a truly nightmarish journey.

I was just glad to be there given my hopes of doing so at around 4.30p.m were standing at absolute zero, and it was all down to the doggedness and determination of the Accrington Clarets who never gave up on the job. Well done all, but particularly driver Steve Todd for keeping my record intact.

Home Park – A long way from home

There had already been a precedent set for struggling to get to a game in the south west due to inclement weather when Burnley travelled to Home Park, Plymouth during the decade of the eighties.

Peter Toner, affectionately known as 'Steamy Windows' to his mates, and brothers Martin and Colin Slater had driven down to our house on the Friday night in readiness for a quick getaway early next morning for the arduous near 500 mile round trip on a treacherous Saturday of January 9th, 1982.

So it was an early 6a.m. rise for me to prepare the local Stoke delicacy of cheesy oatcakes for my guests. Overnight, the snow had turned to slippery ice.

We were away at 7a.m. albeit very tentatively out of our council estate cul-de-sac knowing that it was going to be a very tough journey ahead.

And so it proved, with each passing hour came a deeper intensity of snow forcing hundreds of vehicles to be abandoned both on the hard shoulder and inside lane of the motorway.

Once we got past Bristol the conditions had got so bad we were now driving at no more than 15 m.p.h. on thickly packed ice. It was just like the surfaces seen on the television series 'Ice Road Truckers', because just like those rudimentary thoroughfares there was no moving traffic in front of us.

Information from the car radio was virtually non-existent in regard to football updates during that era and so we were left to pull in to the service stations along the way to ring the Devon Club.

At Taunton Deane, Cullompton and finally Exeter phone calls were made, and each time to our amazement we got the same assured reply from the cheery receptionist.

"Oh yes! The game is definitely on. We've got no snow at all down here ma love".

It was hard to believe given the atrocious conditions we had so far endured for the past six hours with no other vehicle prepared to continue the journey into Devon. But given her comprehensive assurance that the city was clear there was absolutely no choice but to carry on.

That we did, still tentatively, as in our eyes there was nothing more than the same frozen expanse of iciness ahead.

Then within five miles of Plymouth, like magic, there was no snow or ice. It really was as if we were visiting another country.

We knew of absolutely no one else who had come down from Lancashire by car and made the game. As for those hardy souls that had caught the overnight train from Piccadilly , Manchester hoping to get there for breakfast time, they had to battle through eight foot high snow drifts to just make the 3.pm. kick off. Burnley claiming a valuable point with a Kevin Young strike that pushed them up to 19th in the Third Division. By the end of the season just over four months later they would be crowned champions with the same player scoring another vital final goal of that campaign at home to Chesterfield.

26 Cheers to Two Play-Offs –
One Good-One Bad: 1991-1994

I do fancy the odd pint but there are definitely some areas of the country better than others.
10,000 pub visit 1992.

<u>Something in the water....</u>

There is always more than a degree of trepidation when I undertake a football excursion to the South West of England.

It's nothing to do with the spectre of hooliganism, or the long distances involved in getting to my destination. Those are incidental matters as this personal apprehension has much more far reaching consequences. It is all to do with the reaction I have to the locally brewed beers in this area, which I find consistently more disagreeable to my stomach than in other parts of the country.

In particular the neighbouring counties of Devon and Cornwall seem to offer up the most stark inconsistencies to the end liquid product.

Whether that is down to the possibility of hard water being used in the brewing process or an additional element administered to the mash ingredients I really don't know. But what I do know is that my internal filtration system becomes far less tolerant when I partake of a few drinks down in this neck of the woods.

For instance who could forget the near outbreak of World War III when a german visiting party occupied my previously empty dormitory at Exeter youth hostel on my return from a heavy night out in the nearby town of Topsham, Devon.

I was staying there on the Friday before Burnley played Exeter City after hitching lifts off vehicles down the M6 and M5 motorway. What happened next is well documented in part one of my autobiography 'Got To Be There!' For those that have not read the episode the ten or so pints I had consumed made an unexpectedly violent nauseous return that took the form of an airborne attack from my top bunk, or given the company I was in maybe that should read 'bunker'.

It was reprehensible behaviour that given my penned in circumstances I could do very little about. Apologies for my uncontrollable churning were rightly rebuked with a verbal volley of what I can only surmise were germanic profanities and threats of violence.

Ever since that regrettable incident I have made a conscious effort to pace myself when I take in those areas' rogue beers, for my own and everyone elses sake.

Yet, almost as if to remind me of my short-comings a day trip to Torquay for a Fourth Division game nailed me once again.

I was travelling down by car with two Burnley fans from the Nantwich area of Cheshire. It was only a couple of days after the Christmas of 1990 so it would be fair to say I was a little bit fragile. Bryan was driving and 'Cinc' was the other passenger who himself liked a drink. 'Cinc' had gained his nickname the Cincinatti kid from his prowess as a shrewd poker player.

It was my suggestion to call in at Newton Abbot for several early morning scoops. I agreed to meet them in a designated boozer while I surveyed some pubs. After a few quick slurps I joined them in the chosen premises which happened to be the Olde Cider Bar.

This place is one of the rare few in the whole country that serves draught cider only. As such this substitute to my usual pint of bitter had to be sampled to fulfil my 'pub copping' criterion as there were no alternatives.

It was a strong cloudy scrumpy that looked and tasted about as appetizing as a glass of toilet cleaner. But drink it I did in the restricted time that we had available. Bad mistake!

Within three miles of Bry setting off in his motor I could sense the cider curdling in my gut. I had no choice but to ask him to stop. Scrambling out of the car I heaved my heart up on the grass embankment. The curse of the South West had struck again.

We continued to the ground to witness a poor 2-0 defeat which hardly aided my recovery. But at least we wouldn't be coming back down to the pretentiousness of the self-styled 'english riviera' again this season and their awful ales-or would we?

Our finishing position of 6th ensured that we certainly would, as occupying the spot one place below us were Torquay United meaning that a two legged play off semi-final would pair us together once more. The prize for the winner of the four team knockout was the last remaining promotion place to the Third Division.

'Tricky' Trev had offered his driving services for the excursion in his motor.

After picking me up we 'knocked on' for Steve 'The Veg' in his home town of Wolverhampton.

As it was our inaugural qualification for the recently introduced play-off competition an air of excitement enveloped the car as we journeyed South.

Somewhat inevitably the conversation turned to my lamentable conduct on a couple of previous visits to Devon when some of the less palatable local brews had got the better of me with truly sickening consequences. That led me to make this solemn pledge.

"O.K., O.K.! enough's enough! I can categorically state that under no circumstances will I disgrace myself in their fair county again. Don't get me wrong, I'm still going to have a good drink, but at the same time I will remain fully aware of the affect it may have on my metabolism".

Although there were the predictable guffaws of laughter from them both I'm sure they could detect a serious tone to my statement of intent.

We arrived at our pretty fishing village base of Brixham, unpacked our bags, then caught a cab to do the town of Torquay.

It was a pleasant day, so where better to base ourselves than in a few pubs around the picturesque harbour looking out to sea.

Being the mooring point for its many yachts and boats there is always the feeling of heightened activity in this area as vessels come and go and the laughing seagulls hover overhead for a birds eye view.

Early season holidaymakers were strolling in the late afternoon sunshine. The elderly clotted cream and scone brigade were dining alfresco amongst the many continental style pavement cafes and restaurants indulging in polite conversation, and a steady trickle of office workers were beginning to filter into the bars. A more sedate setting would be hard to find.

Then the tranquillity was shattered in an instant as crash-bang-wallop, brawling bodies spilled out of the pub entrance that we were intending to visit ourselves.

One of the battling figures was instantly recognizable as 'Kaiser' who like ourselves had decided to make a long weekend of the trip.

Looking hopelessly outnumbered we all upped our pace to try and break up the melee, but were beaten to it by a siren sounding, blue light flashing, speeding police motor.

Briskly alighting their panda car two officers immediately grabbed Kaiser in a restraining arm lock before handcuffing him into the back seat of their vehicle.

Another two of his mates 'Diddy' and Dominic were also arrested. Then they were gone, leaving the doormen to dust themselves down and assume their original imposing posture outside the licenced premises.

"What was that all about mate?" I asked one of the shaven headed trio.

"Just some northern bastards taking the piss!" he insisted.

"Hey! We're northern bastards," I protested.

It later transpired that the doormen had been trying to sell tickets for the play-off game at the grossly overcharged price of £25 each.

Kaiser and his pals missed the game with Kais going down for six months, later reduced to three on appeal for his part in the incident.

We made our way to Plainmoor, home of the Gulls and awaited the team bus arrival.

Before our very eyes we observed a bleary eyed Frank Casper who was manager at the time, stumble down the steps along with his assistant Jimmy Mullen.

"Bloody hell Trev it looks like they've both been up all night planning for this one."

"Whatever they've been up to, they had better make sure we win it now," replied Tricky.

It turned out to be a false hope as Torquay eased into a 2 goal lead and protected it for the second leg.

Frank Casper seemed to be kicking every ball, so much so that with five minutes to go he walked round to the frame of the goal and leant on it. Then the referee put 700 travelling fans and thousands more watching on the big screen at Turf Moor that has been erected to accommodate those that couldn't get a ticket out of their misery.

Torquay defended well in the return at Burnley and Burnley's only meagre consolation was a late goal.

I suppose we had made the Play-Offs' for the first time, but the bottom line being we had failed, and impatient supporters were wondering if we would ever get out of the bottom tier.

Casper kept his job, but surely after six long years in the basement division it must be dependent on a good start next time out.

Season 1991-92 will be remembered for one resonating chant. That of:

"Jimmy Mullen's claret and blue army!..."

For it was Jimmy Mullen, Frank Casper's right hand man who replaced him as manager seven league games into the season culminating in a gutless 3-1 away defeat at Scarborough.

After the whistle had signalled the end of an embarrassing ninety minutes, myself and Trev charged to where our manager and his assistant were sitting in the main stand.

"Piss off Casper and take that wanker Mullen with you!" was my angry retort towards their direction which they must have heard.

Half of my advice was taken when Frank resigned, unbelievably the other half of the mismanagement team was upgraded to caretaker manager.

"Bloody hopeless Trev, we might as well resign ourselves to another year at this shit tip!" I commented on the appointment.

How wrong could I be?

Remarkably, Burnley went on to win their next eight league games propelling themselves up to 2nd spot in the division.

After which I had to admit to Trev that I had made a terrible error of judgement with Jimmy Mullen. He wasn't just good at his job – he was brilliant!

I pledged to rectify my misconception of the man by singing his praises loud and proud.

We played at Aldershot a week before Christmas 1991 when we had gone top of the league.

Myself and Trev tried in vain to get it going on the away terrace as we sang,

"Jimmy Mullen's claret and blue army,

We're so good it's unbelievable!"

"Perhaps the second line is too much of a mouthful Trev, we'll just have to abridge it next time."

Burnley won that game as well 2-1, but the result was later expunged as The Shots resigned from the league.

Chesterfield away on New Years Day would be our next attempt and with Burnley fans occupying half the ground we made out way to the very end of the crowd located halfway down the side paddock hoping that a Mexican wave type effect might just kick start the chant in its singular. It did! First a couple, then a dozen, followed by the whole 'L' shape following joined in with an enthusiastic accompanying hand clap.

"Done it Trev's kid! It's taken off, and by the sounds of it that one's gonna stick."

And stick it did culminating in what the The Sun newspaper columnist John Sadler described as the longest and loudest sustained chant he had ever heard on a football ground anywhere in the world.

It came 15 minutes before the end of the 3rd round F.A. Cup replay at the Baseball Ground Derby County which Burnley lost 2-0.

Standing on my seat on the lower level of the double decker stand I broke it out.

The Burnley newsagent sat next to me made some kind of 'nutter' comment, and even Trev looked on shaking his head this time. I didn't care, I persisted with the mantra in an almost hypnotic state until after a couple of minutes it had enveloped both tiers of that end. It carried on for 20 minutes after the final whistle when the players and now our hero manager Jimmy Mullen came out of the dressing room to take the acclaim.

"Not bad for a nutter eh?" I referenced the newsagent who himself had found the enthusiasm to join in. He just laughed and nodded in my direction.

It would never be repeated to such a level, although not through a lack of trying.

If you were there it was a phenomenon that you will never forget, if you weren't I urge you to type the game into the Google search engine on your phone or computer for verification of this defiant stance.

Afterwards a proud Jimmy Mullen was moved enough to declare,

"In all my 23 years in the game I've never witnessed anything like that," he gasped.

"It left my players feeling like they were prepared to die for those people."

And on a balmy Tuesday night at York City at the end of April the players fulfilled our dream of promotion after seven very long years with a 2-1 victory.

I scaled the perimeter railings along with thousands of others to invade the pitch in celebration.

"Burnley are back! Burnley are back! I chanted, and they were, back on the road to recovery.

My disrespectful, heat of the moment rant at both club goal scoring legend Frank Casper and now our new found legend Jimmy Mullen was perhaps somewhat compensated for by that everlasting memory of the 1991-92 season. Promotion to that chant of "Jimmy Mullen's claret and blue army!"

No one likes us either!....

I also have to admit to having a big hand kicking off Burnley's version of the Millwall supporters anthem "No one likes us – we don't care!"

Our rendition never fails to baffle the home fans at The New Den when our away following mimic their tune ending it alternatively with the line "We are Burnley from the north!"

Yet, it is perfectly relevant in the context of a football fans census that was commissioned during the month of December in 2003.

In the poll they asked over 2,000 football enthusiasts various questions regarding their rivalries with other clubs, including their most hated.

Somewhat surprisingly it concluded that Burnley were the second most disliked outfit in the whole of England behind Manchester United which was altogether more predictable of course. Given their worldwide fanbase of glory hunters, massive resources and over-arrogant players and supporters they would always have been my first choice too.

On the back of our new runners –up title The 'Lions' chant was modified, much like Millwall to show our defiance of the voting figures.

But why did we acquire such an unwanted tag in that year. Well, demographics played a large part in the selection process with the neighbouring towns of Bury, Bolton, Bradford, Blackpool, Rochdale, Halifax, Preston and of course deadly rivals Blackburn all placing us in their top three.

Besides always taking a large army of supporters to these locations, which brought about its own problems of crowd disorder, Burnley had traversed the bottom three divisions over the previous quarter of a century making acquaintance with all on a fairly regular basis.

The strength of the longer distance anti-vote of Carlisle, Stockport and Plymouth Argyle do take a lot more explaining, so let me enlighten you.

With the Cumbrians, it almost certainly stems right back to the 1991-92 Fourth Division season when around 8,000 followers made the trip north in the very real hope of seeing their team confirm their agonizing seven year wait for promotion from the bottom tier of the Football League. Burnley fans were allowed to occupy one large side of the Brunton Park ground but sheer numbers forced the occupants to open the gates to the adjacent open terrace and beyond leading to over half their ground having been taken over by the away support. I too would find that hard to take if the roles were reversed.

As it turned out the game ended in a flat 1-1 draw which wasn't quite enough to start the designated 'promotion commotion' fancy dress party that I'd instigated with an impromptu leaflet drop around the town after the previous Cardiff City home game.

The stalemate would go on to seal the host team's eventual rock bottom finish, the consequences of which meant 'The Blues' only escaped automatic expulsion because Aldershot were forced to resign mid-season due to bankruptcy.

Now the case of the Stockport County hatred, which at its peak was second only to that of Blackburn Rovers is a matter of familiarity breeding contempt.

We were both fourth division members playing each other the standard couple of times a season, but by a huge quirk of fate our paths would cross an astonishing twelve times in three years in all competitions, and that is with them winning promotion in the 1990-91 season to affectively exclude our paths from crossing in an additional couple of league matches for one of those years. Whenever a draw was made for either the F.A. Cup, the League Cup, the Leyland Daf Cup, or the Autoglass Trophy it just happened to be a time when we would always seem to pull Stockport County.

The culmination of the animosity peaking in the 1993-94 Play-Off Final when Stockport in 4th position played Burnley in 6th position in the third tier of English football. Ahead by a mighty twelve points, they lost 2-1 to the Clarets in a bad tempered Wembley decider that saw two of County's players sent off.

Which effortlessly brings us to one of the predominant reasons the south west outpost of Plymouth Argyle aren't too keen on Burnley either, even though they are around 300 miles distant.

For it was in the Play Off 2nd leg where what looked like a solid 0-0 draw at Turf Moor would be enough to take the Pilgrims to that very Wembley final of the same year.

The pre-match tannoy was announcing details of transportation to the twin towers, and I do have to admit, as most would that night, we came in hope rather than expectation. But an absolute stunning resurgence after going 1-0 down saw Burnley progress 3-1 within the ninety minutes.

Having already gained an away stalemate, and taking an early 15th minute lead there only looked like one outcome, but Burnley turned the game on its head with two slickly worked goals from an Adrian Heath – John Francis combination with two strikes in as many minutes from the latter, and Warren Joyce adding the killer third.

If that indignation wasn't enough, four years later Burnley condemned the very same Argyle to the fourth tier of English football by beating them 2-1 at Turf Moor in a tense all or bust decider for the drop.

So there you have it, some very unlikely antipathy to a small town club of barely a 70,000 population. But football is all about pride, no matter which club you support, and when that green god of envy sets in, hatred is just around the corner.

It's over twenty-five years since the Premier League was formed in 1992. Top-tier English clubs resigned from the Football League motivated by the desire to negotiate their own lucrative television rights.

In its inaugural season it would be fair to say that the response from the very life blood of its existence, the supporters, was at best lukewarm and at worst apathetic. Stadiums didn't reach three quarter capacity and astonishingly, attendances at Chelsea's Stamford Bridge dipped below the 10,000 mark on a number of occasions.

So what galvanized a division that had an initial turnover from clubs of 46 million to the 1.2 billion that it registered in 2012?

Well love them or hate them its down to the primary reason they broke away in the first place and that is the Sky T.V. package and its accompanying riches. The millions of pounds reward money given to each and all clubs on a diminishing sliding scale dependent upon their final finishing position in the table has ensued that every game from first to last has attained an added competitive edge. This in turn, along with the grossly inflated salaries that can also be attributed to the massive investment of satellite companies has attracted the sought after services of professional footballers of worldwide international stature.

As the consistently highest bidder for broadcasting permission the Sky television organization has cornered the market in bringing top class matches to a global audience. With its enticing pre-match build up, regular analytical contributions from its invited guest pundits, and action replays of every incident it succeeds in triggering debate and discussion from the living room to the lounge bar.

In the first Premier League campaign of 1992-93 there were 22 clubs. They included Nottingham Forest, Oldham, Leeds United, Ipswich, Sheffield United, Sheffield Wednesday, Coventry and the amazing Wimbledon.

As you have probably worked out, none of those eight sides are currently in that division. Each having fallen on hard times to a certain extent, but none more than the original Wombles of Wimbledon.

After being ousted from their Plough Lane home in the affluent borough of SW19 they were franchised out to a consortium and reinvented as M.K. Dons in the football hotbed of a new town called Milton Keynes 60 miles away in Buckinghamshire.

'Football hotbed' being my sarcastic term for a place that has only evolved from the year 1967 to become part of the commuter route for London, giving it about as much history as the mini skirt!

But after reforming as A.F.C Wimbledon and not only traversing the non-leagues but getting promoted from them, they are now proud members of the third tier of the Football League confusingly titled Division One after defeating Plymouth Argyle in the Division Two play-off final at Wembley.

It is the very division Burnley were playing in during the launch of the inaugural Premiership season, but then it was called the New Division Two following the breakaway of those clubs.

Jimmy Mullen was now revelling in his revered status after taking the club out of the depths of old Division Four.

The first season back was a decent one of consolidation with a couple of striking victories along the way. In the first weekend of October Burnley took on top of the table West Bromwich Albion managed then by ex-Tottenham icon Ossie Ardiles. Stevey Harper cutting in off his wing to fire in one of the goals of the season in the opening minute. Mike Conroy adding a second after the break before former Blackburn Rovers adversary Simon Garner pulled one back for a 2-1 finish.

A victory by the same score line at Plymouth in February 1993 courtesy of a rare brace from 'John Pender our defender' would take us to seventh position and flirting with the play-off spots. It was Argyle's first home defeat of the season which for us would end at what would be my second home game of the season at Champions Stoke City, after losing 3-0 in my other locality of Port Vale in early January. The Vale would go on to finish a creditable 3rd before going one better the following season to get promoted along with ourselves.

But if there was one game that reinforced belief in the fans it would have to be our 3rd round F.A. Cup tie at Sheffield united in the early January of 1993. Whether it was finally burying the ghost of John Bond in that epic 2nd round replay at Shrewsbury Town which captured the imagination I'm not sure. But what I am sure is that a good 8,000 plus support crossed the Pennine hills to invade Bramhall Lane in a pulsating 2-2 draw which Burnley would surely have won if two goal Adrian Heath hadn't tangled quite so aggressively with Adrian Littlejohn who was a good foot taller than himself, leading to his sending off.

Burnley lost the replay 4-2 and finished 13th in their first season back in the newly named Second Division third tier.

Burnley's last game was at Stoke who had won the league. A 1-1 draw approved our consolation campaign and there was even better to come – much better!

Promotion through the Play-Offs…

Burnley didn't start the 1993-94 season very well losing three out of their first five league matches, but after ten games they never left the top eight. After disposing of Plymouth Argyle in the Play-Off semi-final 3-1 on aggregate after their final 6th place qualification they knew their next opponents in the decider Stockport County would do absolutely anything to win that game at Wembley.

And what a battle it turned out! Burnley's official ticket take up was the full 32,000 plus allocation which outnumbered the County fans more than three to one in an attendance of 44,806, partly swelled by neutral sales.

After just 118 second the boisterous claret and blue army was silenced when Stockport's captain Chris Beaumont stopped to glance a near post header past Marlon Beresford. It was the quickest goal ever so far in a Play-Off final.

Super Johnny Francis limped off after fifteen minutes clashing heavily with opposition keeper John Keeley triggering a knee ligament strain.

But just before the two-goal hero of the semi-final played his last part in the proceedings Stockport's Mike Wallace was sensationally sent off after a heavy tackle on tricky wingman Ted McMinn with the red card being brandished for spitting.

From then on it was advantage Burnley who drew level just before the half hour mark with a goal fit to grace the national stadium.

David Eyres, our other winger, won the ball on the right of the area, beat two men as he went across the box and beat a third before striking the ball home.

From then on it was simply a question of whether Stockport could hold out.

They didn't help their cause when on the hour scorer Beaumont inexplicably stamped on full back Les Thompson in an off the ball incident right in front of a linesman. County were now down to nine men with his inevitable dismissal and really up against it.

Retribution was swift with the winning goal coming from the highly unlikely boot of Thompson's full back partner Gary Parkinson.

His first touch wasn't ideal when he received the ball on the edge of the penalty area, and his shot also had a hint of fortune about it as a deflection diverted it over the goalkeeper, but no matter he would forever be known as the player who got us promoted to the second tier of the Football League for the first time in over a decade.

My overriding memory of the joyous celebrations at the final whistle will always be the two scorers David Eyres and Gary Parkinson holding the cup aloft arm in arm with their winning medals proudly draped around their necks.

As for me I just danced my way around the concourse to the tune of 'The Clarets are going up!' That's where I bumped into Inchy's missus Jane who I instinctively hugged after planting a kiss on her cheek.

"Yeeees! We did it Jane, and Adrian was great. Well done all!"

Jane possibly shocked by my level of intimacy smiled her wide smile, readjusted the hair I had displaced and went on her way with a nervous,

"O.K. I'll tell him."

Trev, Nick, Michele and myself embraced once again before enduring a good 2 hour wait to get off the car park along with over 200 coaches from Burnley.

The Stats

Wembley, Sunday May 29th 1994

BURNLEY 2	**STOCKPORT 1**
Eyres 29, Parkinson 66	Beaumont 2

TEAMS

BURNLEY	**STOCKPORT**
Beresford	Keeley
Parkinson	Todd (Booked)
Thompson	Wallace (Sent Off)
Davis	Connelly
Pender	Flynn (Booked)
Joyce	Williams
McMinn (Booked)	Gannon (Booked)
Deary	Ward (Booked)
Heath	Francis
Francis (Booked)	Beaumont (Sent Off)
Eyres	Frain

Subs: Farrell for Francis
Lancashire, Williams (GK)

Subs: Miller for Gannon
Preece for Williams (Booked)
Ironside (GK)

Referee – Mr. D. Elleray (Harrow On The Hill)
Attendance: 44,806

Shots on target:	Burnley 8	Stockport 1
Corners:	Burnley 3	Stockport 4
Off Sides:	Burnley 7	Stockport 1

We meet again Mr Bond: 1992-1994

Big bad Bond! John Frederick Bond, Burnley FC Manager from June 1983 to August 1984.
Photo courtesy of Burnley Football Club.

The Hindu and Buddhist belief in 'Karma' can never be ruled out in this world. Their religious faith harbours a firmly held opinion that a person's actions in both this and previous lives affects their future fate. In layman's terms, that equates to 'What goes around, comes around.' This theory was put to the test in astonishing fashion one night in Shropshire.

The legacy he left behind...

In part one of my memoirs, 'Got To Be There,' I covered the John Bond era in the chapter entitled 'We've Not Been Expecting You, Mr Bond.'

It detailed the agonising demise of the club as his audacious attempt to rocket Burnley to promotion imploded spectacularly. Bond's revolutionary master plan centred around the recruitment of a number of his previous signings to form a nucleus of the team.

Even in the early Eighties, when football was not so money laden, transfer fees involving these players were numbered in the millions of pounds. But they were in the main overpaid, over-rated journeymen, and they replaced a host of promising, up-and-coming youngsters as well as our more established players who had formed the basis of what was potentially a good squad.

Little wonder then, as Bond claimed himself, he was booed from the moment he walked round the perimeter of the Turf Moor pitch before his very first home game in charge. His subsequent statement at a hastily arranged question and answer session with supporters, that he had felt less wanted at this club than at any other, should have come as no surprise.

A very mediocre campaign with Bond at the helm achieved an equally average mid-table finish of 12th in the third tier of English football, and that after Burnley had been installed as white hot pre-season favourites by the bookies, who had factored in the signing of so many former big name players.

Then sensationally, with only five days to go before the start of the new season, Bond's contract was terminated after he gave the board of directors a self-righteous ultimatum after a fall out with chairman John Jackson, demanding either Jackson go or he would.

When the news broke that he had left the club in the lurch, the supporters were incandescent with rage and Bond immediately became public enemy no.1.

He was never forgiven and certainly could never be forgotten as at the end of that campaign, Burnley slipped disastrously into the Fourth Division for the first time in more than 100 years of history. In the eyes of the fans, there was only one man to blame, but he was long gone and our paths would never cross again – or would they? As in all good Bond films, the villain can crop up in the most unexpected of places.

Fast forward a few short but painful seasons.

As any supporter will tell you, there is nothing to beat the anticipation of an FA Cup draw. It can pit the minnows against the giants, or your team against its local rivals, and there's also the chance of facing ex-players or even an ex-manager.

Of course, there's usually a lesser degree of interest shown in the earlier rounds unless there is the added ingredient of a particular opposition to provide some added spice. This was that piquant moment.

"Burnley" .... there was the standard pause to ratchet up the air of expectation as the next ball was picked from the velvet bag, and then: "... will play Shrewsbury Town."

Normally, this unexciting pairing against a fellow lower division club would be noted quietly with little significance attached, but one critical factor gave it a far greater magnitude. John Bond was now their manager.

After leaving Burnley, he had bossed both Birmingham and Swansea, being sacked by each club, before returning to football in 1990 as assistant to Asa Hartford at Shrewsbury, eventually replacing him as the gaffer.

We hadn't encountered Bond in the subsequent period until now!

The taming of the 'Shrew'...

The tie in question was to be staged at Turf Moor on Saturday, December 5, 1992, more than eight years since the day Bond left, and with New Year approaching, this was one old acquaintance that certainly would not 'be forgot.'

I would say there were three categories of opinion regarding Mr Bond's 14 month Turf Moor tenure. A small, and I mean small, minority considered that he had suffered bad luck with injuries to key players. In particular Kevin Reeves who was forging a regular goalscoring partnership with Northern Ireland international centre forward Billy Hamilton until he was sidelined. However, the majority of fans fell into either the 'dislike' or 'hate' camps, such was Bond's inglorious handling of the club's affairs.

During the interim period after the club saw the back of the vanquished JB, the hatred had festered like a running sore. Remember, Burnley had gone downhill fast after his departure, taking a full seven years to claw their way out of the basement division, during which time they languished without the proverbial 'pot to piss in.'

Rightly or wrongly, Bond had been blamed for everything from the team's demise to the quality of the pies. It had become a warped kind of degradation to the extent that if it was raining, it was Bond's fault; if the car wouldn't start, it was Bond's fault; if the missus had a headache preventing a leg-over, it was Bond's fault.

So with Christmas approaching and the prospect of Burnley's very own pantomime villain coming to town, all the talk turned to the reception he would receive at 'The Turf.'

It seemed for all the world as though destiny had taken a hand in returning the accused to the scene of their alleged crime. Bond would be obliged to take to the stand for his trial and face the wrath of the soon to be assembled judge and jury that would gather in the Turf Moor public gallery.

However, as in real life, there are sometimes instances where the defendant fails to make an appearance in the dock, or in this case, the dugout.

In the week leading up to the game, a number of press reports had suggested Mr Bond might not be coming to the game. Indeed, one Sunday newspaper claimed he had been mailed a photograph of a group of gangsters with the message "We're waiting for you" scrawled upon it, and was considering police advice on his attendance. Soon after these sinister revelations came to light, he confirmed he had received correspondence from parties he termed "gangsters from Burnley's underworld," advising him not to enter their town.

As a result, a short statement from Shrewsbury Town FC was issued which read: "Our manager John Bond has decided not to travel to the FA Cup fixture at Turf Moor, Burnley on Saturday, December 5, 1992. Mr Bond has taken this decision having considered all the circumstances and feels, in the interests of football, he does not wish the possible consequences of his presence to reflect adversely on the game."

Summarising the story for the Burnley Express newspaper, sports writer Edward Lee wrote: "There is little doubt that Burnley fans – many of whom cannot forgive Mr Bond for releasing great young players and replacing them with ageing 'stars' – would have given him a hard time. Other supporters directly blame Mr Bond for the seven long years spent in the Fourth Division and intended to let him know all about it on Saturday."

The Burnley police chief at the time was Superintendent Clive Fothergill, who after releasing the Shrewsbury statement said: "I have assured Shrewsbury Town FC that if he came, we would take appropriate measures to ensure he could come and go as any other manager would."

"Where's your manager?"...

On the day of the game, the non-appearance of their manager failed to quell the dogs' abuse meted out to the small band of away followers who had made the journey up from the county of Shropshire.

The initial tamely mocking inquiry of: "Where's your manager?" to the tune of Middle of the Road's 'Chirpy, Chirpy, Cheep, Cheep' soon gave way to some more robust rhythmic phrases.

"Bond is a bastard" reverberated down the full length of the Longside terracing, and so as to leave no one in any doubt about the degree of the resentment expressed, a collective chant echoed around the ground in a repetitive moronic mode, to the tune of the 'Dambusters Theme'. The words were simply: "We all hate Bond and Bond and Bond, Bond and Bond and Bond and Bond, and Bond and Bond and Bond, we all fuckin' hate Bond."

All things considered, he had probably made the right decision to stay away.

On the field, Burnley and Shrewsbury played out a 1-1 draw, but more fuel was added to the flames of the already belligerent antipathy that had been relentlessly doled out to both the visiting Shrews supporters and players when Town defender Dean Spink was given his marching orders after clashing with fans' favourite Roger Eli. That set everything up for the replay to be played in a powder keg atmosphere.

In truth, it had been a decent, hard fought 90 minutes, memorable not only for the acrimony surrounding the fixture but also for the abject psychedelic choice of shirts worn by each team.

In the early Nineties, this style of kit was an amazingly common sight. It was manufactured for many professional football clubs in the forlorn hope that it would trigger mass appeal among the fashion conscious youth of the day. With the prominent themes of bright, vibrant colours and assorted shapes, they didn't just cross the borders of bad taste, but rather crashed through the barriers with sirens wailing and blue lights flashing.

Burnley's polyester version featured a base of traditional claret and blue imprinted with sketchy white crosses against diagonal flecks. Such was the messy effect, fans nicknamed it the 'pigeon shit shirt.' The offering from their Salopian rivals had a primary yellow undercoat with additional blue horizontal diamonds attached to a series of vertical straight lines. Both outfits gave credibility to the theory that they had been salvaged following an explosion in a paint factory.

And so Mr Bond had eluded all the vilification that had been targeted towards him, but it was surely only a temporary reprieve. The replay was scheduled to take place in 10 days' time at the opposition's regrettably named 'Gay Meadow' headquarters, and he would have to show his face there no matter what the level of intimidation was going to be.

Bond's position as team manager would require a commanding visual presence in order for him to marshal his team. Or would it?

Karma chameleon...

On police advice, the game was made all ticket, and demand was predictably high for the 2,500 tickets allocated to visiting supporters. Prices back then were £7 for a stand ticket and a mere fiver to stand on the away terrace.

The game represented something like a 200 mile round journey on a cold Tuesday evening in December. Quite a trip for the early stages of the FA Cup, but Burnley fans have long memories when it comes to what they perceive as managerial misdemeanours, and they had some unfinished business to attend to after Bond's truancy at the Turf.'

The raucous mood on the terraces resembled that of a hunting party and it was obvious quite a considerable number of the inebriated congregation had taken a day off work to fire themselves up at one of the many boozers in this pretty market town.

As kick off approached, reports from protesting groups awaiting Bond's arrival outside the players' entrance confirmed no sightings of their quarry as yet.

A small number of the Shropshire Constabulary were assembled in a straight line at the back of the tin shed, not much bigger than a bus shelter, which formed the away end. They were ready to act at the first sign of disorder, and they didn't have to wait long.

When an obscene banner was unfurled advising Bond, in far more derisory words, to 'go forth and multiply,' the police moved in to confiscate the offending flag from the miscreants. But they were in no mood to comply and the tug of war which developed from the resulting confrontation escalated into a major breach of the peace.

Frustrations were already running high and the out-numbered police bore the brunt of the Burnley fans' ire. Helmets were scattered like the targets at a fairground coconut shy as reinforcements arrived to quell the disturbance. Myself and loyal driver for the night 'Tricky' Trev handing back a couple of the items of discarded headgear to their rightful owners.

Some semblance of order was restored as the two teams emerged from the tunnel, but there was still no sign of the man in charge of Shrewsbury's team selection and the cause of the spontaneous outbreak of violence.

All eyes scanned the touchline hoping for a glimpse of Burnley's most wanted – 'Big Bad Bond.' Many stood on their tiptoes priming themselves to deliver a vitriolic salvo of abuse, but once again there was no outlet for their anger as he was nowhere to be seen.

The game kicked off with hundreds of craned necks still bobbing around like a colony of meerkats.

"Where is he? Where's Bondy?," I asked Trev.

"Looks like he hasn't turned up again," commented a nearby observer.

"Nah. He's got to turn up at their own ground. He's their boss," said another.

"Hold on a minute," I alerted Trev, pointing to the centre of the main stand to our left. "Why are those spotlights following someone up the steps?"

"It looks like a camera crew is tracking a steward into the directors' box. There must have been some trouble there too," I suggested.

"No, look," chipped in Trev. "The steward's taken his 'hi-vis' jacket off along with his cap, and he's wearing a suit and tie underneath. He's only gone and sat among the dignitaries."

Then it dawned on me. "Eyup then! It's John bloody Bond isn't it? He's sneaked into the ground disguised as a steward!"

Word spread like wildfire and an instantaneous chorus of boos accompanied a cacophony of anti-Bond shouts from the visitors' Station End terracing mixed with uncontrollable laughter.

"We can see you sneaking in," sang the away end choir.

"Can you believe what you've just witnessed? The manager of a football team going to such lengths to avoid being seen?," I remarked to Trev.

"You couldn't make it up, could you? But whatever the threats were, he's certainly taken them seriously," Trev replied. "We must have some nutters following us, that's all I can say."

Payback time...

Now the mission to locate our victim was complete, all attention turned to events on the pitch with only the occasional reference to the 'man in the jacket.'

In the original tie, we had come from behind to force an equalising goal and we would have to do the same in the replay as the Salopians took the lead with 16 minutes left.

The vibes on the away terrace were dark, and fast descending into frustrated aggression. Some of our party spotted local youths hanging around outside the ground and pelted them with a variety of debris, and the additional police personnel drafted into the away end braced themselves for the anticipated backlash if the result went against the visitors.

Our powerhouse midfielder John Deary had been sent off and with the clock ticking down, it appeared the 'silver fox' in the main stand was going to get sweet revenge for being so viciously ridiculed.

Burnley keeper Marlon Beresford had already saved a penalty for us and was under more pressure, and I turned to Trev, saying: "Well, I'm not in the mood for stacking bloody supermarket shelves after this showing, mate." I was referring to the temporary Christmas employment I was currently engaged with at my local Asda store. I was due on the night shift later that evening and would just about make it with a swift departure from the ground after the game.

Then, out of the blue, our defender John Pender headed in the equaliser to spark joyous scenes in the away end.

"Looks like you won't be, Dave," answered Trev, referring to the 30 minutes' extra time that now looked imminent with only three minutes of normal play now remaining.

But there was to be a final twist as Mike Conroy, the centre forward who had scored our goal in the first game, steered in the winner in the last minute of the ninety.

Cue absolute delirium, as not only would I be making my Asda shift, but much more importantly, we had got one over on the individual who many thought had dragged our club into the gutter.

Stacking shelves had never been so much fun that night but my mind wasn't on sorting the peas from the pies. It was now focused on whether we would blunt the Blades of Sheffield United in the next round of the magical FA Cup.

In fairness to Mr Bond, if you haven't met someone, it is hard to form an accurate opinion of them. My only encounter with him was when I was forced to cycle to Burnley for a Boxing Day fixture against Bradford City and he strode across a zebra crossing I'd stopped at in Wilmslow, Cheshire with his two long-haired Afghan hounds. Little more than pleasantries were exchanged.

There are, however, a few people I know who have met him privately, including my mate Tricky' Trev. He had called at Bond's house to collect a few autographs for a book called 'The Clarets Collection' which painstakingly collates every player who has stepped onto the field to represent Burnley FC in a competitive first team game since World War Two. It also lists all the post war managers, hence Trev's visit to the Bond household for his signature.

Trev painted a picture of a generally private individual with an air of eminence about him who comes across as very courteous, but retaining a hard edge to his firmly held beliefs.

Another more detailed examination of Bond's complex psyche can be gauged from a rare interview granted to a good friend of mine now based in the south. Phil Whalley, in his role as editor of the London Clarets' supporters' club magazine then titled 'Nothing To Write Home About' conducted an excellent, in-depth question and answer session with him about his controversial tenure as Burnley boss. The gist of this enlightening insight into his character was that he admitted to making some big mistakes by trying to do too much too soon. For that admission, I give him credit.

As for my view of him as our manager, I would say his intentions, though overly ambitious for a small town club such as Burnley, were nevertheless in all probability quite honourable. It was just that it simply didn't pan out that way, resulting ultimately in his humiliating foray into the dressing up box to avoid detection at his own place of work.

In Memoriam

John Bond passed away on September 26, 2012 at the age of 79.

He had played 444 first team games for West Ham and perhaps the last word on the man should go to someone who really knew him well.

Ken Brown played alongside Bond in the Irons' defence and would later be his assistant at both Bournemouth and Norwich.

In his eulogy, he commented: "John was a great character. He said what he thought and at times, he riled people. But he was honest, and felt he had to say what he felt had to be said. You always knew where you were with him."

Operation Trelleborgs: 1994

Burnley's deep-rooted rivalry with Blackburn Rovers was entrenched before the turn of the 19th Century. From thereon the battle for local supremacy has been fought with venomous hostility ever since.

A palpable buzz of deep contentment emanated from the away end at the Den on Wednesday 14th September 1994 amongst the few hundred away following.

Not only had Burnley secured a hard earned 3-2 victory over Millwall, but so had a little amateur club going under the name of Trelleborgs from Sweden. They had just beaten our fierce rivals Blackburn Rovers by the same scoreline on the previous night to knock them out of the U.E.F.A. Cup.

This is how the national newspaper reported it.

"Blackburn's multi-million pound team were the laughing stock of Europe last night.

They were turfed out of the U.E.F.A. Cup by a bunch of Swedish part-timers who had been reduced to ten men for most of the second half.

And it was a 25 year old accountant who grabbed the goals to set up the biggest Euro upset for more than two decades.

Not since another Swedish team 'Atvideberg' knocked out cup winners' cup holders Chelsea in 1971-72 has an English club suffered such a HUMILIATING DEFEAT!

Ouch! Trelleborgs was to become the most used Swedish word in the town of Burnley with the Scandinavian 'Smorgasbord' coming in a distant second.

The following night a phone call to a house in the West Midlands is answered by 'Steve The Veg.' On the other end is myself. The short transcript of the ensuing conversation went like this.

MYSELF: "Trelleborgs"

THE VEG: "Oh Yes!"

MYSELF: "I think we need to show a gesture of our appreciation for their valiant efforts by twinning Burnley with Trelleborgs. Can you rustle up a painted sign?"

THE VEG: "Sure thing."

A tactical discussion follows detailing a plan of attack, the proposed site for the sign, and an earlier pick up time to implement our stratagem.

What follows is the Veg's personal diary of that night's proceedings in his own published words.

"Friday evening was when the serious work started. A blank side of wallpaper was given a white emulsion coat as it lay on the living room floor.

Enter Ashley, a 4 year old 'Veg junior' to play a significant part in the drama."

"Daddy is this wet?" he asked whilst admiring the footprints he had bestowed upon this rapproachment of the Swedish and East Lancs footballing cultures. A good start eh?

"At 9 o'clock the canvas was given its second coat of emulsion. Thankfully it dries promptly and Mrs Veg is free to give me a hand lettering the sign at around 10.30pm. Next, permanent marker is used to colour in the letters.

11.15pm and it just isn't working. You can clearly see through some of the figures. Well, it's a good thing the little fella's in bed as it will just have to be his poster paints to finish off the job.

1.am sees a very tired Veg going to bed. The paint now looks better, but it won't completely dry so it requires an early awakening and an additional coat of varnish to protect both the poster colour art and sign.

Saturday morning turns out to be sunny so the paper notice is left to dry in the back garden. Luckily Mrs Veg is still in bed, and isn't on hand to object to her jigsaw board being appropriated to form an excellent backing to the work of art.

After surreptitiously smuggling the jigsaw board into the car, there's the masking tape to pack in order to fix it to the metal sign posts. There's a near accident as a sudden gust of wind inverts the placard, but the piece holds firm and we're ready to go."

That abridged version of events demonstrates the attention to detail of Steve's workmanship. He was determined to make a good job of it.

The Veg picked me up at my usual venue of Keele motorway services on the M6 and we headed north to execute our twinning operation.

The large proclamation simply reads,

"TWIN TOWN TRELLEBORGS as we pull in to affix it to the first boundary notice which states,

"Welcome to the Borough of Burnley."

Located on a straight open road heading into the town in a small village called Dunnockshaw it is the ideal placement on a busy thoroughfare.

A secure wrap of adhesive binding attaches it to the two supporting posts below the border indicator and part one of our exercise is complete.

Mr. Nutter …

We drove on into town and before I settled in for my pre-match drinking session I had one important phone call to make.

The Burnley Express formed the well established local paper, but contacting them may have aroused suspicion, and so from the High street kiosk I dialled the number for the more far reaching Lancashire Evening Telegraph which besides being published daily had a much broader readership circulation throughout the county.

Getting through to their receptionist I immediately asked for the news desk. The reporter duly took my call and after introducing himself, asked how he could help.

By now with Steve giggling in excited anticipation I began to work myself up into a suitably appropriate lather in keeping with the 'Mr Angry' character I was about to portray.

Then, in the most convincing Lancastrian accent that I could muster the luckless news hound got both barrels.

"'Ow can ya 'elp? 'Ow can ya 'elp? I'll tell thee 'ow ya can 'elp.

Get thee sen darn to Dunnockshaw ta see what Burnley bloody council 'ave done. It's a bloody disgrace I think!"

Reporter. "Excuse me sir. Can you calm down a little. What's a disgrace?"

Myself: "What's a disgrace? I'll tell ya what's a disgrace! Burnley twinning their town with bloody Trelleborgs so soon after they've knocked us out of the U.E.F.A. Cup.

I've seen it with ma own eyes just coming through th' illage this morning. Utterly spiteful it is, utterly spiteful!"

Reporter: "Where exactly is this sign located again sir?" he asked sniffing a good story.

Myself: "I've told thee! On the Manchester Road by Bradwood Works mill going into Burnley through Dunnockshaw."

Reporter: "Alright sir. Thank you very much for letting us know. And your name is?"

Myself: "It's Mr Nutter from Darwen. Bloody ridiculous it is...scandalous!"

With that I put the phone down, giving the Veg a high five hand slap.

"Consider it done youth, I reckon he's taken the bait."

"You were pretty convincing Dave. Even ya hands started shaking with rage, and that name was certainly very appropriate for you," added The Veg smiling.

The surname Nutter wasn't an unusual one for this part of East Lancashire. In fact it has been calculated that there are more 'Nutters' per capita here than any where else in Great Britain. Even the last witch sentenced to death at the Pendle witch trials 400 years ago was called Alice Nutter.

We'd had a good laugh pulling off the prank yet Burnley went on to spoil the day for me, but even more so for

Steve, as they lost the game 1-0 to his home town team Wolverhampton Wanderers.

Nonetheless we had both cheered up a bit quicker by Monday evening as news came through that an article as well as a photograph of the phantom twinning boundary sign had been featured on the inside page of that night's Lancashire Evening Telegraph.

The caption underneath the photograph reading,

"Clarets fans were chuckling today as Burnley unveiled it's unofficial twinning link – with the Swedish village of Trelleborgs.

The first leg U.E.F.A. defeat of arch rivals Rovers by the part – timers was good news to some Burnley supporters who had a giggle at the expense of the Blues from down the M65 on this sign on Burnley road Dunnockshaw."

It was a timely reminder to them all, that they may have been gone a while but they certainly hadn't been forgotten by us the Burnley fans.

However, the same could not be said for an ever growing army of Rovers 'sheep' who attracted by the team's success had latched on to them totally unaware of the deep seated hatred between the two towns as my next story proved so convincingly.

Rovers fans fail basic history exam...

My summer holiday to Cyprus the following year perfectly illustrated this very point revealing that to some, historical implications counted for little as we headed towards the Millennium.

I was exploring the well known Troodos mountain region of the island wearing my distinguishing Burnley Football club home replica shirt of claret and blue.

As I meandered up to the isolated long and winding road for a picturesque photo shoot I spotted a threesome walking down the steep hill towards me. It temporarily stopped me in my tracks, as even from such a comparative long distance there was no mistaking the instantly recognizable blue and white halved tops that they wore as anything else but Blackburn Rovers colours.

'Endsleigh', our insurance sponsors of many years was boldly emblazoned across my garment and so there was no misinterpreting it for any other strip but their sworn enemies.

I braced myself for the inevitable merciless ribbing that was about to come my way by preparing a few throwaway retaliatory comments. But with them winning the Premiership title and us being relegated to the third tier they would certainly be favourites to claim the higher ground that they already occupied on their descent down the trail.

There was no one else on the walkway, and indeed these were the first folk I had seen in over an hour such was the remoteness of the area. So I was thoroughly cursing my bad fortune at the unlikely coincidence of having to confront of all people, fans of our victorious neighbours.

As we passed I decided to face them off by looking at each straight into their eyes before greeting them with a casual

"Y'alrate lads?" enquiry.

In turn they gave me nothing more than a cursory glance responding with a cheery "Hello." There was no acknowledgement whatsoever of our divided loyalties as they carried on along their route.

More than a little affronted at their lack of expected antagonism I stopped them to ask if I could have my photograph taken against the magnificent mountain backdrop. For my pose I purposely pointed to my club crest almost inciting a measured riposte.

But no, there was still no flicker of a reaction from the father and his two teenage sons. This was completely alien to me as always, not sometimes, when these pair of diversely coloured shirts meet there is at the very least an exchange of friendly banter, and at worst an exchange of punches! Today there was neither, nothing, nowt, zilch, diddly squat! I might as well have been wearing the local Omonia Nicosia top given their impassive response.

By now I was almost inviting them to take a pop at me. Just one snidey comment, or reference of mild abuse would suffice so that I could fire back at them. It was almost verging on intimidation as I asked,

"Do you know whose shirt this is?"

The father looked at it before replying,

"Yes it's Burnley's strip. Isn't that a town near Blackburn?"

"What! A town near to Blackburn," I repeated his quote "We only happen to be your deadliest bloody rivals."

Seemingly nonplussed he went on to calmly explain that to them the ubiquitous reds from Old Trafford were regarded as their antagonistic adversaries given their current status.

You see, this family hailed from a small town called Wells in Somerset and had only fairly recently adopted their chosen club. "I wonder why?" I knowingly asked myself.

To them, and no doubt thousands of newly acquired paying customers they simply knew no different as it had been over twelve long years since their traditional foes had engaged them in any kind of competitive fixture. We had gone one way and themselves the other. So from the time that these three had pledged their allegiance to the Rovers cause it's highly likely that the word Burnley had hardly been mentioned in dispatches or even given a second thought. They would have all undoubtedly failed their football history exams that is for sure.

As with any Premiership title winning outfit they had spawned a new creation of admirers far more geographically spread than in the past. The considerable kudos that goes with purporting to follow a winning team being their falsely attained status symbol.

In terms of divisional stature it was true that we were poles apart at the time, but within a comparatively short five year term we would soon be once again on a level league playing field. Our century old feuding would be reignited and the uneducated second – hand fans that still remained with their relegated club would find out first hand what a 'real' derby game is all about.

27 A Longside Epitaph: 1994-95

The last fan to leave The Longside and even the stewards look saddened.

To be evicted from your spiritual home of many decades is heart-rending enough. But when that home is demolished, the emotion turns to heartbreak.

Taylor-made football grounds …

……, ……, soldier, sailor, rich man, poor man, beggar man, thief!"

Do you remember it? Part of a simple schooldays recital that I'm sure most of you, young or old, have performed at some time during your youth. Each character in the short verse equated to the number of plum or prune stones remaining after the consumption of this school dinner dessert. The said fruit was usually found within a tapioca pudding of bog-like consistency, or 'frog spawn' as it was known to us kids.

So, you may ask, what's this narrative got to do with football? I suppose it could rightly be claimed that examples of all these diverse members of society watch our national game on a regular basis.

But that isn't the issue on this occasion. No, the reason to recall the saying is because it is my particular way of highlighting how the primary reason for attending a match drastically changed for the first time in more than a century during the decade we know as the Nineties.

The more observant will recognise that the rhyme is incomplete as there are two key words omitted from the beginning of the text. "Tinker" and "Tailor." Yes those two simple words, with a slight change in spelling, provide the perfect description of a man who altered something which provided the very fabric of English football, namely its atmosphere.

The primary dictionary definition of the word tinker is "someone who meddles or botches." That seems quite an apt appraisal of Lord Justice Taylor, who through his much heralded report into ground safety singularly stipulated that all-seater stadiums should be compulsory for all Premier League and Championship sides, almost 50 per cent of the original Football League.

And with that mandatory command in place, smaller clubs who have relocated to new, purpose built, identikit grounds appear to have adopted it as the norm. In addition, the annual relegation of a trio of Championship incumbents to the third tier has meant the proportion of Football League clubs with all-seater stadiums is probably around 80% and rising.

"It had to happen if we were going to make stadiums safer," is the well rehearsed mantra from the very people the ruling didn't affect, ie those punters who sat in the stands anyway.

But my firm and eternal belief is that such wholesale changes didn't have to happen, though more modern and user-friendly grounds certainly did.

In my view, the 1989 Hillsborough Disaster will go down as a preventable one that would have occurred whether the ground was all-seated or not. A combination of gross police ineptitude and a deadly ground layout were the two major contributing factors to the outrage. The crucial fact is that it was a strictly all-ticket game for the whole of the ground, so when the fateful decision was taken to open the perimeter gates at the Leppings Lane End, the badly designed stadium outlay took over, meaning capacity would have been breached whether the area in question was for seated or standing fans.

This long considered opinion has been formed primarily by viewing the revealing television documentary on the tragedy and also attending the Burnley v Newcastle United FA Cup semi-final at the same venue in 1974, when Clarets fans were allocated that ill-fated terrace. Even before the erection of pitchside fencing which prevented an escape route for these poor souls, the unnecessary parallel railings within a short space of terracing behind the goal compacted fans into a small area like canned sardines, with the only entrance and exit via a dark tunnel.

Of course, terracing can be safe if the correct measures are taken to marshal these areas, and there are moves afoot to reintroduce so-called 'safe terracing.' What a blessing that would be, because for the supporter that kicks and heads every ball, there is just nothing like a standing section.

And with that in mind, the following is my own tribute to my patch, my terrace, my second home, the one condemned to history like so many other famous rendezvous by Justice Taylor – The Longside of Burnley.

"Long, Long, Longsiders... Long, Long, Longsiders!" Our booming chant announcing our home territory doesn't have the same ring to it when we're sitting down, does it? These oh-so-simple lines which glorified our tribal home are now no more than a distant memory.

Blood, sweat, tears and emotions of joy, laughter and sorrow have all been shared by the seething masses. It looked out over our very own venue of legends, and bore witness to the likes of McIlroy, Lochhead, Pointer, O'Neil, Irvine and Coates in the Sixties to Dobson, Noble, Stevenson, Hamilton and James in the Seventies. Add Laws, Phelan, Flynn, Eli and Grewcock from the Eighties and Francis, Eyres, Conroy and Davis up to its closure in 1995, and the memory brings a lump to the throat of every Longside devotee. The regular Burnley players who became managers, the likes of Casper, Miller, Adamson and Potts, also deserve a place in the Longside hall of fame, as do many more.

As if relegation from the old Division One in 1976 after a hard fought promotion and then a tumble down the divisions wasn't enough to bear, two decades later we also lost our cherished Longside thanks to the say-so of one man and his report, that certain Mr Taylor. For this reason alone, 1995 proved to be a tremendously sad year, but throw in the destination of the Premier League title which was in effect purchased by our bitter rivals from down the M65, albeit for only 12 months, and perhaps calamitous becomes a better description for the time it took the earth to go once around the sun.

The Battle Zone ...

So all-seater stadiums became a reality for Burnley fans and for many, including me, it wasn't a change to be welcomed, to put it mildly.

Besides the substantially higher cost of admission, the cramped seating and the sterile atmosphere associated with row upon row of vacant chairs, there's the irritating 'stand up, sit down syndrome' to contend with. You know what I mean. First the latecomers disturb the assembled, then someone wants to go to the toilet or grab a pie. And every time the ball gets into the opposition half of the pitch, there'll be one bright spark who stands up in hopeful anticipation. This in turn triggers a chain reaction of bobbing heads. It's the equivalent of thousands of battery hens in an intensive farming programme.

At Turf Moor, there are no more mass migrations from the Longside to the Bee Hole End as the game draws to a close and fans head for the exits like thousands of iron filings being drawn to a huge magnet. In addition, there are no more traditional Longside goal celebrations like the manic leaping up and down to the "um, bah, bah" of Malcolm McLaren's hit single Double Dutch, the terrific surge down the terracing, and the male bonding as you embrace someone you've only just met at the match but who shares your hopes and aspirations for the club.

All this has gone, and the orgasmic reaction from the terrace has been substituted by a standing ovation akin to a call for an encore at an opera house.

Watching football is about generating passion for the club you follow, whether it be Burnley, Barnet, Bognor or Bamber Bridge. It's your adopted team and you're entitled to show your exuberance big style.

It's not that I'm against change full stop, more that I don't think making every ground all-seated is a wholly adequate strategy. With a little thought, a standing area could quite easily be restored and retained at most places.

I must concede that on the positive side, every refurbishment has brought with it a much higher standard of hospitality. For example, my landlords at Burnley never showed any concern for basic hygiene in the toilets either at the back of the Bee Hole End or behind the Longside at any time in their 40 year existence. It seemed these public conveniences were regarded as an inconvenience to the club. Such a huge chore as placing disinfectant cubes in the gulley of each latrine was rarely undertaken and there was simply no excuse for the disgusting stench that emanated from the Bee Hole End bog, which was located downwind of the neighbouring cave-like snack bar.

Could you ever imagine any of our directors undoing their flies with total abandon and joining the communal half-time sprinkling ceremony on the grassy bank behind the Longside, or even in the comparative luxury of our twin open-topped parallel-walled 'restrooms?' I don't think so somehow, and that's further evidence of the 'us and them' mentality that existed in the past. Make no mistake, as far as that department went, when the Longside was rebuilt, toilet facility-wise it was like moving from workhouse to Wetherspoon's.

The Longside has also been the scene of many pitched battles between rival fans, especially before there was any type of segregation. The infiltrators would mingle, remaining silent until their team scored a goal, when with cover blown by a celebratory leap or even restrained applause, they would be stalked by the Longside's resident Neanderthals until the chase reached its inevitable conclusion. Frenetic 'Keystone Cops' type scenes would follow as the hard pressed Lancashire Constabulary, with truncheons drawn, would chase the procession of would be warriors around the ground. I've witnessed knives pulled out by the Coventry and Spurs lunatic fringe and West Ham fans using bolt cutters to get through the wire fence at the back of the Longside in order to engage in hand to hand fighting as they tried to breach our fortifications. Lines of police would tightly form into a human barrier with the thankless task of keeping the two mobs apart when Liverpool, Everton, Leeds or Manchester City were the visitors.

But easily the most frightening battle of the Longside took place on Tuesday, September 12, 1978, when 30,000 people turned up for an Anglo-Scottish Cup first round, first leg tie against Celtic. Around 8,000 crazed Jocks took offence at the Burnley fans' incessant chants of "Ar-gen-tina, Ar-gen-tina," the host country of that year's World Cup Finals when Scotland had been humiliated by Peru and drawn with the football minnows of Iran.

Although all Burnley fans had been subjected to a body search after previous dart throwing incidents, the Celtic fans crucially had not. Consequently, it rained bottles all through the game to such an extent that my overriding memory is of police dogs being carried down in the arms of their handlers from the no-man's land area between the fans. The glass was becoming so concentrated that it was forming a layer on the terraces and effectively becoming embedded in the animals' paws.

Parts of the railings were then uprooted from their concrete bases and used as crude spears by the Celtic violators. Combine that with a pitch invasion and fierce hand-to-hand confrontations on the Bee Hole End, and you'd be forgiven for thinking this was some historical re-enactment of a scene from the film 'Braveheart' rather than a tie in some menial football cup competition.

Yet the Longside remained in English hands, the Claret protectorate being held, as its defenders stood firm to repel all invaders. They were helped by the fact that a large part of the segregation fence remained in place. If it hadn't, I fear the Scottish hordes would have overrun the ground. On this occasion, the home fans had prevented even more wholesale disorder by standing their ground to defend themselves from these savages.

And why shouldn't they have done? I'm not advocating violence, but if your own domestic premises were broken into, you would surely put up a resolute resistance to preserve your domain. Safeguarding their home terrace was mirroring the actions of a householder defending his property for those Longsiders that night.

On the same distasteful but relevant subject, I think the last time the Longside was 'taken' deserves an airing.

I have to cast my mind back to Easter Monday, 1976. The world's worst glory hunters from Old Trafford were the visitors. We lost 1-0 in front of 27,000 and were relegated once more from the old Division One.

It was clearly announced that no tickets for the Burnley section of the Longside would be sold on the day of the match, but as it happened, thousands upon thousands were relinquished to the 'red sheep,' who invaded our enclosure and carried out a series of extremely nasty assaults, some of them on women and children. Whose fault was that farcical ticket situation? The club or the police? Wherever the blame lies, it was a total disgrace and some of us who have long memories don't forget such stark scenes.

The Longside was the very pulse of the body that was Turf Moor. Once the volume was cranked up, it seemed in turn to activate the Cricket Field Stand, the Bee Hole Enders, and on occasions even the more restrained residents of the Bob Lord Stand. The ground would reverberate with a crescendo of noise and our home was widely regarded by opposition supporters as one of the top ten most atmospheric grounds in the whole country.

And then we were told to close it!

Eviction Day ...

All too soon came the time for the final day of Longside occupation, Saturday, September 16, 1995. Uniquely for a league match in modern times, the wire mesh and segregation railings had been taken down so the away section could be given over to the home fans. This would enable as many as possible to experience the unique atmosphere of the Longside for one last time.

Hull City were the visitors for this emotional occasion and their supporters were accommodated in the Cricket Field Stand behind the goal. To add a little more personal significance to the last farewell, poignantly for me the match referee was Jim Rushton from Stoke-on-Trent, someone I knew personally from playing Sunday morning football.

In keeping with the sombre mood of the day, I dressed in funereal black, with the tie, trousers and shoes topped off with a black bowler hat. I was serious faced, damned serious, as any occupant preparing to be evicted from their residence of almost 30 years would be. Any fan of any team who has gone through the same experience would empathise with the numbed shock I felt as the ordeal progressed.

I'd taken my daughter Clarette to sit on a crush barrier there just before her first birthday in August 1990. Even then with the modest attendances we had that season, she would be more captivated by the singing off the pitch than the action on it.

But now it was my turn to be hypnotised as I purposely strode along the full length of the terrace. Gazing up at the steep concrete terracing and thin asbestos sheeting that combined with the green-painted interlocking support structure to form a shelter from the wintry elements, I had to hold back the tears.

Basic as the Longside was, and it was basic, it retained an elegance in its vastness. It was simply a meeting place for thousands of worshippers whose sole intention was to stare at an open field of play for 90 minutes. The feeling was incomprehensible to people who hadn't taken in the match day atmosphere, but incomparable to those who had.

Before the game started, I placed a simple commendation written on a piece of cardboard against the perimeter fence recording the occasion and ending with the line "R.I.P. THE LONGSIDE." That very same plain notification would be used as the cover photograph for The Longside...End of an Era!' book 10 years later.

It was incidental but fitting that Burnley won the game 2-1 but when that final whistle blew, it signalled a period of nostalgic reminiscence among the congregation. Along with Tricky' Trev Slack, I knew I had to join the hard core assemblage that was belting out songs of defiant tribute at the back of our stronghold. A full repertoire rang out for a good half an hour before the stewards were directed to clear the ground.

After varying degrees of protestation, the majority left as requested, but a breakaway group reassembled, chorusing a confrontational rendition of "We shall not be moved," aimed towards the crowd controllers. Eventually they did, after what it must be said was a good deal of tact and sensitivity administered by the coercing officials.

With the terrace clearing, I remained, saying nothing and just staring blankly in the direction of the oncoming, brightly jacketed eviction squad. I must have resembled the defiant Yozzer Hughes from the 1980s TV programme 'The Boys from the Blackstuff.'

After politely being asked: "Could you make your way to the exit now please?," I put out a restraining arm to the two heavy-handed stewards attempting to physically remove me."

"Just give me a minute, mate," I asked forcibly.

They realised the importance of the moment and after getting the nod from their team leader, they released their grip accordingly. Then, fixing my eyes forward and with just the small posse of police and security now in front of me for company on the now near deserted terrace, I subconsciously thanked the Longside "for all the good times" before doffing my hat and slowly walking towards the single exit gate. Touchingly, a spontaneous round of applause greeted me from the small group of fellow Longsiders remaining outside the exit gate as the trail of officialdom shepherded me out.

A Burnley Express newspaper reporter witnessed the commotion and asked me for a few comments. After initially telling them "I didn't feel like talking under the circumstances," I decided they might be just the medium through which I could express my disgust at the closure of one of the greatest terraces in English football, the legend that was the Longside.

So there you have it.

The end of degrading toilets with not only no soap or water but no means of drying your hands and no sit-down cubicle either. No more protecting your territory from various burglars, but also no more euphoric chanting from many famous victories.

But above all, the Longside left a lasting legacy and gave every fan who stood there a real sense of being a vital part of Burnley Football Club through being a 'Longsider.'

First Day back at 'Roboboro'

It's Middlesborough away for the opening game of our 1994-1995 football season. After an absence of eleven years, my club Burnley F.C. are back in the first division. However, its not the introduction they would have chosen to renew their acquaintance.

To begin with, there's a certain 'Bryan Robson' mania sweeping across the smallest county in England. There's also a batch of ex-premier league signings secured for around three million pounds, and all primed to make their debuts. As if that wasn't enough to contend with, the additional spur of a brand new 30,000 all-seater dockside stadium is about to be constructed, illustrating the already high expectancy of success. Incidentally, the approach to this pristine complex will bear the unlikely upmarket name of 'Ayresome Boulevard'. Perhaps it would be in keeping with this snowballing mood of events to have the ground officially opened by that most famous of social climbers 'Hyacinth Bucket' (pronounced Bouquet of course). Allow me to enlighten the unitated who have not visited this inhospitable but hardy industrial town. The scale of change in the last six months or so, if represented on a 'swingometer' would be quite stark. Perhaps akin to Kevin Keegan being put in charge of neighbouring Hartlepool United, and bringing half a team of his mega-stars to play at a purpose built super-ground entitled let's say 'Victoria Marina'.

Of course, the only way to form a considered opinion was to see for myself. Therefore, it was with an enhanced degree of anticipation that I prepared to set off on my Claret pilgrimage to Ayresome Park, located in the pseudonym county of Cleveland. Now there's an obscurity if ever there was one! Surely the colloquial term of 'Teesside' would be more appropriate for this boundary, in preference to a meaningless and rootless appellation. This would also instil a sense of origin to the population as a whole. But I digress.

I had long since designated this fixture as one for the 'magic thumb', which is my expression for hitchhiking. I have used this method of transportation to over one quarter of the near 1,500 Burnley F.C. games that I have attended during the previous twenty five years. This has produced a grand running total of 159,400 'free' road miles which is updated annually. From my village near Stoke-On-Trent, Staffordshire it is an estimated 330 mile round trip to Middlesborough and so an early start was imperative, I therefore decided on a departure time of 10.30a.m. from Keele motorway services on the preceding Friday.

First to be packed were my four cardboard hitching signs painted with the relevant destinations I required en-route. Not forgetting a change of clothes for my base camp, enough sandwiches to last a couple of days and various items essential to personal hygiene.

Then last, but certainly not least my lucky humbug! Forty years old I may be, but a lot of cautious supporters as well as their footballing counterparts either retain a lucky talisman, or perform a regular habit forming ritual. Going to such lengths in the belief that it might just be the tiny deciding factor to influence the right result.

Well I'm no different, and so my yellow and brown striped confectionery accompanied me as the current flavour of the month. This magical sweet being a donation completely out of the blue, and offered to me as I was cycling to my departure point for the important 2nd leg of last season's Division 2 play-off at Plymouth. It then subsequently journeyed to Wembley stadium where it played a vital part in the 2-1 defeat of Stockport County to gain a precious place in the First Division. To all the doubters reading this article I would suggest a video viewing of these two deciding matches where victory was procured against all the odds. Therefore for the moment, as a measure of personal importance it ranks alongside the 'Koh-I-Noor' diamond in terms of inestimable value.

Friday morning came and the local motorway services was reached. After engaging in what must have looked like an imaginary game of tennis with a swarm of hornets which were infesting the nearby blossoms, my first chauffeur came along. A lift to the M62 was gained terminating at Hartshead Moor services. This was courtesy of a very excitable contract harvester on holiday from an outback ranch in South Australia, who had more than a touch of the 'Jethro Clampitts' about him.

An exasperated driver returning from an emergency trip to Liverpool passport office, and a Harrogate toffee delivery van ensure I arrive in the fine city of York for 2.15p.m. I've spent a combination of days and nights in the vast majority of towns and cities nationwide following Burnley and for me York comes top of the good night-out league. Marvellous pubs, good people and a great atmosphere within a picture book setting. An absolute must for any fan en-route to the North East. Exiled Burnley supporter Lorne Hayhurst would once again be my host.

An early moring telephone call I requested from Carol, a Preston based Claret was administered with precision at 8a.m. on Saturday morning. After walking to the ring road of the city on the A19, I was rewarded with a lift from an exiled 'Boro' Fan now residing in Sheffield. Friendly banter ensued throughout the journey and I was deposited outside the impressive Red Rose pub near the ground at 11.15a.m. No visible 'Robomania ' in here, and so around the corner to the commanding 'Cleveland' tavern, where clear signs of the addiction were apparent on these premises, and this was further accentuated in the Albert Park and Yellow Rose strongholds. This mainly took the form of portrait printed tee shirts with accompanying red and white army slogans. Then, approximately at 1.20p.m. in the Yellow Rose pub a modern phenomenon occurred. The bustling pair of bars filled with upwards of 300 drinkers predominantly outfitted in the now outdated I.C.I. sponsored home shirts suddenly fell silent. Has the beer run out? Has Kim Bassinger popped in for half of 'Samson' bitter, or has Robson resigned? My answer came as I gazed at the scores of transfixed faces viewing the television where their messiah was giving an interview. I decided against a mock enquiry of 'Who is it?' and watched passively with the rest. He seemed to cast a spell over them not dissimilar to the former North Koreen president 'Kim Il-Sung', but this seemed more genuine.

I progressed to the ground and purchased a programme where an enclosed insert offered the opportunity to invest in a commemorative pottery plate printed with 'Robo's' image. I couldn't help thinking that their fanzine title, 'Fly me to the moon' was more over the top than a 'Baggio' penalty, or perhaps it was an indicative wish on behalf of the supporters. Not wanting to be left out of the party spirit an over-zealous constable provided a heavy handed impersonation of 'Robocop' whilst carrying out the customary body search. Then on to the terrace to take up my position amongst my own tribe of claret and blue after my in-depth probe behind enemy lines. We were in good voice too with 'Burnley are back' celebrating our own resurrection via a harmonious chant, and adding to a good atmosphere. By the way there was also a match played, and we came second. Well, would 'Captain Marvel' be able to navigate his own starship enterprise to the Premier galaxy? One thing's for sure they'll all be watching the next instalments of 'Roboboro!'

The signs seem favourable even this contrived title forms an anagram of the partnership. As for my lucky humbug, it gets one last chance!!

28 My Club 18-30 Holiday – Aged 42: 1996

Miss B'stard shows her delight at being appointed interim secretary of the Ibiza branch of the Burnley Supporters Club.

Do you ever wish you had travelled more when you were younger? Perhaps you regret not experiencing an out of the ordinary adventure or something a bit more daring, risque or even downright outrageous? When the unlikely opportunity came along to achieve my particular objective, I certainly wasn't going to miss it. If you ever wonder what goes on with trips of this kind, maybe the following chapter will enlighten you.

Whoah! I'm going to Ibiza ...

With Burnley's week long pre-season tour of Northern Ireland already pencilled in and some spare time before it took place, I had the chance to try a holiday that had always passed me by in my youth.

After the team had finished a disappointing 17th in the third tier of the Football League, I was in need of some light relief. Now, I'd visited many different countries on five different continents, but one outstanding challenge remained. I had never witnessed the carnage that passes for a 'Club18-30' holiday.

In addition, I had never partied on Ibiza before either, so the advertisement in the window of the travel agents, a Club 18-30 trip to the Spanish island, looked more and more appealing. I could remedy those two remaining voids in my life with one stroke.

If you think you can detect a distinct hint of sarcasm in my text, you would be absolutely right. Neither were actually on my 'must do' list as the years passed by, yet I was intrigued enough to wonder whether I could keep pace with Britain's hard core party animals.

The only way to truly find out would be to experience such a holiday myself on a personal investigative level. I wanted to observe at first hand whether or not the company's well renowned reputation for overseeing excessive drunkenness and debauchery were indeed warranted. And of course, as all good, comprehensive researchers do, I wanted to sample a large slice of it myself along the way without coming home with something that required a prescription ointment on my return.

However, there was one major stumbling block to my plan. The year was 1996 and I was now 42 years of age, a full 12 years above the group's upper age limit.

I studied the advertisement and its reduced price again as I tried to evaluate my prospects. They could only say no, couldn't they?

Just under the departure details, it stated as its selling point: "Two weeks of partying. A young at heart deal." That enticing summary sealed it. I was now determined to give it my best shot.

Now, I've always considered myself to be in the 'young at heart' bracket, and I certainly liked to party on a regular basis. But would I be able to convince both the travel shop staff and the tour operator that I was up for it?

The following day was Saturday which meant I would have enough time to prepare myself to be as convincing as was physically possible.

I shaved twice, smoothed lashings of Oil of Ulay moisturising fluid into my face and spiked up my hair with fixing gel in an attempt to attain a much more youthful appearance. A pair of American style baseball boots, my Lee Rider tight jeans and my brother Shaun's Fred Perry leisure shirt completed my James Dean look.

I strode into the 'Going Places' premises displaying a hint of an attitude swagger, as I chewed my mint gum enthusiastically. Sophie happened to be my attentive booking clerk and she immediately asked if I needed any help.

After I expressed an interest in the offer advertised in the window, the young assistant sat down to methodically read aloud the fine details of the economy deal, glancing upwards to gain a nodded affirmation of each condition from myself. Upon completion of her lengthy recital, she paused to take a deep intake of breath before puckering up her lips in a thoughtful considered manner and addressing me once more.

"OK. Those are the main terms of the holiday contract but there is just one minor problem regarding yourself," she said.

"Here we go," I thought. "All my preening and pampering is going to be in vain as she asks me for proof of age."

I composed a ready response in my mind along the lines of: "I may look older than I am, but it's because I've had a hard life," hoping the quip might allow me to avoid showing documentary evidence.

But she carried on where she had left off with the words: "I'm afraid because you're travelling alone, you will incur a single room supplement charge of £50."

Now it was my turn to pout my lips in a mixture of surprise and satisfaction.

"Ah well. That's life I suppose," I replied in a resigned manner before eagerly snatching the booking form from her hand.

"Sign here, do I?"

Paying up in full, I thanked her before strutting towards the door, maintaining my cool pretence.

In truth, I was probably doing more of an impression of one of the late Dick Emery's comic characters than a hip dude, but nevertheless I was on board, ready to join Britain's partying elite for two weeks of uncontrolled mayhem.

Once outside and out of sight, I punched the air in self-congratulation.

"Get in, my son," I said to myself. The oldest swinger in town was on his merry way to what clubbers call 'The White Isle.'

Romantics would have you believe that term is a reference to Ibiza's expanse of glorious sandy beaches, but the more knowledgeable recognise that it's because of the easy availability of the powdered form of a certain drug over there.

Slipping into situ ...

In readiness for my full-on rave fortnight, I now needed to get into the same suitably bawdy sartorial elegance favoured by the testosterone pumped youths I'd be mixing with.

With that in mind, I bought a pair of knee-length Hawaiin print floral shorts that seemed to be all the fashion rage at the time, and a couple of acceptably lewd tee-shirts.

The first of these carried the slogan 'England Drinking Team' emblazoned across a cartoon caricature of a cross-eyed drunk clutching a foaming beer tankard in each hand. The second read 'Fashion Police Officer' as the headline, adding underneath the words, 'authorised to take down your credentials upon demand.'

At two for a fiver, the tacky garments were probably overpriced by £4. but it would be money well spent if they gained me acceptance by fellow members of the '18-30 Club.'

Ibiza's been a clubbing destination since Freddie Mercury and Grace Jones made it a cool place to visit in the 1980s. Its reputation for a place to have a good time has grown year on year and its drink and drug excesses are well documented, an example being the daily sunset boat parties where up to 300 revellers go for a cruise through the night with the sole intention of getting absolutely blasted with alcohol, drugs or both.

I'd be depending only on drink for my legal high, but there would be a limitless supply and that would be more than enough to ensure a good time.

Mine was a midweek flight as was the case with the majority of the cut price, bargain bucket deals.

After the plane landed on the island in the early hours, a coach was waiting to take myself and around 30 hard core clubbers of a far younger age to the party capital of San Antonio, or 'San Ant' to the initiated.

My hotel was the Rosalia in Santa Rosalia resort. It boasted exactly 100 rooms, and after the standard, laboriously long checking in process, I was allocated the 'top of the shop,' room no. 100. It was one of relatively few single rooms and was located at the very peak of the towering complex.

The tiny lift was out of order so I was forced to climb 10 floors by traipsing up the stairs with the holdall which constituted my luggage. By the time I had reached my room and then made a point of locating the emergency fire exits, a procedure I undertake at every hotel, hostel or 'flea pit' in which I stay, it was approaching 3.30am.

Now time wouldn't normally be an issue, especially with an '18-30' holiday which must be an insomniac's dream vacation, but this particular day was different.

In transit from the airport to the numerous accommodation drop-off points, we'd been given notice of an early rise by our club rep. Adrian – "but you can call me Adey" – who had taken to the microphone requesting all aboard to attend a mandatory 'meet and greet' get together at 10am the same morning in the hotel lobby.

He said it was to inform us of the next fortnight's events which had been lined up for us, including special promotions, attractions and excursions. As a further incentive, as if one was needed, the company was laying on – wait for it — free punch.

Bloody hell! The frantic pace and sleepless nights were already starting.

Getting down with da kidz ...

I did force myself down to the induction, though I was just as bleary-eyed as the rest who had dragged themselves out of bed at this early hour.

The gratis alcoholic concoction had so much fruit floating on the surface that you needed a dredger to get to the liquid at the bottom of the bowl. Once there, the first swig confirmed my preconception that the punch was punchless. In fact, it tasted more like the fruit drink Vimto.

Then Adey got down to his patronising spiel, pitching the various glitzy shows and nightclubs that were available before coming out with his 'Too Good To Miss' offer, which was two weeks' admission to all the nightclubs and discos in 'San Ant' for just £110! His sales technique was convincing enough to entice everyone in the room to part with their cash – except for me.

I certainly wasn't going to spend that amount of money before I checked them out for myself and that's just what I told Adey when he attempted to cajole me into doing so. He didn't pursue the matter with much conviction as of course a 99 per cent sales success rate meant a nice enough wedge of commission for himself.

However, spotting my tee-shirt with 'England Drinking Team' lettered upon it, he tried one last sales pitch, offering me a discount ticket for that nights 'Chubby Brown Tribute Evening' at a local club with unlimited free lager until midnight.

Again, I politely declined Adey's offer while he collected a tenner apiece from the rest of the gathering.

That night, I checked out the comedy night mentioned and found that it was free entry anyway before 10pm and that beer was on sale at cut price promotion rates.

It was the same for all the clubs and discos in the town except for the exclusive Pacha nightclub which was located way out of the capital and required a rather expensive ticket purchase.

I decided on a routine of taking advantage of the early doors 'happy hours' from around 7pm as it was certainly not a problem to go into a sparsely populated premises for a couple of hours before it filled completely with the younger latecomers. I tried a different one every night, usually lasting until around 2am, just when the joint was peaking in terms of activity.

I was going out three or four hours before the 'in crowd' and was getting burnt out a lot sooner than everyone else, but I did want to go all the way until closing for one night at least.

I chose Es Paradis, at the time the most popular dance venue in San Antonio, for what was to be my 10 hour bender.

After the usual bar crawl down the 'West End,' I got in before the costly admission charge kicked in. I'd already had plenty to drink, so I concentrated on the object of the exercise – to dance my arse off!

It was a real test and, because of the sheer length of some of the tunes, quite exhausting given the speed of the dance routines whipped along by the accompanying strobe lights. But I persisted, and kept on raving to the heady beat right through to the morning.

I jerked, I flipped, I shook and I quivered to the monotonous musical hubbub until at last the resident DJ closed the show with the last few songs accompanied by a 'foam finale.'

The industrial sized foam machine spewed out its soapy mass to a chug-chug mechanical sound that actually combined well with the short, sharp thump of the rhythmic pounding. It not only engulfed the room, but eventually submerged the clubbers under a sea of bubbles.

As dawn broke, it was time to wind down by disrobing, slipping on my trunks and jumping into the neighbouring swimming pool provided by the club in order to wash away the sweat and cool down.

I then walked wearily back to my digs with the early morning sunshine gently warming my face.

The night had been a weird but wonderful experience, and I could certainly understand its mass appeal to young people. Besides giving them the chance to chill out and de-stress, it proved to be the perfect exercise and equivalent to a full body workout for the vigorous dance participants.

At long last, I felt I had fulfilled one of my more obscure holiday ambitions. Having partied from the early evening to the early morning, I'd 'got down with da kidz' at one of Ibiza's and probably Europe's major rave venues. I had fully embraced the trend of dancing manically to a raft of continuous electronic tunes, not only on the floor, but also upon the high podiums constructed for that purpose. Indeed, my 'poseur's' gyratory sequence had been substantially enhanced by the rapid bright flashes from the in-house strobe lighting system.

My exertions had left me dripping with sweat but the mandatory foam party and final cooling dip that closed the event were the perfect solution to any personal hygiene problems.

It may have taken me until middle-age to achieve my objective of partaking thoroughly in the unrestrained revelry of an '18-30' holiday, but my exhausted body and mind were testimony to the fact that I had well and truly nailed it!

A siesta fiesta ...

It would be around mid-afternoon each day when I retuned to my room after a lengthy sunbathing session by the hotel pool with a few San Miguel's for company.

I would take a shower to wash away the residue of the remaining 'factor 15' and was then ready to settle down for a traditional siesta before hitting the bars in town to take advantage of the early evening promotions.

With my room being located at the very top and the only other adjacent accommodation being as yet unoccupied, this floor was probably one of the quieter parts of the complex.

But one afternoon, just as I was about to nod off to dream about my first 'two for one' cocktail offer, the comparative peace of the day was suddenly shattered. The lift doors slid open to the accompaniment of a wail of shrieks, screams and general caterwauling with the excitable chatter and laughter of young girls clearly audible through the paper thin walls.

As it happened, there turned out to be only two of them, but they made the noise of many more as they almost battered down the entry to the adjoining living quarters. It looked like I'd gained the neighbours from hell.

All I knew for certain was that they had disturbed my revitalising 'kipette,' my personal term for a short power sleep.

The high spirited pair hardly took time to take breath as they chatted on, and the longer I eavesdropped on their compelling conversation, the more intrigued I became.

What follows is the gist of the duos enrapturing introductory 'gab-fest' purposely reproduced in their mother tongue of a colloquial broad Yorkshire dialect.

"Wha-hey! We made it Trace. An 'ole week away from our parents. No nagging from ma mum about what I wear, and no lectures off me dad tellin' me what time I 'ave to be in for. We're freeee!"

"Yeh, it's great, innit Shaz? Ey, 'av just thowt. We'll be able to get absolutely 'ammered coz they don't ask for ID over 'ere. Daz Higginbottom came last year an' 'e's only 16. Mind you, 'e did say 'e grew 'is tache and sideburns to look older. We can 'ardly do that, can we Shaz? Well, maybe thy can. Ha, ha, ha, ha."

"Did tha 'ear about Daz? Well, ya know what 'e's like, 'e doesn't give a toss about nowt. 'E towd 'is mates that one morning, he woke up wi' a sore bum.

"So 'e goes to that shop on Railway Street where old Albert Titley works and says: "Nah then Alb, does tha' sell arse cream?"

And Albert says: "Aye lad, we do. Does tha' want a Magnum or a Cornetto?"

Cue delirious cackles of laughter from both girls, and I have to admit restrained chuckles from myself as I listened in on the tale.

"Can ya believe that, Tray? E's a nutter, i'n'tee?

"Mental, Shaz, mental. Anyway, it's time ta start the party. Crack open yon vodka and pump up the volume. From now on, it's gonna be sun, sea and shaggin'!"

More lewd references to sex followed before Shaz advised: "Tracy! Shhhh. Ya don't know who might be listening."

It was sound advice, but it had come too late. I'd kept perfectly silent and still as I took in every despairing sentence.

In less than five minutes, Sharon and Tracy had unwittingly encapsulated the holiday ambitions of a large sector of British youth. The holiday company's reputation had obviously preceded it, and represented the chief reason the pair had expectantly and specifically booked an '18-30' break. They wanted it rude, crude and probably nude.

Believe me, I'm no prude, but I'll admit to being more than a little dismayed by the blunt conversation I wasn't supposed to hear. Having a young daughter of my own Clarette, of whom I was naturally very protective, I was beginning to wonder after overhearing the shameless aims of this pair of teenagers if this was a true but sad reflection of our society back in England. It was not only perceived by each as expected behaviour but perfectly normal.

Although I was confident as I could be that Clarette would be sensible enough to reject such shallow-minded, ribald actions when she grew older, what about the more naive and vulnerable members of our community?

Granted, my total rationale for travelling to this party isle was to sample the same pursuits, but I was an experienced 42-year-old, while these were no more than kids. It just seemed totally blatant and felt so worryingly wrong.

So, suitably perplexed by their boorish manner, I decided to formulate a ruse to teach them a timely lesson.

Having been on the island for almost a week now, I had gained a half-decent mahogany coloured tan, so much so that with my dark hair I could pass for one of the locals.

I'd had convincing success on previous occasions abroad masquerading as both a Greek and French waiter in order to fool British tourists just for laughs, but today I wasn't going to impersonate a menial server. Oh no, my chosen character would yield far more authority than that.

I put on my shorts and sandals before draping a strategically placed towel over my bare shoulders to cover up my Burnley F.C. based tattoos, which would clearly have been a giveaway. I was now ready to meet the girls who had transferred their impromptu festivities to their outside verandah.

'Pedro, 'ead of 'otel security' ...

In a swiftly cobbled together mixture of broken English and completely shattered Spanish, I made a grand, assured entrance onto my adjoining balcony.

"Ola!," my voice boomed out, making the girls jump, one of them emitting a very unladylike "What the fuck!" exclamation as she leapt out of her seat.

"I Pedro, your 'ead of 'otel security. I am also your neighbour. Welcome to beautiful San Antonio," I said, and extended my hand in a friendly gesture to ensure a response as I tried to keep a straight face.

Still looking more than a little startled by my over-dramatic appearance, and decidedly anxious upon hearing my status disclosure, they were now both nervously rocking on their white plastic chairs.

One of the teenagers then politely stood up to seal a handshake while the other disconsolately used her arm as a chin rest.

The first girl greeted me in her trademark deep Yorkshire brogue.

"Oh, 'ello Pedro. I'm Sharon and this is ma friend Tracy. Pleased ta meet ya."

For sure she wasn't, and I could tell from her wide, forced smile that her words were insincere. She was about as pleased to meet me as she would her dad, if he had turned up uninvited.

Accordingly, I carried on the conversation with additional roguish intent.

"I really 'ope you both 'ave a very nice time at our 'otel, but it eez also my duty to inform you of some...'ow you say?... guest regulations that must be obeyed, por favor."

After asserting my 'jobsworth' power, I also felt obliged to give them a stereotypical slimy Spanish gaze, brazenly looking them up and down in their skimpy shorts and bikini tops. I wanted to make them feel even more uncomfortable and let them know Pedro was a 'playerrr.'

I must have been pretty convincing as their smiles had now withered and a distinct look of trepidation was etched on their faces.

But I was unrelenting, as I delivered the house rules from hell.

"First, no loud music playing. Courtesy for our other guests."

A crestfallen Tracy turned off her ghetto blaster accordingly.

"Second, all lights must go out for 11 o'clock, then finish because everybody sleeping."

Both Tracy and Sharon let out a collective sigh of disbelief as they looked at each other aghast.

"Well, that's OK, because we'll just be going out," replied Sharon sarcastically as she directed her eyes to her mate trying to make light of the restriction.

"And finally, definitely no alcohol drinking in either da room or da balcony."

For good measure, I ended my declaration of intent with a final coup de grâce, a statement of complete contradiction.

"Eet is so everyone can 'ave a nice time and enjoy their stay at the Rosalia 'otel you understand? Bueno."

Of course, they didn't understand such a stringent set of rules at all, particularly after their friends back home had given them the clear indication that it would be the complete opposite of 'Pedro's' enforcement order. Having taken it all in, they could now see their dream holiday crumbling before them.

Observing their distress was painful, and I felt a right bastard to be honest as I watched them go from a state of unbridled joy to the pits of bewildered disbelief, all within the space of a few minutes. But heart-rending as it was, I kept up my pretence in the knowledge that it would all end happily.

"So what you ladies doing first?," I asked rather insensitively.

"Goin' tot' supermarket ta buy some razor blades, uttered Tracy, who seemed to be taking the terms of her newly revealed tenancy agreement a lot harder than the more subdued Sharon who continued to stare aimlessly into space.

I continued my questioning unashamedly.

"You come from England...yes?"

"Yeh, we're from England, Pedro," answered Tracy with a distinct air of resignation.

"Where in England you come from?"

"A place called Baaaarnsley," replied Tracy lazily.

"Ees that near to London?," I asked, feigning ignorance of the geography of the country.

"Nah, nowier near," said Tracy curtly.

I could see by their strained expressions that they were both fast tiring of my played-out inquiries.

"Is eet near Scotland then?," I fired back, continuing the irritating cross-questioning.

That ridiculous notion succeeded in galvanising the until now almost comatose Sharon into life to deliver her verdict.

"Yeh, it's near Scotland mate," she exclaimed stressed out by all the goings on around her.

It was clear by the perceptible sarcastic overtones of the reply that she wanted to terminate the annoying chit-chat right away, and she got her wish as I just couldn't contain myself any longer.

It was time to reveal the real me.

I pulled the towel down from around my shoulders before laughing out loud and reverting back to my Potteries vernacular.

"Barnsley? Near to bloody Scotland? You didn't get your geography O level, did you, Sharon?"

Trace and Shaz flicked their heads around simultaneously, their faces resembling rabbits caught in a car's headlights.

As they clocked my tattooed Burnley crest, realisation dawned. A surge towards me with their fists thumping my bare chest followed then a concerted tirade of good humoured abuse.

"You bastard Pedro.... you absolute bastard! I bet ya not even called Pedro, are ya?," squawked the previously constrained Sharon.

"Ya nearly ruined our 'ole flamin' 'oliday," added an animated Tracy.

"What's ya real name anyway Pear Drop?," she teased.

"Call me Ralphy," I insisted, pointing to the nickname lettered upon my left bicep.

"I did have you going though, girls. didn't I?"

"Yeh. We do admit to thinkin' that ya were serious 'coz ya suddenly appeared from chuffin' nowhere," sighed a greatly relieved Sharon.

"Well, I couldn't fail to hear you chatting when you came in, and because you sounded a bit over-excited, I thought I'd wind you up for a laugh. And if you remember, I think it was Sharon who warned you that you never know who might be listening in."

"No hard feelings, eh?," I added, offering my hand which they shook with considerable justification now I'd admitted to play-acting.

That remains my most convincing imposter impersonation to date, my very own 'Oscar' performance.

That night, I took the girls down to the town's West End to get them acquainted with the night scene, and from thereon in we became good mates for the duration of the holiday as I won them over to my way of thinking.

More noticeably, the bad language stopped, they turned their music down to a reasonable level, and both had fun without being irresponsible, which gave me great gratification.

Maybe... just maybe, their little brush with 'Pedro' had made them consider that their outlandish behaviour was unacceptable. If it did, I'm sure they've become better people for the experience.

Miss B'stard ...

The first couple of nights of my holiday had been spent down the West End, San Antonio's main strip for bars and clubs. Such was the competition for business between the scores of licensed premises lining the narrow streets, it was by far the cheapest place to get a drink.

Wearing your football team's shirt was fairly de rigueur in Ibiza at the time, so as I was trying to fit in with the crowd, I paraded through town in a choice of Burnley tops.

It is the ever-frustrating norm for Clarets fans that from a distance our strip is always mistaken for first West Ham, then Aston Villa. So when asked if my shirt is either of these clubs' outfits, I give my stock answer of: "No, they copy us."

It's meant as a jocular riposte, because in reality at the beginning of the 1910-11 season, Burnley changed their strip from a predominantly green shirt to claret and blue.

This was done in an attempt to change their luck, and so they actually copied the colours of Aston Villa who were league champions the previous year. And it worked, because in 1914 we won the FA Cup, beating Liverpool 1-0 in the final.

Anyway, there was certainly no confusion on this particular Saturday night as a distinct cry of "Burn-a-lee, Burn-a-lee, Burn-a-lee" rang around the party zone. Had early auditions for 'The Inbetweeners' come to town?

It turned out to be my good friend and regular Burnley fan Mick Holehouse from the small village of Blacko near Nelson in Lancashire. He was over with around half a dozen other Clarets on their Burnley 'wakes' holiday fortnight.

Of course, we retired to the nearest bar where we all agreed to form an Ibiza branch of the Burnley FC Supporters' Club with nightly meetings to discuss footy-related business at the start of the happy hour.

It's always a bonus to bump into anyone who follows football because conversation flows freely from your shared interest, and of course it's even better if the team they watch is your own. It's a bit like when the local police of a town or city allocate a designated pub to away supporters back in England, and so a good weekend of catching up with close season developments and discussing hopes for the future ensued.

And wherever there is a group of people wearing their club colours and enjoying both banter and beer, it always seems to attract other fans of all denominations.

The upshot of all this was that by the time Monday evening came around, the place we met had also become an established meeting place for enthusiasts representing clubs from all four domestic divisions and beyond.

Even a band of Brondby FC fans, who belonged to the hardcore 'Southsiders' group of followers from the Danish club, used it as their focal point. And with the recent defeat of our fierce rivals Blackburn Rovers by fellow Scandinavian side Trelleborgs in a UEFA Cup tie still fresh in the Burnley fans' minds, an instant rapport was established with the Brondby lads as we recalled our bitterest foes' defeat by the Swedish amateur side, and club tee-shirts and tops were exchanged.

Harmony had been maintained in the bar as we hadn't come across any Rovers 'shirt boys' to bait as yet, although there had been as close a call as there could be when a couple of Bristol Rovers fans turned up in their blue and white quartered shirts, as opposed to the 'enemy' and their halved version.

Then suddenly, a young girl came through the open door along with a much older couple who we assumed to be her parents. She looked barely old enough to drink but was served with a vodka and mixer by her two guardians.

Seemingly intrigued by our party, she eventually summoned up the courage to come and talk to us.

"You're Dingles, aren't ya?," said the small, waif-like character, smiling from cheek to cheek.

She had immediately captured our attention by her accusation as we knew that each of our Lancashire footballing counterparts referred to Burnley fans by this disparaging name. It compares us to a fictional dysfunctional family of ne'er-do-wells in the long running 'Emmerdale' TV soap series who are always getting themselves involved in serious trouble.

So straight away, we knew she was either a Preston, Blackpool or Blackburn Rovers follower. We formed ourselves into a circle around her as we began our impromptu interrogation in the order of the teams stated.

"You're not a Knobender, are you?," asked 'Longshanks' from our group, referring to our insulting term for Preston fans.

"A Donkey Lasher?," queried Mick, quoting our label for Blackpool followers.

A quick shake of her head confirmed the worst.

"You're a Bastard!" was shouted in unison towards her, with accompanying fingers pointed in the direction of her head.

"Yep. I'm a season ticket holder as well," she blurted out, confirming her understanding of the Burnley fans' sobriquet of 'Bastard Rovers' for the Blackburn side she followed.

A torrent of light-hearted verbal insults were bravely shielded by the diminutive girl who must have expected such a response given her laugh out loud defence.

It transpired that her two companions were indeed her mum and dad who she was staying with in a hotel just out of town. They invited themselves over for a chat, then after an hour or so, at their daughter's insistence, she was entrusted into our care with the condition that we promised to pack her off home in a taxi at midnight.

This created a bit of a dilemma for us. Just what do you do with an adopted 'Bastard?'

I called an emergency supporters' meeting to discuss the issue. She was only 17 and came from the wrong end of the M65 motorway, Darwen to be precise. She wanted our company because firstly, she had no friends over here, and secondly, she was a bit of a tomboy anyway and enjoyed the company of lads. Her parents didn't mind her staying out as long as she was safe.

After many more pints of the local lager, it was decided that she could be allowed temporary membership of our newly formed supporters branch as club secretary on the strict condition that she answered to the title of 'Miss B'stard' in keeping with the team she supported. This name was taken from Alan B'stard, the character name of the pompous Conservative MP played by the late, and great Rik Mayall in the TV comedy series 'The New Statesman.'

The girl agreed to these terms and conditions and was therefore accepted as a member of our group and became a nightly regular at the bar, even enjoying the naturally frequent digs at her choice of football team. No club colours or reference to her club were allowed as it would certainly be frowned upon by other fans if we were seen to be associating with our sworn adversaries.

And before the clock struck midnight, our little 'Cinderella' was dispatched into a taxi by a volunteer, who oddly enough always seemed to be the 6ft 4in 'Longshanks.'

Furthermore, we had all noticed that as the week progressed, Longshanks's escort service had seemed to spring into action earlier and earlier so we decided to pull him up about this. He went on to admit that he'd purposely walked her along the beach for what he termed "a bit of a fumble" before progressing to the taxi rank. After further enquiries, it transpired that the 'fumble' had included oral sex! After condemnation all round, 'Shanks' tamely apologised for his carnal desires. Strewth! This girl had been placed in our trust. Is it any wonder they call us the bloody Dingles!

A really bad break ...

With regards to all fun gatherings, the three main ingredients for a good time are generally music, alcohol and the opposite sex. All three came together in a bountiful package on this island and access to them was actively encouraged by the club's reps – for a fee of course.

The afternoon booze cruises proved very popular, and they involved a flotilla of small boats transporting revellers to deserted coves and beaches.

My excursion included a light picnic meal, weak tasting draught lager and a choice of rum or vodka shots. Teams were picked to compete in suitably bawdy games of a provocatively sexual nature which also involved the usual high intake of beer and spirits, each contest being actively encouraged by the relentless goading of the organisers.

By the time it was over and we set sail on the return journey, there were a lot of landlubbers looking decidedly 'green around the gills.'

Add trips like this to the substantially higher than normal daily intake of intoxicating drinks and it comes as no surprise to learn that injury numbers rocket in the summer madness of an '18-30' break.

But the worst casualty I saw did not come as a direct result of drink or drugs.

In addition to social activities, competitive sporting events were held between different hotels, and football matches by tradition always sparked the fiercest rivalry.

After attending more than 2,500 professional football matches and playing in around 1,000 amateur games myself, you would think the most disturbing injury to any player I have witnessed would have been in one of these fixtures.

But no. For sheer visual impact and sickeningly horrific damage, the worst incident I ever saw took place on this small island a long way from home.

On the second Sunday of my stay, a game was arranged with a 4pm kick off at a local league ground. My hotel, the Rosalia, were playing the nearby Marco Polo. I'd put my name down as a substitute because the heat was still an oppressive 82 degrees Fahrenheit when the game was due to start.

The venue was a basic, functional arena with one narrow side stand forming the only shelter for the 100 or so spectators, most of whom were already pissed from that day's 'all you can drink' boat trip.

Our lads kicked off to a loud roar from an aggressive, exuberant group who wasted no time in upping the ante by baying for blood. As a response to their goading, there was an intense pace to the game which was surreal given the high temperature. Tackles were flying in with players from each team trying to impress the large number of females in the crowd.

But 15 minutes into the game, disaster struck.

A tall, well built opposition attacker ran full pelt towards our gangly defender who was attempting to control a bouncing ball But he badly mistimed his tackle, missing the ball completely before making full contact with our lad's left knee in a bone crunching challenge.

The poor youth's leg instantly snapped loudly like the bough of a tree breaking. In fact, so bad was the injury that his limb formed itself into an inverted letter C shape comparable to the arc of a crossbow. He was, as you would expect, in absolute agony.

We ran from the bench and tried to rest the stricken lad's head, shield him from the searing sun and douse him in cold water until the ambulance arrived a good 20 minutes later.

The match of course was abandoned after that sickening incident which had taken place no more than 20 yards from where I was sitting. The victim's holiday was well and truly over in horrendous fashion, and he'd have many months of recovery ahead of him.

It could quite easily have been myself out there, or anyone on the pitch, and the fracture served as yet another reminder of the pitfalls of these partygoers' breaks.

Lasting the course ...

By now, I'd tackled most of the tasks I'd set myself and by the time I was due to fly home, I was an absolute wreck after two full weeks of excess.

If you are a parent reading this and have ever wondered what takes place on these sojourns abroad, be warned. It does just what it says on the can...or in my case, on the advert, ie "two weeks of partying for the young at heart" encompassing the three 'S' words of sun, sea, and sex if you want it.

In addition, the potent mix of freely available drugs and alcohol along with the mesmerising rave music made it more a test of endurance for me than a relaxing break.

Even so, such holidays provided, and indeed still to this day supply a winning combination to British youth seeking the ultimate buzz of excitement that can only be gained by pushing physical boundaries to their absolute limit.

Would I go again? No, because fun though it was, there was in my view an over-abundance of self-indulgent participation about an '18-30' gathering. This was unashamedly encouraged by club reps who coerced and compelled the holidaymaker to part with their cash to gain more commission for themselves and almost embarrassed the tourist into taking part in some pretty outrageous acts that they would never dream of doing back home.

Or perhaps that's just me being cynical as a more mature client. Now, where can I find that number to book a Saga holiday next summer?

Dodgy dealing ....

In 1996 the European Championship finals came home to England and there was a new song brought out to commemorate the quadrennial occasion.

'Three Lions' by the Lightning Seeds, ably accompanied by newly established comedians David Baddiel and Frank Skinner became, and currently remains, the unequivocal best football anthem of all time. The emotional lyrics reminiscing right back to the national team's only success when lifting the Jules Rimet World Cup trophy in 1966 also contains that most vital ingredient to any good melody – a rousing chorus rendition.

"It's coming home,

It's coming home,

It's coming,

football's coming home!" reverberated around each and every town and city whenever England played. It was certainly the most exciting football extravaganza in the country since 'sixty six'.

And it proved to be a great tournament, taking the competition to a new plane with entry doubled to sixteen finalists in four groups for the first time, being one of the decisive factors in England winning the hosting rights. However, a side-line of the political process was a trade-off whereby U.E.F.A. insisted that the English FA called a halt to their short-lived campaign to stage the 1998 F.I.F.A. World Cup in favour of France.

Whilst I travel regularly to watch England in both Euro and World Cup contests abroad, I hardly venture down to 'the smoke' to watch them. The high cost of travel, match tickets and a frankly uninspiring clinical atmosphere even in a full Wembley Stadium being my predominant reasons for non-attendance.

Euro 96 was, of course, exceptionally different and the subsequent clamour to be present at the hyped-up event ensured an ebullient mood of guarded optimism towards the nation's chance of success.

Indeed, both the second highest recorded aggregate attendance of 1,275,857 over 31 matches and a 41,157 average per game clearly showed there was still an insatiable appetite to watch top international football.

Although I didn't get to any of the live matches that year, rather by choice than circumstance, there was a memorable personal incident of note which was associated with the proceedings that took place.

The exploit, on the face of it, looked like a decent business opportunity. As I was 'in between' jobs at the time, an advertisement in my local Evening Sentinel instantly caught my eye. It read:

"Be part of Euro 96! Limited vacancies now for football souvenir vendors."

A quick phone call disclosed that I would be selling large colour posters of the England squad at a number of pre-designated football grounds OUTSIDE the stadiums. It wasn't exactly what I wanted but the commission which formed the sole source of income sounded reasonable at one pound for each fiver picture sold.

I collected them in a holdall from Burslem, the so called mother town of the Potteries, inside The Red Lion pub which just also happened to be the former residence of singing superstar Robbie Williams in his youth.

Dan, my supplier, reckoned they would fly out of my bag in a wave of nationalistic euphoria.

I settled for a hundred which, according to Dan, would net me the same amount of pounds for a couple of hours work.

Not bad! I thought as I asked Dan where my first venue was to be. His answer alone should have alerted me to the futility of the venture.

"Your first game is at Old Trafford. It's Germany v Croatia in the quarter finals".

Bloody Hell! Not only would I have to try and sell his wares near to the boundaries of my least favourite club, England weren't even bloody playing there!

But in the spirit of nothing ventured, nothing gained, and because I wouldn't be setting foot inside the place, I decided to give it a try anyway, just to raise a few much needed funds.

After forking out a tenner for my train journey to Manchester, I alighted right outside Lancashire County Cricket ground and made my way down the Warwick Road.

It was a good three hours before kick-off but already scarf, hat and flag sellers had staked their claim for a pitch with hundreds of colourful items flooding their portable tables and stands.

My only form of display consisted of outstretched arms showcasing what on closer inspection looked like a poorly coloured, mass produced print of an out of date first team squad, measuring no more than 20 x 12 inches. The procession of potential punters must have thought so too as there was hardly a cursory glance in the direction of my wares.

In fact, after half an hour of 'trading', my only conversation had been with a shaven headed, man mountain ticket tout trying to off load his various priced categories of admission on me.

So far the day had been an unmitigated disaster with not one sale made and just when I thought that it couldn't get any worse, it terminally did!

"Afternoon sir, Greater Manchester Trading Standards. Can we see your registered licence permitting you to sell these goods please?" enquired the moustachioed inspector, accompanied by a watching police officer.

"What! I didn't realise that you needed any authorisation to sell outside a ground", lying through my back teeth to preserve my freedom.

"Oh you most certainly do sir, and besides that, your products are definitely not official FA approved merchandise. Can you tell me who your supplier is?"

Not wanting to get the mysterious Dan into trouble, I used the "I got them off a bloke I met in the pub" line, which was actually the truth.

Unmoved, the functionary issued me with a confiscation order claiming all the pirate posters for ultimate destruction. I phoned Dan to tell him the bad news, only to get a cursory reply of:

"Dunna worry abite it. They were owd stock anyway and cost me less than a tenner. It's just one of them things yoof. I'll see thee!"

"But, but..." it was too late, my question of any recompense for my travel and time didn't come out as dodgy Dan quickly signed off.

All that was left was to watch the game in the pub which Germany almost inevitably won 2-1 to set up a semi-final with England. I returned home thirty quid worse off but thinking to myself "at least I've been a very small part of it". Yes, very small part.

29 My Top Level Meetings with No. 9 & No. 10: 1996-1998

Jimmy with good friend Coronation Street legend Bill Tarmey who played the always scheming Jack Duckworth.

Rarely are fans afforded even a fleeting parlance with their club's manager, but with a little help from one man, for me it became a regular occurrence.

Inchy's mate 'Jimmy The Dog'...

I first met Adrian Heath in The Thistleberry public house located on a junction in the Higherland district of Newcastle-under-Lyme. The former hotel being just a few miles from his house in the hills, a sought after residence at salubrious Whitmore Heath.

The property and indeed the area are far removed from his upbringing as a child amongst the terraced houses of the mining village called Knutton. It being a tough, close knit community on the fringes of the record breaking Silverdale coal pit.

I was with 'Tricky' Trev Slack and we'd both been invited to meet the manager by one of his lifelong sidekicks Jimmy Doherty, better known as 'Jimmy The Dog' to all.

Jimmy was joined by Adrian's stalwart pal Alan Salt or predictably just plain 'Salty' to his mates.

'Salty' had a distinguishing look about him with his carefully coiffured full head of silver hair. When dressed in his office suit he could easily pass as your friendly local bank manager, or a convincing Gene Pitney the singer lookalike.

His loyal friend who respectfully still addressed him as Adrian followed wherever his footballing or managerial career took him. That would transport him to Stoke City 1979-82, Everton 1982-88, Espanyol of Spain 1988-89, Aston Villa 1989-90, Manchester City 1990-92, then back to Stoke for half a dozen further appearances before rocking up at Burnley in 1992.

The diminutive number 9 striker scoring on his debut in Burnley's first away league game at Stockport in a 2-1 defeat in the 1992-93 newly named Division Two campaign.

'Inchy' had arrived, and he would go on to score twenty league goals that season.

'Jimmy the Dog' called myself and Trev over and duly introduced us to his two companions who gave us a warm welcome. Our combined equitable knowledge of football establishing an instant rapport. From then on it would become a regular meeting place after home matches thanks to J.T.D. where we would discuss the afternoon's game.

Jimmy, if he really was a dog, would be a rare breed. Born and bred in Salford, Manchester he had a natural tendency to support the red half of the city's two football teams. However, once removed to The Potteries instead of legitimately choosing the glory hunting trail, he swapped his allegiance to the poor relations of Stoke-on-Trent in Port Vale Football Club to whom he has remained loyal ever since on more of a 'gory' hunting trail in the main. Both he and Vale fans in general deserving credit for their allegiance to the more unfashionable half of the city.

I bumped into Jim by coincidence when a badly delayed train forced me to catch a taxi outside Stoke-on-Trent station after a night match, in order to wake up early for work that same morning.

Jim was a paragon of a stereotypical cab driver behind the wheel of his vehicle. Knowledgeable, questioning and opinionated, but always in a totally genuine manner.

That chance encounter being a good twenty years before we would regularly meet up along with 'Inchy and Salty'.

J.T.D. had a somewhat unusual claim to fame in as much he actually had his name in Britain's longest running television soap series.

It came about because he and his partner who he called 'Freidabear' had become very good friends with Bill Tarmey and his wife Alma. They had met on a plane going to Tenerife, one of the Canary Islands where they had a holiday home.

Bill of course played the part of the legendary Jack Duckworth in Coronation Street for more than thirty years co-starring with Liz Dawn, his long suffering on-screen wife Vera.

Each played their part perfectly as generally warring spouses that always kissed and made up after a set to.

I was actually watching the episode in question when Jack was behind the bar in his capacity as proud landlord of The Rovers Return. In the clip he was passing on a red hot horse racing tip that he said had been given to him by 'Jimmy The Dog'.

It had come about on one of the many occasions they had all met up for a drink and Jim revealed that he had always wanted to appear as an extra on the 'Street'.

Bill reluctantly informed him that it just wasn't possible as each and every performer on set had to be a member of Equity, the British Actors' Association. However, Bill promised Jim the next best thing and that was to give him a bold mention on the famous 'soap'.

Jim was made up by that grand gesture and it solidified their friendship even more until Bill's untimely death at the age of 71 on November 9th 2012.

The 'Corrie' legend had always struggled against adversity having a heart attack at just 35 years old, a stroke at 36, a quadruple bypass at 56 with a second bypass operation at 60, until his last day in Tenerife. Yet he had a fine voice producing solo albums as well as singing with the world renowned Hallé Orchestra.

Alan Halsall who played Jack's surrogate son Tyrone dedicated a heartfelt tribute to Bill when collecting the best soap trophy at the National TV Award ceremony in January 2013.

My personal best moment as a big fan of the light-hearted character came when Jack sneakily enrolled upon the books of a dating agency as 'medallion-man' Vince St Clair and arranged to meet a rich widow in a bar who just happened to be a wig-wearing Vera, his wife, who had suspected something suspicious was going on all the time.

Meanwhile 'Inchy' progressed impressively with Burnley culminating in a Play-Off Final appearance against Stockport County which Burnley won 2-1 to secure promotion to Division One.

The following 1994-95 season didn't work out so well however as Burnley plunged back down a league with 'Inchy' hardly starting half the games due to injury and loss of form.

It got worse on their return to Division Two and after only four appearances 'The Inch' moved on to team up with his former Everton boss Howard Kendall at Sheffield United as Assistant Manager.

When Jimmy Mullen was relieved of his duties, the new Burnley manager who had overwhelmingly been voted the fans' choice, Adrian Heath, took up the position soon after the birth of his son Harrison in March 1996.

Inchy takes over ......

Although he had an immediate impact with a 1-0 victory at Bristol City for his first game in charge, it would be his only win in nine games. So frustrated was he by the lousy run of form that he picked himself to do better in the away match at Wycombe Wanderers in the starting line up making him the first Burnley manager to play in a competitive capacity for the club. It was to no avail as the recently promoted side thrashed us 4-1, and that after a 5-0 mauling at Oxford United in the previous league fixture.

So the size of the task was all too apparent as Burnley came close to back to back relegations only surviving the drop down by six points with late season victories against Wrexham away and Shrewsbury at home.

The 1996-97 term would be his own, and a chance to stamp his personal authority on the club.

'Inchy' Heath Manager from March 1996 to May 1997
Photograph courtesy of Burnley Football CLub

An opening season win at Luton Town 2-1 provided the best possible start at what I have always considered one of the most antiquated football grounds in the country. Where else would you exit an away end surrounded by Asian families hanging out their washing a few yards below in their terraced housing, or access one side of the 'stadium' to the other by a narrow alleyway?

With a second win against Walsall at home by the same scoreline, Burnley went top of the division only to lose their next three to Shrewsbury, Millwall and Gillingham.

In September 96 we were drawn to play Charlton Athletic in the 2nd round of the League Cup. It was on a ridiculous home and away basis then, when crowds at either of the participants would be sub-5,000 at such a non-consequential stage of the unappealing competition.

We lost 4-1 at The Valley but only after a scorching free kick from outside their goal area was blasted home by wingback David Eyres after just seven minutes to equalize an early Charlton goal. "Get in Eyresy! What an absolute cracker!" I shouted leaping out of my seat to punch the air while everyone else around me glared at me with disdain.

The reason being that I was in the official press box area of the main stand after blagging my way in as a media assistant with bona fide journalist and fellow Burnley fan Ant Dawber from Chorley.

To the utter embarrassment of Ant, I had temporarily forgot myself after seeing such a magnificent strike hit the back of the net.

After signalling me to sit down with a downward wave of his hand, Ant explained the impropriety of my actions in such company. "Ralph," he addressed me cautiously by my colloquial nickname, "You're supposed to be an impartial observer, it's regarded as bad etiquette to celebrate a goal at all, never mind so enthusiastically."

"That's why I'll never make a reporter then Ant. I had to acknowledge that stunner," I replied defiantly.

But judging by the frowned faces of the scribes around me I could see he was right, and so I continued in my agreed menial task of collating corner kicks for his report in a more subdued manner. That wasn't hard from thereon in as Burnley seemed to implode in a seven minute spell either side of half time when they conceded another three goals.

Talking tactics in the boozer ….

After that temporary interlude to the season, soon after we thrashed Stockport County 5-2 with Paul Barnes, a new recruit from Birmingham City for £400,000, notching all five in a superlative display of finishing.

And it was all down to the Christmas tree formation that myself and 'Inchy' came up with on the bar of the Sneyd Arms public house in Newcastle-Under-Lyme. Well, that's what I'd like to believe anyway. Allow me to explain this outlandish statement fully.

The Sneyd had become our new post-match meeting point in order to catch up with a couple of 'Inchy's' other football associates and was only a few hundred yards from our former gathering place at The Thistleberry.

Although Inchy usually only stopped for a couple before ordering a cab home, our early season form was disintegrating before our very eyes and after a 3-2 defeat to Bristol City at home, it was time to stop the rot here and now in the lounge of the Sneyd Arms.

'Inchy' would always greet me with the same question when I arrived in the pub on a Saturday night, or indeed when he had been good enough to offer me a ride home in his slick BMW after a game home or away.

"What d'ya think Dave?" would be his probing enquiry to how I thought we had played.

Now on this particular evening after our damaging defeat by 'The Robins' there was no way I could defend us throwing away a 2-1 lead to lose the game and so I gave him my diagnosis of where I reckoned we had lost the match.

What you can't do is to is attempt to tell the manager how to do his job as no supporter has any right to do that. They have gained their position on merit and that should always be respected. But what you can do if your opinion is actually requested is to make your point in a clear and constructive manner without being too critical.

So we discussed our strengths, our weaknesses and how both could be improved without singling out any particular players for our downfall. More pints were supped as the hours slipped by.

That soon led us to tactics which were briefly halted as 'Inchy' fielded a call to his mobile phone from his missus Jane who was asking why he wasn't home yet.

"Severe congestion on the M6 duck" seemed to suffice, and with a "won't be long now, see ya soon" we were back on the case.

Beer mats were placed on the bar servery to represent players and after a little chess like manoeuvring we came up with what would be a Christmas tree formation once the services of our two wing backs were both available. With that 'Inchy' bid me a fond farewell and was off in a taxi to explain his absence to his wife.

Neither Gary Parkinson or David Eyres who wore the number two and three shirts respectively that season played the next league game at Bury the following Tuesday to implement our configuration and Burnley duly lost 1-0.

But both were in place for the Stockport game which was next up, along with overlapping wingers Nigel Gleghorn and Paul Weller supplying the tip of the tree formed by Kurt Nogan playing just behind the untouchable Barnes, who became the first player to score five in a game since Andy Lochhead against Bournemouth in a 7-0 3rd round FA Cup replay in 1966.

After a spell as Coventry City's caretaker manager in 2007 'Inchy' crossed the Atlantic pond to be appointed manager of USL-1 team Austin Aztex of Texas in 2008.

In 2011 the American franchise did a 'Wimbledon' and moved to Florida to be re-christened Orlando City, although this relocation was on a massively larger scale than 'The Dons' sixty mile northbound hop to Milton Keynes, Buckinghamshire in England.

There they played in the USL Pro division, and 'Inchy' honed his managerial skills to lead the team to three regular season titles and two league championships in his time there. Being named 'coach of the year' for two campaigns in what amounts to the third stratum of stateside football. Now this is where it gets complicated.

In 2013, the team's ownership announced their Major League Soccer expansion franchise bid had been accepted meaning that they were able to join the big boys in 2015 as their 21st member club.

If that's what it takes to get to the top level of the USA pyramid so be it, but if I had been a fanatical follower of the outfit from its conception in central Texas, I would be clocking up tens of thousands of air miles just keeping up with their new homes!

VERDICT: Adrian, according to his father David made a big mistake leaving the managership of Burnley where he thought he could have guided the club to promotion from the third tier and beyond. I have to agree. Inchy's proved his leadership capabilities in an emerging football nation, and one day in the future I think he will in the country that invented the game back here in England.

Although Inchy's achievements in football are many perhaps his biggest one was managing to secure the services of Brazilian great Kaka to join Orlando City in the MLS after their promotion in 2013.

The 32 year old, a World Cup winner in 2002 who was named World Player of the Year in 2007 amounts to a giant coup for the sunshine state club. He would be loaned to his home city Sao Paulo for the latter half of the year before joining the Florida outfit for their fledgling campaign in America's top league which started in March 2015.

Kaka signed for AC Milan in 2003 but switched to Real Madrid for a then world record £45 million six years later before returning to the Italian club in the 2013-2014 season.

Of course having Brazilian millionaire Flavio Augusto da Silva to bankroll you is an undoubted help in persuading a player of his proven stature to join up, but knowing 'Inch' I'd like to bet he instigated the audacious move as well!

After an eight year highly successful asscociation with the stateside franchise just a few weeks before his team played sister club Stoke City in a pre-season friendly in the Orange State, somewhat surprisingly 'Inchy' was relieved of his duties in July 2016.

He is currently serving as head coach of Major League Soccer expansion club Minnesota United F.C. which is set to begin play in 2017.

In Memoriam

Frieda, somewhat unusually spelt with an 'i' for a girl from the North East of England could also be described as the apple of Jim's eye such was the fond regard he had for her. To the end, a subject of Jim's caustic wit with absolutely no malice intended of course, much like his pal's acting persona Jack Duckworth to on screen wife Vera. Jack lost his 'swamp duck' as he termed her in a touching scene in the Coronation Street soap in 2008 at the age of 70.

In June 2016 'Jimmy The Dog' said goodbye to his very own 'Friedabear' aged just 67.

Football Talk Breaks The Ice At No 10: 1998...

About to enter No. 10.
Outfitted in my powder blue suit with Phil standing guard.

A "money can't buy prize" in any competition are few
and far between. But this particular one-off award
turned out to be a precursory, uncanny link to a football
match that fell into the same category.

Question time ...

I enter numerous newspaper competitions for the chance to win prizes. There's a palpable 'feelgood' factor when a congratulatory envelope drops through your letter box to confirm a success no matter how small the award.

Tending to concentrate on entries in my local evening publication, I find that because they attract less 'compers' than a national daily, the chances of winning are proportionately much higher. Even so, a draw full of low value trinketry items are testimony to my theory that although rewards may be more frequent their singular merits are not. This particular hypothesis was randomly blown apart when notification for a quite special anniversary invite was delivered to my house, which I could not refuse.

A year into his Downing Street tenure, Prime Minister Tony Blair issued a call to readers from a number of regional newspapers to "Ask me a Question."

Mr Blair said he wanted to use the exercise as a sounding board on his government's first year record, and also to hear the "views, concerns and hopes of the electorate."

As a devout Labour supporter, having seen the harsh injustices of former Conservative rule, it was a chance to air my abhorrence of what I had termed " inexcusable crime."

In particular, acts of violence to, and the mugging of old people is the single biggest wrongdoing that is guaranteed to get my blood boiling.

It had become an everyday occurrence in England, and to support my case I intended to include a national newspaper cutting of an old man beaten up so badly his face was unrecognisable to his very own daughter.

In almost all other countries in Europe the elderly were revered but it would seem that here in Great Britain such barbarity was in danger of becoming an accepted part of modern day society with an ever more sickening regularity.

Even after capture, the felon is administered with a wholly inadequate sentence that would soon see the accused back on the streets in no time at all, hardly reflecting the severity of the crime, and free to strike again.

My suggestion for such perpetrators of these heinous atrocities would be to subject the accused to at least 12 hours of daily hard labour, much like the continental shift system favoured by a growing number of national companies, but without the perks of extended days off. That may at least inflict a small percentage of the pain to their aching bones in comparison to the severe suffering they had brought upon their victims.

Unfortunately the terms and conditions of the competition restricted the participants' questions to no more than 50 words. This resulted in the following abridged version which was one of nine that received a printed reply in the periodical from Tony Blair himself.

MY QUESTION:
"Why should elderly citizens feel fear and trepidation when leaving their homes? It is time for such apprehension to be redirected at the villain, because without quality of life, they have no life."

THE PRIME MINISTER'S ANSWER:
"I entirely agree with you. Violent crime is, fortunately, still rare in Britain, but petty crime is not. And it does not seem petty when it is your house that is vandalised or it is your family who are threatened by drunken youths.

It is our duty to make the streets safe for all – young and old. Our Crime and Disorder Bill, already going through Parliament, contains a whole range of measures to tackle crime and make our streets safer.

It will end the scandal of repeat cautions for persistent young offenders and cut the time between crime and punishment. It will help to tackle hooliganism and loutish behaviour."

I was pleased to have been one of the few to have had their concerns personally addressed by a serving prime minister. It gave me a great deal of satisfaction to think that he was taking my issue seriously. Gratification fulfilled, f carried on with my everyday life a little happier that I had got it off my chest in such a public manner.

The Prime Minister requests vour presence Mr. Burnley...

The following week, returning home from work I greeted my mother with a customary, double-barrelled questioning entrance.

"Hi Mum, y'alright? Any post for me?"

"Oh yes, dare's t'ousands of letters for you," she replied, only answering the second part of my enquiry in the Pidgin English I had become accustomed to.

My mother's interpretation of thousands was always her stock reply when I had received more than three or four items of mail. Although a gross exaggeration, it did mean that I automatically knew I would have more than my usual delivery.

Picking them up from the telephone nest of tables holding area I casually walked upstairs to peruse them at leisure in the private confines of my bedroom. The top one I fingered open to find a request for my blood. Thankfully, this time it wasn't from the bitter ex-girlfriend, but the Blood Transfusion Service. They were notifying me that my six-monthly donation was due. Although 100 per cent claret in both colour and dedication, its rare type of AB rhesus positive meant that for medical purposes, it was only compatible with 2 per cent of the population.

After writing the date for that appointment on my wall planner, I spread the remaining half dozen letters across my bed.

One cream coloured envelope immediately stood out from all the others which the postman had delivered that morning in late April, 1998.

Not only was it of a thicker more superior quality than the rest, it was also clearly marked on the back with an exclusive sender's address of:

10 Downing Street,

Whitehall,

London,

SW1A 2AA

"Bloody Hell! What's all this about?", I muttered to myself. "A letter from No. 10!"

Then my mind went into jocular overdrive.

"It'll be either Tony Blair requiring my opinion on the ongoing Middle East crisis, or fellow Claret Alastair Campbell saving postage to ask my view on our imminent do-or-die last game of the season against Plymouth Argyle."

It turned out to be neither of these prominent figures, but the next best thing, the invitations secretary requesting my presence for afternoon tea at No. 10 on Friday, May 1 from 2pm to 3pm. The actual wording being "The honour of the company of Mr. D .Burnley." How important does that make you feel?

Yes! I had only won my local Evening Sentinel newspaper competition to ask Prime Minister Tony Blair my question in person to mark his first 12 months in office.

Even so, London was a long way to go for tea and cucumber sandwiches. However, the prize did include the return rail journey, a visit to the Houses of Parliament and a chance to look around probably the most iconic terraced house in the country whilst chatting to one of the current, truly eminent world leaders.

My first trip was to browse around our local charity shops where I secured a suitably stunning set of 'threads.' The lightweight suit in a powder blue colour purchased for the princely sum of eight pounds would be the perfect match for my diagonally striped claret and blue official Burnley FC tie.

In truth, I probably looked more like a poor man's Don Johnson from the 'Miami Vice' cult TV series that was aired in the Eighties. Unorthodox maybe, but I had fully embraced my cut-price ensemble and it was going to be my choice to enter the distinguishing seven segmented overhead portals of No. 10 Downing Street.

I was allowed one guest to accompany me, and as circumstances panned out at the time, there was only one man who deserved that invitation.

It just had to be exiled Burnley fan Phil Whalley. Not only was he a 'Claret', but his main subject of study at nearby Keele University was politics.

Keele Uni. forms the biggest campus outside any town or city in the country.

So much has it extended that it now resembles the size of a large village. As such, scholars from both home and abroad reside here.

Once Phil realised how close we were to each other he got in touch to discuss everything Burnley. Our love of football also led to him playing covering goalkeeper on a couple of occasions for my Sunday league team Madeley White Star. He came on good recommendation and even though he had played for Blackburn Rovers at a junior level, he didn't let us down.

I phoned Phil to see if he was up for the expenses paid excursion to the capital, and after a consultation with his tutor he was granted the day off as it was deemed hugely beneficial to his coursework.

With the preliminary tour around the House of Lords scheduled for 10am, it meant a 5.30am rise to prepare for the outward bound journey.

I had already visited the upper chamber in the 1970s before Burnley played a night match at West Ham. For that trip I queued up with the rest of the public, but this one gained us preferential access and included the services of a guide.

With no more than a few minutes to spare we met up with the other regional competition winners and their guests who numbered around 40 in total.

As the tour came to a close, we were informed that it was regarded by many to bring good fortune if you stroked the feet of Winston Churchill's commemorative bronze statue in the Commons Chamber on the way out. Given that we needed every bit of luck going to win our last game of the season the following day against Plymouth Argyle, I rubbed his shoes until they shone.

Myself and Phil made our way towards Whitehall on the Underground. There was still a good hour before our appointment so we retired to the nearest pub to No. 10.

In the Red Lion, we discussed whether or not my planned unconventional greeting to the first lady Cherie Blair might be regarded as breaking the rules of etiquette for such an occasion. As her Christian name sounded like it had a French connection, I wanted to give her a suitably Gallic salutation. It was to be no big deal, just my way of making the day a little bit more special for all concerned.

Phil smiled his not so sure expression before concluding: "Go for it, Dave. I think she'll be flattered."

Inside Tony's den ...

After a couple of pints of quite strong Youngs Brewery Special bitter, we took the short walk to the tall, black railed gateway of Tony's den. I wanted to take in as much of the internal splendour of the premises as I could. Having collected the grand sum of 12,000 pub interiors at the time, I thought I would be ideally suited to detail this building, which I describe accordingly for the benefit of the millions who will never get the chance to visit such an intriguing establishment.

The unpretentious front of the Prime Minister's official residence is deceptive as it is actually made up of two houses that were joined in 1932. So here is my version of the T.V. panel game show 'Through the Keyhole'.

Once inside the entrance hall, there is a tall, elegant looking brown leather upholstered Chippendale hooded chair and photographs of a painting depicting Sir George Downing, a property speculator from whom the street takes its name.

Leading on from here are the Inner Hall and corridor which share pictures and sculptures by Thomas Gainsborough and Henry Moore respectively. Further on is the most important part of the premises – The Cabinet Room. This forms the Council Chamber and is the regular meeting place of the Cabinet where life-changing decisions are made. The extensive wooden table has been made boat-shaped so that everyone sitting at it can see and hear everyone else. To prevent the chance of a devastating terrorist mortar rocket attack, the walls are reinforced to a 12 inch thickness.

On the floor above is a suite of three drawing rooms (White, Green and Pillared) all linked by wide double doors and outfitted with 18th century furniture, although there are also some modern additions.

Both a small dining room and a state dining room can be used to entertain visiting VIPs. Each has mahogany wooden panelling and matching sideboards.

Besides more impressive pictures of eminent British scientists, busts of Isaac Newton and Michael Faraday can also be spotted.

Staffordshire made pottery figures of Wellington, Peel, Palmerston, Disraeli, Gladstone and Cobden are other items of interest from my area of Stoke-on-Trent.

At the back of No. 10 is a mansion which overlooks the perfectly manicured lawned garden.

In the rear portion of the house, the 18th century staircase links the former ground floor hall to the present first floor. Our group was invited up to meet the welcoming party at the top of the stairs.

An impressive series of prints and photographs of prime ministers lined our route from Sir Robert Walpole onwards.

Being around halfway down our assembly, I could just make out our "meeter and greeter in chief." It was the Premier's press secretary Alastair Campbell, a lifelong Burnley fan.

Now numerous people in the political profession purport to follow their chosen football club only to make the odd cameo appearance now and then. Alastair gets to as many games as his time will allow and is a regular face on the away end, which is how I had got to know him.

As I climbed the steps I wondered if he had checked the guest list to see who was visiting these hallowed grounds.

Within the next few minutes I had my answer which was a definite no!

His much practised "Good afternoon and welcome to No. 10" gave way to a much more exclamatory reaction that only just about avoided any profanities that may have slipped out.

"What the heck! Dave Burnley, what are you doing here?"

Alastair rocked back on his heels and his jaw dropped to the floor as a look of open mouthed incredulity spread across his face.

Before I could answer his question, he called out loudly to one of his smartly dressed lackeys who raced to his aid post-haste. After whispering a message in her ear, I began to explain that I was a genuinely invited guest fearing that he may have thought I was an imposter and was summoning the Downing Street police protection force.

I needn't have worried. It turned out that he had sent a somewhat bewildered housemaid to fetch his camera in order to capture the moment. It's fair to say the remainder of the queue looked on in sheer astonishment, possibly contemplating some sort of outrageous Jeremy Beadle stunt for his popular 'Beadle's About' television show.

Alastair excused himself for a moment to pose with myself for a couple of snaps before regaining his equanimity and returning to his welcoming duties.

Thinking about it realistically, given our island's then 60 million plus population, the chances of coincidentally bumping into someone that you know from the general public whilst carrying out his particular job must have been pretty infinitesimal. Which may account for the shocked expressions upon the onlookers' faces, as for a few brief seconds they convinced themselves they were witnessing a serious breach of security.

Delighted to meet you Cherie ...

Greetings over, we were all then asked to form a line in readiness for the formal presentation to the Prime Minister and his wife.

Preserving etiquette, each person was ushered in one by one for a brief chat and a photograph of the meeting.

Then it came to my turn. I'd already rehearsed my lines in preparation. Determined to leave my mark on the event, I put my modus operandi into action.

My name was called out in a very formal style.

"Mr David Burnley representing the city of Stoke-on-Trent," announced a lady-in-waiting implementing an almost regal tone.

I confidently strolled up to first greet Cherie Blair who was standing directly alongside her husband. She was dressed smartly in a fetching cream coloured costume. It was an Indian style wrap around sari outfit complete with a vicar style buttoned down collar. Her alluring chic aura was the perfect foil for my planned compliment, and she really did gracefully look lovely.

As she offered out her hand to shake, I cupped it with mine. Raising them both to chin level, I planted a gentle kiss on the back of hers and delivered my salutation of "Enchante Cherie" in my best French pronunciation. It seemed to work, my accolade had been accepted.

Cherie immediately spasmed into a half-curtsy as her trademark zig-zag smile lit up her face in unanticipated excitement, giving way to a sporadic attack of the giggles.

"I like the dress too," I added, giving her a few seconds to restore her composure.

My reward was a deeply appreciative: "Oooh! Thank you."

By now a distinctly blushing Cherie asked who I would like my complimentary pictorial brochure of the premises signed to.

"My friends call me Ralphy," I replied.

It earned the following clandestine response on the inside page.

"To Ralphy. Best wishes.

Cherie Blair X"

Meanwhile, her husband's usual sangfroid disposition gave way to a disapproving frown to curtail me openly flirting any more with his missus.

Quickly side-stepping to the right in his direction to dissipate any ill feeling l wholeheartedly congratulated him on what I considered to be a genuinely good first year in office.

Now it was Tone's turn to smirk with pride as his hallmark Cheshire Cat grin beaming from ear to ear showed that he'd already forgiven my lack of protocol.

"Thank you so much," said Tony in grateful acceptance of my tribute to himself.

He continued: "Alastair informs me that you too are a Burnley supporter, and a rather keen one by all accounts.

"Yes, you could say that," I admitted frankly.

"Well, you can always tell when Burnley have lost as Alastair keeps a very low profile for the first few hours of a Monday morning and I take care not to disturb him," he replied.

"I know the feeling all too well. It's part and parcel of being a Burnley fan, I'm afraid. You yourself are a Newcastle United follower, aren't you?"

"Yes, I do keep an eye on their results, but I rarely get to St James' because of the demands of my job," Tone replied honestly.

That said, it was time for me to move on as there were others eagerly waiting in line hoping to have a chat with them both.

Phil's greeting was more orthodox, although still amused by Cherie's reaction to my playful introduction, he managed to gather himself enough to engage in a brief conversation with the two dignitaries.

After which the four of us posed for 'one for the album', taken by the official house photographer. In that picture, obtained exclusively by the Evening Sentinel newspaper and featured on page 391 of 'Got To Be There!' Cherie still looks visibly thrilled by my gesture.

However, it didn't turn out to be a keepsake for either Phil or myself as the cherished photograph had a staggering purchase price of an extortionate £32.50 per copy! With no cameras allowed in for security reasons from our party, as you can imagine there were very few takers.

Niceties over, everyone was allowed to mingle freely, although somewhat predictably because of this the Prime Minister became surrounded like a pop star.

Our choice of beverage was Earl Grey tea or Brazilian coffee with either orange or apple juice as a cold drink option. A silver tray of sandwiches being passed around, triangularly shaped with all crusts trimmed off, as predicted they included plain cucumber as an option which I just had to choose. A veritable array of petits fours graced the accompanying cake stand.

With Tony otherwise engaged with over-keen enquirers, I strolled back over to Alastair for what would be a meaningful discussion albeit in a completely different context.

It was about tomorrow's crucial game against Plymouth where the winners had a chance of staying up, but the losers would definitely go down. Their fate, being exiled to the unforgiving football world of the Fourth Division, as it was, or League Two as it has metamorphosed into today.

Burnley had gone through a disastrous season under manager Chris Waddle. They had failed to even score a goal in their opening six games, or win a league match in their first ten. Unsurprisingly, given our dreadful start, the club never went higher than 19th position during the length of their nine month campaign.

But only on the Tuesday just gone Burnley had blown a golden chance. Leading 3-1 at Oldham with the home side down to 10 men, we had allowed them back in the game to steal a 3-3 result. If Burnley had held on to that scoreline, they would have been able to afford a draw to preserve their status.

Travelling support made up more than half the crowd in an attendance of just under 10,000 with many Burnley fans locked out.

Crucially, after only picking up a mere 20 points from the first half of the season, the second half had garnered 29 putting them in with this last gasp chance of survival, and a relegation scenario not seen since the 'Orient game' in 1987.

After crunching the numbers we came to the conclusion that given the combination of the vast distance between the two clubs and the assured backing of a partisan crowd, Burnley held the edge.

With that, I looked at my watch. It was dead on three o'clock.

"Well, Alastair. This time tomorrow we will be in charge of our own fate as we'll just be kicking off. Keep the faith, eh?," I said.

"We have to, don't we?", added Alastair.

Before our departure, I asked directions to the gents loo, in order not only to relieve myself but of course check out the standard of the convenience.

I found that what is usually regarded as the smallest room in the house is a very good barometer to the worthiness of any premises, be it Portakabin or palace.

As you'd expect, the lav. was in a pristine clean condition with the gleaming gold-plated towel rail and taps the stand-out features of the modern fixtures and fittings that included a shower and bath.

Looking around there was no evidence of an Alastair's 'Burnley FC OK' or a Tony's 'Geordie Boys, we are here!' graffiti etched into the wall that you might find in a public toilet in either of these locations. Yet they came across as two champions of the working class that could well have done such deeds, rightly or wrongly, in their teenage years. The point being that throughout the afternoon we had all been treated as equals.

I still hadn't managed to approach Tony about my competition winning question, but now it was time to bid farewell.

"Everything crossed for tomorrow's game, eh, Alastair?," I suggested.

"For sure, Dave. Up the Clarets!," he responded, shaking my hand firmly.

"Best of luck for the rest of your term, Tony," I wished the PM with an equally solid handshake.

"Very much appreciated David, and here's hoping you get that win you need tomorrow, for both our sakes," he chuckled, glancing towards Alastair before taking a phone call from a French dignitary and walking away.

That left the patiently waiting Cherie.

"Nice meeting ya Cherie. I wish you well," I whispered, instinctively leaning forward to kiss her on the cheek as Tony's attention was diverted.

She looked back at me mischievously before flicking me a cheeky wink of her eye as once again her face turned a crimson hue.

But I ask you. Where else could you do that and get away with it?

What I do know is that I regard myself as a pretty good judge of character and in truth, I don't believe Tony Blair realised just how close we came to trading places on that May day back in 1998.

On the Saturday morning, of course, my benefactors for the trip, the Evening Sentinel newspaper, were naturally keen to report the story of my visit for that night's edition.

I admitted to them that I hadn't actually got the opportunity to pose the question I had been sent down to ask. Adding that because he had been corralled into a corner by the more eager members of our assembly, I had a retrospectively, equally serious conversation with his press secretary Alastair Campbell who also happened to be a Burnley fan.

As a consequence the evening's headline ran: "Football Talk Breaks The Ice At No. 10."

The great escape ...

Now all that remained was to win our clash to save our third tier Football League status and hope that relegation rivals Brentford would either lose or draw at Bristol Rovers to give us any chance of staying up.

I was as nervous as the next Burnley fan. I'd really had enough of the drudge and grind that was Fourth Division football after our seven year exile there throughout the mid-Eighties and early Nineties. We were now staring that scenario in the face once more.

Just under 19,000 supporters attended that game and before the match, I dealt with the pressure in the only way I, and probably hundreds of others, knew how – by having a skinful of beer to anaesthetise the pain.

As I exited the Wellington pub where I'd had a last couple of pints, crossing over to Belvedere Road and my entrance to the ground meant we had to cut across the main body of Argyle fans who were getting a police escort to their Cricket Field End. They numbered a few hundred.

"You've come a long way for nothing, lads," I commented in the desperate hope my quote wouldn't come back to haunt me like it did after my inference that it would be "Fifteen-love today" in a taunt to Wimbledon fans when their non-league outfit knocked us out of the FA Cup in 1975.

"Well said, Dave," quipped 'Mash', a loyal but malcontent member of the Burnley 'Suicide Squad'.

"Let's hope I'm right, mate," I answered, not totally convinced I would be.

The match kicked off at a feverish tempo with Burnley looking as psyched up for the battle as the fans. The front pairing of the two Andys that were Cooke and Payton would prove ideal partners.

After 12 minutes, a cross from the mercurial super Glen Little, who incidentally made the bench at Wembley in March 2013 for Wrexham in their Carlsberg Trophy Final victory some near 15 years later, was headed in by Shropshire lad Andy Cooke. 1-0.

Plymouth equalised after 25 minutes to initiate a quick riposte and it was also bad news in the main fixture that affected our plight. Bristol Rovers, who remember we needed to win, had a goal disallowed and were already reduced to 10 men.

I swear only when I'm angry. Now I was angry as I turned to loyal pal Tricky' Trev Slack for support.

"For fuck's sake, Trev. What's happening? It's all going fucking pear-shaped.' We cannot go down a-fucking-gain!," I stormed, fearing the worst.

Trev just grimaced, not saying a word, chewing his gum in identical disbelieving fashion.

Then dramatically it all turned. Both Paul Weller and Glen Little hit the woodwork before Cooke once again snatched back the lead with his second headed goal.

Within moments, there was even better news as against the odds Bristol Rovers had scored and a mounting crescendo of cheers pierced the afternoon air.

However, the celebrations were short-lived. Brentford had levelled.

Burnley had to defend like demons, and they really did, holding on for a 2-1 win. Bristol had gone back in front and it was yet another occasion when nothing but a pitch invasion would do the day justice.

I danced arm in arm with passionate Claret Andrew Short, always known as 'Elly,' his ginger hair and matching 'tache skipping along to the most appropriate tune of that moment, 'The Great Escape.'

We had survived!

In Memoriam

'Mash,' however, who I'd been drinking with before the game, did not survive long after this so crucial of fixtures. A victim of a brain haemorrhage, his young life was cut short. He might have been a bad 'un' in some eyes, but he was Burnley through and through, and at least lived to see his beloved team stay up on that momentous day.

---

30 The Jersey Boys: 1998 (World Cup Finals in France, Part One)

Undercover to France on the St. Helier to St. Malo ferry. Me and Weedy get in situ.

With the likelihood of England ever, once again being the host nation for the World Cup tournament diminishing by the year, when the chance came along to take the short hop across the Channel to France to be part of this massive event, the avid fan had to give it some serious consideration. Let me take you on this enlightening journey of two halves.

Message in a bottle ...

Myself and regular travelling companion Pete 'Weedy' Read were determined to make the 1998 World Cup Finals in France as they were taking place so near to home.

But what we gained in terms of ease of travelling by their close proximity, we lost on the extra tight security surrounding the chosen locations.

Police forces from both countries had issued more than the usual advanced statutory behavioural warnings along with diligently enforced entry requirements to the Gallic nation. By imposing these stringent measures, they were hoping to control the biggest invasion of French shores since the D-Day landings.

In order to carry out their containment strategy, an unprecedented raft of transport conditions were imposed.

Besides the by now mandatory procedure of convicted football hooligans having to hand in their passports to their local 'cop shop' well before commencement of the competition, teams of police 'spotters' were deployed at all major seaports and airports to apprehend known troublemakers. Anyone receiving a previous conviction against their name would have to be verified by having their details checked on the national computer database to see if they posed a threat of disorder.

In addition, no fans would be allowed to travel without match tickets and adequate funding for the duration of their stay.

It was these last two stipulations that concerned myself and Weedy. Neither of us had any chance of pre-ordering tickets as we hadn't acquired enough ticket stubs from previous internationals to qualify, and our daily allowance for our planned month-long trip was a mere £30 a day to cover everything.

So stretched was our funding that we had borrowed a three man tent from former village neighbour and good friend Chris Edwards, a joiner by trade. Add to this the fact that our transportation plan throughout the trip was to hitchhike, and you begin to gauge the magnitude of the problems we faced in order to fulfil our ambitions.

First and foremost, we had to get into the country.

On one particular day in May just prior to our planned departure, our employment had taken us to the Leicestershire town of Melton Mowbray. Melton is of course famous for its delicious pork pies, but after finishing our work, it was more a few delicious pints we were looking for, and our search for such refreshment took us to a place where we unexpectedly found a solution to our problem.

In a centrally located pub called The Crafty Fox, we came up with an equally crafty idea. Twiddling an empty beer bottle which had been left on our table, I noticed a flight offer promotion on the label at the back of the vessel.

It read: "Collect two of these limited edition stickers to qualify for a special £49 return fare to the island of Jersey," which of course lay just a few short miles from the French mainland.

I looked at Weedy.

"That's it, Weed. We'll go to France the back way to avoid detection," I said.

A couple more of the same bottled beers purchased to acquire our promo codes, followed by a phone call to the firm's marketing department to impart our credit card details, and we were on our way.

Through the back door ...

It was Tuesday, June 16, and the quest to get to the World Cup was about to begin.

I awoke at 4am to get everything ready for our 5.30am lift from our fellow villager and former Sunday league football manager Gil Adams. He was driving us over to the M1 motorway service station at Trowell, Nottinghamshire, where we were hoping to hitch a ride south-east to Stansted Airport in Essex. Gil was a national sales manager for a domestic furnishings company based in Ilkeston, Derbyshire, only a couple of miles from those services where he was to drop us off.

Half an hour into the journey, I removed my bob-hat to reveal my newly dyed, bleach blond crop of spiked hair. Although the little quiff at the front had turned out distinctly ginger, it perfectly enhanced my 'Tin-Tin' appearance and resembled more of a 'Burger King Flame Whopper' amalgamation, but at least it made my companions chuckle.

However, once we arrived at the designated services we realised it was a bit of a logistical nightmare with scores of parked trucks causing major blockages. It wasn't going to be an easy hitch.

After an hour and a half, we eventually secured a lift from an HGV to a quiet slip road just past where the M1 and M6 merge. Another hour and a half then passed before a crusty old farmer and his dog took us along the A14 near to Corby.

Once again we waited and waited until another hour and a half passed. It was now 12.45pm. Our flight left in two and a half hours and we were still more than 60 miles from Stansted Airport.

Then, right on cue, a couple of black lads in a car picked us up and deposited us just an agonising four miles from our destination.

We walked for a mile with our luggage before reaching the plush Hilton Hotel where, with time running out to catch our plane, we noticed a sign announcing that a courtesy bus service to the airport was due to leave in 10 minutes.

We bought a couple of beers at the hotel bar and as the driver called in to pick up passengers for our flight, we gathered our bags and hopped on the bus as if we were guests of the premises. No questions were asked and we made it for the short check-in time, which we would certainly not have done had we walked. With no taxis passing, there was no doubt our initiative had saved us.

But we had only attempted hitching rides for one day and had already hit problems, so it seemed pretty clear that for two six foot plus blokes in their forties trying to get across France, the next month was going to be anything but easy.

On the plane, I was sat next to Sister Theresa, a nun from the Little Sisters of the Poor religious order, who was on a week's retreat to Jersey.

Weedy mischievously asked me to inquire if there was any room at her accommodation on the island, but after a short deliberation, I considered this wholly inappropriate and refrained from doing so.

Upon landing, we caught the local bus to the capital St Helier where we did a quick 'recce' of the town, and after eliminating a number of possible locations to erect our tent for the night, we decided to head for a local park after the pubs had closed.

But as everyone knows, when alcohol is involved, there is always a flaw in even the most well considered plans.

We drained a gallon each in eight different pubs before locating our chosen spot for camping. Of course, by this time it was not only past midnight but pitch black too. The wrought iron park gates were locked and the only way in was by scaling a 10 foot wall.

It was like attempting an army assault course while blindfolded and it took more than half an hour for both of us to conquer the fortification, with numerous attempts at leg-ups, pull ups and even 'jump-ups.'

But that was the easy part.

We decided to attempt our pitch at a site in the far corner of the park beyond some trees. We huffed, puffed, pulled, prodded and pegged before giving up and collapsing into our sleeping bags under any raised canvas we could locate in the partially erect structure. Trying to put up the shelter in an inebriated condition without the merest glimpse of visibility had proved all too much for the two of us.

At first light, after a largely sleepless night, we awoke to view what looked like a five-year-old's first attempt at a Meccano set. The two metal arches of our tent supported each end, but the fabric cover had been pegged incorrectly leaving us only three-quarters protection.

At 6am, a park-keeper began emptying the litter bins at the entrance so we dismantled what was left of our sad-looking structure and made a swift exit, only to notice a particularly stern warning on a raised wooden sign outside the park gates.

It read: "Howard Davis Park. Anyone found sleeping in these grounds is liable to prosecution. They will also be made to leave the island with no return for a period of six years."

"Bloody Hell," I said. "That's a bit harsh, isn't it Weedy? Looks like we had a close call."

Sarah and Bob ...

Next day, we moved to an official pitch at the Rozel camp site a few miles out of town.

We hitched a lift into St Martin and went into a pub called the Royal.

After ordering the drinks, I was instantly aware of two pairs of eyes staring at my Burnley shirt followed by a whisper of: "Yes, it is Burnley."

"Was it friend or foe?," I wondered.

I turned around to find two smiling faces, one male, one female, which confirmed the former.

"Are you a Claret?," I asked spontaneously.

"Yes, we both are," came back the reply I was hoping for.

The couple turned out to be Sarah and Bob Burke, who lived and worked on Jersey but watched Burnley when they could.

So instantly we all got chatting and within an hour they had offered us accommodation in their spare room located on St Saviours Hill, a road leading out of St Helier.

Of course, we immediately said yes. What were the chances of that happening in an isolated boozer out in the country? It was a truly serendipitous moment.

That night, we went around a number of bars celebrating an Irish festival of music with Sarah, Bob and a few friends of theirs from the office where they were employed.

We drank and danced the evening away in their company and towards the end of the night, one of their friends, Terri, a 42-year-old dressed in distinguishing tight, snakeskin patterned trousers, invited me back to her apartment.

I therefore informed The Weed' that he would have to make his own way home to Sarah and Bob's, who had left earlier, thinking there would be no problem as it was close by. He just gave me the nod with his usual toothy smile and carried on dancing.

I returned to our digs the following morning but Weedy was nowhere to be seen. He eventually rolled in at 11am after apparently losing his bearings and walking the streets until crashing out exhausted on a town centre bench.

'Wandering Walter,' as I now dubbed him, had got completely disorientated negotiating a distance of no more than a mile. Remarkable!

We had placed a couple of postcard adverts at strategic locations in a bid to save a few pounds.

The first in a local newsagents offered the return part of our flight for £20 each, which we reckoned was a real bargain. As we planned to come home from France by the more popular ferry route, both were superfluous to our requirements.

The second notice was a request for a working passage across to the French coast which was displayed at the posh St Helier Yacht Club.

It was no surprise that we received no response to either.

Our host Bob had tried even harder to arrange our transit needs. He had driven us to the main depot of Danny Clinton's, the island's major removal firm, to see if there were any vans booked to make the journey to France which we could hitch a ride on. But we had no luck, and we were left with no alternative but to book a single ferry fare to the French port of St Malo.

After a week of exceptional hospitality from what amounted to no more than a pair of complete strangers we had come across in the most unlikely of circumstances, it was time to say goodbye to the generous couple. After presenting them with a small gift as a token of our gratitude, we promised to keep in touch.

But we had one night left on the island and knew exactly how it would be spent.

There had been a promotion running during our stay whereby an inked stamp was collected in a passport-style folder when a pint of beer was purchased in any pub supplied by the local brewery. As we had accumulated more than 50 stamps each, it qualified us for a gallon of beer redeemable at any of the participating outlets, along with two cotton T-shirts to acclaim our feat.

Our last port of call on the night was the Victor Hugo wine bar, where we were to collect our free garments. It was a pretentious kind of place with a name that meant nothing at all to me, and yet it was a title I was going to come across again very soon in the most utterly bizarre way imaginable.

The World Cup tournament had by now got going, and England, after opening their campaign with a 2-0 win over Tunisia, now faced Romania in Toulouse in their second group game, which we watched in a pub on Jersey simply called 'The Sports Bar.'

True to form, they had lost 2-1 with substitute Michael Owen getting the consolation goal. It meant that we needed at least a draw against Colombia in the city of Lens on the following Friday to qualify for the knockout phase.

This was the game we had targeted as our potential first appearance, and it was now time to set sail towards our destination.

Peaceful hooligans …

Besides our tent and sleeping bags, we had brought along another camping essential, the Calor Gas stove. As well as providing us with boiling water to make a brew of tea, we could also prepare our meals as we had also packed a saucepan and frying pan.

But there was another equally important reason for their presence. We were hoping to pay for our black market match tickets, of which there are always plenty due to people's greed, by selling traditional hot dogs and boiled onions in finger rolls, all of which we planned to buy on the day of sale.

I'd reckoned that England fans would be appreciative of traditional footy match day food, particularly as we had brought over those two 'must have' accompaniments in the form of plastic bottles of Heinz Tomato Ketchup and Colman's Mustard.

Upon arrival at St Malo, we booked a pitch for one night at the nearby campsite which was located on a windswept beach. To even peg out our tent in daylight without it blowing away was a stern test, and the continual sandstorm ensured that we would be transporting a multitudinous amount of grit particles around for the remainder of the trip.

It was an early start in the morning to reach our first cultural stop of Mont St Michel, a revered religious outpost.

We continued our journey by hitching, and initially got a lift from one chap, then a good lift through Lower Normandy to Caen from a young couple getting exactly the same reaction from both drivers when we told them we were English and were over for the football.

"You're not football hooligans?," each had asked in all seriousness.

We found ourselves having to reassure them immediately that we weren't, as they gave us the impression that they weren't prepared to take us if we did not do so. It was a question that we would be asked time and again on our journey, such was the fear of English hooligans.

A town called Arras was the last major stop before our destination of Lens, so on reaching there by Thursday afternoon, we booked a room at the OK Hotel, which just about lived up to its name.

For breakfast the following morning, a traditional 'cereal bowl' of coffee was served along with some chocolate bread. Then it was the short journey on to Lens to get the best pitch for our hot dog venture.

And there's always one guaranteed place where you'll find the maximum number of English fans, whether they are travelling abroad with club or country, and that is the main town or city square.

It's easily identifiable by the massed collection of Union Flags that hang from every vantage point of the many bars that are usually arranged around its perimeter. Lettered place names on the material, along with the title of the club the owner of the flag supports have become territorial statements in each location they occupy.

There is generally also some kind of distinguishing statue or obelisk in the main square, invariably commemorating a past statesman or major military leader.

Lens was no exception in all the above respects, and this plaza would provide the perfect base for our new business project.

'Dogs 'Я' Us' ...

Having carried out a big shop at a local supermarket upon arrival, we now had around 60 freshly baked rolls, a bag of French onions and dozens of vacuum packed, good quality frankfurter hot dogs to serve up.

So we set up our cooking utensils on the steps leading up to the sculpture on the square and placed alongside it the 'Dogs 'Я' Us' cardboard sign I'd written out to advertise our wares.

The onions were peeled and sliced then boiled, while the sausages were gently warmed, and before you could say "Hot dogs! Hot dogs! Get ya hot dogs!," they were ready for their finger rolls to retail at around a pound each.

It was a sunny day and we were set to sell, so scouring the square for potential customers, I headed for what looked like the busiest bar with a trial run of 10 'dogs' on a drinks tray I'd borrowed from a nearby table.

The vast majority of the outside drinking area had been taken over by what looked like a block booking of West Ham United supporters who had made the trip over.

Now, I don't know what it is about fans of West Ham, or 'Boiled Ham' as I call them, but when they travel to watch the national team, they come over all elitist because a trio of their players were in the victorious England side which beat West Germany 4-2 way back in the 1966 World Cup Final. It would be fair to say that the triumvirate of Bobby Moore, Martin Peters and Geoff Hurst played a huge part in the outcome, but so did the remainder of the team. Yet their arrogance remains undiminished, as I was about to find out.

Clad in my favourite 1994 promotion home shirt sponsored by Endsleigh Insurance, I expected some stick as I leaned over the fence surrounding the bar and shouted: "Who wants a hot dog, then?"

A number of heads spun round in response before one of their party yelled back in a Cockney accent: "Whose fackin' colours are those?"

"Burnley," I instantly replied.

"Fack yerself off then," came the retort from the same foul mouthed bloke.

The rest turned away, so unperturbed, I concentrated on the 'lippy' one.

"I'll tell you what then, Try one for free with the Heinz Tomato Ketchup and Colman's Mustard I've brought from home, and if you don't like it, you don't pay the 10 Franc charge. I can't say fairer than that, can I?"

I'd singled him out and now I'd put him on the spot in front of his mates.

There was an awkward impasse until one of his pals urged: "Go on. Lennie. Try one."

He finally took up the offer, albeit reluctantly, adding boiled onions and tomato sauce to his sausage. Taking a large bite, his face then transformed from looking like a bulldog that had swallowed a wasp to one of appreciative satisfaction.

"Not bad, I suppose. Give us another one," he conceded, and gave me 20 Francs for the pair.

His friends followed until the tray had been cleared, so I headed back to Weedy to re-stock my goods.

"Keep 'em coming, Weed. They're lovin' 'em," I quipped.

I worked the square until we ran out of rolls. We had made 600 Francs, which less the 150 Francs cost of the food, gained us a tidy profit of 450 Francs within an hour.

Selling a quality product at a fair price had worked. Now it was our turn for the beers before attempting to get tickets for the game.

It's party time ...

The stadium in Lens was surrounded by a triple ring of security which was almost impenetrable without the required ticket.

With the black market rate way out of reach even for a low key game against Colombia, we decided to try to find a bar, and as the match had now started, I gave a running report on the game to Weedy using my small travel radio.

Then Darren Anderton scored for England, resulting in wild scenes all around a back street we had strolled down in search of a beer.

As we leapt around punching the air, just a few yards ahead a couple of young kids playing football beckoned us over whilst pointing through the window of a house at a television that was showing a replay of the goal. The front door was open and upon inspection, we saw about 30 people in the house having a footie party for the event. The couple living in the premises waved us in, offering us free beer and snacks to consume while we watched the game on their TV.

And if that wasn't enough in terms of surprises for the night, sitting on the floor among the invited guests was regular Burnley and England fan Craig Stansfields from Trawden near Colne.

"Of all the bars in all the world, you had to pick mine," was my jocular greeting to Craig who had also been priced out of a match ticket and fortunately had wandered in the same direction as ourselves to be greeted with this great French hospitality.

It was yet another inconceivably lucky meeting with a Burnley fan in what was fast turning into a string of improbable coincidences.

David Beckham added a second and England went on to win 2-0 and qualify for the next stage, and then as none of our party had anywhere to stay, we were asked by the very trusting tenants if we would like to sleep at their place for the night. Given the fact that they had two young children, this really was a massive gesture and one that we gratefully accepted.

The next match for England would take place on Tuesday, June 30 in St Etienne, a plum last 16 tie against one of our bitterest adversaries, Argentina.

After thanking our hosts for their outstanding hospitality, we said goodbye to Craig as we prepared ourselves for the long hitch south.

Having just witnessed at first hand the level of security in Lens, we at least now knew what to expect. With thousands of ticketless England fans making the trip, it would be doubly difficult to secure a ticket for such a high profile tie. Yet it was a game we both desperately wanted to see given its significance.

My only souvenir from the Lens visit was a discarded VIP neck lanyard that I had found near to the ground after the final whistle which I kept for possible future use.

We got three separate lifts to our first base of Dijon. A male college lecturer who before dropping us off took us back to his place for a dinner of crepe pancakes and wine, an elderly couple, and finally a young female student who went out of her way to drop us near our choice of accommodation.

In fact, it was now two weeks into our journey and we still hadn't come across the haughty French stereotype that we had regularly found on previous visits. So far, we had encountered nothing but good experiences in the provinces.

On the day of the match, we set off from Lyon where we had booked all but our sleeping bags into the left luggage office at the railway station after a morning selling hot dogs to the many England fans milling around the station approaches. We knew it was going to be a long night.

Taking the train from Lyon Part-Dieu station, we arrived in St Etienne just after 1pm and were still drinking outside the transport hub at 3pm in the hope of landing a couple of black market tickets.

But the cheapest asking price were the equivalent of £200 each, well over double what we were prepared to pay, so with options running out we headed for the stadium. Yet here too, tickets were rarer than rocking horse droppings as the people who had them weren't, it seemed, opting to sell at any price.

France 1998
Blag my way through to the turnstiles with the help of a
Canadian girl.

Blagging it in ...

The police and military were out in force once again with four lines of validation checks to be passed, which were causing major crowd congestion as kick off time approached.

"It's every man for himself, Weedy," I shouted across the swell of the waiting thousands as they pushed us apart. "Meet ya back at Lyon station after the game."

Within five minutes, I saw 'The Weed' being escorted away by two burly security personnel after a failed attempt to sneak along an adjacent railway track on all fours in shorts and sandals. It was just like a scene from the World War Two Far East prisoner of war series Tenko!'

Meanwhile, in the crush I'd got acquainted with Liz from Ontario, Canada, who was attending the game alone. She was getting ever more distressed by the scrummage behind her.

"Don't worry. I'll get you through, Liz," I said. "Just give me your ticket to wave at the checker and I'll sort it."

I slipped the VIP lanyard over my head, and though it was clearly marked for the Colombia match, such was the pressure the officials were now under, a quick glance at the precious ticket we held together was sufficient to allow us access through the first, second, third and finally the fourth checkpoint that stood between us and the turnstiles.

"If we get through here, I'm going to marry you, Liz," I blurted out excitedly, in jest of course. It would have had to be the World Cup Final itself for me to consider such a pledge.

But Liz needn't have worried as I was brought down at the final hurdle.

"Deux personnes, s'il vous plait," I vainly pleaded while displaying just the one admission ticket and pointing my finger between myself and Liz.

"Non, non, non...impossible!," came back the reply from the turnstile operator. "Qu'il est impossible, monsieur," he repeated.

After further pleas while showing him my outdated lanyard, he still wouldn't budge, so to save Liz missing the game, I kissed her goodbye and thanked her for trying. A last desperate bid in the form of a 100 Franc bribe also failed to budge the operator, and I walked away to avoid the possibility of being arrested.

So there I was, just yards away from the live action but having to listen to it on my portable radio with my sleeping bag as a seat.

I'd tried so hard but just failed. Or had I?

It seemed to be the high tempo game we had expected as the commentary became ever more frenetic after an Alan Shearer penalty leveller followed an early Argentine spot kick success. Then came more drama.

"It's Owen. He takes a touch with the outside of his left boot, he beats one man, goes wide, darts past another. It's a tight angle...he shoots...and scores! A remarkable goal."

I was still conducting my solo celebration when I saw a latecomer dressed in a suit banging on a large metal sliding door as he tried to get in. He too was wearing an identification lanyard.

An elderly steward slid the door open to allow him in, so seizing my chance, I strolled up right behind him, flashing my ID necklace while coming out with the only French I could muster at such short notice.

"Bonjour, mon amie. Tele..vision. Merci beaucoup."

I brushed past him as he showed no resistance. Maybe he presumed my TV equipment was inside my sleeping bag, or did he let me in for my sheer audacity? I will never know, but I was at last in the Stade Geoffrey Guichard.

And whatever he made of my next manoeuvre will probably stay with him for the rest of his life.

I still had to get past the stewards who were checking

tickets at the top of the concrete steps which needed to be climbed to access the end the England supporters occupied.

Then something extraordinary took place.

In celebration of Michael Owen's wonder goal, hundreds of our fans were spilling down the terraces towards me in a conga line, joyously singing: "Let's all have a disco, let's all have a disco. Nah, nah, nah, nah. Nah, nah, nah, nah."

It was a perfect opportunity to catch that human train and dance my way up to access all areas, and I wasn't going to miss it.

Joining the long chain as last man, I skipped up into the stand as the security personnel looked on in amazement, carrying on right down the centre aisle until peeling off right behind the goalmouth. I was in at last! Two more Burnley fans, Nik Race 'N.R.' and Gary 'Rocket' Jenkins had seen me dance in and came over to greet me.

It had been a night of sheer good fortune for myself off the pitch, but on it, England were fast unravelling against the 'Argies,' who equalised just before half time.

After David Beckham's petulant schoolboy kick out at Argentina's snidey Diego Simeone who fell like he had been shot by a sniper while the England man was still on the ground, which led to his inevitable sending off on 47 minutes, our chances of victory appeared greatly diminished.

But to their credit, the gutsy 10 men battled on to earn a 2-2 scoreline after extra time. Indeed, they could quite easily have won it only for a legitimate Sol Campbell headed goal to be ruled out for a Shearer push directly in front of the prematurely celebrating England fans.

That meant it was time for the dreaded penalty shoot-out at which we usually fail miserably, and tonight would be no different with shocking misses from Paul Ince and David Batty losing us the tie on spot kicks 4-3.

So it was game over, not only for England's World Cup hopes but also for our fledgling hot dog business. "Trust England to ruin our lucrative sideline," I thought as I made the long walk back to the station.

After a few beers, I arrived back at Lyon at 1.30am, where I met a welcoming committee of dozens of the local gendarmerie with their accompanying salivating Rottweilers.

As the masses of England fans who had been jam-packed on the train slowly moved out of the station concourse, I tried a waiting room door which to my surprise was open. There was only one other youth sleeping there so I rolled out my sleeping bag and lay down in the corner.

Another two full trains came in, and on the second one I spotted Weedy and called him over. There were too many distractions throughout the night to get any sleep so we gathered up our bags for an early dart out of town.

Our football interest may have been over but our holiday certainly wasn't.

31 Fifty Shades of Grey... Y...Fronts!: 1998 (World Cup Finals in France, Part Two)

'La Coup De Monde, c'est fini...'

As the reality dawned that our interest in the World Cup was over, I had to admit it was no surprise. In more than 50 years of false expectations, it would be fair to say that we now followed England abroad more for the experience and the atmosphere than the football. If we do get a game or two in, all well and good, but if not we always factor in a contingency plan whereby we explore the country regardless. Having been let down by the national team so many times, we have inevitably done a lot of exploring.

A French fancy. Pascale's friend Monique in the Irish bar, Senlis, just north of Paris.

A taste of things to come!

Heading south for the vineyards …

At the point where the A7 joined the E17, the fast road to Avignon, we waited for more than an hour before securing a lift from a Japanese couple who were decidedly the worse for wear after visiting a nearby vineyard for a wine tasting excursion.

This was an experience we were also planning, and we had lined up the famous Chateauneuf-du-Pape plantations for a visit. The stark difference was that our friends from the Far East had purchased crates of the stuff while we were only going for the free samples that were on offer at the scores of 'degustation' cellars in the area. But that was for another day.

In the mean time, we had a great session in Avignon centre on the night France played Italy in their quarter- final. The French were victorious in a nail biting penalty shoot-out as their opponents last spot kick dramatically crashed against the bar, while Brazil beat Denmark 3-1 in another last eight match. That set up what many thought could be 'La Classic' final as both sides should realistically dispose of their respective semi-final opposition.

As a result, this area of Provence was absolutely leaping. 'Happy hours' drink promotions sprung up from nowhere and competition for business intensified as the partying frenchies hit the town to celebrate their achievement.

Not ones to miss out on a good knees-up, the 'Weed' and I embraced their jubilation wholeheartedly in the only way we knew how. With plenty of beers and a large kebab apiece, we did it in the traditional British method, before finally hitting the canvas at 2.30am.

The following day we designated 'Wine day'.

No busses ran to our Chateauneuf-de-Pape destination and so the magic thumbs were utilised once more. Somewhat remarkably, a mother with a sleeping young daughter in a baby seat, picked us up and drove us directly to the wine village. And it turned out to be an epic day as we listened to the mandatory chat at about a dozen wine caves before sampling around 30 varieties of top quality grape produce with a couple of brandies thrown in, all for free!

We hitched back into Avignon to finish off the night in an area called 'The Red Zone' where we went through our animated rave dancing routine repertoire for a few hours before calling time at 2am. It was a top day costing just a few Francs.

Hitching a ride.
My sign is almost a worded premonition of England's hopes.

Our sleep was understandably sound given our excessive alcohol intake, resulting in a hitching departure at 11am a lot later than planned. Toulouse was our next target city, but rides proved elusive as it was a quieter than normal Sunday.

It took us more than two long hours to get our first lift, which was courtesy of a Belgian bloke going to Montpellier. We got him to drop us off at a service station some 15 miles short of the city to give ourselves a better chance of our next lift – or so we thought.

By 5pm we had only travelled a distance of around 40 miles in six hours so we had to make alternative arrangements in regard to our journey's end. Eventually, a Tunisian lad stopped to pick us up. He was only going as far as Carcassone, some 80 miles further on, but we accepted the lift.

After scouring our French campsite guide, we settled for an idyllic location set under the panoramic picture postcard vista of the imposing castle and surrounding fields of sunflowers. Our fee for a pitch for one night was just 4 Francs, 15 cents the equivalent of around £4.50.

We then observed, our by now standard pitching ritual, of each purchasing a large bottle of the always excellent strong French cider from the camp stores to consume while we erected our tent. Otters scurried into the nearby river as we later took the walkway into town for what was a more reserved night than the previous one.

Next day was another bad hitch as we traversed no more than four miles in the same amount of hours. Well behind schedule, and with the temperatures hitting 100 degrees Fahrenheit in the sun, we were getting nowhere fast so a change of itinerary was necessary.

Bypassing Toulouse, we chose to stay at a town called Montauban where we booked into a cheap hotel recommended by our invaluable 'Berkley' guide to France, in order to clean ourselves up a bit.

The many students in the area had just finished their exams so we indulged ourselves in their jubilation at a beach party promotion night which lasted until 4am.

But that meant we paid for it big style the next day when our 8am alarm kicked in mercilessly. After breakfast, we walked to a layby with the aim of getting as far as we could towards Bordeaux.

Once again, the going was tough and after two hours, we had only travelled about eight miles to just beyond the Napoleonic bridge on the far side of a town called Moissac.

A young farmer drove us as far as the Agen toll booths by 6pm and that's where we stayed. This had proved to be our least productive period of the tour travel wise, as we registered just 40 miles in seven and a half hours, and were still 85 miles short of Bordeaux.

We pitched up alongside the motorway toll bridge after my request for a night in the cells was politely refused by a patrolling gendarme. We then watched the Brazil v Holland game at a local truck stop and saw the South Americans triumph on penalties after a 1-1 draw to go through to the World Cup Final against France, who had beaten Croatia in their semi-final to set up a contest most fans had hoped for.

Next day, an early rise got us the ride we needed to Bordeaux. However, because of our slow progress, we were well behind our timetable to get back, and so just booked one night's accommodation in the city at a Formula One hotel, which we had used before as the chain represented great value.

To make up for the hours lost, we bought train tickets, initially to Paris Montapanasse station then onwards north to Senlis, a random choice well clear of the capital. The town offered university accommodation whilst the students were on holiday and it was also close to the busy A1 which would take us back to the port of Calais.

Out for a quiet night – not! …

At first glance, it looked a sleepy place but it was Thursday evening so we weren't expecting a big night out anyway. How wrong could we be?

It had been a long travelling day so I suggested to Weedy that we just dump our bags, have a quick swill and go out to find a few bars as it was getting late. Accordingly, we kept on the same clothes we had worn since the morning to save time.

Upon inspection, the only life of any note in Senlis appeared to be centred around a nest of four drinking venues located in the equivalent of the high street.

We had a drink in the first three which were uninteresting 'locales', before moving on to what seemed the busiest spot. This took the form of an overpriced Irish themed pub of a type which would be largely outdated in England at the time, but which appeared to positively thrive on the Continent as alternative entertainment outlets. In fact statistically there are 10 times more Irish bars located worldwide than in the Republic itself.

It's pseudo-interior boasted the usual Irish type clutter arrangement of articles of bric-a-brac around the high ceiling borders, along with the omnipresent Guinness advertisements in various forms.. Wooden compartmental seating replicated Emerald Isle furnishings and the repetitive sound of the 'diddly-dee' style Irish jig tunes were the epitome of tedious brackground music.

Yet for all this, the place was quite crowded, noticeably with a large percentage of the fairer sex, two of whom were sat on the next table and were giving out flirtatious tell-tale signs of interest in our direction. Their fleeting glances towards us were accompanied by kittenish smiles while they stroked their hair.

"I'm getting good vibes from this pair, Weedy", I said. "I think it's time to reel 'em in."

Weedy instantaneously produced a manic grin to reveal his main attribute, a full glistening set of pearly whites. Showing his big teeth seemed to have the desired effect as the watching girls went into a giggling fit as they observed what resembled a toothpaste advertisement.

I beckoned them over to join us and we introduced ourselves to their continued amusement.

Their names were Pascale and Monique and were both employed as nurses at the local hospital. They were attractive 'chicks' with Pascale wearing her straw coloured hair in a raised manner while Monique's shoulder length dark locks were curled under stylishly. Metaphorically speaking, it turned out that they would each be letting their hair down too as they had a day off tomorrow.

As the night wore on, I found myself being drawn to Pascale while Monique kept Weedy occupied in conversation, with most of the talking being done by herself.

Last orders at the bar were called just before midnight but the girls said they knew a club that served late which we could all go to and they could get us in. It sounded too good to miss so Weed jumped in Monique's Renault car to the venue while I travelled in Pascale's Citroen 2CV.

French call for a general erection! ...

Within five minutes, we had pulled up outside the door of 'La Clique,' an isolated building located down a back street. Classy it was not, and the flashing neon lighting illuminating silhouettes of naked ladies against a pink backdrop showing up on the exterior glass signage left us in no doubt about its main form of entertainment.

A swift embrace and kiss for each of the girls from the two muscular doormen was followed by a nod of acknowledgement to ourselves, and we were in.

It was a quite spacious, split level, cave-like premises with a raised J-shaped, dimly lit bar servery. So, with dance music, beer and erotic artist scheduled, it certainly ticked all the boxes with regard to a decent finish for the evening.

As the clock progressed towards 1am, there was a noticeable migration of men making their way up to the layered steps of the railed balcony area, staking their claim for a good view of the upcoming performance.

"Looks like the cabaret's coming on Weed. You'd better get yourself a prime spot." I teased.

Sure enough, the lights were faded out to be replaced by a lone, broad, funnelled spotlight beam that followed a tall, voluptuous black girl to the centre of the raised dance floor.

The attractive Naomi Campbell lookalike introduced herself as Caprice, before launching into a raunchy, provocative dance routine to the Michael Jackson song 'Thriller.' Dressed only in sparkly sequinned matching bra and briefs, she got an enthusiastic response from the appreciative audience including ourselves of course.

More songs from the same 'Jacko' album followed as the girl seductively pressed her huge 'dairy cannons' into the faces of eager punters while cavorting around the room. It was the usual kind of tawdry show I'd witnessed on several occasions on lads' nights' out.

Caprice then stopped dancing before making some sort of gestured request in French to the gathering which yielded no participants.

"What is she asking for, Pascale?," I inquired.

"She wants a volunteer to join her," came the reply. "But no one will go on."

Not wanting to spoil the show and being quite intoxicated, I offered myself for the position by raising my arm in the air. A big round of applause greeted my passage to the floor followed by shrill whistles and cheers.

"They must know something I don't," I forewarned myself as I leapt into a showman's dancing routine to MJ's 'Billy Jean' opposite the vivacious Caprice. When it had finished, I acknowledged the considerable acclaim afforded to me with a customary bow.

More harmonies from the Michael Jackson portfolio were played including "Wanna be Starting Something" as the real centre of attention then gestured towards me to undo her bra. I obliged in an instant and her well developed, mountainous 'chesticles' poured out of their retaining cups to the sound of ever-increasing co-ordinated handclapping from the now captive assemblage.

Off came my tee-shirt and beer stained white vest to the strains of 'You Are Not Alone' as Caprice removed my garments one by one to the musical medley.

She then progressed to my cut off cargo trousers, first undoing my top button, then unzipping my fly before pulling it down sharply to reveal anything but 'pulling' pants. To complete my derobing Caprice undid my black leather belt.

Of course, making a guest appearance as a striptease artist's assistant hadn't been factored into my itinerary for the evening, so it would be fair to say that my alcohol-fuelled initial enthusiasm was possibly misplaced.

I had temporarily overlooked the fact that I was still in the same gear that I'd been in all day, including my 'travelling undercrackers' which were my designated comfort pants whilst out on the road.

Best described as 'lived in,' the battleship grey Y-front budgie smugglers were so well worn that the surrounding edges encircling each leg incorporated their own frayed design. A threadbare elasticated waistband was just about holding everything together although splayed tentacles of rubber precariously sprang out of its centre, spider leg style. Add to this an over-used gusset unavoidably flecked with a patterned amalgamation of sweat and isolated spots of wine meant David Beckham fashion wear they certainly were not! To the great amusement of the gathered clubgoers of course, who were now in raptures of uncontrollable mirth.

But if that had raised a laugh, my next interaction brought the house down. My trouser belt had been doubling as a bolster for the far from fancy underwear and so with no additional prompting, they headed south down my legs to nestle around my ankles as tracks from the 'Bad' album began to ring out.

Caprice then asked me to lie prostrate on my back with my lower limbs apart. She then removed her knickers to reveal a well trimmed patch of lady garden, to the tune of "The Way You Make Me Feel."

So there I was, stark bollock naked except for a pair of naff white socks I only wear when I don't have a clean set with me.

Caprice then began to lower her torso closer and closer to mine as Jacko's 'Beat It' blasted out across the disco. The finale came when she eased herself briefly onto my lifeless todger that had remained stubbornly flaccid throughout the show.

Placing a metal bucket full of ice over my fully aroused manhood to cool my expected ardour should have been the crowning glory to finish off her act, but I was so wrecked through a combination of booze and tiredness that all I could raise was an apologetic smile.

I was however escorted back to the dressing room on the stripper's arm with tumultuous applause ringing in my ears. The crowd had obviously enjoyed the unorthodox spectacle.

Not so Caprice, who told me in not so many words that I was the first man in her long career who had not 'stood proud' during her act, but she too saw the funny side all the same.

I gently pulled our nude bodies together before giving her a kiss that she seemed to accept willingly, but just as I finished asking her "Do you fancy a shower so I can make it up to you?", a large black chap who I presumed to be her minder sidled up to me.

"She ain't going nowhere. Boy!" he boomed. "Now put your clothes on, and for your trouble get your complimentary drink from the bar with this ticket."

I certainly wasn't going to argue, particularly in my condition, so with a quick wave 'au revoir,' off I went to collect my prize.

There was a lot of pointing, smiling and pats on the back for me for the rest of the session, most of which were in sympathetic ridicule, I might add.

It was perfectly summed up by a couple of young French blades queuing up for the gents' toilets unaware they were ahead of me. After the first one clearly described my escapade to his friend, he flicked down his index finger to signify that I hadn't risen to the occasion before loudly crying out. "English man!" amidst concerted laughter from the cubicles.

However, more importantly, Pascale and Monique gave me a hero's welcome on my return to our table, whilst Weed could only comment on my choice of underwear as he repeatedly lurched forward and back from his waist upwards, still bent over with laughter after my impromptu stage presentation.

Crashing out for the night ….

It was time to leave when Pascale asked if we would like to stay at her place at Lorteil, some 30 kilometres north of Senlis.

Nonchalantly, I said "I'll have to ask my friend," knowing full well Weed wouldn't turn his nose up at a bit of bonhomie. In fact, he would probably salivate at the chance.

As I relayed the offer to him, his eyes started to sparkle and his freshly flossed gnashers were put on show once again as he eyed Monique up and down like a fox sizing up a chicken.

"What about our stuff?" he inquired.

"No problem. They're willing to drive to our digs and wait while we pack," I assured him.

That settled it, and off we went to our university accommodation to collect our luggage.

Once there, I got the distinct impression Weedy had taken some kind of performance enhancing drug as he zipped up the stairs two at a time with all the speed of modern Olympic sprinter Usain Bolt.

In fact by the time I'd reached our seventh floor room and begun to gather up my toiletries from the bathroom, The Weed had already strapped his holdall bag across one shoulder ready for an immediate downward descent.

I just had to take a minute out to have a quick word with him and lower his all too apparent expectancy.

"Hold your horses, Blue." I advised him, 'Blue' being the alternative nickname I gave him for such moments when he buzzes around frenetically like an agitated blue bottle fly.

"Don't get yourself over-excited. I know you want a shag but you're like a dog with two dicks! You're making us look desperate. If they really are interested, they'll wait for us. If not, at least we've had a lift back home."

He tried to explain his hurried actions.

"No Ralph, I'm thinking more about getting a ride 20 miles north towards Calais."

"Course you are Blue. Course you are. Judging by that swinging pendulum motion in your strides, it looks like you'd be happy to travel just six inches north. It's a dead giveaway. Now pull yourself together and take a deep breath."

I do have to admit it was a relief to see that the girls' cars were still waiting for us as we exited our very temporary lodgings, although I would probably have changed my mind if I knew what sort of journey I was letting myself in for.

Monique nominated herself as lead driver and Weedy compliantly got in her motor whilst I took my place in the passenger seat of Pascale's older looking model.

Once out of town, it became increasingly evident that both girls were well over the drink limit. They repeatedly weaved from side to side along the narrow country lanes and even pulled alongside on wider roads as the speed dial hit 60 kilometers per hour so they could accompany each other in singing along to a track by a dodgy sounding Gallic artist that was being played on both car stereo systems at a high level of decibels.

I gestured to Pascale to slow down and to her credit she did, leaving Monique to surge ahead once more.

Then disaster struck as her friend misjudged a sharp bend, clipped the kerb and ended up in a shallow ditch, narrowly avoiding a large tree.

"Sacre bleu. Monique!" cried Pascale as we screeched to a halt a few yards behind the tilted vehicle.

But before we could get out of the car, Monique furiously revved the engine, spewing dried mud all over Pascale's windscreen in the process. And after a few thousand rapid revolutions, the Citroen span out of the ditch and with a loud toot of her horn to signal both her and Weedy were OK, they continued apace without further incident.

"Monique, Monique. She is a crazy driver sometimes," laughed Pascale, more in relief than condemnation as the now slushy mud on her windscreen limited the visibility to the sort of view you would associate with a farmer's tractor cab in a ploughed field.

I laughed too, but deep down I knew their behaviour was totally irresponsible. Myself and Weedy were also guilty by association and it starkly highlighted the risks you take when you drive under the influence.

Briefly my mind flashed back to 1978 in New York when myself and fellow Brit Gaz Poole from Sheffield accepted a ride to Brooklyn from a couple of drunken Swedish lads who we'd been drinking with in downtown Manhattan.

They'd offered us a lift to the actual discotheque where the movie 'Saturday Night Fever' was filmed. We thought it was too good an opportunity to turn down until the driver wrapped his motor around a lamppost on Brooklyn Bridge.

Gaz and I carried onto the club on foot that night, shaken but unscathed, yet the point was that I hadn't learned the lesson of two decades ago because again I go into the car with someone who was clearly pissed. My only defence was that on both occasions I was myself at least as inebriated as the driver when I accepted this high risk strategy.

We did eventually reach Monique's house in one piece, and carried on partying over a bottle of the finest French brandy.

Giggles began to turn into laughter and tender looks were transformed into tactile touches before Pascale leaned over to administer the most subtle of French kisses before whispering: "My room has a green door".

I was tempted to reply; "That needs painting then," but resisted and instead asked to take a shower before retiring to her bedroom.

La Place de la Victor Hugo ...

I needed to wash as I was both sweaty and grubby after a long day and night. Scrubbing myself clean, I analysed the evening, wondering if there was some kind of ulterior motive to the girls taking us home to their isolated cottage in the woods.

Were there some burly 'Frenchies' hiding in the house, ready to rob us of our meagre possessions? Were they themselves going to execute the deed with the aid of some hidden weaponry? Indeed, were they themselves 'femme fatales'? Just why were they willing to take a chance on a pair of reprobates such as ourselves?

They had found us both in a fairly bedraggled state, bereft of enough funds to buy them a drink. Frankly, we could hardly be classed as a good catch even on a quiet midweek night in a sleepy 'one horse' town.

And after all, on our very first meeting, Pascale had seen me buck naked, except for a pair of tasteless white socks even Albert Steptoe would have tossed in the rag bag! She'd also clocked my emaciated pair of garish grey y-fronts that had dropped despairingly to the floor through a lack of adequate support.

But perhaps most damming of all, the girl had witnessed no visible signs of arousal from my joystick, though it was certainly not for the lack of trying from the sexy seductress Caprice who had wiggled, cajoled, teased and even straddled me during the floor show. Or maybe it was my erectile dysfunction that had pleased her.

Whatever it was, here we were, and as the time was fast approaching 3.30am, there was now no other choice but to face the consequences of our actions, if indeed there were to be any.

I passed by a very glazed looking Weedy, and a patiently waiting Monique who were occupying separate but adjacent sofas, both still with glasses in their hands. I bade them both "bon nuit" and winked at Weedy in a gesture intending to signal "Have a good night."

I climbed the steep stairs to the green door and entered the bedroom to find Pascale propped up against a fluffy nest of three pillows set within a queen-sized bed. As our eyes met, she gave me a longing look of desire, and that was the moment I knew her intentions were genuine.

Teasing her soft cascading tresses of golden hair I became intoxicated by an evocative scent of a clearly high class french perfume as I caringly pulled her head towards my lips to administer a kiss aptly named after her homeland. Pascale dropped her head down slightly to nuzzle my neck with a salvo of tender kisses heightening the sensation.

Taking off my decent change of packed underwear, I slipped under the smooth silk bed sheets. A session of gentle fondling quickly giving way to heavy petting soon followed. Caressing both ample breasts like a baker lovingly kneading his freshly made dough to mould a large cob, I first licked, then teased her pert nipples gently between my pursed lips until they stuck out like two proverbial chapel hat pegs. Her sharp nails scoring lines down my back in appreciation of the act.

Pascale, like myself, was getting ever more turned on to the extent of no return as she grabbed my erect member and fed it feverishly into her open mouth sucking the shaft right down to the nuts. An immediate 'soixante neuf' manoeuvre being adopted to juice her up accordingly within her sensuous petal like folds.

Reverting back to an upward facing role I slowly slid a gyrating forefinger into her inviting, well maintained velvety groove using the resulting wetness to further moisten the inner and outer folds of Pascales labia before seeking out that sometimes elusive 'man in the boat.' Yet I have found that perserverance is the key and once you do locate that all important sensory clitoris at the front of the vaginal entry, with a little tender loving care and light flicking of the bean, once fully engaged that woman is yours.

It may be like trying to find that literal needle in a haystack but the orgasmic wails of pleasure and tightening embrace will inform you that the spot has been hit, along with a sticky residue of cum ejaculated from the most intricately complex bodily organ every woman possesses.

Now fully aroused I skimmed her most private hole with an index finger to enhance the pleasure which soon led to our two bodies becoming one. Our lovemaking gathered frenzied momentum until we both reached a satisfying simultaneous climax with Pascale whispering an appreciative 'Je taime' softly in my ear, after disengaging from our 'doggy' position.

Yet bizarrely, at the height of ecstasy, Pascale had let out a strange cry, shouting out loudly; "Ohhh! La Place de la Victor Hugo!"

"What the f…" I didn't even finish my exclamation as I stopped dead halfway through my vinegar stroke.

Initially, I thought I must have stumbled into the 'out of bounds' orifice unintentionally, but I clearly hadn't as her continued thrusting testified.

Pascale then collapsed into a heap, uttering a prolonged sigh of satisfaction before kissing my forehead and cuddling up to me affectionately.

But just what had she meant by her impulsive outburst? And just who was Victor Hugo anyway, besides coincidentally being the name of the last pub, we had visited for a drink before leaving St Helier.

Was it a reference to a past illicit liaison, or maybe a romantic location from years gone by? Perhaps it recognised her favourite Parisian market square, or had she indeed visited that very same bar in Jersey where we had redeemed our beer passports? I have to admit that the latter seemed highly unlikely.

Whatever the significance, I had never heard anything like it in my life, and even to this day, years after the most puzzling of encounters, the meaning of the phrase is unknown to me and any relevance to intimacy is completely lost.

After considerable research, I did discover that old Victor 'Marie' Hugo, to give his somewhat dubious full title, was the founder of the 'Romanticism' movement and lived from 1802 to 1885.

As an exponent of such a crusade in France, he was revered as a poet, playwright, novelist, essayist and human rights activist, with most of his literary fame stemming from his poetic talent. With novels and plays including 'Les Miserables' and 'The Hunchback of Notre Dame' among his many credits, he was obviously a very talented man and eminently well respected by the French population.

Therefore, I can only conclude that Pascale had made her exalted place name reference in her personal moment of eroticism because it was a location renowned for its romanticism. Tres bon! What more can I say?

In the early afternoon, Pascale dropped us both off on the road to Calais. 'Au revoirs' were exchanged then I whispered that key phrase in her ear. "La Place de la Victor Hugo."

She just blushed, looked longingly into my eyes and gave me a prolonged hug. And then she was gone, probably never to be seen again.

What an enjoyable but truly strange set of circumstances, I concluded. We were very lucky, and got one lift directly to the French port, and sailing back to Dover on the ferry a few hours later I read through my holiday diary to recap on the month.

My view of French people had completely changed after this adventure. Even when the many ordinary folk could only communicate in their own national vernacular, they went out of their way to try to understand us.

From single women to mothers with children, from old couples to young girls and lads as well as fully grown men, all had contributed to a truly great experience from start to finish culminating in a deeply passionate alliance of pure lust.

So if you're reading this chapter in bed I suggest that you look lovingly across to your partner and whispering softly in their ear ask them if they are in the mood for what I personally term a 'France 98!'

You won't be disappointed.

A wide cross-section of the French public had come to our aid, not only by stopping to give us a seat in their vehicles, but also to offer us hospitality ranging from complimentary food and drink to an invitation to a party in a family home in order to watch the football. The ultimate gesture was of course an invitation to the bed of a highly sensual and emotional female.

We had only used public transport when absolutely necessary and over the month, I reckon we hitchhiked a distance of around 1,200 miles free of charge.

As documented, we were two fully grown males well into our forties, so it was never going to be easy getting lifts, and our two large holdalls with additional tent and sleeping bags added to our handicap.

But with the right planning and application, we had proved that it could be done, even when tarnished as "English football hooligans".

32 "We've Signed Wrighty": 1999-2000

What a coup!
Ian Wright confirms his place in Burnley F.C. history.
Photograph courtesy of Burnley Football Club

It's a stark fact that the lower down the English League pyramid your team slides, they are much less likely to make national football news. Unless of course something extraordinary takes place that warrants nationwide attention. This was that day.

"I don't belieeeeeve it!"...

I heard it for the first time on the Monday afternoon while listening to the radio in my kitchen. I'd just awoken after doing a Sunday night shift and was about to make my first invigorating cup of tea.

It was the memorable date of February 14th, 2000. St Valentine's Day, when menfolk are cajoled into the commercial maelstrom of buying cards, flowers and gifts for their partners.

As a youth, I willingly participated in sending smutty rhymed messages of lust to someone I fancied, under a cloak of anonymity. But the 'Guess who?' sign off retains little mystery when sent to a known partner these days. So like most blokes, I would donate my present largely to keep the peace, but also to vastly increase the chances of getting a leg over later in the night. Sorry girls, but that's just the way it is.

Yet that's just a lewd aside to the happenings that unfolded this first Valentine's Day of the new millennium.

Back to the radio, where by laboriously tweaking and twiddling the broken aerial to and fro at the precisely required 45 degree angle, I could just about receive a partially audible broadcast from BBC Radio Lancashire which kept me up to date with the latest goings on at my football club. Our Staffordshire location is probably only about five miles south of perfect clarity as gauged by my experimentation process on many car radios while travelling back from the North, but here at home reception was patchy. However, I settled in to glean any information I could from the sports bulletin which would follow the news.

A loud crackling transmission kicked in something like this.

"Today... craaaack...craaaack... Burnley FC manager Stan...craaaack Ternent...craaaack...was hoping to secure the signing of...craaaack...craaaack...ex-Arsenal and England international...craaaack...craaaack...Ian Wright."

I addressed the electromagnetic device with: "Whaaaat? Who is this newsreader trying to kid? It's Valentine's Day, not April Fools, isn't it?"

Then 'Stan the Man' himself came on to confirm that he had indeed been in talks with Ian Wright. I managed to hear him go on to say once the T's had been crossed and the I's dotted, he was confident that "Wrighty," as he affectionately termed him, would become a Burnley player by this evening.

"Bloody hell! That's a bold statement to make," I shouted loudly in sheer disbelief. Then I thought to myself: "Why would he choose to go to a team in the third tier of English football?"

By now, hungry for more flesh on the bones of this astounding claim, I frantically tried to maintain the intermittent signal by grasping the aerial with one hand while adjusting the volume control with the other.

Then into the room stepped my 'German au pair receptionist' *aka* my mother. Alerted by the commotion surrounding our second hand ghetto blaster, she'd come to investigate proceedings.

"What you doing? What you doing?," she asked in her own inimitable way.

"Shush, quiet," I implored her as I tried to hang on every word of the broadcaster's dialogue to try and keep pace with ongoing developments at Turf Moor. My mother stood transfixed like a statue in the doorway, wondering just what could have captured my attention so much which warranted such intense scrutiny of the airwaves.

In an attempt to give her a charade-like clue, I began to excitedly jump around the dining table with the clenched fist of my gyrating right arm held aloft, chanting in the accustomed manner: "Ian Wright-Wright-Wright...Ian Wright-Wright-Wright..."

I repeated the verse half a dozen times in the hope of triggering a responsive acknowledgment of his iconic status. But no, it was a totally alien reaction from my mother, who had probably never heard of the bloke given her token interest in football over the years. Still retaining a look of sheer puzzlement on her face, she shuffled back into the living room. I afforded myself a chuckle as I heard her mutter: "He must have won on the horses or something."

I hadn't, but Burnley Football Club would certainly hit the jackpot if this particular signing came off. For the uninitiated, in a nutshell, we were on the verge of obtaining the services of one of the top footballers of the 1990s decade.

Over the following four hours, I made sure I stayed within the vicinity of the kitchen in order to catch all the snippets of information that emerged from the half-hourly news intervals.

Then the verification I was hoping for came through as a home affairs programme was interrupted by a newscaster's announcement that "a press conference has been called for later in the day when it is hoped the signing of Ian Wright will be confirmed."

He finished the statement with the line: "Remember where you heard it first, right here on Radio Lancashire."

For supporters of teams outside the Premier League, it was the sort of incredible newsflash they may be lucky enough to hear once in a lifetime, if at all.

Communication meltdown ...

Then the phone began to ring...and ring...and ring....

Both my 'brick,' the name I'd given to my oversized mobile, and my landline were being answered at a frequency more associated with traders on the Stock Exchange floor.

First up was Christine Marsden, wife of Pete 'Nuzzler' Marsden, like her husband a fanatical Claret, followed by at least half a dozen more people, all hoping to be the earliest bearers of the good tidings.

It became infectious and I too had to share the moment. 'Tricky' Trev Slack, my longstanding match day companion, seemed surprised to receive a call from me at the beginning of the week rather than the end when I usually ring to sort out my lift to the game.

"Eyup, Trev. What about it then?"

"What about what?," Trev asked.

"Haven't you heard who we've signed?," I queried.

"No, I haven't been listening to Radio Lancashire today. What's gone on?"

"We've only gone and signed the services of one of the biggest names in football, that's all," I announced proudly.

You're not going to tell me we've signed Zinedine Zidane..., are you? That's a big name," he chuckled.

"Nooo, closer to home. England international," I teased.

"England international? Us?. Who? Not 'Incy'?"

Feeling an unremitting urge to inform him after the impasse at the other end of the phone, I blurted it out.

"We've signed Wrighty, Ian Wright," I said, going on to divulge the full details.

Trev then asked the same question I had just asked.

"Why us though? I can't see that somehow," said an unconvinced Tricky.

"It's the Crystal Palace connection from when Stan was assistant manager there. Turn your radio on. There's a special programme going out now," I assured Trev before bidding him farewell.

Next up was The Veg,' and I just knew he would take even more persuading.

"Oi'll believe eet when I see eet," was Steve's initial appraisal in his trademark Black Country twang.

"Eee isn't going to play though is he Dayve?," he continued dismissively.

"But it's been confirmed and Burnley are holding a press conference right now," I tried to embolden my statement, offering him a little food for thought before leaving him to draw his own conclusions.

These two calls to battle-hardened Clarets just showed how sceptical our supporters had become over the years with regards to our ability to attract big name players.

The press conference went ahead as scheduled with phenomenal media interest from newspaper, radio and TV companies giving the breaking story the extensive coverage it warranted as the rest of the football world looked on with envy.

Ian Wright corroborated that he was signing up for Burnley probably until the end of the season and when asked: "Why Burnley?," he answered: "Probably the only person that could have persuaded me to make a comeback was Stan Ternent."

The esteem in which Wright held Stan was a glowing tribute to the man and he deserved great credit for pulling off such a sensational coup.

It emerged that our boss had phoned Wright to ask him if he was doing anything at the moment, and if not, would he like to do him a big favour by teaming up with his good mate Mitchell Thomas, our current full back, for a short spell. Stan had been first team coach at Crystal Palace when Wright had burst on the scene and forged a fearsome goalscoring partnership with Mark Bright, so he knew him well.

They'd obviously remained in touch and as a gesture of good will, one of the most famous players in England at the time had refreshingly agreed to take a dramatic cut in wages and provide his services. His weekly pay would still be disproportionate to that of the other players and outside the club's wage structure but this would unquestionably be recouped through increased attendances and associated merchandise.

Wright-mania! ...

Right on cue, Burnley FC's marketing department sprung into action to take full advantage of this unprecedented association. Personalised 'Wright' T-shirts and team jerseys flew off the shelves in the club shop with more than 1,000 of the latter being sold in the following two days. This man was clearly 'big business.'

His debut against Wigan Athletic was a sell out in the home sections but the Latics were well aware of Wrighty's potential and he was well shackled in an uninspiring 0-0 draw. However, the fervour stoked up by 'Wright-mania' boiled over when one of the worst outbreaks of violence for a long time saw around 200 Burnley supporters attack both the Wigan supporters and the mounted police outside the Clog & Spindle pub on Yorkshire Street after the match, with multiple arrests being made along the length of the road.

The notorious 'Suicide Squad' were once again implicated as being at the hub of this serious confrontation. Subsequent local press coverage of the following court appearances even reported that Phil Holmes, one of the gang's leading members, had been charged with picking up a police dog and hurling it back at the members of the Lancashire Constabulary during the fracas. Although his defence may have pleaded it was softer than a brick, it was still to no avail as the 'dog chucker' got sent down.

The following week, we visited Colchester United at a near capacity Layer Road, and our new acquisition was the reason for the near doubling of their usual home attendance.

However, there were many among the home section of this big crowd intent on giving Wright a hard time. A torrent of personal abuse directed at the modern day legend cascaded down from the Barside Terrace. The Burnley following on the Layer Road End were enraged by this show of poisonous hate with a number breaching police lines to try to confront the instigators first hand. It was a totally undeserved outburst against a man who always gave his all for both club and country and those guilty Us' fans who took part in chanting those hateful songs on that day should hang their heads in shame.

It was left to defender Steve Davis to exact divine retribution and secure a deserved 2-1 victory, with the Burnley supporters rubbing salt in the wounds of the home fans by chanting "You're only here 'cos of Wrighty" as they exited the ground.

We then lost back to back home games, first against promotion rivals Preston North End 0-3 and then Luton Town 0-2, making it four matches without a goal for our England international. It appeared the viciousness of the recent verbal onslaught was affecting his confidence.

Wright was named on the bench for the next fixture at Wrexham where regular centre forward Andy Payton, known to the fans as The Padiham Predator,' notched the game's only goal. It was also his 200th career goal which he gleefully advertised by revealing a pre-written message lettered on the vest under his shirt which proclaimed him as a 'Natural Born Claret.' The cross for the goal came from workhorse Andy Cooke who formed part of the spearhead Stan Ternent described as the best strike force in the division.

Wright came on as a substitute in the next two games, breaking his duck by converting a late chance to earn a crucial 2-2 draw at Gillingham, and then again scoring late on in a 3-0 home victory over Reading. A Tuesday evening fixture at Blackpool followed which ended in a 1-1 draw with the striker failing to score.

Meanwhile, Stan was slamming national press speculation claiming Wright was unhappy at the club. In truth, Ian had other things on his mind, not least the two match ban he was to be handed by a Scottish FA disciplinary committee that week after his sending off for pushing one of the officials while playing for previous club Celtic against Kilmarnock.

The ban meant Wright missed the league games at home to Bury and away to Cardiff City. A last minute equaliser from Ronnie Jepson earned us a 2-2 draw against The Shakers and we then hung on for a 2-1 victory down at Ninian Park after talismanic winger Glen Little had been sent off with 17 minutes to go after kicking out at former Fulham player Richard Carpenter.

Wrighty returned from suspension to make an appearance as substitute for the final seven games with inspirational effect. His first touch at home to Notts County was a shot into the top corner which secured a 2-1 win in the very last minute. Then at Oxford United, his lightning acceleration enabled him to keep in play an over-hit ball that everyone else had given up. The resulting cross found midfielder Paul Weller who guided it home to give us a third consecutive 2-1 win. The only defeat in this period came when fellow promotion hopefuls Gillingham saw us off 3-0 at Turf Moor in a Tuesday evening game.

Next up were Millwall, who were at the time occupying third spot in the table, and they brought 1,500 supporters to Turf Moor, the best following I can remember them having at our ground, for a real six pointer of a game. Burnley tore into the Londoners to deservedly go 4-0 up after just half an hour, but then the transformation from total football to total panic had to be seen to be believed as the Lions clawed three goals back before referee Jeff Winter blew for time.

More ugly scenes sadly ensued with ripped out seats, thunderflashes, smoke canisters, coins and bricks all being used as missiles inside and outside the ground as the police helicopter monitored the two sets of warring fans from above.

An away win at another London side in the shape of Brentford gave Burnley a share of second spot in the league, with two goals from John Mullin and one from that man Wrighty completing a 3-2 win. Then Burnley claimed second place as their own in the penultimate match of the season thanks to a 2-0 success over Cambridge United. A brace from Andy Payton did the damage and took his season's league goal tally to 27, only two behind Willie Irvine's post war record of 29 in 1965-66.

Sunny Scunny ...

That win left just one fixture to complete the campaign, which would be a decider at already relegated Scunthorpe United for the second promotion place, as Preston had long secured the Champion's title.

My village travelling companion Pete 'Weedy' Read was up for this one as I planned to make a weekend of the trip. Every time Burnley have won a promotion, the town goes absolutely crazy, such is the closeness of the community, and I intended to be part of it if we achieved our aim.

Catching the train to Stockport, we met up with 'Tricky' Trev Slack and 'plain' John Smith. Trev. drove us over to the Morris Dancers pub in Colne where Alan 'Beeky' Beecroft had organised a coach with an early morning departure. The beer stop was Pontefract, West Yorkshire, about 40 miles short of our final destination.

We'd only been given 2,000 tickets for the game, so a big screen had been erected at Turf Moor to accommodate the additional thousands who wanted to view the action live. In fact, 7,270 turned up, which was 1,408 more than the

5,862 attendance at Glanford Park and the fifth highest in the division that day.

The build up to the match was tense with stewards and police confiscating a number of poorly forged tickets outside the teeming turnstiles. I purposely positioned myself near to one of the seemingly hundreds of fans who had brought along their radio headsets to keep up to date with the critical game at Wrexham, whose opponents Gillingham had drawn level with us on 85 points but who had a far superior goal difference.

Then, a roar. Yeess!!! News filtered through that Wrexham had taken the lead through Mark McGregor, a player who would later sign for Burnley in the 2001-2002 season. But Scunthorpe, though already doomed, were playing as though they had to win to stay up, and after a spell of pressure, they went ahead on 20 minutes with a stunning strike from Lee Hodges which hit the underside of the bar and bounced over the line.

A cloud of gloom descended over the South Stand visitors' section, but just before the break our comically named powerhouse Micky Mellon let fly with a 20 yard volley into the bottom corner to level it. On the hour, Glen Little came on as sub and 11 minutes later, 'Super Glen' rattled a shot past keeper Ross Turner to make it 2-1, the favoured scoreline of the Clarets over the last month or so. Scunthorpe pressed hard to even the game up but we held on and the whistle sounded to signal a mass pitch invasion.

However, there were still four minutes of injury time to be played at the Racecourse Ground, Wrexham. We prematurely danced, sang and hugged each other until a Wrexham victory was at last confirmed.

I embraced Weedy, who didn't go to the game but had followed events in a nearby pub before making his way onto the ground.

"We're up, Weed. We're up!," I shouted.

"So I've noticed," he casually replied, looking around at the celebrating hordes.

Just then, I glanced across at the home supporters in the North Stand who'd stayed behind to applaud. It was a magnanimous gesture considering they were going in the opposite direction to the promoted Clarets so myself and a couple of others led a reply of applause towards them.

Then manager Stan Ternent and the players, chairman and directors came out above the tunnel to take the deserved ecstatic acclaim.

Speaking to the reporters after the game, Stan said: "It's been a long hard season, and I'll have a bottle of champagne for Flynny in the morning."

He was referring to ex-Burnley player Brian Flynn, who still lived in the town but was that day managing the Wrexham team which had just done us such a huge favour.

Slowly we drifted back to our coaches in jubilant mood, but not before I claimed a small clump of turf as a memento to commemorate the extraordinary climax to a remarkable last quarter of the season.

Just another day in paradise ...

After a few pints with the lads back at the Morris Dancers, myself and Weedy headed for Burnley town centre some six miles away. The party had started straight after the pictures being beamed back from Scunthorpe had confirmed promotion, and was already in full swing.

As I'd expected, all the bars were heaving, but there was one in particular which was physically shaking with music, noise and excitement, and that was 'Paradise Island' near the bus station. There was a notice affixed to the front window announcing "No trainers or tracksuits," and luckily Weedy and I wore neither that night, thus allowing us access past the fearsome looking, shaven headed bouncers who were diligently guarding the door with added zeal given the vast crowd.

Once inside, we squeezed past the seething masses of humanity that were jiving erratically to the booming tunes belting out from the raised DJ deck, and tried to get a drink. And amazingly, there behind the bar serving the booze was none other than the scorer of the winning goal Glen Little. He was working flat out as well as having the inevitable chat and banter with the customers. It really was a selfless effort and showed the growing bond between the town and players.

But this was ultimately the story of a legend, the man who without question was the catalyst to our promotion from Division One of the Football League. Yet as other members of the first team squad filtered in, there was one notable exception. The hero of the promotion charge Ian Wright wasn't among them. Perhaps, I concluded, the humble gas lamps of Burnley didn't compare to the bright lights of London.

However, I was later to find out from one of the other players that Wrighty had tried in vain to gain admission to Paradise Island but had been vehemently refused entry by the doormen because of their strict 'no trainers or tracksuits' policy. He had come down town in both, and the boys in the monkey suits just weren't budging, reciting the well rehearsed cliche: "If we let one in, we'd have to let them all in."

Even after concerted protests from fans and players alike, the bouncers remained adamant that rules were rules and pointed at the dress standards notice. I'm sure the goal ace was welcomed in other bars all over town, but in an ironic twist, we as fans were, metaphorically speaking, in Paradise Island, while the principal character in our success story had to play the part of a castaway.

Ian Wright had done his bit to put Burnley firmly back on the football map but Scunthorpe would be his last match for the club despite Stan Ternent trying his best to convince him otherwise. He now has a blossoming television career, which has already seen him front his own chat show entitled "Friday Night's All Wright," as well as introducing "The Guinness World of Records" and "Sing It Your Way," and has also lined up a show with US star Will Smith. Wrighty currently has a regular phone in show on BBC Radio Five Live and is a respected columnist for The Sun newspaper. He was also a regular pundit for England internationals including the ill-fated Euros in France 2016.

Subsequently, the following summer he travelled to Buckingham Palace to officially become an MBE for services to football, and during the ceremony he confirmed to no less a figure than Her Majesty the Queen that he was to retire from the game for good. So it was goodbye to Wrighty, and time to thank him for all he did for Burnley FC in those vital last few months of a sensational campaign. A man who achieved legendary status at Burnley within such a short space of time.

Get 'em off! ...

I arrived back from my Scunthorpe sojourn late on the Sunday night. I'd already booked the Monday off work in the hope that promotion would be achieved, knowing that if it was, I would need time for the celebratory alcohol excesses to wear off.

So that Monday morning, it was a happy but bleary-eyed figure that made his way to the garden bench at the front of our house to take the air. Already sat having a cup of tea on the corresponding long seat outside the house next door was our neighbour of many years Dorothy Rowley, husband of Alan, a pal I'd grown up with.

Dot, as she was affectionately known, opened up the conversation.

"I see you did it then. You've gone up another division."

"Oh yeah! That's right," I confirmed, once I realised what she was referring to.

Dot, you see, rarely talked football as she wasn't really a follower of the sport, hence my hesitation in replying. But it seemed Dot's interest concealed a hidden agenda as she continued: "You'll have to keep your promise now then."

"Promise? What promise is that?," I inquired in a bemused manner.

"To do a streak around the village," Dot fired back instantly.

"Whaaat!" I exclaimed, vigorously rubbing my eyes with the knuckled index finger of both hands before pulling them away sharply.

"Yeeees," she stated assertively. "You said a month ago you thought they were too far behind, and when I said "You never know," you said if they did go up you'd do a streak around Madeley Pool."

"I can't remember saying that," I immediately replied.

Then a distant voice piped up.

"Oh yes you did. I was there when you said it."

It was Dot's partner Alan, who up to that point had been turning over the borders of his lawn with a fork at the far end of his garden.

"Oh, right. I'll have to work on that one then," I said, still believing they had both lost their marbles.

But no, I was doing them both a disservice because as the week went on, another two people who must have heard my pledge confirmed it to me. I concluded that I must have made such a throwaway remark while under the influence, but nonetheless if I'd given such an undertaking, I knew I'd have to do the deed.

The following Friday's lads' night out was designated as the time for my streak. As planned, I returned on the last bus from our Newcastle-under-Lyme drinking venue and Julie, my girlfriend at the time, was dutifully waiting by the bus stop in her car.

I'd decided I was going to tie claret and blue ribbons around my lower appendage for the duration of the streak to signify the reason for the event, which I only succeeded in doing after a little gentle stimulation from 'Jules' as the fabric was secured. It certainly wasn't the ideal moment to get 'brewer's droop,' but as the clock struck midnight, I just knew it was perfect timing, and I disrobed to begin my streak.

The bus I'd just disembarked from was about to pull away, and on board that very bus was none other than Miss Badhead, my ex-girlfriend and mother of my daughter Clarette. Her look of abject disgust as I gave a cursory wave on passing the vehicle was absolutely priceless.

Even the driver tooted his horn as he slowed down to drive alongside me for the first 100 yards of my journey, looking on in amazement as he did so. The Jules Rimet Trophy it certainly wasn't, but my own celebratory gong it definitely was!

I circled around the large pool, a distance of around half a mile, before jumping into Jules's car and making good my escape before the village police were alerted.

I felt fully accomplished as I had fulfilled my promise and no more than half a dozen folk had seen the spectacle. It was my fourth streak through the village in all, each one coming after consuming vast amounts of alcohol. But, you know, it is always an invigorating experience feeling the cool air waft against your skin and being at one with nature. I would recommend every adult on the planet should try it at least once in their lifetime.

Next day, I saw Dot pottering around in the front garden doing some weeding and confirmed to her that I had carried out my allotted task on the stroke of midnight.

"Oh no. You haven't, have you?" she rasped back, with a genuine look of disappointment that would have been understandable if she had missed seeing the real Crown Jewels, never mind my personal version.

"If I'd known, I would have stayed up especially to see that and got the whole street out to organise a midnight party."

Whether she was being serious or just behaving facetiously, I couldn't help but smirk as I left her to her gardening, thinking to myself: "I sometimes wonder about our Dot."

33 The Rep Without A Car: 2002

Off to work I go!
Some of over a hundred hitching signs that take me around the country.

As more and more potential employers expand their business networks further afield, it is a distinct advantage for any jobseeker to have access to a motor vehicle, or at least to be able to drive, in order to secure that well paid post. Non-drivers can therefore rule themselves out of opportunities that require driving as a condition of their employment. Or can they?

"Gizzajob!" ...

The problem with a reliance on temporary contracts and working for the many agencies I have registered with over the years is that when your stint ends, so does your steady income.

You then have to search for another job, and of course when you do, it soon becomes clear relevant qualifications can 'fast track' the applicant. And realistically, three mock 'O' levels don't carry a lot of credence these days.

In addition, I have never had the inclination to drive, and therefore that is another clear hindrance to gaining prestigious positions.

Nevertheless, when an application form for a vacancy inevitably includes the question 'Do you have your own transport?', I always tick the 'yes' box.

It's a legitimate reply as I do, albeit in the form of a 12-year-old 'sit up and beg' bicycle. Undeniably, it's not quite what the employers are looking for, but it does remain a factual answer, and the bike is my main method of getting to a local workplace. How the potential employer interprets my answer is open to conjecture, right up until the moment when I may or may not be asked to elaborate.

In this particular instance, that simple upward stroke of my pen was going to have huge implications, seemingly assuring me of far-reaching employment opportunities with the incentive of rich rewards. It would prove to be the most audacious endeavour to gain an opportunist opening I've ever attempted thus far, and it's questionable whether a similar stunt has ever been attempted by anyone before or since.

I had applied for the position of lorry driver's assistant, a post which required the applicant to travel nationwide on a daily basis. The vacancy had been advertised in my local Evening Sentinel newspaper, and I submitted my details over the phone to the agency dealing with the recruitment drive.

It was late March in the first year of the new millennium, and all of Burnley's midweek, difficult to reach fixtures had been completed, which allowed me a few precious months to accumulate some funds without the need to take days off for matches.

An offer of an interview for the job then came via the telephone, with the meeting to be conducted at my local Job Centre.

A lady called Caroline had come all the way from the company's headquarters in Devon to conduct the formal questioning. She proudly informed me that they were a brand new enterprise called British Ceramic Tiles and were already regarded as the largest producer of such a product in Europe. She stressed that BCT manufactured an innovative type of sophisticated, modern kitchen and bathroom tile.

Caroline then said that having just won a prestigious contract to supply their product to all of the 175 stores owned by the well known Focus DIY chain, BCT were recruiting as a matter of urgency. Their aim was to set up 10 regional teams by the following Monday to distribute their expensively priced wares to various destinations across the country within a 10 week period.

At the interview, I displayed my extensive geographical knowledge of Great Britain, gained from following Burnley, and it seemed to leave a favourable impression. I then completed a short examination with few problems, and therefore awaited her communication regarding whether I had been successful with a certain degree of optimism.

A telephone call on the Thursday confirmed my confidence was well placed as a start date in four days' time was confirmed. I was told I would be picked up by a company HGV at Keele motorway service area, located on the M6, conveniently just four miles from my house.

An introductory package was delivered to my home the very same day containing a photo identification badge and a couple of high quality BCT branded leisure shirts to wear when I took up my new occupation.

The hourly rate of pay wasn't great. However, it was probably commensurate with the task involved because my job was to help unload the cargo for delivery to the shop floor, and as there were considerable distances between each branch, I expected to spend a good proportion of my time just being driven along in the cab of the HGV.

But by the Friday of the first week, my remit had changed in dramatic fashion.

The phone rang. It was Glenda, the BCT site manageress who was in charge of transport logistics. She had only been in touch yesterday to inform me of my assignment, but today, she seemed a little bit flustered.

"Hello David. Glenda from BCT here. I'm ringing you regarding our store replenishment project which is due to begin at the start of the coming week.

"We're...err...hoping you may be able to help us out in another capacity. I'm sorry to say that due to the limited time we have been allotted to fully complete our refit, we need our personnel to work alone now, so there's been a change of plan.

"I see that according to your application form, you do possess your own transport. Is that correct?"

"Well, yeeees, I do," I hesitantly validated.

But before I could tell her that my only form of carriage was a humble pushbike, she continued the conversation apace.

"We were suitably impressed with your written text at the interview and would like to offer you a position as merchandiser of our goods.

"The company will reimburse your fuel costs at a generous 40 pence per mile and your hourly rate of pay will be enhanced by £3 per hour to compensate for travelling time to and from the site. The cost of any overnight accommodation will be reimbursed where necessary.

"Dispatch of the tiles each day should mean a delivery time between 9am and 11am and placement of our product on their allocated shelving should take three to four hours. So are you aboard, Dave?"

Aboard? I'd been knocked overboard by her expectations of me. Ker-ching! Pound signs flashed before my eyes as I totted up all the lavish benefits she had instantly proposed.

And now that it had been established that the consignments were going to be transported to their place of display by the firm's carriers, I reasoned that all I had to do was to make sure I was at the required destination on time.

Up to now, she hadn't directly asked me if I did indeed possess a car, merely assuming, wrongly of course, that the transportation 'tick' on my form must denote an automobile. I hadn't been forced into lying just yet, but surely it was just a matter of time before Glenda asked about my driving record.

She eventually did, and I swerved the question once again.

"Do you have any points on your driving licence, David?"

"No I don't, Glenda," I replied truthfully, seeing as I didn't hold such a document in the first place.

"Good. So, what do you say?"

"Errrr," I paused, delaying matters deliberately as the full implications of the operation spun round in my head.

Once I satisfied myself that there was a sporting chance I could achieve their objectives without the use of a motor car, I answered affirmatively, if somewhat hesitantly.

"Err, OK Glenda. That seems achievable. Let me know where my first job is once it's been confirmed."

"Oh, great. Well done, David. You won't regret it. I'll be in touch and thank you very much. You've saved my skin."

"If only Glenda realised," I said to myself.

I bid her goodbye before flopping back on my bed to take in the full gravity of my self-inflicted dilemma.

All I knew was that starting on Monday morning, I would somehow have to get myself to their chosen retail outlet, which would be anywhere within a radius of 80 miles, for around 9am. Depending on the nominated location and the difficulty in getting there, my mode of transportation would have to be either train, coach, bus or hitching a ride.

I was representing a major retail company and had the responsibility to honour my contract with them by helping to oversee a regional strategy of establishing the company within a well-known retail chain, and all this within a stringent time scale.

What had I done?

My timetable for the week arrived in the Saturday post and so I was now officially 'The Rep. Without a Car.'

On the tiles ...

Whoever drew up the roster which I was allocated had treated me comparatively kindly.

I was to be seconded to Focus DIY branches in Chester, then the Derbyshire town of Ilkeston, followed by Fenton near Stoke-on-Trent, then Nottingham, and finally finishing the week by setting up a display at the Focus store in Crewe, Cheshire.

At 40p a mile, my travelling expenses would not only cover the cost of my fares on public transport, but would make me a considerable profit. And as long as I got to my appointed site on time and did a good job, I figured we would all benefit. Car or no car, everyone's a winner.

So on the Monday morning, I made sure I was up with the birds to catch a bus that would take me the whole 35 miles to Chester. And although it took almost two hours to get there as the journey accommodated a multitude of stops, I arrived soon after 9am at the chosen store which stood on an out-of-town industrial estate.

I introduced myself as the representative for British Ceramic Tiles and was asked to sign the visitors' book which also requested me to state my time of arrival and car registration number. For the latter of course, I had to give a fictitious plate number and would say that I'd left it some distance away if asked about its whereabouts.

The truckload of goods hadn't even arrived yet and so I was allowed access to the staff canteen while I waited. Then at around 10.30am, the shipment turned up in the delivery bay. However, only two pallets of tiles were unloaded.

The driver jumped from his cab looking agitated, before going on to explain the shortfall.

"Thu'rrre 'avin' a blody nightmare down thurrre, they are," he said in his Devonian lilt. "They just can't produce enough tiles to go round so thu'rre rationing them and giving so many to each store, they arrre."

From what I could gather, the strict time limitations attached to the restructuring of the supply to the DIY chain had meant production couldn't keep up with the quantity required.

I phoned Glenda to advise her of the shortfall, and from what she said, I gathered that the Focus group was in the process of being taken over, hence the requirement for an early completion. But it had not been possible to create the substantial order in such a short time even with a 24 hour assembly line. Therefore, she had made the decision to share the part of the order which had been produced evenly between the various stores.

It was a situation I was to come across on a regular basis over the next few weeks. As far as I was concerned, it made my job infinitely easier, because Glenda concluded that as I had been sent to each store by the company and the shortfall was their fault, I would receive a full day's pay irrespective of the amount I had merchandised. It was their problem, not mine, she pointed out. As far as I was concerned, it was 'happy days.'

Now, don't get me wrong, I would have done the full job to completion no matter how long it took. But their misfortune turned into my good fortune. On that first day, my task was complete after an hour and the rest of the afternoon was spent 'copping' a few pubs before a leisurely commute home by bus with a couple more refreshment stops along the way.

My Arriva bus company 'day rover ticket' had taken me all the 70 miles there and back for the princely sum of £3.50. With a £28 allowance for petrol, that represented a £24.50 gain. Of course, fuel receipts had to be coerced from friends for authentification purposes on my expenses form, but that was it. To all intents and purposes, in their eyes I was just a regular everyday rep.

The rest of the week followed the same pattern. Mid-morning deliveries of depleted stock to each of the shops were followed by a swift dispatch of the goods into their relevant positions.

Ilkeston had been the most difficult destination to get to but even then, I made a 10am arrival which was a good hour before the curtain-sided truck clocked in. I'd earned a good wage and even been paid both travelling and waiting time. It wasn't just a 'good number,' it was a 'bloody good number.'

In the next few weeks, I was asked to work at more than a dozen other locations within that 80 mile radius, as well as some of the stores I had already been to as an ever increasing amount of the baked clay blocks became available.

If the venue was easier to access by hitching a ride on the motorway, I'd do that, or even make use of the National Express coach network if that was a convenient way of reaching my target store.

After a month, I'd fulfilled all my obligatory duties and was even receiving high praise form Glenda for doing a decent job of it. My weekly 'top line' was more than £500 which was probably three times as much as I would have received as a simple driver's assistant.

They were happy. I was happy. Things couldn't get any better, I thought. But they did.

Glenda made her regular call to my mobile phone for her usual Friday afternoon update on proceedings. She began the conversation by saying how appreciative the company were of my efforts, before almost apologetically asking whether I would be interested in working at locations further afield as they were still behind schedule.

Additionally, Glenda asked if I knew anyone who would like to assist me to speed up the task.

"Hmmm...," I said, pausing deliberately as I tried to supress my delight at her proposal. It worked.

"We would be willing to up your petrol allowance to 50 pence a mile to compensate for wear and tear to your vehicle, and of course accommodate you at a hotel of a reasonable standard for your trouble. What do you say?," she said.

"OK Glenda. You've talked me into it," I replied, winning her over even further with my false air of reluctance.

"Oh thank you, David, thank you. And can you recruit a competent assistant?," she inquired.

"Yes. I think I know just the man," I assured her.

"Great. I'll send out your itinerary straight away. Thanks again David. Byeee"

Two 'reps without a car' ...

It was like lighting up all the bonus lights on a fruit machine at once. More miles, more money, more pubs.

But the stakes were higher now. Much, much higher.

I immediately phoned my mate Weedy, who was a self-employed piano haulier.

"Eyup Weed. I'm gonna make you an offer you can't refuse."

"Ha,ha....l bet you are, Ralph," came back his sarcastic reply.

"Well, if I told you that you could make two grand in the next month, and afford to have a good drink every night of that month, what would you say?"

"I don't beleeeeive it!" came back his second sardonic reposte in his well practised Victor Meldrew mode, which was getting a little wearisome now.

"So you don't want the chance to earn big bucks then, Weedy?," I replied, giving him one last opportunity to take my proposition seriously.

"Yeh, sorry Ralph. I got a bit carried away."

If there's one thing that instantaneously captures Weedy's attention, it's the threat of him losing money.

He was all ears now as I fully explained this unmissable business proposal, and after asking a few questions, he rescheduled his spasmodic forthcoming appointments to sign up with BCT.

A day or two later, British Ceramic Tiles sent us their 'must do' list of sites to be visited. It was extremely ambitious with a car, and highly improbable without one.

Our addresses to reach were at Ashington, Northumberland on the Monday and Tuesday, then down to Hastings, East Sussex for Wednesday, King's Lynn, Norfolk on Thursday and Haverfordwest, Dyfed, Wales to finish off the week.

I'd always calculated my distance from the chart in the Great Britain Road Atlas, and this little lot came to around 1,600 miles, equating to shared expenses of £800. Along with our paid travelling time and wages, if we accomplished the formidable odyssey, it would represent my best pay ever for a week's work.

But the vast expanse between each outlet and the tight scheduling involved would necessitate a plan of military precision to complete the task, so we weren't getting carried away.

At this point, Weedy's usefulness in being the holder of a current driving licence would also come into play.

We hitchhiked to our first venue in the North East on the Sunday to ensure an early start in the store on the Monday morning. After completion of our task early on the Tuesday afternoon, we then once again hitched it, this time heading home.

We made it in time to give us a couple of hours to freshen up before boarding the National Express coach to London. A return train ticket out to Sevenoaks in Kent then got us far enough out of London to hitch directly to Hastings along the A21. Job done, but we were shattered after that coach ride to 'The Smoke' and another National express coach home once we had made it back into London from Kent.

A car was hired for the next two assignments to King's Lynn and Haverfordwest respectively as both represented gruelling cross country treks. Even so, a top line of £820 each was earned for the week which, even after expense deductions, was a great return.

Over the next month, we became Glenda's 'troubleshooters,' being sent to places far and wide to redesign shelving placements which had been incorrectly displayed, all the time using a combination of hitching and public transport to generate maximum profit from our lucrative travel expenses.

There were only two occasions when we were nearly, but not quite, caught out by our frugality.

The first was when we had both managed to hitch a lift to an assignment at Carlisle in Cumbria. Although it was a near-300 mile round trip, it only required us to negotiate one motorway as the route was straight up the M6.

However, maybe our habitual end of the working day drinking session had been extended longer than usual due to the lure of the delightful, warm summer sunshine, as we didn't find ourselves occupying a position at the head of the motorway slip road ready to hitch it on our long journey back until 6pm. That meant that even with the perfect lift all the way, we were still around two and a half hours short of our home base.

Tonight it really did appear that our late stop over would cost us dear, as three fruitless hours passed without a hint of any vehicle obliging. Then, just as dusk was closing in, a car did pull up. The lone male driver was going to Holmes Chapel, a small town in Cheshire near junction 18 of the M6, and agonisingly just 18 miles short of our destination.

Nevertheless, we were on our way and grateful to meet this accommodating chap who it transpired had attended the evening horse racing meeting at the nearby Carlisle track. He was enraptured by our reason for being at the side of the road, and genuinely amazed that we were travelling the country to carry out a job that normally requires a car to fulfil the role.

It turned out that his name was Charles Yates and that he was TV editor for The Sun daily newspaper, and he intimated that our employment adventure would make a cracking story for his tabloid. However, as we were still reliant on the company for our income for a few more weeks, we had to politely decline his proposition for comedy stardom.

We reached our intersection and thanked Charles for our free transportation, but it was now 11.30pm and pitch black with little or no traffic passing by.

Yet somehow against all the odds, a motor slowed down, and the occupants of the car turned out to be a mother with her daughter aboard. The mum stated that she'd seen our Stoke-on-Trent sign, and because they were heading home to Stockton Brook, a small hamlet north of the city, she was happy to help. Of course, she added that standard cautionary note of: "I don't usually pick up hitchhikers, but you both looked clean and tidy so we both agreed to stop since we were going your way."

They kindly dropped us of in Hanley, regarded as the hub of the Potteries conurbation, from where we got a taxi home. We'd made it back in time to prepare for the following day's workload in Nottinghamshire, but we knew that only a few minutes had spared us from a miserable night in the open air.

An unexpected twist ...

If that previous episode had illustrated our fortitude, the next incident, which involved another bad hitching day, embodied our aptitude.

Our posting was to Walton-le-Dale, a couple of miles south of Preston, Lancashire. We'd made it up the M6 by our regular rule of thumb within a couple of hours, and by our arrival time, the full consignment of pallets of tiles were being delivered to the unloading bay of the store.

That proved to be no problem as the two of us could replenish the shelves with a full new stock within three hours. What did turn out to be a problem was the awkward location of the premises which happened to be on a dual carriageway spur road to the industrial estate, with no footpaths along the three mile stretch to our required junction and little sign of a bus link.

So after getting the job completion papers signed by the branch manager, who we'd got on very well with, by mid-afternoon, we said our goodbyes and decided on this occasion it would be wise to head back closer to home for a drink, given the store's isolated location well away from the 'main drag.'

But it took us a full hour to get a short lift from a male customer at the store, and even that was to just a mile down the road to what amounted to little more than a lay-by, which the chap misguidedly thought would be better for vehicles to pull into. However, because it was a straight stretch of road, drivers were apt to accelerate, being reluctant to slow down on such a fast paced downhill descent with little scope to stop safely.

And so we waited...and waited...and waited, until it had gone 7pm. We had managed to go one mighty bloody mile in four and a half hours! Because of a lack of pavement in either direction and only vast, open, green fields behind us, we had conspired to get ourselves marooned on a short piece of tarmac with cars flying past us at great speed. We were well and truly stuck, and even passing taxi drivers gave us short shrift, nonchalantly shrugging their shoulders in their time honoured manner.

Then came a highly unlikely development, one that five hours ago we could scarcely have imagined. At last, at long last, a top of the range Volvo braked sharply and turned into the narrow pull-in. As it screeched to a halt, I immediately recognised the figure behind the wheel.

"Bloody hell, Weedy. It's the store manager. Quick! Name a major part of a motor car that can break down," I asked, not being conversant with such intricacies.

"Big end, Ralph. Big end," Weedy responded promptly.

"No need for personal insults, Weed," I joked.

The Focus boss slid down his automatic passenger window.

"What the heck are you two doing here?," asked the clearly bemused head of operations.

"You'll never believe it, but the big end packed in on our motor soon after we'd left you, so we've had the car towed in to a local garage," I ad-libbed.

"Hop in, lads. Let's get you out of here. We'll talk about it in the car," urged the driver.

"So why haven't you gone with your car?," he asked, quite legitimately.

I carried on with our story, which in essence was true.

"Well, unfortunately we've got to get to our next job at Hoylake on Merseyside tomorrow, so we rather unwisely thought it better to try to hitch a lift home so that we'd be ready in the morning to pick up our hire car. From all accounts, our motor is going to be a big repair job."

"And you've been stuck here ever since in an effort to make sure you both get to your next appointment. You know, I think that's truly commendable. You're a real credit to your company and I'll be saying as much to them tomorrow."

"There's really no need. We were just making the best of a bad job," I offered.

"What?" the boss came back. "Waiting hours in a god-forsaken lay-by in order to guarantee your presence on their behalf?... No, you're being way too humble. Your actions were beyond the call of duty."

Dropping us off on the slip road of the 'big slab' that is the M6, he bid farewell to us with a cheery: "Well done lads, and the very best of luck," before going on his way.

"What about that then Weed? High praise indeed," I laughed.

"Yeah. We'll be flavour of the month with Glenda once she gets to hear of our resolute endeavours," I suggested as we managed to catch a lift home before dark.

Sure enough, soon after our arrival in the county of Merseyside next day, Glenda made an early morning call.

"Good morning, David. How are you today after the terrible bad luck with the car?"

"Oh, not to worry, Glenda. It was just one of those unfortunate things."

"No David, it was a demonstration of a truly admirable work ethic in your determination to literally go that extra mile in the course of your work," Glenda insisted, She went on to say

"Well, the branch manager has been in touch to tell me the full story of how it left you both stranded, so we're putting a £50 bonus on to your salary this week as a token of thanks for your commitment and the inconvenience caused."

"That's very kind of you. Thanks a lot, Glenda."

"No, thank you both very much. Bye, David. I'll be in touch," and she was gone.

Myself and Weedy did an impromptu jig, dancing around each other's outstretched arms to celebrate.

The incident formed the pinnacle of our 10 week tenure. Our daunting mission was soon over and the money earned as 'reps without a car' went on to fund our three week holiday cheering on England in the European Championships at Holland and Belgium that summer.

Once again, however, our interest ended prematurely with a 3-2 defeat against Romania in Charleroi, Belgium. Ah, well. At least the beer was good.

34 My Mother's Tales Of The Unexpected

"What a kafuffle!" My Ma is genuinely bewildered to see the Little Britain characters Lou Todd and Andy Pipkin outside Tussauds at Blackpool.

My 'ma' seems to have built up quite a fan club following her starring role in Chapter One, "The Big Kick Off" from Part One. That is where I shared some of her shall we say, more unpredictable moments with the reader. So back by popular demand are a few more outrageously funny, frequently toe curling episodes from 'Herta's School of Life'.

Gordon Banks O.B.E. beaten in the last minute by an 80 year old German gran …

Now that's a headline I bet you would never have thought you'd ever see, but metaphorically speaking it really did happen.

Although now fairly inoperative due to her numerous debilitating ailments my mother still retains the power of voice to bark out the orders Sergeant Major, or maybe more appropriately Feurer fashion from the living room where she now permanently resides. This she relentlessly does until all her requests are met.

Of course, both myself and my brother have become accustomed to her insatiable demands so we let her stew a while until she adds those most important of words – 'please' or 'thank you'. It's just to let her know that we won't respond to her continuous beck and call.

Her unorthodox approach to most social situations remains remorseless, particularly so when she gets the rare chance to be transported outside in her manual wheelchair.

She did have a motorised version, but it had unfortunately laid idle in the garden shed for many years. In fact from the moment she acquired it at a knockdown price from the widower of a deceased neighbour, just one day after her passing, Herta didn't venture out on it more than half-a-dozen times in five years.

My mother's wholly thoughtless assessment that, "She won't be needing it anymore now", was probably enough to numb Bob, the stricken husband of the recently departed lady, into a shock quick sale. Tactless? Unquestionably…. priceless? Definitely.

After having a few futile attempts to master the basics of driving it, she put the conveyance back into storage claiming,

"It's too bloody dangerous!"

On the very rare occasion I had seen Herta out on the battery version her regular penchant for creating untold mayhem continued apace.

Take for instance the grand opening of our brand spanking new village community centre, a state of the art complex with an adjoining residential home building for assisted living.

We had the honour of the inauguration ceremony being performed by village resident Gordon Banks O.B.E., the former Chesterfield, Leicester City, and latterly Stoke City goalkeeper. The man who won 73 England Caps, and was of course custodian on that unforgettable day in 1966 when we actually won the World Cup 4-2 against West Germany after extra time.

Regional press and radio representatives were all in attendance, as well as a few hundred locals who had all been looking forward to this long awaited, prestigious event.

The council dignitaries went on to make their introductory speeches, and then Gordon himself regaled the audience with football related anecdotes which drew enthusiastic applause from the appreciative gathering.

All the time that this had been going on my mum had been very restrained, almost disinterested in the preceding speech that was taking place. But curiosity got the better of her as she strained to hear the words of the famous orator, eyes squinting to focus on his silhouette.

Completely unaware of his identity she had a look of sheer nonchalance on her face until suitably intrigued by the loud clapping and laughter Herta asked matter-of-factly,

"Who's speaking?"

Even though I thought that there was a chance it could evoke a reaction, I simply couldn't resist telling her directly who this mystery man was in a purposefully mischievous manner.

"It's Gordon Banks, England's goalie when we won the cup 4-2 against 'GERRRMANY' in 1966", I replied making sure I emphasized our Germanic rivals purely for my mother's behalf.

Now I watched the game on our black and white telly at home, and of course witnessed the disputed Geoff Hurst extra time goal for England as it happened. For those few that may not have seen the incident, when the ball famously struck the crossbar before rebounding down to be cleared up field, it was extremely controversial. And because the Russian linesman gave it is as over the line it still rankles with my ma to this day as she also watched it live on TV with me.

Realising she had a renewed connection to that fateful day with one of the opposition right in front of her, it seemed to trigger a recurring bout of post-traumatic stress that had laid dormant for many years.

"Grrr…No gold!" bellowed my mother, using her usual misinterpretation of the word 'goal', waving her walking stick aloft at Gordon as if he was personally culpable for the decision.

"You bloody swine. That wasn't a gold!" she reiterated crudely.

"You can't say that to Gordon Banks, he's a national bloody hero!" I advised her, before telling her to keep quiet or she'd be in big trouble.

Gordon, the attending media and the majority of the crowd had heard her outburst as I went on to inform them that she wasn't feeling very well, leaving my by now wholly embarrassed eldest sister Susan to tell her to "shut up!"

The uncalled for outcry was partly my fault as she was only protesting the validity of the strike in her own inimitable way as happened whenever I tease her.

I wouldn't mind but she had lived in the East German Democratic Republic when she was a child before fleeing to the west when the Russian army invaded her country. Nevertheless, the affinity was there.

Thankfully 'Banksy' dismissed the untimely outpouring of dissent with his characteristic smile.

Now whether that was the catalyst for her next shocking manoeuvre, or more probably because our host had announced that refreshments would be served from the in-house cafeteria immediately after the ceremony, we will never know for sure.

But before the ex-keeper could cut the ribbon to officially open the premises, my by now agitated mum rocked to and fro impatiently in her motorised 'killing machine' before pressing the activation button that propelled her forward through the crowd. With her walking stick stuck out in front of her like a knight in armour lance, and wearing her trademark fashion accessory ensemble of pink plastic cap with green fluorescent gloves, after a couple of loud toots on her air horn she breached the assemblage like a modern day Moses parting the Red Sea!

"Scusa me, scusa me. I have to come through now!" shouted my mother rudely.

"Bloody Hell!" She's like Ironside on drugs!", quipped one watching spectator, comparing her to the wheelchair bound detective from the 1970s television series.

To his immense credit a bemused Gordon Banks finalised his duties with the same wry grin that he had displayed in her initial "No Gold!" protestations while my mum positioned herself at the very head of the refreshment queue to the chagrin of those behind her.

"All I can say is she must be desperate for a cup of tea," joked Banksy.

Fortunately her actions failed to spoil a memorable day for the village even though the local equivalent of the German Panzer Division had breached their lines.

The German au pair/receptionist …

My pet name for the head of the household is the 'German au pair/receptionist.'

This tag denotes her nationality, the job she successfully trained for in order to come to England, and also her self-appointed meet and greet duties that she has bestowed upon herself when someone either knocks at the door or rings our telephone number on the land line.

Her eagerness to be the first point of contact for an incoming call has in the past proved most disconcerting for my brother and I, not forgetting the callers themselves.

For even if me or Shaun do get to one or the other of the two cradle phones first, it's only a matter of a few seconds before the click of her 'hands free' set is heard as she plucks it from the stand; this appliance always residing by her bedside in case of an emergency.

She will then begin to conduct her own suspicious inquisition accordingly.

"Hell…0!.... who's speaking?" is her hardly welcoming opening line.

Then once a reply has been received a curt, "What you want?" quickly follows.

If either myself or my brother are requested, a sharp "What you want them for?" forms her next question before further investigative work begins.

From this point on the victim at the other end of the line has approximately 10 seconds to convince the au pair/receptionist that their call is genuine and intentions are honourable before she will slam the phone down to the same insulting retort each time.

"Chupitch nut!", she will yell. 'Chupitch' as stated being her misconstrued word for stupid.

Now the problem with these brief exchanges, as funny as they might sound, is that legitimate friends, potential employers, agencies and business contacts are left shell shocked and discriminated against as if they are also unwanted callers. So now a password system has been brought into operation to ensure proper communication.

However, there is a plus side. We certainly don't get half as many cold callers as we did anymore.

In fact the last one that I can recall was from an unfortunate advisor claiming to be from the Lloyds Bank based at a Philippines call centre. After giving the foreign speaking woman short shrift by slamming the phone down after a few seconds her interpretation of the unfortunate enquirer was,

"She was a ching chong chung talking itch, mitch, titch, tutch, tatch!"

A storm in a teacup …

The day had started much like any other now that I had become a full time carer for my 86 year old mother Herta Maria.

It was Tuesday February 2nd 2016 and I was more eager than normal to attend to my mum's many needs as I was hoping for an early afternoon train departure that would transport me to our Championship League, night match at Sheffield Wednesday in South Yorkshire. Having made provision for my absence with my sister Susan until my return in the early hours of next day I set about my domestic tasks.

Her routine, like most Brits began with an early morning cup of tea, which I duly delivered to one of a nest of small wooden tables from where she always drank her hot beverage.

I administered the first of three blood pressure tablets that Herta was required to take, then set about boiling some hot water so she could bathe herself, saving a little to clean out the plastic cup that housed her set of false teeth.

'Italia 90'
The excitable Italians like to let you know when they've won a game.

'Italia 90' You just couldn't make it up!
England Fans queue in the 90°F heat to obtain match tickets from
a lone 'Fanzone' caravan in a random field.
Note: 'Zippy', centre in a yellow vest, denim shorts and a man bag
doing a good impression of 'Stavros' the kebab seller.

A saucy seaside postcard.
It's a 'dying fly' manoeuvre on our 'Tarts Weekend' to Margate for
my 10,000 pub celebrations June 1992.

The marriage of our High Priest Jim, Margate 1992. Exposed vicar 'Tricky Trev' performs the wedding ceremony with best man Barney looking on as Jim places the ring on his £10 bride.

Mullen Out!'
The turn your back to the pitch protest against Crewe Alex at
Turf Moor. 0-1 February 1996 at precisely 3.33pm. 48 hours later
Jimmy had gone.

The last kiss.
Before I leave my spiritual home The 'Longside of Burnley' a final
Farewell to the spot I've stood on for the last quarter of a century.
Saturday 16th September v Hull City 1995.

R.I.P The High Priest.
Jim Purcell taking a break from his highway patrol policing duties.

'Zippy' and 'Bungle' force a smile after paying me up my football bets.

How it all started.
'Father Ted!' a.k.a Reggie Bradshaw pops into town for a pint.

Lifelong drinking partner 'Weedy' recovering after running into a
lamppost when the pub closed!

Two legends for the price of one!
Brian O'Neil, 'The Bedlington Terrier' to the right and Mr.
'Perpetual Motion' Ralphy Coates as guests of Turf Moor.
Photograph by Adrian Ashworth

I raise a glass to toast
my boyhood hero Ralph
Coates at his wake held
at White Hart lane,
Tottenham.
Died Dec. 17th 2010.

Nice touch.
A magnanimous
gesture from
The Royals in our
final away game.
2013-14

Quirky fact.
More Benedictine spirit
sold in Burnley than
anywhere else in the
world.

Champions at Charlton
Burnley Fans in the background acclaim our First second tier
Championship since promotion to the top tier in 1973.

Hyped up!
How one tabloid
promoted the upcoming
Man. United v Burnley
game played Sat. Oct 29th,
2016, Premier League.

Noticing that her gnashers weren't in the receptacle, on my return to the living room I asked my mum if she had placed them in her mouth which she sometimes did in preparation for her breakfast.

"No, you had dem in da cup," she replied assuredly in her broken English twang.

"No I haven't, there were no teeth in the cup", I countered with equal surety as I cleaned out 'Jethro' the cockertiel's cage.

"Well, where they gone den?" Herta asked more urgently.

"They not here! You must have chucked dem in da rubbish. Find dem David, I can't eat without my teece," she wailed stating the bleeding obvious.

"Well they must be in here somewhere because you had them last night and they haven't walked off themselves have they?" I responded, ever more annoyed by her dramatic over-reaction.

I strode back into the kitchen to start a clothes wash in the machine, all the time thinking if I had been careless enough to have thrown them into the household rubbish that I had squashed into our wheelie bin and placed by the gate ready for our fortnightly collection around mid-morning.

But I always keep her falsies in the cup with my hand placed over them to minimize contact whilst first draining, then swilling with warm water before, topping up again with hot. Surely I couldn't have been so absent minded to have inadvertently jettisoned them out with the waste could I?

By now Herta, who often worked herself up over any incidental issue, hence her high blood pressure, was now so beside herself she resorted to playing the blame game by accusing me of some kind of warped prank in a repetitive tirade of nonsensical deliberations.

"You've had 'em! You've chucked dem out with da rubbish or in da garden. Go and look to find dem!", she cried desperately.

Now she was getting silly I told her,

"Why would I want to put your false teeth in the garden. They're not going to grow another pair overnight you know."

In an effort to placate her I told her to calm herself, have a drink of hot tea, and lie down on the bed while I looked for them in the lounge.

Without even considering a sip of the tea placed in front of her she painstakingly shuffled herself to the edge of the bed before rolling herself onto it in undignified fashion still muttering unintelligible lines of gibberish under her breath.

For the next half-hour I ferreted around feverishly delving into every possible nook and cranny. I looked under, behind and between the sofa, chairs and carpeting before returning Herta back to her armchair recliner in order to carry out a full strip down of her bed. Nothing! Absolutely no sign whatsoever of the missing porcelain.

Drawers, boxes and all surrounding shelving had been thoroughly searched but to no avail. I had even checked the parrot's cage just in case I'd unwittingly placed them in Jethro's seed box. But no, I had turned the place upside down just as thoroughly as cops would conducting a drugs search, without success.

Now my head was in a total spin with the relentless caterwawling from my ma bleating about her eaters.

"Day will cost two hundred pounds for a nudder pair because you've trone dem out".

Her constant accusations had by now sewn some seeds of doubt in my head making me contemplate the unthinkable – that maybe, just maybe, in my haste I had plonked them with our kitchen waste, which was now currently residing in the wheelie bin outside.

What a load of rubbish! ....

Time was of the essence as I heard the powerful jaws of the refuse collectors lorry loudly munching it's cargo in the next parallel street to our own. I knew I had to work fast to rule out any slight possibility that in my hurry I had jettisoned them out with the rest of the trash, so out I rushed!

Grabbing the top two black bin liners I undid the knotted end and delved into each bag at a frenetic pace in a bid to beat the imminent arrival of the 'Biffa' truck.

Placing the squishy-squashy waste in an individual line across six pages of our laid out Sun newspaper I pulled out a mixture of numerous 'Tena Super' panty liner pads, not to be confused with the similarly sounding alcoholics can of choice 'Tennants Super'. I waded through a batch of my mother's used incontinence pads of which there were many, mixed in with paper tissues, apple cores and a range of washing up scourers and cloths. I was just glad that separate food bins had been brought in a few years previous or else it could have been even messier.

I had filtered through the scattered rubbish with all the thoroughness of an elite forensic team and as predicted there wasn't a sign of her chewing tackle.

Dashing out to catch the bin wagon before it left I managed to chuck my last couple of bags into its cavenous rear mouth before it swiftly exited the cul-de-sac. I disinfected my hands after the futile search racking my brains for further hidden locations.

Now I was really puzzled.

"Where the bloody hell could they be?" I whispered to myself as I entered our front door to relay the bad news to her majesty.

"Sorry mum, they're nowhere to be seen. You're gonna have to phone my sister Susan to see if she can help you out O.K." I asked as reassuredly as was possible under the circumstances.

"Look you haven't even drunk your tea. It's cold now, so I'll have to make you a fresh one before I go", I uttered grudgingly as I picked up her cup.

The accusations continued ever more vehemently as I left the room.

"It's you! I know it is, no one else has been here! Where are day David tell me pleeeease", she pleaded, illogically believing in her own head that I must have taken them as some kind of perverted punishment.

Angered to think she thought I would even consider doing such a cruel act I switched on the kettle and hurled the cold tea into the metallic sink. And you would never believe what fell out! No, not a tea bag, but her full set of false teeth that rattled into the basin like a couple of spanners in a washing machine.

All became crystal clear now! Herta had mistakenly dropped her dentures into her tea cup, blissfully unaware that she had mistook it for her warm water soaking mug nearby. Because they were completely submerged in the brown coloured liquid neither of us could either see or even consider that this would be their novel new resting place.

I must admit that after a stressful morning brought about solely by my mother's lapse of concentration or darn poor eyesight my instant reaction was to pick up the dentures, take them to her and demand a full apology for her many false 'teeth' allegations.

However as soon as the said objects revealed themselves I could not help but laugh out loud at the sheer preposterous absurdity of the whole episode, so I let her off with a mild scolding with no admission forthcoming.

Besides, I was downright relieved that I could now set off on my journey to the game at Hillsborough where Burnley went on to earn a creditable 1-1 draw on a wet and wild evening, very much like the day I'd already had back home with my mother!

Astoundingly, next day my ma explained away her delirious outbursts concerning the sorry teeth debacle by claiming that the grilled cheese on toast I'd made at home the previous day for her tea had given her nightmares about her falsies and their whereabouts.

"But you only have nightmares when you're sleeping!" I told her, before thinking about it and concluding,

"No, you're right mother, you certainly had a nightmare yesterday morning!"

April Fools Day is no joke in our house ....

The only way to describe my mother's sense of humour would be blissfully simplistic.

For instance, her most watched television programme is the BBC sitcom 'Some Mother's Do 'Ave 'Em' from the 1970s. Starring the multi-talented Michael Crawford. It is farcical entertainment at its best.

Whilst her taste in comedy films take in such timeless slapstick classics as Laurel & Hardy, along with the antics of Groucho, Chico, Harpo and Zeppo from the Marx Brothers series, Herta's most raucous belly laughs are saved for the asinine high jinks of the irrepressible 'Mr Bean' picture shows. The rubber faced buffoon classified as essential viewing in my mother's mind.

Which might go some way to explaining why she seems to go completely off her rocker once the calendar comes round to April 1st or 'All Fools Day' to give it a more recognisable title.

It's the day when her early morning efforts of tomfoolery emerge with a regular predictability. Such well-worn proclamations that,

"Dare's a spider on da ceiling!" are immediately followed by a loud shout of "April Fool!" well before any of us have had time to take in her statement, never mind look up for the imaginary arachnid.

Her lack of subtlety always met with a shake of the head from all her victims such is it's predictability to family members. Which is more than you can say when she decides to go public with her chuckle crusade on that commemorative date.

I'd imagine it's no laughing matter for our milkman when he's loudly informed that,

"Dare's a maggot in da milk bottle!" especially with half the street in attendance on the doorstep.

Or when the local Co-op store staff and its customers recoil in sheer abject horror as she bellows across the shop,

"A big fat black rat just run across the floor!"

Her guffawed laughter being only briefly interrupted by a cry of "Only Jokesing", not remotely enough to pacify the shell-shocked audience who by now have collectively clasped both hands across their faces as a direct result of her ill thought jape.

In fact I was always relieved when the clock ticked past midday to traditionally signal the end of her interpretation of the centuries-old English custom, and all the ensuing mayhem that she left in her wake.

Then I knew that we could all get back to some semblance of normality until next year, whatever that normality may be in our household.

35 Kaiser's Japanese Torture: 2002

'Kaiser' in angry mode.

I've known 'Kaiser', real name Stephen Rimmer, for more than 35 years now, travelling to football matches with him many times at home and abroad. He's always vehemently defended anything he believes in, and remains fiercely loyal to his football club, the national team and above all his friends. As a consequence of fighting his corner on their behalf, he has been involved in a number of scrapes in the past, but never to the extent of this truly harrowing episode. This is Kaiser's own account of a World Cup trip that went drastically wrong.

Welcome to Nippon ...

After watching England play abroad for many years, when I heard Japan had been chosen as co-hosts for the 2002 World Cup along with neighbouring South Korea, I just knew I had to be there in the Land of the Rising Sun. It was the chance of a lifetime to see a country I wouldn't normally dream of visiting for a holiday.

I got in touch with some good mates of mine, who were also regular England fans who I'd met on previous journeys following the national team, to see if they were interested in making the long trip.

Their club side was West Bromwich Albion and one of their 'top boys' was Eammon Payne, who took the role of their spokesman. After the necessary consultation process had been carried out, Eammon phoned me back to confirm that seven of his lads were up for it. My pal Mark Morris, or 'Mooner' to his friends, who was based in Bury and was also a Burnley fan, said he fancied going too, which meant a party of nine would be making the long trip to the Far East.

I'd been to games before with Eammon and two of the other West Brom lads, John and Bailey, but I didn't know the rest. John booked the flights for around £550 along with a national rail pass valid for a month, which was necessary to cover the long distances between each match.

Mooner and I travelled down to Great Barr in the West Midlands to meet up with the 'Baggies' lads in their own boozer, where we discussed how much spending money we would need.

I said I had £2,500 in my pocket which I hoped would be enough when Eammon pulled out a thick wad of dollars.

"There's five thousand there, Kaise. That should cover it," he said gleefully.

Taken aback by such a huge amount, I quipped: "Fucking hell, Eammon. Have you just printed 'em?"

His knowing glance back and quick nod gave me the answer I didn't want to hear. "All in fifties, Kaise. All in fifties."

We boarded the mini-bus taking us to Heathrow thinking no more of it.

The first leg of the flight took us to Austria as part of the economy route, and from there a connecting flight took us to Narita Airport in Tokyo. 'Welcome to Nippon' was the greeting at passport control.

I had match tickets for the first three England fixtures, against Sweden in Tokyo, Argentina in Sapporo and Nigeria in Osaka.

We had landed in Japan four days before the opening match against the Swedes which was due to take place in Saitama, a suburb of the capital, so that allowed us a good first week of drinking and getting to know the locals who seemed very friendly towards us.

As for the game, England only managed a 1-1 draw against the Scandinavians but that was predictable for the inaugural tie.

Sapporo city beckons ...

Myself, Mooner and Eammon decide to head straight up to Sapporo on the train for the next match against our old foes, the Argentinians. The remaining six members of our group stayed in Tokyo.

I reckon it took about eight hours on the super-fast express, and I stayed awake supping a few cans while Mooner and Eammon got their heads down.

We arrived at our destination late at night, yet there were still plenty of locals about willing to direct us to available accommodation, and our eventual choice turned out to be a top hotel. I took a room on my own to guarantee some much needed kip, leaving the other two to head for the bar after their revitalising snooze travelling up.

The day before the game, we caught the train to the ground for a few photos with my Burnley union flag.

We got chatting to one of the locals who told us about a bar where you paid a 3,500 yen entry fee, which was the equivalent of about £25, but you were then entitled to eat as much food, and drink as much beer as you wanted for a period of 90 minutes. You chose your own grub and cooked it yourself on a heated griddle. We had a bit of fodder and a whole lot of beer.

Eammon had smoked a few cannabis spliffs through the night, and this along with a large intake of alcohol within a relatively short timescale was seriously affecting his judgement. That could be the only reason he decided to pay the bill with fake dollars instead of yen.

We left in a taxi to sample the nightlife in a busy part of the city. Hustlers tried to coax us into their clubs, one of whom stood out more than any other. He was a huge coloured bloke sporting an 'Afro' hairstyle and looking for all the world like Huggy Bear, the sidekick of fictional TV cops 'Starsky and Hutch.'

He immediately caught our attention so after a chat we decide to go into his premises. The cost to gain admission just happened to be $50, but I warned Eammon against using his fake dollars as the Antonio Fargas lookalike spoke with an American accent.

"He's a Yank, Eammon. He might notice something's wrong with 'em."

But it was too late. Eammon was blasted on both drink and weed so simply paid the man.

Inside, you could tell quite easily that it was a 'clip joint,' a fact that didn't escape Mooner as he disappeared upstairs for a 'massage,' while myself and Eammon got the drinks in and watched the scantily dressed hostesses perform their exotic dance acts.

We'd barely been in there 30 minutes when I got a tap on my shoulder.

"Can you come to the door, please?," asked the bouncer politely.

We obliged, thinking that maybe Mooner had got into some kind of dispute upstairs with the escort girl. But as we got to the entrance, we were met by the sight of more police patrol cars than I'd ever seen in my life.

"What the fuck!" turned out to be the last exclamation Eammon or Mooner would hear from me for a very long time.

The cops physically manhandled us all into separate patrol cars then drove us to the local police cells.

In the words of the Monopoly board, it was a case of 'Go straight to jail. Do not pass go!'

The nightmare begins ...

I was thrown into a padded cell and had to sleep on the floor. No one could speak English so I hadn't a clue what was going on.

After a few days stewing in basic surroundings, during which time our luggage was collected from our hotel and every single item photographed and listed in minute detail with nothing left to chance, I began to be subjected to the daily monotony of the interview procedure.

A bell would sound at 9am and the police officers would escort me to the reception desk where two foot print markers denoted where you had to stand. I was handcuffed as I faced the inspector with a rope around my upper body which was tightened as I was led to the interview room. I felt like a bloody dog being taken for a walk!

I answered the questions through an interpreter whose introductory advice was: "When you are arrested in Japan, you must admit your crime straight away." Upon hearing this, I pointed out that "In England, you're not guilty until proven," which failed to impress the inspector.

The intense interrogation had a daily timetable of 9am-11.30am, 2pm-5pm and 6.30pm to 9.30pm. That was three sessions a day for, as it turned out, 56 days.

Every single day was both physically and mentally demanding with not even the compensation of a decent meal to revive our flagging spirits.

Let me give you an example of the chefs typical menu of the day. BREAKFAST: Cold rice served with a bowl of miso soup, made from fermented soya beans, that had the appearance and taste of dirty dish water. A great way to get going with the most important meal of the day.

DINNER: Noodles of varying texture and consistency. Bearable but boring beyond belief.

TEA: Raw fish, and as a sweet treat, fish bones coated in treacle.

My polite request for cottage pie and spotted dick gained a frosty response.

I just couldn't stomach it no matter how hungry I felt. It was shit before it became shit and consequently I hardly ate anything. Because of this, they started to add bread with each dish in the hope that it might sustain me. But it didn't so I had to adhere to the 'Nippon weightwatchers diet plan.'

Back to the interviews, and I provided to the police statement after statement that filled reams of paper, in which I had to account for every hour that I had been in their beloved country. I told them as much as I could without implicating anyone.

It turned out that upon inspecting one of our travel bags, the police had found £5,000 worth of fake dollar bills, all in $50 denominations, along with 95 grams of cannabis resin.

Assured that it wasn't mine, all I could say when they asked me the inevitable question was: "I don't know anything about it."

Realising they couldn't implicate me for the possession of either of the illegal packages of goods they had found, I began to relax a bit more. That was until they decided to pursue another line of inquiry with potentially far more grave consequences.

After a brief discussion between themselves, they accused me of being the 'Mr Big' behind the operation, or 'crime boss' as they dramatically termed it.

They then went on to point out my tattoos, the body art favoured by their country's gangsters. The word 'Burnley,' which was the common denominator of my tattoos was construed as some sort of gangland affiliation in England.

The fact that I was the eldest of our trio affirmed the belief in their eyes that I was the organiser of a plot to flood the country with counterfeit notes to bring the economy down, with Eammon and Mooner my accomplices.

Besides converting dodgy dollars to yen, we were also apparently supplying a drugs cache to the 'Yakuza,' the word which denotes the Japanese mafia.

Up until that point, I'd been fairly compliant in answering their questions but these latest allegations were pure fantasy and I had to make a stand.

"I think you've been watching too many American movies," I replied curtly to their insinuations.

Changing the subject quickly, one of the investigating officers then bizarrely asked what I knew about the war. Maybe the only films they get to see involve the conflict.

"Which war? First World War? Second World War? Korean War?," I offered.

"We mean the war between Japan and America," announced another sharply.

They were getting to me now so I answered their question with the contempt it deserved.

"Do you mean that cowardly attack on Pearl Harbour?"

The interpreter translated my statement back to the speaker who went ballistic, helping the guards to manhandle me back to my cell in a rough fashion. I was later told his father had been a Kamikaze pilot in the Japanese Air Force, hence his aggressive reaction and abrupt suspension of proceedings.

A cruel game of bluff ...

Over there, the police can only hold a suspect for a maximum of 20 days without charge, so when this period elapsed, they told me I was being released.

My holdall was returned intact and amazingly still contained my money, passport and rail pass as well as both flight and match tickets. I then said my goodbyes to my fellow inmates on the prison wing and felt made up to be leaving this hovel at last.

How wrong could I be!

I was taken to a room filled with all the various inspectors involved with the case who took great delight at laughing in my face and generally taking the piss. It soon became clear I was going nowhere.

They'd set me up, probably because they didn't take kindly to some of my derisory comments during their cross-examinations. I was, to be blunt, fucking furious, but I knew I had to keep my cool.

The bastards! I had been convinced I was on my way home, but as I was led back to my cell, I had to unwillingly accept the fact that this was their modern version of Japanese torture. Even my hardened fellow prisoners thought the charade was bang out of order and expressed their condolences at my plight.

Apparently, for some reason, the 20 day ruling didn't apply in my case so I was left with no alternative but to reluctantly readjust to life inside Sapporo police station, with all hope of seeing any further World Cup football now gone.

After 56 days of relentless interrogation, I was eventually moved to a real prison called the Sapporo Detention Centre, where I was housed in a cell 24 hours a day.

During all this time, my only physical contact was with my consular officer from Tokyo's British Embassy, a Mr Julian Fletcher. He happened to be a Nottingham Forest fan so an instant football rapport was established.

I was of course worried about my BMW which was still parked up in West Bromwich, as well as my job as a plasterer with Rochdale Council and my mortgage, but Julian along with my lawyer sorted it all out.

The car keys were posted to England so a couple of mates could pick up my car and my ex-partner Deslie saved my job by getting in touch with my bosses at work to explain the ongoing situation. They kindly put me on unpaid leave for the foreseeable future.

Friends in Burnley held fundraising parties to cover my mortgage for two months, and my dad and Deslie deposited enough money into my account to cover my outgoing bills. A massive thank you to all concerned. Without you, I would have lost the lot.

But life inside was really getting me down now and my captors were succeeding in breaking my spirit. After persistently being told where we had been and what we had done, I was forced to concede defeat.

According to them, my fingerprints had been found on both the dollar bills and the weed even though I knew I hadn't touched either of them.

I was guilty purely by association, but my law attorney Mr Tadashi Furuyama informed me that a 'not guilty' plea meant it could be 12 to 18 months before the case went to court. I couldn't handle the demoralising prison regime for that long so I decided to follow Tadashi's advice and plead guilty, hoping it would lead to a suspended sentence.

While I waited for the impending trial, I found out that Eammon and Mooner were also in the centre but on different wings. I hadn't had any contact with them since we were nicked and I wondered how they were coping with the overly strict methods of depravation which constituted the daily routine of a miserable existence, all carried out to a precise timetable.

Imagine this itinerary if you will.

Besides living under virtual lockdown, your meagre 'meals' were served through a small hole in the door. You sat on a mat about two feet square with legs crossed and little more to do other than watch your toenails grow. There was no standing up or lying down allowed until 6pm when your bedmat could be rolled out.

We were walked to a shower room twice a week where you could also have a shave. However, no eye contact could be made with any other inmate and all ablutions had to be completed in an allotted 10 minute period, which was regulated by a stop watch. Complete silence had to be maintained at all times.

If it wasn't raining, from time to time you would be escorted to a single berth outside cage measuring about 15 feet by 8 feet to get your legs functioning a little. On one such occasion, I was placed next to an enclosure where Eammon was housed. I couldn't believe it. I hadn't seen him for months. Although talking was banned, I managed to have a whispered chat to him without detection before the guards took me back down.

Any kind of communication helped me cope with the tedium of prison life. I received the News of the World every week from my old man back home which was my primary link to the outside world. In addition, letters from Kev, Jack, Damo and Dave Burnley kept me updated with the more local news and footy results, which were all appreciated.

Remarkably, one day I had a visit from the Immigration Control Police asking the ridiculous question of why I had overstayed my visa and informing me that my passport had also run out. After explaining the bleeding obvious to them ie. that I was currently otherwise engaged, I promised to renew my documentation once free, whenever that might be.

Up before the judge at last ...

More long months passed until eventually our court date was set.

The three of us were brought to the dock together, the first time we had all met since that last night of freedom in downtown Sapporo. We each had our own supporting attorneys who we relied upon to do a good job representing us.

The prosecution claimed that we had collectively tried to bring the Japanese banking system to its knees and reiterated the police inspector's view that we were in league with the reviled Yakuza Japanese mafia. Both were very serious charges.

They requested two years hard labour for myself and Mooner with a term of three years for Eammon because of his alleged drug ownership.

All the testimonies made against us were well over the top and were exaggerated to maximise the level of shock the disclosure would cause.

Five thousand pounds worth of 'Mickey Mouse' bank notes and a wedge of weed were serious amounts, but they were hardly going to impact on either the monetary reserves of one of the richest countries in the world or the power of the drug barons of the Far East, now were they?

Yet that didn't stop our knees going weak and the colour draining from our faces.

We were all ordered back to prison for two weeks so that the judge could decide on the case. None of us said a word while we were in transit as the reality of what could happen suddenly hit home. Two years without Burnley was unthinkable.

It was the longest fortnight of my entire life, except perhaps for a previous summer holiday I spent on a rain-soaked Morecambe campsite.

Don't be fooled. I can joke about it now but only as light relief and in hindsight. It really was a horrific experience.

I didn't get a lot of sleep in those two weeks of waiting until at last 'D-Day' arrived. As we walked into court, I noticed that occupying the press seats were the immigration men who had interviewed me about overstaying my visa. "Are they waiting for me?", I thought.

The three of us stood in front of the judge as each of our defence lawyers took it in turn to make a convincing case for each of us.

The tension was tangible as we awaited our fate, but it seemed the judge had already made his mind up as he made his closing speech. Then came the sentences after our forced admission of guilt.

"Stephen Rimmer – Two years in prison, suspended for two years, and deportation from Japan at your own expense. Also a ban from visiting the country for 10 years."

Mooner got exactly the same punishment, with Eammon getting three years suspended and an identical banning order.

We just looked at each other and allowed ourselves a half-smile. At last we were going home.

Or so we thought. Wrong again!

We were taken back to the detention centre to pick up our luggage, each of us handcuffed to one of the accompanying immigration officers who had awaited the outcome of the proceedings. They then took us, still handcuffed, to Sapporo Airport where we boarded a plane for Tokyo.

Once there, we really thought we'd be put on the next plane to London, but for the second time it proved to be another false dawn as all three of us were shipped to an immigration centre prison without a word of warning.

As you can imagine, I was absolutely gutted.

By all accounts, the prosecutor had two weeks to appeal against the judges' decision on sentencing. I was beginning to wonder if I'd ever get home.

In my new prison, I shared a cell with a Nepalese bloke who spoke good English and a Mongolian who didn't, but there were some positive outcomes to the change in our place of incarceration.

We could buy decent food with our money and there was also a kettle to make a brew, and for the first time in six months, I had someone to talk to, which for me was the most pleasing aspect after more than half a year of solitary confinement.

Eventually, the appeal failed, and soon after the British Embassy renewed my passport and we paid £650 for a one way flight home.

We were made to sit at the back of the plane like naughty schoolboys and told that we were barred from drinking alcohol. However, once we were airborne, the pilot informed the 'trolley dollies' that he had no problem with us having a few snifters on the nine hour flight, so of course we did.

After landing at Heathrow, we said our goodbyes to Eammon who had his missus Jackie picking him up, and she forthrightly advised him straight away to "Put some better ink in your fuckin' printing machine!

Myself and Mooner then forked out £110 for a Virgin train to Manchester, eventually arriving back in Rochdale at 11.15pm that night.

Nobody knew I was being released, so it was a bit of shock when the new slimline Kaiser turned up for the Clarets' game at Leicester the following Saturday morning.

It was now the middle of September, 2003, but I was finally home.

I still think I was hard done by because as I'd previously stated, my only crime was being guilty by association, but then again, that was my own decision. What I knew for sure was that after my hideous ordeal I was just glad to be back.

I'll always be indebted to the British Embassy in Tokyo, and in particular consular officer Julian Fletcher, so much so that later in the year I sent him a Christmas card as well as a match programme from our 1-0 victory against his team Nottingham Forest at Turf Moor just to rub it in.

Hey, come on! You should know that some things don't change whatever happens in life!

Up the Clarets.

Kaiser

Su-Su-Suicide!…

In 2016 'Suicide Squad', an American superhero film came to the cinema screens. Based on the DC Comics antihero team of the same name a secret government agency recruits imprisoned supervillains to save the world from a powerful threat, in exchange for reduced sentences.

By coincidence it also happens to be the same title as Burnley's breakaway hooligan element. Formed in 1985 as a backlash to the football club's first ever relegation to the fourth tier of the English pyramid in over a hundred years since its formation, the malcontent followers kept the town's

Suicide Squad The Movie
Not based on Burnley's notorious hooligans, yet the violent
overtones of gang warfare are uncannily similar.

name in the football headlines for all the wrong reasons. From York in the north to Plymouth in the south. From Scarborough in the east to Wrexham in the west, all these locations and many in between had been left with indelible images of visits from Burnley's Suicide Squad and the "Su-Su-Suicide" chant ringing in their ears.

But where are they now as we approach 2018? The truth is the vast majority have either been banned from not only attending matches but also have to adhere to an exclusion order preventing any movement within a ten mile radius of Turf Moor. That is why you are more likely to find them watching the game on T.V. in a pub around Todmorden, West Yorkshire which complies with their restrictions.

There have been several serious football related incidents in the town since the new Millennium, two of which have regretfully resulted in deaths.

On Saturday December 7th 2002 a group of Notts Forest fans had agreed to a pre-arranged meet with members of Burnley's Suicide Squad. They didn't make the proposed venue outside of town but were found assembled in the centrally located Yates's Wine Lodge which the Burnley contingent entered. Remarks were exchanged and the Forest fans left the pub. One of them was punched in the back of the head as he left. Burnley fans followed with one hitting him over the head with a pint glass. He got up and started to walk away but collapsed and died next morning of massive brain swelling and brain damage at Royal Preston Hospital. A nineteen year old teenager later being charged with manslaughter and sentenced to seven years youth custody and banned from matches for the maximum ten years.

After another Division One (Championship) fixture at Turf Moor against Sheffield Wednesday rival fans clashed outside the same pub on Saturday April 26th 2003. Burnley had been thrashed 7-2 in the early kick-off by a team already relegated so feelings were running high amongst the locals.

The defendant was asked to move on from the scene of a clash by what he termed an over-zealous policeman. Discontented by their attitude he entered the back beer garden of the Yates's establishment and was suitably fired up to throw two heavy glass ashtrays over the wall in the direction of the Wednesday fans. By sheer bad fortune a Mrs O' Meara who was 79 and just 4 foot 6 inches tall was hit by one of the projectiles as she was doing last minute shopping prior to a dancing holiday in Blackpool. The lady suffered a fractured skull and a blood clot dying two months after the incident when becoming unconscious following an operation. A 21 year old man was jailed for four years after pleading guilty to the charge of manslaughter along with a six-year football banning order.

And it was Sheffield Wednesday who were once more the visitors when a gang of Burnley fans dubbed part of the 'Suicide Squad' were jailed for a total of 23 years for attacking the Owls supporters who had pre-arranged a drink at Burnley Miner's Club after the game. The match itself had ended in a 1-1 draw on January 18th 2014. However the said club is less than 100 yards from two of Burnley's Clarets' stronghold pubs The Turf Hotel and The Princess Royal which was always going to be a potential problem.

One police constable who was first on the scene described it as the 'most volatile incident' he had ever encountered in ten years on the force.

19 men and a 17 year old boy were jailed for between five and 22 months for their part in the proceedings, all of which were Burnley fans. Bans from all football stadiums for between six and ten years were also dished out.

In December 2014 a Southampton fan apparently trying to escape after-match clashes outside the cricket club drove off in a panic knocking over a 13 year old girl. He failed to stop but was arrested on the M6. He received a 27 week prison sentence suspended for 12 months whilst the victim who was thrown over the bonnet of the car received head injuries.

These represent the worst incidents of involvement associated with Burnley's hooligan firm although nowadays police intelligence prevents the vast majority of public disorder in the town.

But perhaps, no not perhaps, definitely the biggest accumulative sentences handed out somewhat predictably were after clashes with sworn local rivals Blackburn Rovers.

On Sunday 18th October 2009 Burnley were at last due to play the enemy at Ewood Park for the first time ever in a Premier League fixture.

Because of the inflexible security arrangements for this high profile fixture I had to set off a full 27 hours before the official 1p.m. kick off the next day to ensure my place in the 500 yard queue that filtered onto the waiting convoy of around 40 buses and coaches which were ferrying our restrictive ticket allocation of only 2,800.

Burnley lost the game 3-2 in the first time we had played Rovers in the top flight for 43 years. A number of the 'Suicide Squad' decided to commemorate the importance of this match by organising an attack on one of the Rovers' fans stronghold after match gathering points at The Station pub on Preston Old Road in a suburb of the town. Cars and taxis ferried them to the venue where around 60 opposition supporters were waiting. The Burnley element charging towards them not only encountered a hail of beer glasses and bottles but a charge from mounted police who had been tipped off by the following force helicopter who were tracking the offenders.

12 men were sentenced to a total of 32 years and tough banning orders totalling just short of 100 years.

Chief Constable Andy Cooke describing the accused as "half-wits and remnants of a bygone age".

But has that bygone age disappeared?

Besides Burnley shamefully topping the league for banned fans in 2015 when they were relegated for the second time from the Premiership, the passage of time over three decades of hand to hand combat have seen many members retire early from either their accrued injuries or the onset of old age and not being up to the task.

Then of course there are those that go on to meet their maker either naturally or in these two cases unnaturally.

The first of which has to be Norman 'Knuckles' Jones, a prolific hooligan who featured in the Injury Time chapter 14 of Part One.

As leader of Burnley's notorious 'Suicide Squad' in the 1980s his participation in their many confrontations from then onwards have contributed to the vast proportion of his 150 plus convictions, which must have filled a number of scrapbooks detailing his crimes in newspaper cuttings and charge sheets.

At the age of 60 Norman had received his fourth banning order from Turf Moor after police described him as one of the oldest and most prominent members of what they called the 'Burnley risk group'. A constable involved in the most recent arrest codenamed 'Operation Fixture' from the Lancashire police football banning unit commented,

"A football banning order will make our life a whole lot easier".

In his defence Norman insisted that,

"I have had enough now I've reached 60. That is the end of it!"

That was in May 2009 after his release from prison but in June 2010 he was convicted once more and sent back to jail for 360 days.

In later years Norman, a former fit and active ju-jitsu instructor and football coach would find himself battling a cocaine addiction.

In his 30s he was jailed in America after killing a man who pulled a knife on him in a New York nightclub. After serving 15 years of his sentence, including five in San Quentin he was deported back to the U.K.in 2001.

Although banned he would still continue to orchestrate his troops for missions as far away as Southampton appearing in person as their figurehead on regular 'away days'.

There can be nothing but condemnation for his catalogue of criminality, and yet I always got on socially with the serial offender whenever I bumped into him.

Perhaps the best example that expressed his devout loyalty to the area came when I was out on the beer in the party district of Hammerton Street on Halloween night Saturday after a home game on 31st October. Burnley with its Pendle witch connections is probably one of the epicentres of the traditional celebrations anywhere in the country.

The many pubs were packed to capacity and in one of the late night dens I happened across Mr. Jones himself. He gave me his usual welcoming hug which he did whenever we met, then asked me what I was doing up here. After informing him I'd been a corporate guest for the day and was staying over I enquired,

"And what are you doing in Burnley Norm?" knowing that he lived in Nelson around 5 miles away.

His reply just epitomized his belief.

"What am I doing here? This is my town!" added the man decisively.

Norman Jones passed away in July 2013, yet his name is to this day emblazoned on flags and banners carried by his previous legion of followers into football grounds across the country as a sort of hooligan homage to their previous leader.

Of the same fighting ilk was baby faced Iain McKay who was a regular fan both home and away even in the bad days of the old 3rd and 4th Division seasons.

Easily distinguishable by his curly blonde locks Iain was also a bit of a chancer. To make an income he would go on regular tobacco and alcohol trips across the channel selling on his contraband to assorted clients, along with a few illicit substances.

One of his customers reportedly owed him between £1,200 and £1,600 and a meeting was arranged to sort out the debt at a Lovers Lane car park to avoid detection that evening in October 2000.

Having been lured there Iain demanded his dues be paid up as soon as, to the 22 year old Asian youth.

But the only payment he received was in the form of a lead bullet to the back of the head. Police found him with his arms folded across his chest with muddied knees suggesting he had been forced into a kneeling position before death. A small entry wound to the back of the head causing a massive exit lesion from the barrel of a sawn-off shotgun.

In May 2001 his killer was sentenced to life imprisonment for what the judge described as the gangland execution of a small-time drug dealer. Upon review, after pleading that he wasn't the person who pulled the trigger the Royal Courts of Justice in London ruled the defendant should be free to apply for his release after 16 years, which of course happens to be 2017.

In 2001 Burnley had its own race riots which affected a number of towns and cities in the north of England which was widely proclaimed as due to social deprivation and high unemployment, making it fertile soil for the growth of resentment leading to violence. Add to that the case of Iain McKay's brutal slaying at the young age of 31 which bred revulsion amongst all Burnley supporters that knew him, and it is far easier to see why the town of Burnley kicked off with a week-long orgy of looting and rioting.

Although hooliganism is relatively rare at Burnley these days with no Lancashire rivals in their midst and numbers depleted as explained, the following Lancashire Police report from their successful 'Operation Fixture' dawn raids gives a precautionary insight into what could happen upon their reformation.

"Burnley F.C. have the dubious and unfortunate honour of being the unwilling host to a group of hooligans that are larger in number and more vociferous in their behaviour than clubs of a similar position in the league. The hooligan element at Burnley proudly refer to themselves as the Burnley Suicide Squad. The self-imposed title is derived from previous behaviour at away games where the single-minded involvement in violence against overwhelming odds could be described as suicidal."

36 Stand Out Fans

*There's football crowds, and then there's those individuals who
stand out from the crowd.
Photo by Gary 'Rocket' Jenkins in V striped shirt*

Most football clubs have a number of 'larger than life'
supporters that follow their team. Some are regular
attendees whilst others are less frequent spectators,
but their very presence and subsequent antics of such
characters inject a welcome dose of humour into the
match day experience.

Let me introduce you to a truly eclectic mix of some of
Burnley's most colourful personalities from around
the country.

'Pete The Claret' at home with a tinned version of this pre-molten soup.

Pete 'The Claret' Carding …

I'll start with the story of a fan that I know close to home. In fact, not only does he live in the Potteries, but his residential flat was little more than a stone's throw from Stoke-on-Trent railway station when I first met him.

Going under the name of Pete Carding or Pete 'The Claret' Carding as termed by his work colleagues, he has supported the club since 1963 and is one of a nucleus of around forty followers in the region. All can only attend matches infrequently due to a combination of family, financial or employment commitments.

As in Pete's case, because his portering job at the local National Health Service hospital insisted on weekend shifts as part of his contractual agreement, like the majority of these exiles, when the opportunity to watch the team perform locally comes along, they seize the chance.

To guarantee his attendance, once the fixtures were confirmed, Peter would request a day off from his holiday entitlement well in advance before other employees took up the slot. Well, that was the theory anyway, but on this particular occasion, to his utter dismay, the chosen date had already been booked by someone in his department. Nevertheless he hoped his application would be given due consideration.

At this point allow me to pose you, the reader, a couple of associated queries.

Assuming that you are an avid football fan, which is a strong possibility, given that you have chosen to peruse this book, let me ask this pertinent question -

"What lengths would you be prepared to go to in order to get to a game?" Additionally, "What level of pain would you be willing to endure to further that aim?"

It is highly unlikely that many would resort to the drastic measures undertaken by this man as told in the following, fully corroborated, extraordinary tale of devotion to the cause.

Only a few days before the scheduled 'run of the mill' Division Two fixture at nearby Crewe Alexandra that Peter had hoped to attend on Saturday February 1st 1997, his expectations were shattered. One of the catering staff had been taken ill and, with no available cover, Peter was told -not asked – that he would be required to fill that position in the cafeteria for the next few days, which, on this occasion, included the weekend. Pete's protestations that he had already made plans fell on deaf ears forcing him to take up the alternative duties as specified in his Conditions of Employment.

As you can imagine, Pete was devastated that it looked like he was going to miss the match he had set his heart on many months previous, and he was more than a little aggrieved that he had followed the correct procedure rigidly when applying for a day's holiday to take the time off. It now looked like his match ticket would be wasted.

Pete had been transferred to the works canteen and put on indefinite serving duties. Although rightfully rankled in his new role, he turned up to fulfil his obligations on the Wednesday afternoon shift. But by Friday his festering anger at the injustice of his treatment came to a head in somewhat sensational fashion.

Sick to the back teeth of being treated like a nonentity, he put into action a drastic plan that would turn out to be on the very outermost of the desperation scale.

Lifting the industrial sized soup ladle out of the deep rounded tureen to serve a customer, Pete purposely slipped, spilling its entire contents down the front of his chest. Falling to the floor in agony, a panicked member of staff threw a large saucepan of what turned out to be warm water upon his prostrate body in a dramatically failed attempt to neutralise the effect of the boiling hot liquid.

"Stupid bastard!" shouted Pete as the second wave of fluid only exacerbated his excruciating pain as he writhed in agony on the ground.

Indeed, it was too late; the damage had already been done. He was rushed to the Accident and Emergency department, which being within the hospital complex, was fortunately for him only a short distance away.

Peter suffered second degree burns to his upper torso causing immediate reddening of the skin and painful blistering.

He was carefully wrapped, first in gauze, then wide bandages that formed a broad swathe across his body, before being relieved of all duties and sent home to recuperate from his ordeal.

That night he followed the doctor's advice and rested accordingly. The following day he joined a couple of thousand Burnley fans at Crewe Alexandra's Gresty Road ground.

We'd met up before the game in The Brunswick pub on Nantwich Road, one of our designated gathering points. There he had showed me his padded up mummified body and told me the story behind it.

At first I doubted his tale, putting it down to excitable match day exuberance until receiving ratification from his workmates a few weeks later. In effect, Pete 'The Claret' had 'gone for the burn' for Burnley and there was more pain to follow.

With both teams competing for a top six play-off position, it looked like The Alex were going to claim the points with a goal scored soon after half-time, but with just two minutes to go top goal scorer Paul Barnes nicked a point with an equalizer.

As an instinctive reaction a burly Burnley fan grabbed Pete around the shoulders hugging him in an impromptu celebration of the goal, purely because he was the nearest bloke to him.

Peter let out an agonizing "Arrrgghh!" but the attached heavyweight interpreted his scream as a triumphant reciprocal roar and continued to squeeze the life out of him in sheer joy.

Hardy Pete went on to make a full recovery bar his superficial scarring with even the more suspicious of his colleagues concluding "No one would ever go to such extents in order to attend a simple football match -would they?"

Cozo.
Well, would you buy a second hand car from this man?

'Coz' forever NOT blowing bubbles ...

It is well documented in the opening chapter of Part One how I came to support Burnley Football Club. My life-changing declaration occurred when village mate Reggie Bradshaw had put me on the spot to pick a team after he had predictably pledged allegiance to newly top of the table Liverpool way back in the Easter Bank holiday of 1964.

I randomly chose Burnley only because of a memorably distinctive picture that appeared on the back page of our daily newspaper. It featured an upper body shot of the club's cantankerous Chairman Bob Lord that had been indelibly etched into my mind.

My simple selection process would from there on determine every decision on how I would conduct all aspects of my future existence, although I did not know that at the time.

In effect, fate had taken a hand in my own particular situation and although admittedly, such stories are the exception rather than the rule of a lifelong devotion to a football team, how about this following bizarre example.

Now firmly settled, he is based in the sedate surroundings of the West Sussex coast, along with his long suffering wife of many years Lynette. He plies his trade as an established, somewhat stereotypical second hand car dealer.

Going under the full title of Bernard Richard Cozi, this man of Italian descent is fast approaching retirement age. Known simply as 'Coz' to his friends, there is no denying that he is in possession of what some would chronicle as an amiable, lived-in face that would make many a bloodhound's heart race. This, combined with an incessant banter, and a knowledgeable half fact-half 'bullshit' persuasive manner, give him the necessary qualities to run a successful business in this field.

Described in his own words as 'an angry excitable extremist', Coz was born and raised in the East end of London on Boleyn Road, just half a mile from West Ham United's football ground.

On the 2nd February 1959 it was Coz's 9th birthday. Amongst his presents was one from his grandmother. Excitedly ripping through the colourful wrapping, he opened the parcel with great expectation. Glimpsing a claret and blue jersey he didn't need a second guess to ascertain what the prized garment was – or so he thought.

Holding it aloft with both arms, his eyes were immediately drawn to the eye-catching club badge that had been hand sewn on to the replica gear.

But facing him wasn't the distinguishing crossed hammers emblem denoting his home town team West Ham, but a more traditional heraldic coat of arms signifying Burnley Football Club. His grandma had bought him the wrong top!

Of course being brought up in the district, she understandably thought that what she had purchased from her local market stall could only be what thousands were wearing in the area where she lived. It obviously wasn't, and with a young Coz yet to pick a chosen football club to follow, his grandmother's misapprehension had decided that choice for him. From that day to this, and to his immense credit considering the intense pressure put upon him to 'ditch the shirt', he remains a devout follower of the true 'Clarets'. Attending a good number of games each season since, with an appearance at the FA Cup Final against Spurs in 1962, part of his prestigious supporting CV, he remains a good mate with many a story to tell!

Coz is also a friend to the stars, and this well respected pillar of the community within the leafy suburbs of Worthing has mixed with many past and present day footballers, not only through his business but also by virtue of his attendance at numerous charitable functions over many years. His enduring love for the game, both as a former local league player and now a supporter, remains undiminished.

Indeed, he claims that his close friendship to ex-Burnley player and manager Brian Miller extended to putting him up overnight on several occasions after attending meetings at nearby Goodwood racecourse. I wouldn't bet against it!

When you get up front and personal with Coz, he will inform you of his ambition in life which I have to say is some aspiration. He declares in all seriousness...

"One day I want to be Chairman of Burnley Football Club. That's an awful lot of used cars you've got to sell Coz!

Ever the optimist Jordan displays his 60 match accumulator bet.

The irrepressible Jordan Croisedale ...

As a visitor to Burnley, some away supporters still choose to ignore police advice and unwittingly stroll through the compact town centre sporting their team colours on a Saturday afternoon.

This preventative warning from the Lancashire Constabulary is made with good reason and, as such, should be taken seriously, for a lack of prudence could easily spoil the traveller's day out.

But it's not the threat of being attacked by the partisan locals that is the main concern, as on the whole the force regularly monitor possible flash points to avoid confrontational issues, keeping them to a minimum.

No, it's potentially far more frightening than that, and as yet is something the cops have not found a solution to. That peril is the very real danger of being 'JORDANED!"

Jordan Croisedale is a 32 year old man who has had his finger on the pulse of everything connected to Burnley Football Club since he was a teenager. A literal 'larger than life' character who suffers from an Attention Deficit Hyperactivity Disorder, which may be a contributory factor to his ungovernable social skills and his ability to eat one potato more than a pig!

With his distinctly protruding forehead atop a tall sizeable torso, his invasive manner to the uninitiated could easily pass as aggressive behaviour, but in the dog world Jordan would be 'Scooby Doo', the affable Great Dane in the popular childrens cartoon series, always on the lookout for a 'Scooby snack'.

Wired for sound with his ear phones plugged into the radio, big Jord's morning shift constitutes the breakfast run, whereby he checks out the deal of the day on the cafe menu boards. His predatory senses being immediately ignited by the seductive waft of bacon, sausage and egg frying on the griddle. Once locked in to his sensory radar, just like the bulbous character 'Wimpy' who appeared in another cartoon series 'Popeye', he will follow the aromatic smell to its source. Once found, there'll be a quick but chilling peer through the steamed up windows of the cafe to assess the price of his indulgence. This ritual will be repeated at up to half a dozen establishments until the best value offer is located.

After refuelling, Jord will bounce about town with an added spring in his step, keeping an eye out for opposition fans to accost in order to ask their views about the present state of their club and a predicted result.

Anything but a winning forecast for the home team will be met with disdain, an unforgiving frown and an in depth analysis of why theirs is the wrong prognosis.

In fact, the most hilarious example of Jord's over exuberance took place only five games from the end of our automatic promotion season to the Premier League in 2014.

Middlesbrough were the visitors to the town in a game that could have sealed runners-up spot if results had gone our way elsewhere. Four 'Boro' fans in their early twenties just happened to stroll into our meeting place for a pre-match drink.

Jordan's enemy tracker latched straight on to them as soon as they entered. With a loud snort through his nostrils, Jord sprung out of his seat and rampaged over to the unfortunate quartet, cutting off their path to the bar.

Expecting an imminent assault, the four young lads all pinned themselves to a central wall as a slobbering, spitting Jordan delivered his 'in their face' greeting:

"You've not come here to spoil our party, have ya?" he asked in his inimitable brusque but innocent manner,

After shaking their heads in bewildered denial to 'The Jord's' icebreaking enquiry, they were obliged to answer a few other football related questions before being allowed access to the servery in a state of delayed trauma. Unbeknown to them, they had just been 'JORDANED!'

The gentle giant's next task will be to call at all the bookies along the way to pick up and peruse his football coupons for that days bets before joining us for the 'Saturday Morning Club' in the Brun Lea Wetherspoon's outlet just off the main drag.

Our 'Saturday Morning Club' has become a pre-match meeting place for the early arrivals that want to discuss all things football to which Jordan is a regularly enthusiastic contributor.

Not that Jordan confines his pearls of wisdom to us mere supporters. Oh no! There was an occasion when he spotted our then Manager Stan Ternent walking around the ground. Armed with the latest news and rumours from the internet, Sky TV, and assorted papers, he approached Stan as he had done many times before in an attempt to confirm the speculation. But Stan, somewhat irritated by this regular unwanted attention, pre-empted his questioning by yelling out,

"Who've we signed today then Jordan?" inferring that Jord knew more about proceedings than himself.

Previous to Stan, when Chris Waddle was in charge for the 1997-98 season, suitably vexed by his regular daily inquisition he was moved to inform him accordingly.

"Blood Hell Jordan! I see more of you than my wife and kids!"

In 'Spoons' however he knows that he has a captive audience made up of scores of Burnley fans.

A few away fans do stray into here as it serves decent real ale at cheap prices and more significantly it is just down the hill from Manchester Road railway station.

As demonstrated, Jord will do a recce of the premises to first locate, and then acquaint himself with the opposition by way of his big broad smile before firing the first of many questions into the faces of the shell-shocked drinkers. After being showered in spray from Jordan's quick fire repartee, the punters usually make an early exit in a daze, shaking their heads in disbelief and vowing never to go back there again!

An uncalculated gamble ...

When we all move on, 'The Jord' will catch us up in the next bar on our route to gleefully wave his wad of betting slips in the air. They're generally all for small stakes but there are no doubles, trebles or four folds for this man; Jord will unfurl a copy of his predictions that resemble a Dead Sea scroll. His attempt to guess the outcome of anything up to twenty matches as one accumulator wager often gives him a potential, but extremely unlikely pay-out that will almost exceed the million pound maximum.

Of course, he generally gets nowhere near collecting a pay-out leaving him forlorn and frustrated. Yet there was one instance when he convinced himself that he'd won a considerable sum only to have his dreams shattered by an oversight – his.

It was Saturday February 5th 2011 when a Jay Rodriguez goal proved the decider in a 2-1 victory against Norwich City at Turf Moor in a Championship League game.

The match itself still had five minutes to run when big Jord came charging down the steps of the main stand like a runaway juggernaut to make a startling announcement. Swishing his lengthy Coral wager above his head in an animated fashion, he declared, "I've won! I've won!" There was a short pause before he excitedly continued, "I've won over seven thousand pounds!"

Of course congratulations were offered all round as he passed his duplicate betting slip copy around for all to see. And indeed, it stated that if all of his choices were correct, he would indeed be richer to the tune of £7,619.

But the match was still in progress as it entered added on time so we had to calm him down until the referee blew his whistle and the points were ours.

"Now then big lad just what have you won your bet on, and are you sure you're right?" I asked him.

"Each game had to have two goals or more in it to win" beamed an excited Jord.

"Great! Well done lad, now get the beers in!" was my final sentence as we left him to claim his winnings.

However, at 7.30pm, drinking in a Manchester pub, I received a phone call on my mobile off a disconsolate Jordan. Apparently the bookmakers hadn't paid him a penny; the actual terms of the wager being that each game had to have OVER two goals or more and not just the two or more that Jord had mistakenly misinterpreted it as.

Oh dear! Poor old Jord, out of luck again.

'Knock off' Nigel photo-bombs the triumphant Lancashire title winners.

'Knock Off' Nigel …

Nigel Standige lived in Walsden, a small village near to the town of Todmorden, West Yorkshire, a location that forms a considerable catchment area for Burnley fans when these particular tales took place.

Nige was given his dubious moniker initially, simply because he shares the same Christian name as the roguish wheeler-dealer portrayed in a past television advert, its intention being to dissuade the general public from buying illicit goods on the cheap that have been stolen or 'knocked off'.

However, our Nige is partial to a bargain too and is always on the lookout to seal a good deal or seize that golden opportunity, but since having this defamatory title bestowed upon him, he seems to have progressively tried to emulate this persona.

His quality of jokes probably gives the best insight to his character. Try this representative piece for a taster. He asks,

"Do you know anyone that wants to buy a sixty inch plasma TV for a hundred quid?" He added, "The volume button doesn't work but at that price you just can't turn it down."

Besides keeping an eye out for a personally beneficial ruse, dodge or scam, his subterfuge chicanery now seemingly knows no bounds.

Take the following instance for example.

Let's start with an illustration of his misrepresentation exposé.

Knock Off goes global! ...

For sheer 'brass neck' audacity, this 'gate-crashing the party' episode takes some beating at any level.

On Saturday 17th September 2011 Burnley were playing away down at Peterborough and I'd taken another Friday off work to make it a long weekend.

Before catching my train to Cambridgeshire, I was enjoying an early morning pint and the usual good value traditional breakfast at The Wheatsheaf, Wetherspoon's outlet in Stoke town centre.

I was just about to tuck into my first Lincolnshire sausage when my mobile phone rang.

It was 'Knock Off Nigel. He had travelled down to Taunton on Thursday to give his support to Lancashire Cricket Club in their 'do or die' match against Somerset who they duly beat to clinch their first County Championship in 77 years. After exchanging a swift greeting, I berated him for his bad timing just as I was about to dine.

"This better be good K.O., I've got a full English with my name on it right in front of me!"

"It is, I promise ya," he assured me confidently. He went on "Have a look at today's Times newspaper. I'm on the back page joining in the celebrations with the Lancashire team on the pitch."

"What, a little dot in a crowd scene? I enquired, mockingly. My question triggered an instantaneous response.

"No, it's the official group photo of them receiving the cup, take a look."

Our brief conversation ended and after wolfing down my 'brekkers' I headed for the newsagents.

Sure enough, there was K.O. looking flushed in the face from his heightened state of excitement. Similar photos also appeared in the Daily Mail and The Telegraph.

I caught up with him at the match and asked,

"How the heck did you manage that K.O.?"

He went on to tell me that after being stopped by a steward from getting on the cricket pitch to celebrate the momentous occasion after the game had finished, he informed the security official that he was part of the camera crew. When asked for identification to back his claim, 'Knock Off' produced a C.A.M.R.A., Campaign for Real Ale membership plastic wallet. Pointing to the large lettered acronym on the front, he was amazingly allowed through with nothing more than a boozing pass!

He went on to be photographed in the team pictures that were being beamed worldwide by the Sky Sports television channel, as well as subsequently appearing in a wide selection of newspapers and magazines.

Full credit to K.O.'s opportunism. It was a priceless "I was there!" moment and a tale he will regale for many years to come – and believe me he does!

'Rocky'

Derek 'Rocky' Mills ...

My support for Burnley Football Club now spans six decades of attendance. Throughout that time scale, I have come into contact with a myriad of loyal fans that follow their team with a genuine ardent desire.

However, some more than others do distinguish themselves by their very presence and outgoing demeanour. One such diehard falls effortlessly into this category.

That man is Derek Mills, or Mr Derek Sylvester Mills, to give him his full title. But that isn't the name he is known by to his legion of devotees. No, to them he is plain and simply 'Rocky'.

The obvious link being that his rarely heard off middle moniker is the same as the Christian name of the world famous Hollywood actor Sylvester Stallone who, of course, played the boxer Rocky Balboa in the 'Rocky' movies. But there is more to the connection than merely word association.

The fact is that our 'Rocky' also used to have the ripped physique of a prize fighter after pumping iron as a bodybuilder for many years. By all accounts he was a muscleman of some repute in the Lancashire region going on to win numerous macho man competitions along the way. Being such a hugely distinctive individual, Rocky would certainly have featured in Part One of my fan related story collection if only I had been aware of him. And believe me, at any match he's hard not to notice as his thunderous trademark rants are clearly audible in whichever part of the ground you occupy.

In truth, I hadn't either seen – or more to the point – heard any of his vociferous shrieks between the duration of those years covered from 1964 to 1987, and can only conclude that like many others, his support over these years had lapsed. Either that or he had temporarily lost his voice big style!

I do know that young Derek was taken to his first game way back in 1958 but I would estimate his real resurgence began with the 'Orient game' in May 1987 when my first half literature ended. That defining ninety minutes being the pure embodiment of inspiration to literally thousands of previously disillusioned followers.

Since then his commitment to shouting on the lads has grown into the fanatical classification of support. He continues to make a point of letting all and sundry know his feelings in rudimentary terms at each and every fixture he travels to, which is the vast majority.

On match days at Turf Moor the 'Rock' can be found outside the 'Bob Lord Stand' selling the club's half-time 'Goalden Gamble' draw tickets. He drums up trade by intermittently yelling out his hallmark Red Indian style battle cry. The very same one that he uses in the ground in a vain attempt to put off the oppositions goalkeeper when he takes a goal kick from the six yard box. I think that I've only seen it prove effective once in the last twenty years and that may have been an unfortunate slip from the custodian.

The remainder of Rocky's expletive riddled beratement or encouragement takes the form of short sharp shouts of limited vocabulary that rarely extend beyond two syllables and are despatched in a loud bellowing tone.

"Attack! Attack! Attack! Attack! Attack!" is probably his most positive reposte, with the more aggressive screech of "Get into them" rattled off with such machine gun rapidity that three words are amalgamated into one to make "Gerintoem! Gerintoem! Gerintoem!"

Besides firing a few 'F' words to all three match officials, even the fourth member of their party gets a volley of abuse if to his mind the wrong number of minutes flashes up on the electronic scoreboard to signal added time.

But of course, as it has always been, the greatest amount of discord centres around the referee with all disputed decisions greeted with his regular solo rendition of 'Wanker! Wanker! Wanker!"

'Rocky'
8 Snatch squad police haul the legend out!
Last game of 1998-99 season at Northampton Town 2-2
Div. 2 (Old div 3)

The Rocky horror show ...

Rocky generally travels down on the 'Boundary Clarets' coach, so named because their service picks up in the surrounding areas around the town.

As he lives on a smallholding along with his missus Jean Wylde Mills and an assortment of farm animals out in the sticks, he owes a huge debt of gratitude to the two Burnley stalwarts that ran the away trips.

Both Bill Hadfield and Neil Conway keep the miscreant on a tight rein and their 'old school' style of discipline seems to command the necessary respect from Rocky whilst in transit. But once in the stadium, and off the leash, he is a lot harder to control. With cries of 'Rocky! Rocky! Rocky!' ringing out from his terrace fan club just like scenes from 'Sly' Stallone's films, he becomes intoxicated by the atmosphere and plays up to the desires of the crowd.

Within most away grounds around the country the local police and stewards do seem to make allowances for Rocky's regular stream of profanities. This may have something to do with them being tipped off about his behavioural patterns by the Burnley based football intelligence officers who travel to each fixture on the road to maintain order and spot hooligans.

There again, some regional constabularies are only willing to take so much as demonstrated at a game at Northampton Town's Sixfields stadium in the late nineteen nineties.

After one too many of Rocky's Tourette like outbursts, a section of Northamptonshire police decided enough was enough and began to manoeuvre their way into the away stand to arrest him for foul and abusive language.

What they didn't realise is that a lot of Burnley fans regard the 'Rock' as their very one deferential Dalai Lama and will protect him at all costs from any insurgent forces.

Like worker bees defending their queen in the hive, Rocky's army of foot soldiers formed a human shield around their hero. The boys in blue drew their truncheons in an aggressive response to breach the angry flesh and bone barrier. After a fierce exchange of blows and curses, the blockade split open and the 'feds' moved in to grab their troublesome quarry.

But, true to his name, Rocky wasn't going easily and in the end it took eight burly policemen to apprehend an old timer!

His wife Jean Wylde Mills also hit the headlines as well as the interest of the regional TV company when a misplaced football slammed into her during a home game.

So upset was she over the incident that a case was prepared to sue Burnley Football Club for negligence which didn't go down well with their fellow fans. However, common sense prevailed and after a bit of coaxing, the allegations were dropped.

Mr Mills, having recently celebrated his 70th birthday, shows no sign of toning down his own particular brand of enthusiasm. Metaphorically speaking, this will be music to the ears for his legions of fans who class him as their favourite 'coffin dodger'. For football and Derek go together like firework and lighter.

So make no mistake, if you happen to ask folk in this part of North East Lancashire "What their favourite Rocky film was?" most would reply "That Football Tribes one, that our Rocky starred in on Sky TV".

Selwyn – The Court Jester.

"Magic our Selwyn, magic" ...

Last but certainly not least is 'Selwyn', yet another Derek. Real name Derek Colclough, he was dubbed this nickname due to his resemblance to veteran comedy actor Bill Maynard who played the bumbling title character in the 1970's sitcom 'Oh No, Its Selwyn Froggitt'.

In the television series whenever Selwyn got one over on his adversaries, his on screen associates would join in with a cry of..

'Magic our Selwyn, magic.'

The same seal of approval could also easily apply to our 'Selwyn'.

After Burnley's painfully slow decline through the divisions, I had watched them on all 92 grounds by 1987 and as supporters numbers decreased, you get to know the diehard fans that were still believing, of which Selwyn was one.

He lived in Hebden Bridge near to the town of Todmorden, West Yorkshire. An archetypal jolly ice cream seller, he worked purposely restrictive hours in his van to make himself available for games.

His quick wit and tinder dry humour were always evident when you bumped into him at the match. A big lad with a belly so large it warranted its own post code, and testimony to the number of match day pies that had passed that way through the years. But his bulging waistline didn't bother the man, in fact he was self-effacing enough to compose this terrace chant that was taken up nationwide to insult less than svelte looking footballers, fans, stewards and police. It went like this:

"Who ate all the pies? Who ate all the pies? You fat bastard! You fat bastard! You ate all the pies!"

Magic our Selwyn, magic.

I have two standout everlasting memories of Selwyn, one in a serious situation, the other funny.

The first took place at the previously well documented top of the table fourth division clash with Cardiff City at Ninian Park on Saturday February 29th 1992.

It was bad enough being bottled and stoned on the away terrace after that 2-0 victory but even before that powder keg atmosphere, Selwyn's mini-bus that he himself had driven down with his mates aboard had been tipped over on its side by Welsh yobs intent on trouble.

Not withstanding the Bluebirds fans' fearsome reputation, they had innocently pulled into a city pub on the way for a few beers that just happened to be a stronghold of Cardiff's infamous 'Soul Crew' hooligans. They, in turn, had given our lads a typical Cardiff City welcome.

As he made his way up the terracing steps towards our mob in the ground after his terrifying ordeal, looking pale and clearly shaken, he blurted out a classic Selwyn line in his unbridled anger,

"Next time I'm coming in a flamin' Sherman tank!"

It was the epitome of his character, making light of a dangerous escapade.

Sumo Warriors …

The second incident was far more frivolous and couldn't be further removed from the ugly scenes in the Welsh capital. It took place at Adams Park, home to the altogether more sedate surroundings of Wycombe Wanderers Football Club. A picturesque location set amongst woodland.

In an old Division Two (3rd tier) fixture that took place during the late nineties Burnley were once again trailing at half-time, which for some reason, always seemed a regular occurrence at this venue. It just added to the overriding mood of despondency that particular season.

Yet the day was brightened up hilariously when in a spontaneous show of machismo, two of Burnley's heavyweight supporters whipped off their XXXXL club shirts to challenge one another in a sumo wrestling contest. There for all to see was the biggest show of flesh outside Soho!

It was, of course, Selwyn taking on his good friend and equally amply proportioned contender Jock Bannerman.

In a series of earth shattering clashes they battled it out, very large belly to belly, behind the goalmouth at the front of the terracing. They resembled two warring bull elephant seals feuding over a sea cow. All that was missing was a narration from David Attenborough to complete the spectacle.

It really was a side-splitting sight as time after time their full colossal bulks collided like two planets from the solar system. Proceedings only coming to an end as the second half was about to commence when a watching policeman came over asking them to replace their shirts with the comment "You're far more entertaining than watching the match lads, so spectators might get distracted."

That was good 'coppering', adding a touch of humour to diffuse any antagonism towards himself and his colleagues.

The several hundred Burnley fans finished the performance with an enthusiastic repetitive rendition of...

"Sumo Sumo Sumo!"

Both combatants taking a bow to sustained applause from all parts of the ground. Half-time entertainment was never the same again.

These were just a couple of the many japes and scrapes Selwyn got himself into following his football club, his unwavering funniness staying with him until cruelly struck down by the evil that is cancer.

Now this was the biggest fight of his life. It lasted for eleven months during which his huge frame diminished drastically and he became almost unrecognisable as the Selwyn we knew.

Throughout his variation of treatments to resist the disease, he would still try to arrange appointments in between Burnley fixtures whenever possible. And despite struggling badly with his condition, which in the latter stages had spread to his liver, lungs and bones, he would insist on travelling. He was helped and escorted by, amongst others, his siblings, devoted driver Lisa and of course his loyal mate and fellow sumo wrestler, Jock.

Only a week before he passed away, aged just 50, I'd seen him at the Peterborough United away game on 17th September 2011.

He never gave in or complained and carried on regardless and one of his last messages to his family was "Don't worry, be happy."

A bravery and courageousness to be admired from a true Claret to the end.

37 Nine Lives Used: 2005

Battered and bruised.
My sheikh shades hide my battered face on the Bradford Burl
outing 1996.

Throughout our time on this planet we will all experience close calls in life that threaten illness, injury or in some cases, even our very existence. Many of these instances can be self-inflicted situations we put ourselves in, whilst others are randomly guided by the fickle finger of fate, when you are simply in the wrong place at the wrong time. Here are some such cases.

Have you ever wondered why some folk believe in the common myth that 'cats have nine lives?'

Well, the main reason moggies got a reputation for reincarnation is because of their durability to survive dangerous situations. Whether they are running out in front of cars or falling from a great height, their resilience is renowned.

In fact they have been known to jump off high rise buildings, or even skyscrapers hit by an earthquake, and still remain alive.

This is because of their amazing ability to twist very quickly in the air by what is termed a 'righting reflex'. Possessing a flexible backbone as well as having good balance and instinctive reactions has helped to nurture this misconception of having a multiple actuality.

Then again, maybe it is not the false notion that it seems to either 'puss' or person, as my personal log of perhaps narrowly avoiding making an early acquaintance with the 'Grim Reaper' demonstrates.

These are my nine chances used so far, some of which are naturally football related as you would expect, with a potent mix of alcohol and bravado thrown in for good measure to produce a hazardous combination under any circumstances.

No. 1. 1967. The tragic roundabout ...

As teenagers, it is common to go through certain rites of passage to prove your masculinity. One of my given tasks was to leap on to a speeding children's roundabout that was being spun furiously by my then best mate Paul Lukic, who also just happened to be the cousin of John, the Arsenal goalkeeper of the 1980s.

"It will definitely be a new record if you can climb aboard this baby Dave," encouraged Paul.

The idea being to complete one full 360 degree spin to claim the title of 'Supreme Champion'.

So jump on it I did, tightly grasping one of the holding bars that were affixed to the core hub of the structure.

But obviously not firm enough as I didn't even last a single revolution, with the sheer power of the centrifugal force sending me flying through the air backwards.

Knocking my head heavily on the hard ground as I landed, rendered myself 'sparked out' unconscious.

The muscular Paul picking me up and carrying a lifeless body draped over his shoulder like a sack of potatoes the few hundred yards to my home.

There I distinctly remember coming round to see my mother administering her own form of first aid which consisted of applying the flat side of a kitchen knife, complete with a knob of butter, to my throbbing bonce. It would probably be a case of being rushed straight to Accident & Emergency these days, but back then, the old remedies were deemed sufficient.

A bad injury to any part of the cranium can have far reaching consequences, thankfully after using the first of my nine lives, this one didn't.

No. 2. 1971. Mob rule ...

Being attacked by two or three youths at any one time can result in a collection of black and blue bruises to your body.

So imagine the consequences of up to two hundred perpetrators trying to 'duff you up' simultaneously in order to gauge the extent of such a beating.

That is exactly what happened to me and 'Rock Steady' Eddie Simmons from Leeds on an August Bank Holiday evening in Preston.

As detailed in Part One under the 'Injury Time' chapter three of us just happened to come across the wrong crowd outside the town's railway station.

Burnley were playing a Division Two fixture at Deepdale and we had arranged to meet up for five o'clock at the booking office.

No shops, pubs, cafes or even takeaways were open, so the streets were deserted at tea time. That is, all but for a rampaging mob of opposition supporters that introduced themselves to us by way of a rubber cosh to our temples.

Myself and Eddie got duly battered from head to foot, so much so that by the end of the sustained assault we both gave a good impression of looking like smurfs or modern day Avatars, such was our distinct blue hue.

By the time the Lancashire constabulary intervened, the remaining member of our party made an appearance. Pete Horsfield from Knaresborough, near Harrogate, had quickly sidestepped the slaughter, presumably only returning after the fracas had subsided with the intention of identifying the bodies.

Make no mistake, this was a truly horrific incident that could quite easily have had that grisly outcome.

No. 3. 1974. The underground crypt ...

This one could certainly have been avoided if only I had backtracked from entering a Burnley underpass before a home game against Wolverhampton Wanderers.

But pig-headedly I didn't, and walked straight into a fifty strong pack of 'Wolves'.

Way before the police had started their regimented shift, the away fans had gathered either side of the subway that connected the retro El Greco cafe to The Cat's Whiskers night club en route to Turf Moor.

A couple of young kids had even warned me in their colloquial accent that "There's Wolves down yon!", as they scurried up the concrete embankment to safety.

It was to no avail as I strode purposefully down into the tunnel with my knotted Burnley F.C. silk scarf leaving them in no doubt where my loyalties lay. I wasn't going to be intimidated in my own team's town!

After retaliating to the first punch thrown, the inevitable onslaught followed where I literally had the 'shit kicked out of me!'

Yet somehow I managed to put up a good enough retaliation to gradually, yard by yard, limp my way towards the steep exit and the eventual refuge of the Yorkshire Street 110 Club.

By my own admission it was a foolhardy show of misplaced bravado in what I termed 'my' adopted town, but if nothing else, I had at least made my point.

In reality, that day I made a crazy decision to enter what to all intents and purposes could quite easily have become my underground tomb!

No. 4. 1980. 'Pneumonia One' ...

I slept rough regularly throughout the 1970s decade both at home and abroad.

There were two primary reasons for this. Back then the customer couldn't book ahead to secure discounts of over fifty per cent on both train and hotel chains. Everything was a set price which wasn't particularly good value. Today each is proportionally much cheaper.

So even though I was in full employment during those ten years, my budget still did not extend to regular nights of accommodation or full price travel.

Circumstances would also take a hand as last trains or coaches home left well before you could connect with them after night matches.

This was the case for a period of a few years after games at Turf Moor when the last direct bus to Manchester was indefinitely suspended due to vandalism that the company claimed was caused by returning home football fans.

It meant undertaking a series of three journeys just to get me to Manchester where, after exhausting all the late night bars and discos, I settled down with the homeless in the Piccadilly Gardens Arcade shopping centre to await my first early morning train home before going to work after a quick wash and brush up.

Sleeping out on the continent wasn't as bad because I only went abroad in Summer, but the cold winter months on the streets of Britain's town and cities brought on a quite severe bout of pneumonia diagnosed by my village doctor as relatively serious to my wellbeing; the lung condition being stubborn enough to last for a full three months before clearing up. As the medical warning starkly states – "Pneumonia kills!", but fortunately not on this occasion.

No. 5. 1983. Tombstoning in Sardinia …

During a three week holiday on this Italian island I busked around the northern tip with New Zealander Brett Fleetwood. I sang my mostly made up songs, through a swimming snorkel as an improvised microphone, whilst Brett played guitar for an hour each night, raising enough in donations to eat and drink quite well.

It's where I met a 16 year old Italian girl student called Annalisa Columbo who hitchhiked with me after her parents had given their blessing. Although I only had a week long relationship with Annalisa, such was our instantaneous

A forced smile for the cameras before my 100ft leap ...

intimate bond, hers would form the middle name that I would give to my future daughter Clarette.

On one of our beer and picnic stops we chanced across a group of local youths taking a perilous 100 foot leap from a jutting-out rock face into the sea.

Sipping our cold beers we marvelled at their bravery jumping from such a height. Some of the group approached us and asked if myself and Brett were interested in doing the same daredevil stunt.

"I don't think so!" I politely replied, awaiting Brett's answer which was, to my surprise, affirmative.

Now Brett had informed me that he was an accomplished deep sea diver, so if anyone was going to take up the challenge, it would be him.

We both walked over to the take-off platform hewn into the cliff to get a better view. Painted on to an adjacent overhanging precipice in white paint were the numbers 30.3 metres confirming a 100 foot fall into the ocean below.

After psyching himself up on the rim for a full five minutes, I expected Brett to take a jump but he eventually retreated claiming it was far too dangerous. I accepted his expertise as a skilful diver of many years and carried on drinking my beer convinced he was right.

However, one of the group wasn't going to let our non-participation go unnoticed and started taunting us with a chicken sound as he flapped his angled arms to the side in a rapid motion of sheer piss-take.

"English chickens hey?"

"Cluck – cluck – cluck – cluck – cluck – cluck – cluck-cluck – cluck!" he kept on and on, until I decided enough was enough, I was going to do it.

Now I'm anything but a good swimmer, although when a pretty girl askes me the same question I assure her that l am a champion breast stroker! But now I had committed myself to the plunge with the clapping, expectant crowd looking on. There was no turning back, unless that is, I was willing to accept what would be a barrage of contemptuous ridicule.

I wasn't, and so I gingerly made my way to the tipping point to look down on the daunting sheer drop from its precipitous edge, even managing a forced smile for the cameras.

As I don't do diving very well at all, my plan was to go into the water feet first, with my arms tucked in tight to my side in order to lessen the impact. This was what most of the participants were doing anyway, an act that is now known as tombstoning.

... and down I go!

Taking one last deep breath, I counted to three and took the plunge. Instinctively my arms pulled away from my body resulting in a loud slap as I hit the sea.

I'd had the bottle to take on their challenge, but now I had to survive the task. Since my school days I'd only dived ten feet at the baths to pick up a rubber brick to gain my first badge of achievement, now I was plummeting almost to the depths of the ocean bed.

Down down, deeper and down, to quote a Status Quo line, it seemed that I would never ascend such was the great height I had hurtled through the air.

My descent finally levelled out and I was now faced with the ordeal of a return journey to the top.

Desperately trying to hold my mouth closed, I straightened my arms to cut through the massive expanse of water until finally after what seemed like an absolute age, I broke the surface sucking in the light sea breeze.

The bathers broke into loud applause with accompanying cheers to herald what I have to admit was an act of sheer stupidity that could quite easily have cost me my life in a watery grave.

Even more chilling, upon enquiry we found that all the other participants were established cliff divers!

No. 6. 1985. Almost killer cholera …

I was at a very low ebb to begin with as I set off on my 70 day round the world tour a week after Burnley's relegation to the Fourth Division of the Football League. This was to be my convalescence trip of a lifetime to take my mind off the ignominy of my club playing in the basement of the English game for the first time in their history.

It certainly wasn't going to be a luxurious trip as I had less than five pounds a day to survive on. That's how I found myself attempting to live like the locals in Old Delhi at my first stop in India, for 25 pence a night.

With the temperature touching 100 degrees Fahrenheit in the shade and my room having no air conditioning and little ventilation, it certainly wasn't conducive to a comfortable night's sleep by any stretch of the imagination.

Litres of bottled water were being consumed to avert dehydration, as well as the ubiquitous cups of 'chai', sweet milky tea. Yet within days I fell ill big style. Severe bouts of diarrhoea followed, combined with a complete loss of appetite and an incapacitating restriction of movement.

So much so that I could only just about bring myself to getting up to go to the toilet, which in one day alone amounted to 32 visits ticked off on my already graffiti ridden walls as an unwholesome reminder.

As a result, my weight plummeted by a massive 20lbs in only 10 days, the last four of which not seeing a single morsel of food pass my lips as I slipped into a moribund decline.

After initially being diagnosed as the parasitic organism that carried the scientific name Giardia Lamblia, which is a species of a single-celled protozoan microscopic animal that colonises and reproduces in the small intestine, even worse medical news was to follow.

Transmission of this particular bug is via the faeco-oral route, which basically means a lack of sanitation as it is usually passed on through contaminated drinking water.

This is generally the case for the second more serious type of illness that attacked me. That turned out to be a common strain of cholera which included severe, watery diarrhoea, stomach cramps and continuously feeling sick as its symptoms.

Without treatment, dehydration can quickly set in leading to a sudden massive drop in blood pressure which in the most severe cases can prove fatal. To prevent this I drank regular doses of powdered glucose to sustain me.

As this book proves I did survive, after intermittent onward visits to hospitals in Australia, New Zealand and finally back home in England.

It would take a good six months to finally clear up. But at that time, just over 30 years ago, I really did think that the final whistle was about to be blown.

No. 7. 1986. 'Pneumonia Two' …

Ask any rough sleeper which weather conditions they fear the most and nine out of ten would say the severe cold. Because while fierce winds and rain do make street life considerably more miserable, those elements can be protected against within an enclosed shelter. Shielding yourself from an acute drop in temperature is far more challenging.

That is how I believe I got 'pneumonia one.'

Then, soon after my first bout of lung inflammation my travel luck changed. Making my way round from the Longside terrace to the Bee Hole End after a 1-1 draw with Shrewsbury on a Tuesday night in a competition that carried the inanely contradictory name of the Anglo-Scottish Cup, I bumped into a Burnley fan that I'd last chatted to outside Arsenal's Highbury ground in 1969.

It was August 1980 when 'Tricky' Trev Slack first greeted me and then informed he was living in a village just outside Stockport. His offer of a lift was instantly accepted by myself, meaning that I could catch that vital last train home. From thereon in, my newly discovered chauffeur would be the difference between a night out with the vagrants or a night in the comfort of my own pit!

However, although Trev travelled to a good number of away matches in the lower leagues, there were still quite a few long hauls that still necessitated an outside sleep-over, particularly the numerous far flung destinations in the Third and Fourth divisions.

As a consequence along came 'pneumonia two'. But this time more virulent and debilitating. Coughing up deep seated phlegm is a horrible side effect of the illness but even with antibiotics to kill the bacteria, it took another long three months to fully clear such was its hold.

The second attack had further weakened my lungs with the doctor's final appraisal confirming my thoughts. "Contract it again David and it could just be the last time you do!" Point taken doc!!

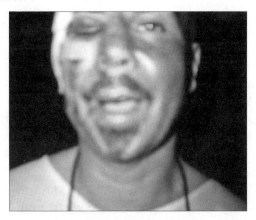

The aftermath of my R.T.A. dressed as an arab for our Bradford Burl outing.

No. 8. 1996. A serious road traffic accident ...

England supporters will remember 1996 as the year they almost got to a major tournament final, but personally I will recall it as a time that I used up another of my nine lives with thirty stitches to prove it.

As the weekend approached I was making last minute plans for our annual 'Burl' outing. Around a dozen villagers were due to travel to my chosen destination of Bradford, West Yorkshire.

With it being a large multi-racial city, our choice of fancy dress for the trip could have been described as not intentionally provocative, but more overtly daring.

We were going as Arab sheikhs, complete with white robe and headscarf. For extra authenticity each of our party were to grow a goatee style beard in keeping with the appearance of many from the middle east states.

As founder member and president of 'The Burls' I had intentionally picked the day to coincide with England's crucial Euro 96 fixture against the old enemy Scotland to add an extra bit of spice to proceedings.

It was going to be our usual early morning departure by mini-bus to take in a full day of drinking so I had made plans to spend a quiet Friday night down at our village local the Offley Arms.

That was until I got a call from Mick Fitzpatrick from Knutton who was generally an infrequent guest on our weekly lads night out. What the heck did he want at this late hour?

'Fitzy' as we abridged him, had been nicknamed 'The 70s porn star' for still sporting an audaciously smarmy 'Magnum P.I.' style moustache that his wife Rose forbid him to shave off, probably because of that very reason. The sort of bloke that would sing 'Islands in the stream' or 'I got you babe' on karaoke night.

Add that to the rumour he was hung like a 'Vim tube' in the trouser department possibly explained why his missus always applied a deep coat of rouge to her cheeks to mask her pallid, worn out look after bedroom exercises from the night before. However, it has to be said Rose always seemed to have a wide smile on her face whenever you met her come what may.

Amongst others he'd also been likened to Kevin Webster, the 'grease monkey' car mechanic from the long running

Coronation Street soap series as well as Bob Carolgees the master puppeteer of 'Spit the Dog' fame, also of the 1970s. So you get the picture, Fitz had 'IT' in the middle of this shortened surname because he thought he was just that.

But why was he ringing me today of all days, he knew I had a heavy weekend ahead.

All was revealed in an impassioned plea, "Hey Ralphy it's my birthday today. Do you fancy coming out for a few pints to celebrate it with me?"

"Bloody Hell 'Billy no mates' don't you realise it's the Burl outing tomorrow? Probably the biggest drinking day of the year!"

"I know it is, I know it is," Fitzy countered, "But I can hardly go out by myself on my own birthday, can I?" he asked forlornly.

At that moment I burst into a quick rendition of Roy Orbison's song 'Only the Lonely' mocking his lack of a social circle of friends. In actual fact having worked in a supervisory role at the local Rists Wires and Cables for over 20 years, a plant that produced integral parts for motor cars, he was very well known. But he'd left it too late to organise anything, hence the desperate phone call to myself.

"It won't be a big session Ralph, I just want a bit of company mate. You are my mate, aren't ya?" Fitzy whimpered.

"Cut that out now Fitzy! You're beginning to sound like a pervert. OK I'll come to ya rescue, but I'll have to cycle in as there isn't another bus for over an hour. Dry those crocodile tears and I'll meet you at The Cherry Tree beer garden as it's such a nice night. See you at 8.30."

"Cheers Ralph, I won't forget this. I might even buy you a pint", quipped Fitz sarcastically.

Fitzy wouldn't be the only one who wouldn't forget the night. As it transpired, neither would I.

With it being such a balmy evening I plumped for shorts and sandals to coordinate with my lightweight tee shirt as the weather forecast predicted another dry night in keeping with the previous week.

In half an hour I had ridden the six miles to Newcastle-Under-Lyme, our customary night out town.

'Vim Tube' was already smugly sitting on a bench table in the grassed front beer garden that overlooked the busy A34 Stafford road. A broad grin spread across his caterpillar coated mush clearly showing he was pleased to see me.

"Happy birthday Fitzy!" I greeted him cordially, "I just hope you appreciate this sacrifice," I added, just to make him feel more obliging.

"Cheers Ralph, I've got ya out of the village anyway haven't I?"

"Don't push it Fitz. I'm only here for a few, because as you know it's always an early dart for the Burl outing".

Fitzy had been to a couple of our trips but had given them a miss lately as some in the recent past had descended into disorder with local youths at our destination venue.

We went a few more pubs and I'd had no more than four pints of ale, half our usual intake on a typical Friday with the boys, before I bid birthday boy farewell at exactly 10.30pm. It wasn't an issue being over the limit on my bicycle as during the last three decades I had regularly ploughed a straight path with double figures inside me finding no hint of a problem controlling the trusty steed.

My lights were on and I was heading home for a good kip before the following days' excesses.

And that prognosis was going perfectly to plan until just a mile outside my village.

I was going quite a lick on a downward stretch at Finney Green, location for the sensational 1970 Hollywood music festival extravaganza that featured Grateful Dead, Traffic, Free, Black Sabbath and Mungo Jerry amongst many others.

I never made it home on the main night of the gig choosing to stay on site to soak up the atmosphere. This time, just outside the same location, I wouldn't have a choice.

Trying to avoid easily the largest pot hole on the route I attempted to swerve around it. Out of nowhere a car sped past me forcing me at speed into the substantial cavity.

The resultant impact bucked me out of my saddle and skewed my bike into the kerbside, yet I still managed to gain enough control to run along what was a deep guttering level.

Now I had the immediate task of carefully extracting my cycle from the narrow ravine back onto the road, knowing that at the 30 mph pace I was travelling, any sudden movement of the front wheel wouldn't clear the steeped tarmac bordering.

Of course gradually applying the brakes may have been an option but alas not one I chose, as I tried to ride out of the crevice hoping my propulsion would be powerful enough to clear the perimeter.

It wasn't! As soon as the rim of my tyre touched the side to edge back on track, the rear of the steering wheel hit the kerb at the same angle propelling me over the handlebars into the middle of the highway.

My head slamming the surface face down, I was temporarily concussed with blood pouring out of my gaping wounds.

A following car had seen the incident and phoned for an ambulance. It later transpired that the offending driver had actually come to a halt fifty yards further up the road before deciding to motor on.

So the combination of his or her recklessness, and a plainly dangerous pot hole landed me in hospital just hours before the 'Burl' outing.

Yet as I lay on that trolley I had ever such a deep sense of inner calmness, an almost out of body experience I suppose.

With my black eye closed and with my wounds cleaned out I had plenty of time to think about what had just happened.

What kind of person would drive off after an accident? A heartless one I concluded, which was sad.

Would I have any permanent brain damage after such a crashing fall?

And how would I make what was now today's trip as the duty nurse wanted me to stay in to recover for the weekend?

Well after convincing my carer that I had to be discharged as I was the sole driver for an Asian wedding booked for Bradford that morning, she wilted, and pulled out all the stops to get the surgeon to apply thirty stitches to my ear, eye and lip transforming my bruised and battered face into Frankenstein's monster.

The blatant, but completely necessary white lie had won me a reprieve and, with no sleep, I took my place at our meeting point in the village to the utter disbelief of our lads, but not before I had all but completed the Sun newspaper crossword to evaluate my intellect. With only two clues unsolved I reasoned I was around the same level as previous, to my great relief.

The police asked me to collect my mangled chariot from the local station on the Monday and, would you believe it, by the end of the week our local council had not only filled in the culpable crater, but also a three mile stretch of the A525 where the incident had occurred. Probably after a police tip off methinks to prevent any liability implications, no doubt.

As for our day out, it really was a good one. The progressive intake of alcohol gradually anaesthetizing my pain, with the rig out of sunglasses and long head scarf doing just enough to prevent me scaring people to death with my newly acquired nickname of 'The Elephant Man!'

The highlight being England beating Scotland 2-0 with Paul Gascoigne scoring one of his most memorable goals ever for his country in the European Championship.

Gazza controlled the ball on the left side of the penalty area, flicked it over centre half Colin Hendry who slipped trying to adjust his footing, before slamming home a volley for the second goal.

This, just a minute after the Scots had been awarded a penalty to equalize. McAlister's shot being saved by the elbows of goalkeeper David Seaman.

Our charity collection raised a handy £150 plus for the Bradford burns unit, and after a full on session of a couple of gallons of beer apiece, our party retired to an amazingly cheap curry house after midnight to finish off our festivities in style at around £3 for a sit down meal.

Reflecting on an incident free excursion considering our risque Arab attire in one of the country's biggest cities, I felt an air of accomplishment from what could easily have been a fractious weekend.

Just then one of our group lamped a diner full on the jaw. It was 'Soapy Suddes' taking exception to a derogatory comment made about his outfit.

The Indian proprietor asked us all to leave or he would call the police. But as the attack took place in the early hours of Sunday morning, I'm not going to count it as spoiling what was really a great day. And after my serious mishap on Friday night I was just simply glad to have been part of it!

No. 9. 2005. Off my trolley ...

Before you read any further let me state from the outset that I am the first to agree that my participation in this story can only be regarded as the height of foolishness bordering on insanity.

It represents the sort of impetuous lunacy more associated with a demented teenager than the 50 year old pillar of the community I was aspiring to be at the time – not!

Let me paint you a picture of proceedings. Myself, along with regular drinking partners Weedy, Fitzy and Zippy, were coming to the end of our weekly Friday night out having consumed our usual considerable intake of beer on a balmy summer's evening.

As we approached a subway to take us under the road to our final pub, there right in front of the entrance is a discarded supermarket trolley.

What would be your initial reaction to seeing an abandoned receptacle a long way from its home?

Outraged by the irresponsible behaviour of the moron that could carry out such a crass and pointless action perhaps?

Then maybe in the morning phoning the particular store that it came from, which in this case was 'Morrisons', to inform them of their abandoned property and giving them the location for collection by a member of staff.

Normally, I would be the first to echo that condemnation and latter course of dutiful conduct wholeheartedly and unequivocally.

But, as we all know after a belly full of beer, clear thinking and due diligence go out of the window.

All I could see in front of me was a vehicle of transportation that could give me the opportunity to re-enact the Jamaican bobsled scene from the film 'Cool Runnings!'

So without further ado I shouted a "Look out, I'm coming down!" warning to any pedestrians within the underpass and prepared for my steep descent.

Taking a short run up I jumped into the metal basket and careered downward at high speed with the only control of its direction being to jerk the front wheel over to the left or right by my body weight.

It was hardly calculus, as anyone will tell you that the wheels on these contraptions have an agenda of their own, flicking every which way but loose.

With the 45 degree dog's hind leg corner fast approaching I figured that the only way to take the bend was to lean my 'machine' over to the right like motorcyclists do in T.T. races.

It turned out to be a totally flawed manoeuvre of course as the extra heaviness to one side flipped the improvised people carrier on to its side before colliding hard into the opposite wall with a loud crash.

I'd managed to roll into a heap on the floor before impact with the trolley's side, forming a barrier between me and the cemented shell, sustaining just a few superficial bumps and bruises. Had I been propelled head first into the concrete interior, there is no doubt I would have suffered life threatening injuries.

And therein lies the lesson. If you do ever consider slaloming down such a steep escarpment at high speed in a supermarket trolley, make sure you:

"Always wear a helmet!"

Naturally the lads just laughed it off as a drunken jape but when I considered the potential consequences of what could have happened in the cold light of day, I knew I had behaved like an absolute 'plank!'

So, there you have it my full quota of reprieves extinguished. Well not quite, as I seemed to gain a bonus award for my endeavours after a party piece dance floor manoeuvre went spectacularly wrong.

It was a celebratory evening as England had just beaten rival opponents Argentina 1-0 in a World Cup match in Sapporo, Japan. That result going some way to avenging our nation's knockout to the same country in that infamous defeat in the previous tournament that I had attended in France 1998.

Of course, I wanted to celebrate the momentous victory well into the night. Which I did with my pal Weedy in many pubs along the way. But I was hankering for a chance to throw a few shapes on the floor. I would get my wish but not quite in the way I intended.

'The Weed' suggested The Revolution Bar would fit the bill as it was student night and accordingly be quite busy. The chain of nationwide Vodka bars does seem to have hit on the formula of how to get many scholars to hand over quite a proportion of their education grant to spend on their grossly overpriced drinks portfolio.

But that was their choice, as it was mine to dance. The venue we'd chosen only had a small wooden floor to perform on and yet at 10.30 p.m. only me and Weedy were doing so, on the upper level of the premises.

"Come on students! England have just beaten Argentina. Why aren't you celebrating with us?", I yelled across the room.

A couple of youths in England shirts did take me up on my request, but their lack lustre jigging hardly compared with my version of a 'Flea dance' and Weed's 'electric shock' manifestations.

To liven up proceedings, goaded on by Weed as usual, I demonstrated my party piece to trigger a reaction.

This takes the form of a hand stand up against the wall, usually where I remain for a few seconds until my loose copper change falls out of my pockets with the more valuable coinage safely tucked away.

No I don't know why either! But it always gets an attentive response from the gathered drinkers.

The only problem being that there was no wall around us, jut the stairway down to the ground floor.

That'll do I thought. It was around five-foot-high so it should meet my temporary requirement.

What a gross miscalculation! Being over six foot myself, as I perform the exercise the propulsion of my legs over the top of the banister went on to flip the rest of my whole body along with it, resulting in my arse being firmly wedged between the base frame and the hand rail twenty feet above the ground level.

Cue the trio of musclebound bouncers who scampered hurriedly up the stairs to roughly prise me out and escort me arm in arm out of the building to the utter merriment of the following Weed.

If my backside hadn't lodged within that stairwell I would certainly have sustained very serious injuries if I had survived the fall at all.

Slightly sore and battered, but still in the mood to finish the night off we turned the corner to access the neighbouring modern day 'Lymes' reincarnation of what used to be the traditional pub titled 'The Bulls Vaults?'

Approaching the entrance rubbing the lesions on my arse cheeks as I proceed we were both brought to an abrupt halt by the outstretched arms of a couple of bruiser bouncers whose gnarled faces might as well as had 'no entry' printed on their foreheads.

"What's the problem mate? There's no dress restrictions tonight are there?"

"You're not coming in!", the lead doorman insisted without choosing to answer my question.

"But why?", I protested aggrieved at his abrupt stance.

"Because you've been barred from the 'Revolution Bar' tonight", he finally explained.

Then it dawned on me that all monitored licenced premises operated a pre-warning system through the two-way radios that they equip their security staff with.

I'd been well and truly rumbled for literally arseing about!

Nine lives my arse! This cat's got a few more to use up yet!

Bénédictine

And whilst on the subject of alcohol did you know during World War I men from the Burnley area were recruited into units known as pals' battalions that made up the Lancashire regiment.

Many badly injured soldiers were withdrawn to convalesce and re-group near Fécamp in the Normandy region of France, which was also home to the Bénédictine order of monks. The story goes that they had developed a herbal liqueur at their abbey, naturally named after their title of Bénédictine. The British casualties were offered this strong alcoholic concoction to ease their pain which became a comfort to them, so much so that after hostilities had ceased, the Burnley based contingent brought some home and passed it on to friends in the town.

Nearly 100 years later, the pubs and clubs of Burnley still do a thriving trade dispensing this sweet spirit, with 'The Burnley Miners' Club' located near to the football ground being the world's biggest single consumer. A 'Benny and hot' (Bénédictine and hot water) is to this day still sold at the licensed bars on the concourse areas of Turf Moor for the hardy few that still partake of this tradition.

38 Any Job

To afford a total passion for football does mean considering any job that becomes available, outside matchday hours of course.

That is why in the past I have taken on 16 hours a day seasonal work, attempted 80 different occupations and suffered the inevitable periods of unemployment when my contract ends. The following extracts are case studies from all three.

Just three hours sleep a day...

So let me start with the 16 hour day placements.

When Christmas and New Year come charging along, I don't need to tell you of the added financial pressures they bring. These days the commemoration seems to carry a prerequisite appeal for you to spend well beyond your means all in the name of nothing more than naked commercialism on everything from food and entertainment to a compulsory Aladdin's cave of gifts and presents.

And for the dedicated football fan monetary matters get even more stretched over the festive break as it can entail up to five matches within a period of just ten days.

That is the primary reason extra provision has to be made for the doubly concentrated outlay of cash. In order to survive this hectic holiday schedule there have been times when I have taken on two daily eight hour shifts to compensate for my outgoings.

Being hired by a pair of separate employers my first shift would start at one of the local Royal Mail depots sorting Christmas cards into the relevant post coded pigeon holes ready for bagging up and collection. That would last until 8p.m., which gave me just enough time to quaff a couple of pints before boarding my agency minibus to the pie factory at Market Drayton, Shropshire working the night shift from 10p.m. to 6a.m. There, I would lift the heavy batches of produce on to my conveyor belt to detect any metal contamination in a quality control capacity.

By the time the return bus dropped me off to connect with my public bus transportation it would mean not hitting the sack until 8a.m. That would allow just three hours sleep before preparing once more for my sorting office job. Reliant for weekly periods of five days on this minimal amount of kip and progressively feeling like a dead dog , I wouldn't wish this sleep deprivation ordeal on any one. However, it has to be said that the two weekly wage packets helped cover the Yuletide and New Year extravaganza.

Temporary occupations generally come the way of agency work for which I was registered with several. They aim to recruit as many suitable candidates as possible to add to their portfolio of workers that will generate them a lucrative daily hiring rate, being paid for by companies that require an immediate ready workforce.

Maybe that is why in my experience the adjudicators of the required designated entrance exams, will in a lot of cases exercise a very generous degree of tolerance.

For example door supervisors or bouncers are never going to win a B.B.C. T.V. Mastermind title but their sheer general enormity and brute strength can make them perfect deterrents for this post. That is why several of my friends of a reasonable, but possibly not required intelligence tell stories of a little 'helping hand' to allow them to proceed to the recruitment process.

In my particular case the invigilator loudly declared that he was going for a ten minute 'fag break' ¾ way through my, and half a dozen others competence test for the position of electrician's mate, in essence an assistant to the main 'spark'. For our gathered candidates that was taken as a signal to cross-check our multi-choice answers, which I certainly did as I simply just didn't have a clue in regard to the vast majority of questions.

The reason for this is I just don't do D.I.Y. and am more likely to return such a request with its acronym of "Do it yourself!"

Don't get me wrong I will always apply the maxim of 'Nothing ventured, nothing gained' when looking for work and would like to think I adapt and learn as I go along in whatever capoacity when faced with tasks and procedures completely alien to me. But once they changed the colour coding to the cables I gave up trying to wire up a household plug and decided to leave any kind of electrical work to the experts.

So the head of recruitment gave us a fifteen minute interval before asking us all back in to announce very enthusiastically that "I am pleased to inform you that you have all passed!"

Well surprise surprise we were all in!

The following Monday all clocking on at what was then the North Staffs Infirmary, now the Royal Stoke hospital on a major Laing O'Rourke contract to re-wire a complete ward.

A quick safety awareness test and within an hour I found myself on wheeled scaffolding tasked with the assignment of drilling out holes in the tall ceiling to insert the metal support rods for the electrical tray that supports the cables along a 100 yard stretch.

That phraseology is second nature now after being amazingly offered subsequent contractual electrical mate's positions, but back then I seriously didn't know my arse from my elbow. So much so that when attempting my first hole drilling manoeuvre, not conversant with the mechanism of a power tool I pushed and prodded relentlessly into the ceiling plaster making absolutely no impression for a good five minutes.

My toil had caught the eye of a proper electrician as he walked past below who shouted up to me, "Hammer, hammer!"

Suitably perplexed and sweating profusely after hardly making any indentations, shattering a couple of drill bits and levelling another completely flat in the process, I blew my top at the passer by.

"Even I know you can't use a fuckin' 'ammer to make holes in that ceiling. It's too fuckin' hard!", I replied in vexatious tone.

The tradesman just laughing out loud before carrying on walking.

"What a stupid notion", I whispered under my breath, wondering why he would suggest such an option in the first place. Then all became clear as I glanced down at my power drill control when I spotted a small hammer symbol on the opposite side of my switch.

Quickly flicking it on I tried drilling again and bingo, it eased into the concrete surface.

Believe me, that 'Mr Bean' moment perfectly demonstrated my total ineptitude as any kind of handyman.

Fortunately I got away with it, and so began my learning curve as an electrical mate which amazingly earned me a number of temporary contracts at new build casinos, medical centres and department stores. My main claim to fame being a consistently flickering counter light that I had wrongly wired up on my last day at a local city centre Primark store that was still giving the till assistant a headache a full week after opening.

Turning on the taps...

But blagging it to an individual is far easier than trying to convince a whole workforce that you are a competent tradesman.

That happened to me when I was posing as a pipefitter in yet another secondment on a six week placement fitting out a new Boots the chemist warehouse at Chandlers Ford, near Southampton, Hampshire.

Now I must have made some kind of favourable impression on this particular assignment as within the first fortnight of being on site one of the locally based painter and decorators sidled up to me before taking me to one side in the canteen Portakabin.

"'Scuse me Plam", he whispered the colloquial abbreviation of 'Plum', short speak for plumber, which by association referenced us as pipe fitters.

He continued, "I was wondering if I could ask you a favour. You see I'm having a new bathroom unit delivered next week and I thought I'd enquire if you would be interested in fitting it for me as a foreigner?" A 'foreigner' of course being the slang word for cash in hand.

My initial reaction was, 'Bloody hell, he thinks I'm a proper bloody tradesman!", but quickly thinking on my feet I fabricated a get-out clause.

"I'm ever so sorry mate, I would love to but we are under strict instructions from the gaffer that participating in any other work not associated with my employer will result in automatic dismissal. "

"Oh! Really sorry Plam, the last thing I want to do is get you into trouble, but I thought I'd ask anyway".

Phew! That was close to being exposed, yet the final week upon completion would pale that episode into insignificance.

"Ralph, I'm going to take all the hire tools back to the shop. You just stay up here in the cherry picker and if you're asked any questions tell 'em I'll be back soon", was the message from qualified pipefitter and village mate Ronnie Kendrick.

"O.K. Ron, spot ya later", was my goodbye.

Minutes later whilst tinkering around with a spanner to give the impression I was working I heard a bellowing call from down below.

"Hey Plam, cam on darn, it's your big moment. We're ready to switch on the pipes".

"What! Switch on the pipes – what for?" I replied cautiously hoping it wasn't anything too technical.

"It's the big turn on Plam, we're testing the whole factory. So get yaself darn here now."

Looking down I saw around a hundred tradesmen gathered in an arced formation around the cordoned off utility supply unit.

I stepped down out of the cherry picker cage to be confronted by all the plants workers focusing directly upon myself and a set of three vertically positioned wheel shaped dials that were facing me.

My mind was now racing, bloody hell this is the culmination of six weeks of intense graft from a raft of professional tradesmen and here I am easily the least qualified person on site being asked to do the honours.

That was the last time I had to think as the supervisor declared,

"O.K. Plam, let's turn on that water."

From all accounts a short spray of the wet stuff should signal a successful completion.

So, with just a trio to choose from I decided to apply the 'middle for diddle' adage and spun the wheel clockwise with absolutely no reaction.

A deadly silence ensued as it was obviously not the correct choice, so with my back still facing the gathering I spun around with my fingers pointing outwards to deliver a loud "Fooled ya!" response.

Some muffled chuckling broke out amongst the throng proving that a few were treating my act as a joke.

So with one down and a fifty-fifty chance of success on my next pick and the sound of the boss urging me to "Get on with it Plam!", I plumped for the top one. Surely it had to be – but no, once again there wasn't a reaction, and once again I fobbed them off with my two handed finger point.

But this time my 'Fooled ya again!' was interrupted by the ever-more irate foreman's,

"Get on with it Plam, and stop messing about!"

"O.K. boss!" was my final delivery as I switched on the

only other option and a welcome fountain of water spurted upwards to confirm a successful fitting procedure.

Applause rang out amidst unconfined laughter after I took a bow and with a sweep of my arm across my body let out a loud "Da da!".

"You bloody lunatic Plam! Was all that really necessary?" asked the gaffer.

"You will never know just how necessary" , I thought to myself.

"Good job done!", he added shaking my hand firmly before attending to some other related business.

Ron came back from the builder's merchants soon after.

"Bloody hell Ron! What a time to leave me on my Jack Jones" (alone).

"Why, what's happened Ralphy?"

"I've only just turned on the full water works to the whole shabang!"

"Flaming heck Ralph, I didn't know you had it in you!", laughed Ron grabbing both my shoulders with his powerful arms.

"No Ron, neither did I", responding identically to his embrace.

In Memoriam

Ronnie Kendrick helped and guided me through the technical aspect of pipe fitting when we were on location working together as a team.

In September 2012 Ron passed away aged 66 years. He was a larger than life character with a great sense of humour. A great observer of people and situations he formed a great partnership with his wife Joan. If there actually is an after-life you can be sure Ron will be at the forefront of proceedings making them chuckle.

A distinct case of a sense of humour failure ...

If there is one thing that I'll never understand it is the laborious nonsensical complexities of the D.H.S.S or more importantly when you're 'between jobs' the Employment Service.

After filling in reams of paperwork each time you re-sign on, the client undergoes a long drawn-out assessment process which by the staff's own admission they are instructed to adhere to.

Their remit being to almost corral the claimant into a category corner with the option to take any kind of employment with payments suspended for non-compliance.

Which is all well and good you might say, but the reality being that on many occasions the positions offered are predominantly dependent upon having the necessary experience in a particular field.

That said, if you are requested to apply for any such jobs then you have to comply or risk facing sanctions to your benefit money. It does feel like you are being pressured into filling in application forms for wholly unsuitable vacancies.

A feeling I had when asked to submit a 12 page brochure for a simple office admin. assistant. Once again it seemed a futile exercise as almost all such modern day businesses now request a competent level of computer skills which I don't possess.

Nevertheless before leaving for my regular Friday lads' night out I endeavoured to wearily fill in the first 10 of the dozen pages, deciding to finish the final two when I came back from the pub, ready to post next morning to comply with the closing date.

Bad mistake! As any regular drinker will tell you ten pints followed by a lamb doner with chilli sauce isn't the best preparation for the completion of a serious task.

Turning over the last couple of pages to the application form I came to a section requesting my hobbies. Slightly inebriated and additionally ready for my 'pit' to get some shut eye I wrote in the box 'drinking, gambling and womanising', with the thought that it just might give me an edge by appealing to their sense of humour.

Well wrong! It didn't as Sue my job advisor informed me in no uncertain terms on the following Wednesday when I signed on.

From all accounts the employer had been on the phone to the job centre absolutely enraged by the so-called contempt with which I had treated the application process, adding that because of this lack of respect they would not be using the job centre's services again.

"What have you got to say for yourself Mr Burnley? This is a prestigious company that you have completely ridiculed with your crass comments".

"It seems like a bit of a sense of humour failure to me Sue, as I thought that a slightly off the wall set of pastimes would clinch me the job".

"No excuses at all, and as a result of your inadequate actions you will now be required to go on to a mandatory two week course on how to fill in a job application form!" , stormed my mentor.

"But I've filled in literally hundreds of application forms Sue".

"Yes, but not properly in this particular instance. Your first lesson will be at Hanley, Trinity Street next Monday morning. Fail to attend and you'll lose one month's benefits".

There was no getting out of it now, I had to comply and so for the next fortnight I found myself completing the mind-numbing process of something that I had done since school leaving age. Once again it seemed a harsh penalty for what I still regard as a massive 'Sense of humour failure!'.

Kippo's comes calling...

In 1990 I commenced the first of what would turn out to be many subsequent temporary contracts at a company that was then titled Manor Bakeries and now trades as Premier Foods.

Located in the district of Trent Vale or Trent 'Vegas' as it is colloquially termed, the factory lies little more than a mile equidistant from the nearby towns of Newcastle-Under-Lyme and Stoke.

The corporation is a driving force in some of the food industries' most competitive categories with a brand portfolio that includes Ambrosia, Lloyd Grossman and Sharwood's to name but a few. However, at Trent Vale, only cakes are produced.

Using the finest quality ingredients that have been sourced worldwide Mr Kipling has become the firm's flagship product which, as described in the almost iconic T.V. advertisements, 'does make exceedingly good cakes'. Sadly, a phrase that it's new owners want to relinquish.

It also supplies private label brands for many major supermarkets, and leading up to the festive period orders in excess of ten million packets of mince pies are taken on, such is their trusted standing in the ever-challenging global market.

Because of this rapid increase in production, besides retaining around 600 core employees, up to a further 300 temporary staff are recruited to cope with the extra demand between the months of July and December.

Out of that total figure I would estimate that around half the workforce are from a multi-racial background but with few exceptions both the ethnic and white British staff toil tirelessly as a team to produce an end product worthy of the 'Kipling' name.

Even a prayer room has been incorporated into the premises to meet the needs of all practicing religions, making the site a perfect example of how to run a modern day business in this cosmopolitan age we now live.

Although all these points that I've made are admirable they do disguise the primary reason that I came back to work at 'Kippos' year on year, and that is the advantage of choosing the morning shift.

My clocking-on time of 7 a.m., although requiring a 5 a.m. rise in order to cycle the eight miles to the workplace, does mean that I can knock-off at 3.30 p.m. This giving me a good four hours to either catch the train or share a lift to Burnley mid-week matches. For games taking place further afield my accumulative holiday entitlement can be accessed to obtain the necessary time off. However it wasn't always the case.

I had been generally employed in the mixing bay, which as it implies is at the very source of the productive process. Here I both physically and mechanically add the stipulated amount of ingredients as stated on the request sheet to produce the required combination for each mix.

I'd like to think by always being punctual, not having any days off sick and consistently doing my work to the required standard I was given a little bit of essential flexibility in order to follow my team religiously to every game. In other words my fanaticism seemed to have been tolerated, if not fully accepted by the management team.

All cultures are respected for their beliefs and no offence is taken when hard to pronounce ethnic christian names are abbreviated or rejigged to provide an easier enunciation. For instance two regular Indian brothers that I have worked with are Charanyeet and Sukdev Maan who are equally at ease answering to their given nicknames of 'Charlie and S-man' respectively. Other examples include Benny for 'Binoy' and even a simple 'Mo' for Mohammed. Such is the long established bond between the workforce in general. I do have to specify 'in general' as it has to be said some are infinitely more accepting than others, which of course you will find in all walks of life. As I have previously proclaimed my own personal appraisal of an individual begins from the initial few minutes of introduction with points being gained or deducted from that moment onwards. In other words to my mind everyone is an equal, leading their lives how they wish in a free world. Unfortunately some folk seem to take a less tolerant, narrow-minded viewpoint as in this man's case.

He was Phil law, or 'Lawman' to his friends, a point he would succinctly make if womeone he didn't regard as falling into this category addressed him as such.

Knowing Lawman as I do he would have to fall within the classification of a modern day Alf Garnett type character who played the head role in the 1970s' sit-com 'Till death us do part'.

There was also more than a passing resemblance in their looks. Both sporting a closely cropped tight style in an attempt to disguise a fast receding hairline, and each spewing out their nationalistic ideology which had long been consigned to a past era.

The Lawman would also fondly reminisce about his skinhead days regularly confusing fantasy with reality when claiming his small town street gang got the better of the Madeley Mafia at various venues in Stoke-On-Trent.

For example, I bumped into him one evening in Hanley, as stated the biggest of the six towns that make up the borough of Stoke-On-Trent. As I was ordering my pint at The Unicorn pub, an established Victorian boozer almost opposite the flagship Regent Theatre complex, he sidled up to me at the bar. After a swift greeting he began to regale me with stories of his drinking companion for the night.

His face was contorted into a gaze of intense seriousness, an appearance that I jokingly classify as 'well crucial' when confronted with it, as usually it is nothing of the sort.

He didn't disappoint.

"Ya see ma mate sat there, well I'll tell you something for nothing. He used to be the 'ardest bastard in the whole of the Potteries! I've seen 'im take coppers out, put down the leaders of every mob that's tried it on and 'it 'em so 'ard that he could 'ave been done for attempted murder in a bare knuckle fight.

I began to turn my head to observe Conan the Barbarian, but before I could Lawman still rigidly maintaining his 'well crucial' look offered me this cautionary advice as he lay a hand on my shoulder.

"Dunna look at 'im! I'm not kidding ya now, he doesn't like anyone staring at 'im."

I smiled, and did so anyway, only to see the most unlikely looking gangster of pensionable age propped up against the dralon wall seating munching a packet of salted peanuts alongside his half of mild, walking stick in hand.

"Now you are having a laugh Mr Law! He looks like he is going to need help to get to the gents toilet."

Lawman, affronted by my rebuke closed by saying somewhat unconvincingly.

"Well I'm telling ya, he was THE top man in his day!"

Although Phil was as curmudgeonly a person you could meet he was also a fiercely loyal patriot and probably the only bloke that I know personally who actually attended the England v West Germany world cup final in 1966, and we still meet up regularly for a few drinks.

It was also Phil who informed me of the death of my footballing hero, whose nickname I am called by – Ralphy Coates.

The Friday before Christmas I was unusually still employed at the Manor Bakery site. Unusually, as most temporary contracts finish a good couple of weeks before the big day.

A recognizable face appeared at the entrance doors to the works canteen. It was Phil Law motioning me over to him even though it was evidently clear that I was only half-way though my double poached egg on toast breakfast.

"It's urgent!", he mouthed, not being allowed in to the rest area in his work overalls.

I reluctantly left the table to find out the cause of his urgency.

"I've called ya out because it's just been announced on the radio that Ralph Coates has died."

I knew by his serious delivery that there was no way that he would ever announce such a statement without a totally hundred percent assurance.

I said nothing, and took a deep breath I took a couple of steps back.

"Bastard!", is the only word I could utter before thanking 'Lawman' for informing me.

I had texted Ralph a get well message after he had suffered a stroke, and now a double stroke had seen him off. Ralph was only 64.

A phone call to general co-ordinator for all such players recognition and all round great girl Veronica Simpson at Burnley Football Club arranged a pick up for me at Keele Services on the M6 in order to attend Ralph's funeral at Enfield North London on Wednesday 5th January 2011, followed by a wake courtesy of another former club Tottenham Hotspur.

A tragic death in my workplace...

Only the two of us were asked back as regular temporaries at 'Kippos' for the 2012 Christmas run of mince pies at the beginning of August.

Besides myself, the ever effervescent Gary Clowes had offered his reliable services to the company.

Gary would always greet everyone with either a cheery collective salutation of,

"Hello everybody!" or an individually tailored acknowledgement of,

"Hello mister" or "Hello missus" dependent upon their gender.

Gary knew his mixing inside out, and planned well ahead at every opportunity to get on top of the day's task.

His particular shift ran from twelve noon to eight thirty in the evening, and he had just started his daily stint on Tuesday 9th October of that year.

I'd seen him already dashing around to organize his line as I exited the protective plastic curtain slats that segregated my personal works locker from the mixing bay.

Knocking off for my thirty minute dinner break I noted the time at 12.04 p.m. to ensure my return wouldn't be late.

Gary was only a few yards in front of me as I asked how he was doing in my own practised manner.

"Alrate Gaz lad?"

"Go , go, go!" came back the reply indicating his usual level of busy involvement to the job in hand.

I made my daily walk down the metal stairs to the quieter canteen quarters located near to the factory entrance. There I purchased a consistently flavourless powdered soup drink from the vending machine before settling down to pick my chosen horses from the newspaper racecards.

I'd just taken a bite from my first ham sandwich when to my surprise in walked two of the team members from the recently started afternoon shift.

It was Growler and Wazza who had been working on Gary Clowes' line. Both were ashen faced and in bits as they related their harrowing story, clearly distressed, to the listening employees.

"It's Gary", cried Waz. "He's just keeled over in the new bay and I saw his face turn blue!".

"He's in a real bad way", added Growler,

"There's no way I can work after seeing that".

Both turned to leave, each consoling one another as they left.

Hurriedly, without finishing my sandwich I too accessed the rest room's double doors before striding purposefully towards my work station.

I didn't get that far as the intermediate stores area had been cordoned off by nylon braiding either side to prevent through access, normally reserved for when the bulk bag of flour is changed with the fork lift truck as a health and safety measure.

The paramedics had been immediately summoned from the City General Hospital just a short distance away across the A34 London Road and were working frantically to revive him.

Our personnel attempted to carry on working as normally as possible given the circumstances of our popular colleague's plight.

It wasn't an easy afternoon to get through and when a deputation of three representatives from the senior management team asked us to gather round in a circle I feared the worst.

A statement was read out to the remaining workforce, half of which like myself were due to clock off just before 3.30 p.m.

One of the works bosses, Martin Mullaney delivered the dreadful news.

"It is with great sadness that I have to report that one of our employees, Gary Clowes, passed away today after many attempts to revive him from both our staff and the North Staffordshire hospital paramedics. I'm really sorry to have to pass on this sad news.

Anne, one of the cherry sorting girls let out a loud wail opposite me with her other two female colleagues Diane and Wendy quickly following suit. A couple of our lads went over to console them whilst I felt myself slowly wandering over to the wash area in a temporary daze.

This section is where the used plastic trays and tubs are taken to be sprayed clean. It was unoccupied awaiting the change of shift, but I couldn't help myself kicking out at a stack of containers in anger as tears welled up in my eyes.

"Why? Why? Why?", I asked out loud as the pile of trays scattered across the bay.

It transpired that two of the company's first aiders Gary Bennett and Warren Broomhall were immediately on the scene to administer both C.P.R. and mouth to mouth resuscitation but to no avail.

Would a defibrillator have helped?

They say not, but with so many people in a workplace they should surely be as common as fire extinguishers. There is a fifty percent added chance of survival than C.P.R., and that margin alone should be proof enough of its need.

Although 100,000 people in the U.K. suffer a sudden cardiac arrest each year, only 13% of the population have been taught how to save a life and as little as two hours basic training could change all that. It is such a simple procedure on the basis of a skill for life on how to save a life. I'm staggered that such an official mandate hasn't been brought in to date. In Norway for instance first aid training starts at years 7,8 and 9 which is a compulsory part of the core national school curriculum.

I could see that Anne and her mate Wendy had been deeply affected by the exceptionally sad loss of one of their close friends, so as we were all due to clock off I asked if they wanted to go for a drink to give ourselves the chance to take in what was a really distressing episode. The girls, myself and

Anne's partner Russell somewhat appropriately convened in the Jolly Potters pub in Newcastle-Under-Lyme for an hour or so to numb the shock of proceedings.

Appropriately, because Gaz as we knew him, was always a smiling, happy go lucky lad, even after having lost two of his brothers at an early age.

His funeral in a small inconspicuous church in the Boothen district of Stoke town was a particularly fraught service given the circumstances of his passing, all three male siblings being survived by their sister, plus mother and father.

A hooligan confrontation averted – but only just …

Year on year I would be asked back for the Christmas preparatory work which would dovetail nicely with the first half of the football season. I went back most times except when I was employed on a longer building site contract either as a labourer or the aforementioned electrical mate.

But in the intermediate years I was employed there my job would be in what was termed 'The Christmas cake room'. Here, as the name implies, a team of around 25 staff would contribute to build the luxury Marks and Spencer version.

In the confined area of the production line the blokes' conversation would inevitably turn to football and which team you followed.

"I'm an England fan", was my half-truth reply to my questioner, a certain Dave Miles who was an active member of Stoke City's 'Naughty forty' hooligan element. In later years my cover would be blown as my bogus dental and doctor's appointments on a regular Tuesday afternoon to allow me time to travel to home games was sussed by a few of my colleagues who had spotted football related articles in local newspaper The Evening Sentinel.

The upshot of which was regular references to Burnley's lunatic fringe 'The Suicide Squad'. Asking if I knew any of their members I told them the honest answer that I did simply by association in travelling to matches on a regular basis.

But that seemed enough to Milesy and his cronies who after constant badgering to organize a 'meet' for a fight between the two factions I decided to let them have their wish – or so they thought.

"Who's their leader?", asked Milesy's mate 'Big Nose'.

Sensing an opportunity for a little poetic licence I gave him a suitably embellished answer to evoke the air of notoriety he obviously craved.

Now I knew a Burnley fan whose nickname was 'The Nail'. Why he had obtained this soubriquet I never knew but I decided to get a bit of mileage out of Phil's title just to stop their ever persistent urge to set up a face-off between the two parties, so I wound them up thus,

"Yeh, The Suicide Squad's leader is called 'The Nail', simply because after an altercation with a brickie on the building site where he worked he pushed him against an M.D.F. wall and stapled his right ear to it with the aid of an industrial nail gun."

"No way!", cried the two arrangers in unison.

"Yes way!", I answered pressing my point.

"Right! Shall we organise a meet then to see who are the top mob?"

"O.K., I'll get in touch with 'The Nail', I'm sure he can accommodate ya. He never refuses a ruck", I answered mischievously.

And so it was arranged. A fictitious meet somewhere along Penkhull Bank, an ancient village about three miles from the Brittannia Stadium. Kick-off 1 p.m!

I relayed this wind-up to Phil 'The Nail' who himself was suitably amused by it.

The game passed by and on the following Monday Milesy and Big Nose were complaining of a no-show for the proposed scrap.

"Well I don't know what happened, I'll have to ask The Nail at next Saturday's home game, but it must have been a good excuse because The Nail backs down from no one!".

At Burnley the following weekend I related my tale to Phil expecting him to laugh out loud at the jape.

He didn't! Phil went on to tell me that two of his vans full of Burnley fans had been pulled in by police at Sandbach motorway services on the M6 going down to the match. They were both escorted back to Lancashire just after 11 a.m. when the cops had confiscated multiple amounts of beer and spirit bottles along with a cache of weapons.

"What!, Why's that then?", I demanded.

"Because we were on our way to Penkhull to meet the 'Stokies' as agreed".

"But that was just to wind 'em up because they kept pestering me to organise a fight".

"Yeh, I know, but once I started talking to some of the lads about it they decided to take them up on it".

"Bloody hell Nail! Thank goodness you got stopped or else I could have been arrested for orchestrating a flamin' riot".

I relayed the reason for their non-appearance to the main protagonists the next Monday and they were suitably satisfied with that answer as they too had heard about the police operation that turned them back through the media.

So reputations intact to both sides in the hooligan league, and I was just glad it never happened!

The end of my cake run ...

My time at Kippo's came to an untimely and somewhat acrimonious end at the age of 60. Still relishing the task of maintaining the production line to the best of my ability I would always be one of the first on the line in preparation for the daily task ahead.

This day seemed no different as I browsed my menu sheet to determine the type of cake that was being produced first which would decide the type of pastry that I would be mixing to encase the filling.

My dry ingredients consisting of two full base bowls and one lid had been prepared as usual by the early morning shift ready for mixing.

Timing is everything to ensure a fresh pastry product and so I waited for the precise moment to push my 200 kilo. bowl to the industrial sized mixer which is termed a 'collette'.

Immediately I noticed how difficult it was to move the load which was a regular occurrence that us as employees had to endeavour to overcome as our appeal for a change of wheels to make transportation easier invariably fell on deaf ears.

Upon further inspection it became apparent that one of the 360 degree spheres was completely rigid, leaving just the two free flowing alternatives to carry the dead weight.

Working on the theory that the prep. team must have been able to manage the stainless steel container into position by my line 3 I attempted the short push to the one collette which is accessed by four production lines sometimes all at once which necessitates a queueing system.

Having struggled successfully to virtually haul the heavy receptacle into position, once it had been mixed the container gained added consistency resulting in it being barely movable.

As the production team were now in place downstairs along the 200 ft length of the baking belt I shoved the vessel inch by inch to the lifting cage which picks up the bowl and tips it upon the rotating nibblers which make the paste more manageable for the holding depositor one floor below.

Pushing, shoving and turning it I got within a couple of yards of my objective. Figuring one last big push would guide the load in I summoned up all my strength to attempt a final swing of the troublesome cargo carrier. As I did so my full body weight was placed on my knees for the final spin which I anticipated would do the trick. It didn't! My upper body spun round but the bowl didn't as the rear wheel locked solid, which meant my knee ligaments were shredded.

I of course reported it to the foreman Ray Walsh who immediately took it out of service and recommended I book the incident into the works accident book for reference which I did. To my utter surprise a few days later I was summoned into the bay manager's office where a twenty page risk assessment notification had been prepared to review the procedure. It was duly read out to me concluding that the problem had been my fault as I should have stopped work, with a case note warning issued to me which I had to sign for. It was an unfair appraisal and I pledged not to work there again.

Throughout that protracted spell of long service I had implicitly maintained my punctuality for whichever working shift I had been rostered.

Furthermore, having not taken one day or even one hour off sick was a record of which I felt justly proud. Either my monthly accrued holidays or in isolated cases where they had run out, time off with permission was requested to cover travelling to my football fixtures. That was besides, through sheer necessity having to fabricate a few 'little white lie' dental appointments in the early years when no form of absenteeism was tolerated or stipulated in their conditions of employment.

'Kippos' had run its course for me, and when my contract was completed a few weeks later it would be my last.

'Wayne the bane'...

For those of you that read Part One you may recall a short story under the sub-title 'Big Billy' (page 207).

It told the tale of a pretty cantankerous fellow work colleague that I helped to reform in the 1980's era. Andy Williams was his name, christened by me as the far from politically correct 'Big Billy' in reference to the comic book character 'Billy Bunter', the fictional schoolboy also known as 'The fat owl of the remove' residing at Greyfriars public school.

Back then Andy used to go grudgingly about his job, a permanent frown painfully etched across his forehead as he strove to pick upon any minor discrepancy in other people's work enforcing his role of assistant foreman at the local steel warehouse where I was employed. He was just never a 'happy bunny', and I would suggest that if you look hard enough in most work places you will find your very own 'Cloud of doom'.

The stares, the glares, the studious looks in your direction are generally sure-fire signs that a particular individual has got it in for you. My way of dealing with such sad cases was to discreetly take the mickey out of them when they passed by, either whistling or singing along to the tune of the Nat King Cole song 'Smile', in a defiant stance and maybe as a remedy to their sullen looks.

The following lyrics to the tune say it all.

"Smile though your heart is aching
Smile even though it's breaking
When there are clouds in the sky, you'll get by
If you smile through your fear and sorrow
Smile and maybe tomorrow
You'll see the sun come shining through for you
You'll find that life is still worthwhile
If you just smiiiile…."

After repetitive recitals the miserable target soon begins to realize the significance of the words.

He can be compared to the school kid in your class that takes great delight in pulling off the legs of a spider for no other reason than a sheer bloody-minded awkwardness. That is why they tend to prey on those they consider weaker than themselves until proved otherwise.

Although some form of confrontation is inevitable when pressing the point home my continual 'happy' whistling had left an indelible imprint in his head in the case of Andy who went from being a total 'arse' to someone that his friends look to for a good laugh nowadays, for which he continually thanks me.

Well, 'Kiplings' had an 'Andy' too, although this one was actually a 'Wayne'. Wayne Fulcher was only small in stature but tried to compensate for his vertically challenged appearance by being intimidatory. Disguised insults, barbed comments and snidey looks were all part of his duplicitous armoury whenever he happened to wheel his ingredients bowl past me. I reckoned from his sulky demeanour that all was not right at home and maybe he was being given a hard time by his missus which I often put to him. His disparaging response clearly showing that I had hit a nerve although he would never admit to it. Even so, that was no reason to bring his problems to work and try to make other people's lives as wretched as his own.

Events eventually came to a head one day when he overstepped the mark by verbally insulting my football club once too often.

"O.K. Wayne you've gone just too far this time. The only way we can sort this out is face to face, so I'll see you on the car park at 3.30!", I remarked calmly but sternly.

He didn't reply, only offering his trademark snigger as he powerfully spun his hundred kilogram mixing bowl away in an aggressive manner to flee the scene.

At knocking off time I waited for fifteen minutes at the designated meeting point ready to take him on if necessary and possibly risk being sacked. But Wayne never showed, citing the reason for his non-appearance as a late call from shift team leader Mark Shenton asking him to work overtime.

Whether that was true or not I'll never know, but it did have the desired effect as his derisory comments gradually petered out as he generally gave me a wide berth from that day hence.

Wayne left 'Kippos' soon after myself and I now generally bump into him in one of the local bookies when he puts his bets on. Although not what you would call the life and soul of any party, his general disposition is far more affable and his outlook considerably more cheery. He even talks about Burnley in more positive terms, which is all I ever ask of anyone. And whenever I bid him farewell with my intentional line of "Keep smiling Wayne", his immediate riposte is now,

"I'm always smiling mate, always smiling!"

Therapy eh? Another satisfied customer.

Slapdash! The strange case of Matt Smith.

'Matt the chat'....

At the opposite end of the spectrum is the work's wag. An employee whose disposition always seems bright no matter what the challenges of the day. Ever willing to regale you with a tale of what they have been up to, or are going to get up to the previous or following weekend. Always oozing an ebullience to ingratiate themselves with their fellow colleagues through an indomitable spirit of fun.

That man was Matt Smith who may occasionally have been known by some as 'Doctor Who' after his infinitely more famous time traveller namesake.

At work the jovial thirty-something was more commonly referred to as 'Harry Hill' given his striking resemblance in both appearance and manner to the bald bespectacled comedian that featured on our T.V. screens.

But to me he will always be 'Slapdash', the title I bestowed upon him after witnessing the aftermath of many of his allotted tasks. Whether the job involved weighing out the preparatory ingredients from tubs of cocoa powder or filling plastic trays with rapeseed oil ready for the cake mix, you could bet that upon completion his work station would look like a bomb site, with his standard issue white bakery jacket and trousers being transformed into a psychedelic suit at a hippy music festival.

Then one day without any prior warning or given notice, Matt decided to jack it all in. The Kipling court jester had mysteriously and unceremoniously simply just left, probably never to return. Not a single farewell or by your leave to his many colleagues. He had deleted his Facebook account, was uncontactable by landline or mobile phone, and as the weeks went by hadn't been seen out by anyone. As those weeks turned to months there were genuine fears for his safety

It seemed for all the world that this affable all-singing all-dancing entertainer had simply had enough.

Just as his workmates were contemplating a Reginald Perrin case scenario after many further enquiries and investigations proved fruitless, Brett the washman provided a long overdue breakthrough.

"Someone's seen Matt, he's o.k. and has enrolled on an engineering course at a local college".

I did eventually bump into Matt myself at the local Coral bookies in town where I questioned his somewhat unconventional departure from the factory.

"Slapdash" I shouted across the busy betting shop where I'd seen him feeding twenty pound notes into the gaming machines like he was giving a donkey strawberries.

"What the bloody hell happened to you? You didn't even say goodbye to your muckers."

Matt turned round , his trademark frown that he always wore when playing the fixed odds terminals that I had dubbed his 'well crucial' look gave way to a more accommodating smile as he realised the identity of the enquirer.

"Eyup Burl", he addressed me by my colloquial idiom without giving me an answer to my question, so I asked him again the reason for his hasty departure.

His clearly evasive reply of "That's me innit, I just do it!" was plainly not the full story but without wishing to intrude on what could be a far more personal and sensitive issue I didn't pursue my request for information any further.

Instead, after a brief exchange of football related banter I told him that I was pleased to see him, and finished the conversation by telling him to look after himself.

Now whatever the reasoning behind Matt's non-conformist exit strategy maybe only he will truly ever know and that is up to him at the end of the day. However what it does demonstrate is that sometimes that constant happy-go-lucky façade that is evident in a character, like us all can be affected by a raft of external conditions to hide a range of internal emotions that absolutely no one but the person concerned knows about.

So two totally diverse characters working under the same roof. One happy – one sad, but maybe the final question should be; "Do you know which one?"

39 Barely Treading Water: 2002-2008

Stan Ternent

Steve Cotterill

Owen Coyle

Our managers' through the 'noughties'
Stan Ternent   1998-2004
Steve Cotterill 2004-2007
Owen Coyle   2007-2010
Photgraphs courtesy of Burnley Football Club

After finishing 7th in the old Division One for the last two seasons, and as a consequence just missing out on the Play-Offs by the narrowest of margins, the following six seasons would see an erosion of these final placings.

Relegation may have been avoided, but for all but one campaign The Clarets had flirted with that very real prospect in these subsequent years.

2002-03: Final position 16th. Division One ...

An opening start of four consecutive defeats, with three goals being shipped in three of the four certainly wasn't the platform Burnley were hoping for after coming so close to a Play-Off berth in the previous couple of years.

Indeed, after the quadruple loss away at Reading manager Stan Ternent actually considered jacking it in as his team hit the bottom of the table.

Things did improve at the end of September when Burnley put together a run of five consecutive wins against Wimbledon, Sheffield Wednesday, Walsall and Leicester in the league and a 1-0 extra-time victory at Huddersfield in the 2nd round of the League Cup.

But the sit up and listen moment came along at the end of the season when an already relegated Sheffield Wednesday side came to Turf Moor and inflicted a painful 7-2 thrashing in front of a good crowd of 17,435.

This coming just three weeks after centre forward Gareth Taylor had scored a hat-trick at Burnley against Watford, yet still ended up on the losing side of a 7-4 reverse, after going in 5-4 down at the half-time break.

We'd had an absolute skinful of the Hornets for one season. They had not only beat us 2-1 down at Vicarage Road in the return league fixture but also knocked us out of the Quarter Finals of the F.A. Cup 2-0 on their patch. A Sunday game when expectations were high on progressing at least to the semis', but the performance level low, on an afternoon when Burnley simply didn't turn up.

If those were shock score lines they all fell short of the final result on a cold Tuesday night at Grimsby in late October of 2002. Grim Grimsby , a town you wouldn't want to visit by choice even at the height of summer given the waft of fish smell that emanates from the enormous Findus factory complex on the outskirts. But visit we did, coming away with a 6-5 defeat after witnessing some of the most chaotic defending ever seen by two sides in ninety minutes.

The aforementioned fish factory night shift reminding us of the score on a large placard that had been placed by a returning roundabout used by the majority of the away supporters on their drive home. Although the staggering score line wouldn't be enough to save them from their fate of relegation by finishing rock bottom of the First Division table.

There was a battling 2-1 win over Spurs as a highlight in the 3rd.round of the League Cup at Turf Moor back in November, but perhaps the general feeling of an apathetic campaign all round can be illustrated by the lowest attendance I've ever seen at a second tier league game. When just 1,972 bothered to go through the turnstiles as Burnley succumbed 2-1 to nomadic Wimbledon who played this last game of the season at their temporary home of Crystal Palace's Selhurst Park before shockingly being franchised off sixty miles north as Milton Keynes Dons.

2003-04 Final position 19th. Division One ...

This almost felt like a case of déjà vu as three opening defeats to Crystal Palace at home 2-3, West Bromwich Albion away

1-4 and Wigan Athletic at home 0-2, rooted Burnley once again to the base of the division table. They would hover in or around the relegation zone for the vast majority of the season. In fact it would take a couple of back to back wins against Wimbledon 2-0 and Derby County 1-0 both at home in late April to preserve our status.

It had been another war of attrition in defensive terms, with only Wimbledon on 89 goals against who finished in 24th and last in the league, conceding more than Burnley's 77.

Again there were some heavy defeats with the worst three being a 6-1 tonking at Ipswich, a 5-3 loss at Preston and exactly the same score line at home to Norwich.

Even more galling was the fact that Stan had built the foundations of his success at club level with previous employers Bury Football Club on a tight defensive strategy. That aim was now clearly eluding him.

With a week to go to the end of the season the chairman Barry Kilby and his board of directors must have thought the same as they decided to unceremoniously cancel his contract of employment with the club.

Coincidentally his final game would be at home to his own boyhood heroes Sunderland. It finished 2-1 to the Wearsiders whose fans along with the grateful Burnley supporters in a near 19,000 attendance gave him a standing ovation as he completed a lap of honour with tears streaming down his cheeks. Stan had started our long awaited arrival to the second tier of the league pyramid, now who was going to take us further?

Of course any team can have an 'off' day from time to time, but in his six year tenure at Burnley in truth Stan had been in charge of just too many wholly unacceptable damaging results of five or more goals as detailed overleaf.

5 GOALS AGAINST:

DATE	SEASON	OPPOSITION	VENUE	COMPETITION	SCORE
FEB 27th	1998-99	GILLINGHAM.	HOME	DIV.TWO (3RD)	0-5
OCT 25th	2000-01	NOTTS.FOREST.	AWAY	DIV.ONE (2ND)	0-5
APRIL 1st	2000-01	BLACKBURN.	AWAY	DIV.ONE	0-5
DEC 29th	2001-02	MAN.CITY.	AWAY	DIV.ONE	1-5
FEB 1st	2002-03	READING.	HOME	DIV.ONE	2-5
DEC 20th	2003-04	PRESTON.	AWAY	DIV.ONE	3-5
APRIL 3rd	2003-04	NORWICH.	HOME	DIV.ONE	3-5
AUG 11th	1999-00	MAN.CITY.	AWAY	LEAGUE CUP	0-5

6 GOALS AGAINST:

DATE	SEASON	OPPOSITION	VENUE	COMPETITION	SCORE
MARCH 9th	1998-99	MAN.CITY.	HOME	DIV.TWO (3RD)	0-6
OCT 29th	2002-03	GRIMSBY.	AWAY	DIV.ONE (2ND)	5-6
DEC 14th	2002-03	ROTHERHAM.	HOME	DIV.ONE	2-6
OCT 14th	2003-04	IPSWICH.	AWAY	DIV.ONE	1-6

7 GOALS AGAINST:

DATE	SEASON	OPPOSITION	VENUE	COMPETITION	SCORE
APRIL 5th	2002-03	WATFORD.	HOME	DIV.ONE	4-7
APRIL 26th	2002-03	SHEFF.WED.	HOME	DIV.ONE	2-7

Giving a grand total of 14 games played, goals for 23, goals against 78!

2004-05: Final position 13th. Championship …

The man eventually tasked with the job of taking us to the next level was Steve Cotterill, or 'Quiterill' as he was tagged after he walked out on Stoke City after just thirteen games in charge to join ex-England caretaker manager Howard Wilkinson as his assistant at Sunderland.

In his first season in the managerial dugout Burnley went on decent cup runs in both the F.A. Cup and league version.

We were due to play the mighty Liverpool in the 3rd round of the F.A. Cup on the traditional first week in January but the match had been postponed due to waterlogging down one side of the touchline.

It was rescheduled for the 18th of the month which meant myself and Tricky Trev, Slack would have to wait a little longer to see if we would get a return on our individual bets of a £2 and a £5 win on the same score of 1-0 to Burnley at odds of 10/1.

So imagine our double delight when the hapless Dijimi Traore tried to produce some intricate footwork just beyond his own goal line in order to make a clearance out of the muddy six yard box only to turn into his own net for the only goal of the game.

Joyously we returned to the Corals betting shop to collect our bonus winnings which should have been £22 for me and a tasty £55 back for Trev.

Imagine our utter astonishment as we were handed back just our original stake money.

After querying it long and hard we were referred to the statutory betting rules and regulations poster. There in small print it stated that if a fixture is postponed and the rearranged date is more than seven days after the bet was first placed it then becomes null and void. The reason apparently is that a combination of injuries and players suspensions could come into effect to determine the final result after such a period.

It was understandable, yet I would like to wager hardly any punter was aware of the ruling.

Still we were through, and after disposing of Bournemouth 2-0 at home in the next round, would you believe it we drew the old enemy at home in the 5th round.

In a live televised match it ended all square at 0-0 meaning a replay at Ewood Park 10 days later. In a highly charged atmosphere there were no less than three separate attempts by pitch invaders to attack the wind-up merchant that is – Robbie Savage. All were prevented by a combination of police, players and stewards as the significance of a victory against our deadliest rivals brought temperatures to the boil.

We could have done with some of that hot blood on Saint David's Day the date of the rematch. Around 7,000 made the trip to follow Burnley and my plan of smuggling in a rubber blow up doll with, 'Property of Lily Savage' lettered upon it had to be aborted due to an inner and outer ring of full body searches by police and stewards.

Burnley went one nil down just past the half hour mark, then just three minutes before half-time Jamaican midfielder Micah Hyde powered in a viciously struck volley from just outside the penalty area over the head of stranded goalkeeper Brad Friedel to make it 1-1 and send the travelling support into raptures. The first goal scored by Burnley on Ewood soil for 22 years when Derek Scott got a late consolation in a 2-1 defeat more remembered for the rioting Burnley fans that caused a fifteen minute delay.

Hyde's goal deserved to win any game, but it wouldn't as a winning strike four minutes from time gave the home side an identical score line to that notorious fixture back in April 1983.

At the final whistle our players gathered in a circle with arms draped over each other's shoulders as a show of togetherness and 'the huddle' was born.

A massive attendance of 28,691 had turned out on a freezing cold night as the Burnley contingent crunched their way home through the snow, completely blocking the road with a mass of walking bodies en-route to their vehicles.

The season fizzled out after that. We had sold leading scorer Robbie Blake to Birmingham for a then record £1.25 million and his replacement Ade Akinbiyi, a £600,000 acquisition from Stoke managed to sensationally get himself sent off after just three minutes of his televised debut as a substitute against Sunderland for an off-the-ball lash out caught on camera.

Richard Chaplow had excelled in midfield an observation not missed by West Bromwich Albion who broke the transfer record for the second time with a 1.5 million bid on deadline day.

But the shining light of the team would have to be the player of the season Gary Cahill on loan from Aston Villa. From his debut at home to Nottingham Forest, he was the catalyst for six league wins out of the next eight.

However we still ended up losing more games than we had won and that wasn't good enough.

2005-2006: Final position 17th. Championship ...

To his credit Cotterill did snap up a trio of promising starlets from Bournemouth who would turn out to be considerably influential in the future. They were all midfield players too which could give the team an immediate understanding in that department.

So Wade Elliott, Gareth O'Connor and John Spicer joined the other two new faces of Sheffield United defender Jon Harley and Arsenal rookie Danny Karbassiyoon. But the most amazing transaction came when the manager decided to book an away day to Florida U.S.A. to secure the services of Stoke defender Wayne Thomas. He linked up with his former team mates Gifton Noel-Williams, Ade Akinbiyi and James O'Connor from the Potteries. We were fast turning into Stoke reserves!

Another new season – another disastrous start as Burnley went down in their first game at Crewe and their second at home to Sheffield United by the same 2-1 score.

A fairly equal number of wins, draws and losses followed in the next dozen or so games that kept us in the lower region of the table. Then remarkably a mini-run of five wins out of six propelled us up to 6th position.

All the ex-Stoke boys had found the net but one more than any other was playing like a man possessed.

With eight goals banked already Akinbiyi was fast becoming our leading light as Burnley entered the month of November, but nothing could prepare me for one of the most sensational individual displays I've ever come across following the club and the almost surreal circumstances I witnessed it.

It was Bonfire Night, with a Saturday afternoon kick off when Burnley travelled to Luton Town on the back of two home wins against Hull City and Millwall. It has to be said both the town and their football team's Kenilworth Road ground must be the least favoured day trip of most away fans. There are few pubs, and those few are poor, and at the end of it is a destination of dated dilapidation.

That is how I found myself killing a bit of time before the game seeing if there were any spare complimentary tickets going outside the main stand pick up point. Our lads had drawn a blank, but I refused to give up.

Coming towards me was a silver haired gent in a pin-striped suit who gave the appearance of someone important so I took a cheeky punt.

"Good afternoon. How are you today?," followed by an immediate long shot enquiry.

"You don't have any spare tickets do ya, as my contact has let me down".

To my utter amazement he said he did, and invited me up into the exclusive hospitality lounge.

He just happened to be the chairman of Vauxhall Motors, an automotive manufacturing company that was based in the town.

After a couple of drinks to toast my good fortune the boss allocated me a place in the posh seats of the directors box, only on the condition I wear a tie as it was 'house rules'.

He loaned me a spare one he had asked for, and after making sure there was no Luton Town references emblazoned upon it, I tied it around my collared tee shirt.

This really was top draw. In for free, with food and drink included.

I made polite conversation with the amiable chap about the 'Hatters' season so far and settled down for the match with the intention of restricting my level of enthusiasm to polite applause in keeping with what always are controlled quarters.

Town were unbeaten on their own turf so far this season so I wasn't expecting to do a lot of clapping as the opposition anyway. How wrong can you be?

What followed was an astonishing performance given the happenings, with one player surely having the match of a lifetime.

That man was the powerhouse that is Ade Akinbiyi. Burnley took the lead with two stunning strikes from the big man. However all his good work looked like it would amount to nothing as our goalie Brian 'The Beast' Jensen raced out of his goal to deny the oncoming Steve Howard of Luton, carrying the ball out of the area in the process resulting in a harsh dismissal.

We had no substitute goalkeeper on the bench for some inexplicable reason meaning it was left to midfielder John Spicer to volunteer himself for custodian duties, although he had never played there.

Luton pulled one back before half-time and my, up to now well contained euphoria after going 2-0 up, was now quickly giving way to trepidation at the prospect of surviving with ten men and no recognised goalkeeper.

However, ten minutes into the second period saw Akinbiyi race clear only to be brought down for a penalty. Taking it himself he confidently converted past former Clarets stopper Marlon Beresford.

Luton scored again with half-an-hour to go but Burnley held firm to record a stunning victory against all the odds with Ade clutching the match ball.

"Credit to Burnley, that really was an outstanding performance," conceded the amicable Vauxhall Motors chairman.

"I have to agree. That really was sensational stuff!," I nodded in agreement. Then after a post-match pint and a couple of my favourite egg mayonnaise sandwiches, I thanked him for his hospitality and was away.

Ade scored the only goal to beat Stoke City on Boxing Day after a convincing 4-1 victory also at home to high flying Watford and suddenly Burnley were up to fifth.

But Ade, the catalyst for our revival would be lured to Sheffield United in the January transfer window as their then manager Neil Warnock came calling. A total fee of £1.75 million being agreed.

Goals inevitably dried up with former England striker Michael Ricketts drafted in on loan from Bolton as his replacement.

It was to little effect with a run of six consecutive defeats hurtling us to as low as 18th. Andy Gray became another striking option signed from Sunderland and with his help we made safety once again.

Stephen Cotterill June 2004 – November 2007 …

I only spoke to Steve Cotterill face to face on the one occasion, but that brief encounter gave me the measure of the man.

It took place after a pre-season friendly in Austria when we played out a 1-1 draw with Greek side PAOK Salonika in 2005.

The game itself was contested within the most picturesque setting that I've ever watched a football match, in the small town of Abtenau. The stunning backdrop to the open field being a tall range of snow capped mountain alps with fluffy cumulus clouds floating above them majestically like airborne marshmallows over a giant Toblerone chocolate bar.

When the referee blew the final whistle most of the few hundred Burnley fans that had made the trip headed over to the opposition's goalkeeper and former Burnley F.C. favourite Nik Michopoulas who had played under manager Stan Ternent. We knew him more simply as 'Nik the Greek'.

As I walked across the pitch to also shake his hand, my path just happened to cross with Cotterill so I took the chance to introduce myself.

"How are ya Steve? Dave Burnley, all the way from Stoke-On-Trent. Just want to wish you the very best for next season".

"Ah Stoke!", he replied without even the courtesy of a thank you to acknowledge my sentiments for the new campaign.

"I've got a lot of good friends from Stoke", he continued wistfully.

A bit peeved by his vacuous response I countered brusquely,

"I'd like to bet you've got a lot more enemies!" referring to the considerable depth of resentment that I personally knew existed in regard to the manner of his departure from the Potteries.

He seemed to bristle at my quote, inwardly seething that I had the temerity to suggest such a thing, and without a further reply or glance in my direction he shouted out to 'Nik the Greek' before jogging off towards him.

We would all later find out that facing any kind of criticism wasn't his strongest point by any means.

Like a lot of people I had found it hard to take his comments seriously from the outset. For instance in a supporters question and answer session soon after he had been appointed Burnley boss he was asked the following.

"What is your ultimate ambition in football?"

His reply, aspiring as it may be, took most of those present by surprise for its sheer audacity.

"One day I want to be manager of England!" he answered in all seriousness, and no shortage of smugness.

That ludicrous statement given his current standing said it all about a man who had ideas well above his station. Granted, he had more badges than a boy scout, accumulated from a range of football coaching courses, but as we would see his man management skills were clearly lacking, with his excuses becoming ever more tiresome.

2006-2007: Final position 15th. Championship ...

There was no better example of each when from December 2006 to the beginning of April 2007 Burnley went a full four calendar months without winning any game. A run of nineteen matches without a single victory.

This barren spell had easily been the worst sequence of results since we had got promoted to the championship at the turn of the millenium, and had in fact set a new unwanted club record of going winless for eighteen league games.

Slipping ever closer to the abyss that is the third tier of English football,the prospect of which filled me with dread, I began to drink excessively to alienate such a thought. No matter how many times people tell me that over-indulgence isn't the answer, all I do know is that it works for me!

I was getting more and more enraged by a set of circumstances that were out of my control. Cotterill's tactical ineptitude when a game turns against us, his big 'I am ' attitude and the seemingly limitless reasons for the team's failure.

He had dismissed the players as not being the same quality as they were when at the start of the season a top six position had been maintained for three months.

His hardly Churchillian quote after a 2-1 loss at Wolves in February 2007 left a lot of folk completely baffled as he explained away the latest defeat in his post – match interview and his simplistic deducible reason for the bad run of form.

"We haven't scored many goals and we haven't kept many clean sheets, and that's not necessarily a recipe for winning".

Well ya don't say Steve, and there's disillusioned us thinking that was the formula for success. Talk about stating the bleeding obvious!

Then as desperation began to set in he tried to change our luck by reverting to what were our traditional white shorts and socks for one particular game, all to no avail.

As the inevitable rumours circulated about his position as manager at the club he despairingly intimated that we were pretty darn lucky to have him at all when he came out with this self-styled statement,

"I think there's been times where, in the last year or so I could have maybe left the club on three or four occasions, and haven't .

So it looked like we were stuck with a loser that was going to take us down.

Thankfully that grim outlook did not materialize as out of nowhere Burnley went on a miraculous mini-revival which saw us win five of our last eight games to finish fifteenth.

The most remarkable turn around of form which all but extinguished our relegation threat took place on the 7th April 2007 at St Andrews home of Birmingham City F.C.

Manager Steve Bruce was confident his team would return to the top of the championship table after this encounter as did 28,000 of the sell-out crowd.

I'd gone along to this one on train, meeting my daughter Clarette at New Street Station. 'Tubs' as I affectionately term her from her formative years when she was a well nourished bonny child, hadn't had to travel far as she studied at the nearby Aston university and resided in rented accommodation in one of the local suburbs. I was hoping that she could provide that little bit of luck needed if we were going to get anything out of this tough fixture.

Since becoming a teenage vegetarian after crying through most of the 'Watership Down' film about displaced cuddly rabbits at the cinema Clarette has become more svelte than substantial. Making my 'Tubs' nickname which was short for tubby although wholly inappropriate still paternally cute to me, and somewhat awkwardly embarrassing when in company for Clarette.

In the stadium there was a huge siege mentality both on and off the pitch as our 800 strong allocation was firmly wedged into a tight corner triangular away section. We sang our hearts out in an effort to spur them on to maintain what had been a largely stubborn rearguard action in an effort to preserve what just could be another valuable point to safety.

But it was to get even better than that and lead to scenes of unbridled joy when the most unlikely of scorers John Spicer, until then a deep seated midfielder, nicked the ball off the toe of former Blackburn Rovers centre back Martin Taylor, before advancing at speed to produce an unerring finish into the top corner of the net to secure a late 1-0 victory. It has to be admitted that it was completely against the run of play. Did we care? Not an iota.

In Memoriam

Our best result of the season was also tinged with sadness as it was discovered that Burnley legend Brian Miller had passed away that morning at the age of 70.

A Claret through and through, Brian first walked on to the 'Turf' as a fan at eight years old.

As a player he stands eighth in the all-time appearance list.

He was an ever-present in the club's 1959-60 Football League Championship winning team and played at Wembley in the 1962 F.A. Cup Final against Tottenham. Brian was also the only Claret to have featured in all twelve of the club's European ties, and won one full England cap.

After his playing career was over 'Dusty' remained a one club man being uniquely involved in all of Burnley's championship titles in some capacity throughout all four divisions.

As stated, he played in 1959-60 for the Division One championships.

He was first team coach when Burnley took the Division Two title in 1972-73.

The actual manager in 1981-82 when Division Three was clinched.

And finally chief scout when Division Four was conquered in the 1991-92 season. Brian Miller 1937-2007.

Cotterill had now led us to 13th, 17th and 15th in his three years at the helm, or to put it another way, non-achieving, established stalwarts of the Championship!

Some argued that we couldn't hope for anything more given our limited resources compared to other far richer clubs in our division.

I begged to differ on the basis that last season we had lost 15 of our 19 league games by the odd goal meaning we weren't that far away from being truly competitive at the business end of the table.

This led me to the conclusion that something was missing from our play. That vital component was motivation, an ingredient critical to the mix.

This man obviously couldn't supply that crucial commodity, but then who could?

2007-08: Final Position 13th. Championship ...

After just another undistinguished first third of the Championship season Steve Cotterill was relieved of his duties after what amounted to a shocking performance by the team in a 1-0 home defeat to Hull City on Tuesday November 6th.

Long serving player Steve Davis taking over as caretaker manager for the following game at Leicester City which Burnley won 1-0.

Before our next game at home to Stoke City we had a new man at the helm in Owen Coyle.

Unknown to me as a manager yet highly recommended by sources from his home country north of the border in Scotland his first time in charge led to a 0-0 draw with the Potters.

A non-event of a contest with both teams cancelling each other out. So poor was the performance that the travelling contingent of 950 Stoke fans were coming out with a chant of;

"Stand up if you want to die!"

A reference to manager Tony Pulis's lack of adventure going forward, and yet at the end of the season it would be they who took one of the promotion places with the Clarets finishing below halfway once again.

Coyle's record since taking over being little more than steady with an almost uniform mix of wins, draws and losses in his first short tenure.

The club had hardly even been treading water for the last half-dozen championship crusades, and there was seemingly no reason to think that this state of affairs was going to change given that Burnley were now regarded as one of the poor relations of also-rans in the division having averaged a finishing position of an unimpressive 15th over those last six years.

Taking that on board why should us the supporters believe that this apparent status quo would be any different next time around?

We now had a relatively unknown manager in charge, with only limited experience of the intense melting pot of desperate teams that had fallen from grace, all trying to propel themselves out of one of the most competitive leagues in world football to the manifestation of the Premiership nirvana.

I certainly wasn't holding my breath, but by the end of the season I definitely would be!

40 Back In The Big Time After 33 years! 2008-09

Unconfined joy at the 2009 Play-Off final with with Jules, and Clarette. Burnley 1 Sheffield United 0
(Wade Elliott)

An extraordinary epic journey taking in a record 70 games over 25,000 miles in distance. A season when Burnley inflicted 'capital punishment' on London teams in the League Cup which should have taken them all the way to Wembley. Instead, they went there to win promotion to the Premier League through the Play-Offs.

A pre-season friendly frenzy ...

From seemingly out of nowhere Burnley F.C. made the announcement that they would be casting their net stateside in the hope of building foundations that would help them develop and nurture players on that side of the Atlantic.

Senior club officials, chairman Barry Kilby, Operational Director Brendan Flood, Development Director Paul Fletcher and Assistant Manager Sandy Stewart flew out in early June to research two franchises as part of a strategic youth development programme.

They were to visit Carolina Railhawks and Minnesota Thunder of the USL First Division which played in a league, one below the MLS.

Whilst over there, Burnley must have thought they could further their relationship by participating in friendly games against them both, and so dates in mid-July were arranged.

After studying my world atlas I estimated that the span between the two venues was a conservative 1,000 miles as the crow flies, or in this case as Delta Airlines fly. But with no flight found online for under £200 I was going to have to find a more economical alternative mode of transportation to bridge the distance.

I turned up at Manchester Airport for my Tuesday trans-Atlantic air journey to find the Burnley F.C. players and management personnel booked on the same trip that included a change of plane at New York's Newark airport for an onward journey to Raleigh, North Carolina.

Media Manager for the club, the amiable Darren Bentley caught sight of me and invited me over to their party who were waiting in the departure lounge. I'd known Darren and kit man Daryl Bielby through their support of Burnley before their respective appointments with the club. Now for the first time I was being introduced to manager Owen Coyle, assistant manager Sandy Stewart as well as head physio, Andy Mitchell and first team coach Steve Davis.

I shook hands to greet them all, had a quick chat, and then let them get on with their own personal conversations.

Now I've always reckoned that I'm a pretty good judge of character when assessing individuals. Within a few minutes of observing and listening to a person talk, I think that a reasonably accurate picture of the subject can be established through their mannerisms, short speech content and body language.

The problem I encountered with Owen Coyle was made more difficult as he spoke so fast in his deep Scottish brogue that it was hard to understand. Of course I had seen and heard him interviewed many times on both television and radio bringing me to the conclusion that this bloke was indeed the real 'McCoy' or should that be 'McCoyle?'

But there was one glaring omission from his personality C.V. that I had used as an accurate yardstick all my life. The axiom being, "Never trust a man that doesn't drink!"

My theory being that unless someone has a medical condition preventing them from partaking of alcohol they simply can't unwind, let their hair down and truly enjoy themselves or people's company without a few relaxing snifters. In other words, abstinence is socially unacceptable in adult circles without good reason, and according to my suspicious mind he would always be far more clear headed than the rest of us.

Here we had not just a Scot, but a Glaswegian brought up in the rough Paisley neighbourhood of the city defying all logic, but I was willing to give him the benefit of the doubt.

My conjecture having only been proved inaccurate the once with Clive 'Crogger' Read. 'Crogger', being one of three brothers, the other two Pete and Phil having been lifelong seasoned drinkers in comparison to their eldest's total abstinence.

However 66 year old Crog will no doubt point to the fact that until recently he still played competitive football as a goalkeeper at an amateur level because of his teetotal lifestyle. I'm also forced to admit that besides being a trustworthy bloke, he is the regular instigator of witty repartee when in his presence. But my view remains steadfast, that he is the exception rather than the rule, and this contention of mine would once again prove accurate in the none too distant future.

Our plane arrived in the USA and within an hour we were all boarding the next aircraft to our destination airdrome. Although my reserved seat was right amongst the players, there was plenty of room elsewhere so I forfeited my place to let them get on with the regular card school they had formed to pass time.

Once landed, I said my farewells and caught a service bus towards the town of Raleigh. As I did so I kept a look out for the best accommodation deals boldly displayed in daily dollar rates upon the neon motel signs, ready to press the bell and get off as soon as I spied a suitable bargain with dusk setting in.

After sighting many comparisons along the highway, I clocked a budget offer at the Capital Inn offering queen size beds for $40. With the ten dollar coupon discount I'd taken from a local free paper that made it $30, or about £16. The weather had now turned wet and windy.

Showered and changed, I asked the receptionist where the nearest bars were. "There ain't no bars round here mister, except for the Foxy Lady," she replied with a wide smile.

"Well that'll do me, as long as they serve beer," I assured her, and asked for directions.

It was in fact located just 100 yards adjacent to the hotel and turned out to be a lap dancing club. With no other option for miles, I was left with little choice. It turned into a good night, drinking bottles of promotional beer, playing pool with the locals whilst scantily clad nubile women gyrated in the background. Welcome to America!

An introduction to the boldly vivid, but grossly over exaggerated descriptive dialogue of a stateside journalist came next. I got a call on my mobile from Tim Candon who was a Sports Editor for a local newspaper asking if I'd mind being interviewed. I agreed to meet him at the nearest bar, but alas once more there were none close to this isolated stadium that went under the title of WakeMed Soccer Park.

This short introductory transcript gives you a flavour of what could be termed colourful American journalism. It appeared in the regional tabloid the following day.

"When I pulled into the parking lot at WakeMed Soccer Park yesterday evening, I saw a gentleman wearing a claret and blue soccer jersey walking down the sidewalk. He was sipping a 24 ounce can of beer from a pack of tall boys purchased from the nearby gas station.

That's got to be Dave, I said to myself. Sure enough it was. So you think you're a die-hard fan of whatever team you support? Well, bollocks to that!"

Tim then went on to detail the rest of our dialogue in the same somewhat shocking but amusing fashion. Once the match kicked off I would discover more quirky Americanisms. When a far fitter Cary Railhawks U-23s took the lead the tannoy announced the score as '1 zip to the Railhawks'.

During a musical 90 minutes there was a regular rendition of dramatic organ strains at free kicks, whilst the Addams Family theme tune piped out at random moments, and the instantly recognisable score from 1974 film Jaws cranked up the tension as the Railhawks lined up a free kick. Although there wasn't one in Burnley's 2-1 defeat, I gather that a 'P.K.' is the yank's abridged version of a penalty kick.

Contrary to general opinion, off the pitch they have still got a long way to go to capture that essential ingredient called 'atmosphere'.

I had a few beers with those friendly Cary fans at their home pub in town, and one even gave me a lift to my discount digs by the highway where I was due to hitch back to Raleigh tomorrow to get my first Greyhound bus north.

Up at 5.30 am and got a lift to my departure station. The task was to get to a way out place called Blaine near to Minneapolis in Minnesota State by public transport, the benefit being I could save two nights' accommodation costs on the £130 single fare. The downside being it would add around 400 miles to the journey as I had to circumnavigate the massive land mass that are the Blue Ridge Mountains.

Greyhound buses certainly aren't what they used to be. Way back in 1979 when I used them, if there was no room for as few as half a dozen passengers the company would lay on another vehicle to get the customer to their destination. Now with the rising price of fuel and the sheer number of travellers, in order to secure a seat you have to not only get in a queue, but stay in it, as a first come first served policy operates.

After 37 hours and 800 miles I arrived in St.Louis where I broke my trip and stayed the night. A good tour of the massive Anheuser-Busch Inc. Budweiser brewery complex replenished some liquids and a night out around the famous St Louis Silver Arch memorial topped the day off.

Never in a million years ....

Another 600 miles and 17 hours and I had arrived at Minneapolis 2pm on Monday afternoon just an hour before the team had flown in.

I walked around the city looking for somewhere to stay. I tried the Salvation Army hostel where a rag-tag bunch of desperate looking souls hung out. Upon enquiring, the big black lady informed me abruptly of the premises time limits, "In by ten, out by nine! No return until 5pm. $10 a night in shared rooms."

It meant that you had to vacate the premises during the day. I reckoned it was too risky to leave anything in there and so carried on my search.

Then an impressive looking building caught my eye. The Brit's Pub est. MCMXC, which when converted from its Roman numerals represented a rather less impressive 1990 foundation. But that was a certain cue for a drink, so in I popped.

I noticed around half a dozen posters advertising the Minnesota Thunder versus Burnley game dotted about the large interior. That was a good sign. After ordering my pint I ventured up to the roof garden where they had a full size bowling green. Only in America I thought, as I relaxed in the sun contemplating my next move.

Within a few minutes I heard a call from across the other side of the roof that gave me one of the shocks of my life. "Ralphy! Ralphy Burnley, I just knew you'd be here. I just knew it!"

I squinted in the bright sunshine beaming directly into my face wondering who the heck this excitable youth was, knowing that he must be local to Stoke-on-Trent, as that is the only area they call me by my nickname in honour of Ralph Coates, my all-time Burnley hero.

It was quite remarkably a mate called Andrew Marson who had moved out of our small village of Madeley many years ago to find work in the States. I had absolutely no idea where he'd gone until now. Andy informed me that he was currently the Operations Manager at this very pub. So out of all the U.S.A. and its fifty independent states, I walked into a bar in a city fast approaching a million inhabitants and met a bloke whose parents live two streets away from my place. Absolutely stunning, but never in a million years would I have thought it possible.

From there on life got a lot easier. Andy directed me to a youth hostel as well as sorting me out with a lift and tickets for the game 15 miles north of the city.

Needless to say The Brit's Pub became a regular during my stay in this beautiful metropolis which is divided by the wide expanse of the Mississippi river. By further coincidence, it was also going to be the designated venue for both teams' after-match party.

Minnesota Thunder also proved to be a stern test on the Tuesday night of July 15th, but Burnley triumphed 2-0 in front of a sizeable American crowd.

We made our way back to Andy's pub where supporters were welcome to attend. The hot open buffet was truly sumptuous, as is usually the case on these pre-season tours. There's no turned up sandwiches or stale pork pies for our football elite. I mingled unobtrusively with players and fans alike until gone 1.a.m. the following morning before making my way back to my digs.

It wasn't until I awoke mid-morning from my alcohol induced stupor preparing to pack my holdall for the flight home that I realised I had mislaid my 'Stoke-on-Trent Clarets' banner, the lettering of which had been painstakingly painted by Tony 'Arnie' Wilcox who also supported Burnley from the Potteries along with his missus Karen 'ginger minge'. Her highly unlikely nickname originating from a particularly drunken party held at their house straight after victory over local team Stoke City. At the soiree she was outrageously dared to prove that her shock of permed auburn hair was in coordination, or in basic layman's terms 'her carpet matched her curtains?' Karen, well steamed on several glasses of Chardonnay, then proceeded to exhibit the required proof of evidence to a stunned audience for absolute verification. Suffice to say that epithet is now indelibly etched on the mind of all those present.

But back to the story where I retraced my steps, paying specific attention to the many rooms that made up the Brit's Pub premises. It was all to no avail, with no sign of it, meaning I returned home without what had become, thanks to good mate 'Arnie', my very own signature flag. However my nomadic wanderings were far from over in what would become a season of record games played.

Our next friendlies took in a whirlwind tour north of the border to Scotland. Three games within a five day period paired us against Queen of the South in their Dumfries home on the Saturday, Patrick Thistle in Glasgow on Monday night, finishing off at St. Johnstone's beautiful city of Perth location on the Wednesday.

Burnley's traditional annual fixture against Accrington Stanley at their then Fraser Eagle Stadium helped to swell the Accy. coffers, as around three quarters of the attendance is generally made up of travelling Burnley supporters.

It's a great gesture to forge further links with one of the original members of the Football League way back in 1888. Boldly proclaimed as 'The club that wouldn't die' when rejoining the fourth tier after a 44 year gap back in 2006 when they were promoted as champions from the Football Conference.

With little time to spare, I prepared to pack for the following Monday where we took on Jimmy Mcilroy's old club Glentoran in Northern Ireland. The revered Ulsterman invited as a guest of honour to the game. His inked signature on my tee shirt emblazoned with himself in an action shot, my prized souvenir of the night. A game also notable by the fact that our manager Owen Coyle came on as a substitute to play in the second half, scoring the fifth goal of our rout against 'The Glens'.

An away game at Bradford City on the Wednesday night preceded our final warm-up against Inverness Caledonian Thistle on the last Saturday before the actual season took place.

That made it a personal pre-season record for me of around 12,200 miles covered watching the boys in four different countries! It had been one of my toughest road trips for sure, but what did we hope to achieve by journeying the equivalent of half way around the world?

Hopes skydive in opening games ....

Already, I had clocked up more miles in friendlies than I would throughout the whole of the forthcoming season. That made me think. If the compacted nine games of extensive travelling had been gruelling for me merely watching, how must the players feel? I was soon to have my answer.

Our first Championship League game was scheduled at Sheffield Wednesday. Just under 3,000 Burnley fans had made the journey to Hillsborough in a crowd of 23,793.

Former players featured prominently in this fixture, with James O'Conner recently released by the club appearing on the front cover of the programme maybe to install an 'I'll show ya what you've been missing' psyche, and Brian Laws being the manager in charge of the home team who was our previous right back of the early 1980's. Little did we all realise that in around 16 month's time this man would be entrusted with Burnley's team selection.

Referee Clive Oliver blew his whistle to signal the start of a much anticipated season. What happened from thereon in was a complete aberration.

Within 30 seconds, and hundreds of away fans still filing into the ground Tudgay opened the scoring for Sheffield Wednesday to claim the quickest goal of the new campaign.

A disastrous start! Then there's only 3 minutes on the scoreboard as Akpo Sodje thumps a half-volley into the top corner of the net – 2-0.

On six minutes Burnley do pull one back as new signing Martin Paterson crashes in a header beyond their goalkeeper Lee Grant, who would go on to play for us in the not too distant future.

It doesn't take long for the home team to restore their two goal advantage as Sodje gets his second after only a quarter of an hour played. That's how it remained up until half-time.

In the second half Tudgay scored his third, and Wednesday's fourth to seal a humiliating 4-1 defeat. It was Burnley's heaviest opening day deficit since a 3-0 home game reverse to Colchester United in a 1987-88 Fourth Division fixture.

Out of our new acquisitions Martin Paterson was probably our best player on the day. The other two 'newbies' had games to forget. In fact so bad were they that neither would start another Burnley league game again. Peruvian international Diego Penny displayed just how far his national team need to catch us up as he never got close to saving any of their four goals. As for the much heralded Remco van der Schaaf, he possibly saw even less of the ball as he was given the complete runaround in midfield.

It was a calamitous start to a new campaign that anchored Burnley firmly to the bottom of the initial Championship table.

It couldn't get any worse in our next league match at home to Ipswich Town could it? You bet it could, and it did.

The Red Devils parachute display team had been hired for the pre-match entertainment at Turf Moor. Seven members were due to drop on to the pitch one by one in spectacular fashion to present the referee with the first home match ball. The ref just happened to be Ant Bates from Stoke-on-Trent who had played in the same Sunday League team as myself called Madonna Park after the static caravan site where the ground stood at Stableford just in the county of Staffordshire on the Shropshire border.

He was as incredulous as the rest of the watching public when the high drama unfolded.

The inclement weather was denoted by a strong blustery wind that maintained the stadium's flying flags at a horizontal position such was its force. That meteorological condition caused what was about to unfold. The first six of the group had managed to land successfully. However the swirling breeze propelled one of the parachutists who went by the name of Ben Cannon to swing wildly off course, and instead of landing on the pitch, the gale blew him well wide of his target forcing him to touch down with a crash on to the David Fishwick stand. Commonly known as the Cricket Field End due to its location next to this playing oval, its current sponsor and local businessman would go on to form the 'Bank of Dave'. This interest-free lending service to entrepreneurs wishing to improve their commercial organisation gained worldwide media attention after its successful launch.

Burnley fire brigade was called out to the stranded parachutist who was now waving to the crowd as they cruelly sang 'You're not flying anymore.'

A special 100 foot aerial ladder had to be brought over from Accrington to get the man down from the fragile asbestos roof. Safety inspections followed to clear any debris that had fallen under the stand and emergency tape cordoned off an exclusion zone from the 710 visiting Ipswich fans.

There was some doubt whether the game would get the go ahead, but Ant the ref, after consultation with both ground and Fire Brigade officials finally got the match going a full 52 minutes late.

It really was a pantomime introduction to a Saturday afternoon and there was more to come. The Burnley defence failed to deal with not one, but three elementary clearances resulting in a final score of a 3-0 deficit.

That made two games played, one goal scored and already seven conceded. We remained bottom of the league.

Then followed two consecutive 0-0 draws with Crystal Palace away and Plymouth Argyle at home to stem the goals against flow. Neither were impressive results, as the first point at Selhurst Park was against nine men for near on the last forty minutes, whilst try as they might Burnley lacked a cutting edge to penetrate The Pilgrims. Besides, although these two points had taken us to just one place off the bottom, those latest pair of teams we had played lay in 22nd and 21st spot immediately above us.

So Burnley entered the month of September in far from good shape, although they had progressed to the 3rd round of the Carling Cup after beating Bury away 2-0 and Oldham at home 3-0.

The cup that cheers ...

Finally, the team secured their first league victory after a fortnight's international break. It came at Notts Forest with two set piece goals from right back Graham 'Mr Dependable' Alexander.

After remaining unbeaten throughout that month , and with a sensational late goal from young substitute Jay Rodriguez against Fulham at home to secure a 1-0 victory and passage to the 4th round of the League cup, Owen Coyle received the 'Manager of the Month' divisional award. The traditional next game curse materialised in the form of a 3-1 defeat away at Reading to temporarily slow our momentum. But going into November, Burnley fans had only one game on their mind. Chelsea away in the next round of that League cup, sponsored by the Carling lager makers.

I have to say this about Burnley's support. When it really matters, they do turn out in vast numbers. That is why on a cold Wednesday night in November over 6,000 of them made their way to West London in the hope something special might happen. And they duly got their wish.

It must surely have been the greatest game of goalkeeper Brian 'The Beast' Jensen's career as he put his body on the line to repel all raiders. He could do nothing about Didier Drogba's sublime finish in the bottom corner in the 26th minute, but the boastful celebration directly in front of the massed ranks of away fans was met with a hail of coins, one of which felled him momentarily, before he recklessly picked it up and threw it back from whence it came. He received a deserved booking from referee Keith Stroud for such crass stupidity. It stayed 1-0 until half-time.

In the second half Burnley roared on throughout by their travelling army got the equalizer they thoroughly deserved when Robbie Blake released a fantastic chip to Chris Eagles who brought out a fine save from Chelsea's custodian Cudicini. But the ball ran loose to substitute Ade Akinbiyi who caressed it into the same corner that Drogba had found in the first half. What can only be described as an absolute frenzy of excitement broke out on the away terraces.

1-1 after ninety minutes meant extra time. There were chances aplenty at both ends and our Steven Caldwell was sent off for two bookable offences, but the clock ticked by with no further score so it was down to what must be the very height of tension for both players and fans at any level of football. The penalty shoot-out!

Probably the best in the business, Graham Alexander rattled in his spot kick with Mahon, Eagles and McDonald also registering. Only Michael Duff had missed his. Chelsea replied with Lampard, Kalou, Ferreira and Malouda, but two superb saves from 'The Beeeeast' ensured The Clarets triumphed on the night as full internationals England's Wayne Bridge and Jon Obi Mikel of Nigeria failed to register.

Pandemonium ensued as the full significance of the result began to sink in amongst the claret and blue hordes.

Chelsea had previously only lost one game at home out of 86. As for Brian Jensen, that accounted for his fifth success in a sudden death lottery having saved spot kicks in each one, prompting a very apt Daily Mirror headline the following day of 'Jensen Interceptor'.

Burnley were now in the quarter finals after a truly historic win.

Considering the opposition and the standing of each club at the time, that night's achievement was second only to our 4-1 win 5th round victory at Tottenham Hotspur's White Hart Lane in 1983 in the same competition. Absolutely stunning!

Burnley were drawn to play Arsenal at home at this particular 5th round stage. Our cup run had transformed our league performances too, and as we took on the Gunners, a position of 4th in the Championship had been attained.

On a fresh Tuesday night at the beginning of December, the newly adapted catchphrase of 'Capital Punishment' was meted out once more to the Londoners. Yet again, Brian Jensen performed magnificently between the sticks making a good half a dozen superlative saves but the man of the match had to go to Owen Coyle's Scottish prodigy Kevin McDonald who went on to score both goals in a 2-0 triumph.

At work the next day there were hearty congratulations all round from my mixing bay mates, but I wasn't complacent as I knew for certain there would be one dissident objector on my shift. That would be long lapsed Stoke City fan Phil 'Bungle' Law. His back up Gary 'Zippy' Tunstall was on the night shift so he knew that he would have to face me alone.

In preparation I made up a folded cardboard sign resembling a makeshift office desk workers nameplate. Written upon it were the words, "Reserved for League Cup semi-finalists only."

I placed it at the front of the table I was sitting at in the communal canteen for my breakfast break and awaited Bungle's imminent appearance.

Glancing up from my daily newspaper with the match report of last night's game clearly visible on the back page, I sighted my quarry and began to reel him in.

Bungle appeared at the head of the table within an instant.

"Good Morning Mr Law. How are you? You're looking well," I greeted him in a cheerily sarcastic manner.

Without exchanging pleasantries, he pointed a finger at my exclusive sign. "Dave... Dave... whats's all this about?" he laughed out loud before coming out with a more expected stern faced statement.

"I dunna believe it! You can't be serious Dave. I'd be embarrassed! They put out a load of kids."

There was a momentary pause before he added, "Well, Iv'e seen everything now".

He started to pull up a chair, until I showed him the palm of my hand to deter further disruption.

"I'm very sorry Mr Law but you can't sit here. As you can see it is reserved as stated, and I'm afraid Stoke went out long ago."

By now, most of the busy diners were watching our confrontation pan out. I kept both calm and composed.

"Besides, we can only play the team that Arsene picks, and they were no mugs with Silvestre, Wilshire, Ramsay and Bendtner all starting." I added.

"Correct Dave!" shouted Pete the fitter taking time out from his bacon butty. There were more nods of approval leaving Bungle in the minority.

Now Lawman had painted himself into a corner with his ludicrous outburst.

Realising this, he muttered another, "I dunna believe it," before shuffling off with his tail well and truly beneath his legs.

As he left I asked my trademark question to the assembled which I'd done after each successful cup round, making sure Lawman was still within earshot.

"Does anyone know the quickest way to get to Wembley? Would you go down the M1 or the M40?"

Bungle shook his head disconsolately and made for the exit as laughter broke out all around the room. I'd repelled another verbal assault from Mr Law, but he would soon be back once his argumentative armoury had been restocked.

But I would be ready to have the last word, as I invariably did.

The Carling Cup run had inspired the whole squad, with positive results in the League being accredited to this winning sequence.

A 2-2 draw at home to Cardiff City was sandwiched between victories against Sheffield United away and Southampton at home by the same 2-0 score line.

The 2-1 win at Bristol City ensured a happy turkey dinner for the big day maintaining our position of 4th in the table going into Christmas.

Then came Boxing Day and yet another example of the unfairness of the life we all live as Burnley's biggest home league attendance of the season paid an emotional tribute to former captain Ray Deakin who had sadly passed away on Christmas Eve from brain cancer at only 49. A minute's applause was immediately observed by the 16,500 supporters for the leader on the pitch that fateful day of 'The Orient game' 1987.

That sad outpouring of grief for one of their own may or may not have affected some players, but the outcome was a 2-1 defeat to our bogey team from Barnsley.

And the bad form continued with another four consecutive league defeats to Doncaster, Swansea, Preston and Watford plummeting us down to 9th in the table.

In the middle of that string of defeats Burnley had also to play three games in the FA Cup and another two in the Carling Cup. It looked like the age-old problem of playing too many matches within a short period of time could derail their promotion hopes.

With probably the smallest number of playing personnel at his disposal in the division, frustrated Owen Coyle was further restricted as Michael Duff became the 7th Claret to be sent off that season when seeing a harsh red against Swansea City at home in January.

Battling fight back spurs the team on to greater things ...

But we were still progressing on two fronts and about to witness what so nearly was one of the greatest comebacks of all time.

To keep the 'Capital Punishment' theme going our opponents in the semi-finals would be Spurs with the first leg at the venue of our greatest cup shock 26 years previous down at 'The Lane'.

After pitting his tactical wits against such world renowned managers as Luiz Felipe Scolari of Chelsea and Arsene Wenger, appropriately of Arsenal, Owen Coyle now had to go head to head with that wily old fox, Harry Redknapp in early January 2009.

Over 4,000 Claret fans made their way down to North London on a freezing cold January night. As at Chelsea my trusty shredded sheepskin coat 'The Bear' served to protect me from the biting cold.

Burnley were good value for their first half 1-0 lead as Martin Paterson notched his 15th goal of an ever-productive season with a close range strike. However in the second half Tottenham pressed forward relentlessly to inflict a 4-1 defeat on the battling Clarets.

Manager Owen Coyle summed up the task ahead perfectly in the return tie by saying, "We've left ourselves with Everest and a little bit more to climb, but we will give everything we can to win that second leg and restore some pride.

My boyhood hero Ralphy Coates who attended the first leg after playing for both Burnley and Spurs gave his, as it turned out uncanny premonition in this quote, "Everybody seems to be saying it's a foregone conclusion, but funnier things have happened than a Burnley triumph. Obviously, if I was a betting man, my money would go on Spurs getting through, but I'll not be 100 per cent surprised if there was a turnaround."

Wise words Ralph, and as I was most definitely a betting man I put my couple of quid on the only possible score that would get us back in the tie-a 3-0 victory to Burnley after 90 minutes at 66/1. It would be an inspired prophetic punt.

I remember the reaction to this day as I went around the Longside Upper Tier with my Coral's betting slip in my hand asking each supporter the very same question as I showed them my wager.

First was Alan 'Captain Beeky' Beecroft, a follower all his life.

"Do you believe my son?" I enquired in lay preacher terms.

"I believe you should be bloody certified!" was Beeky's discouraging reply.

Undeterred I continued to ask other members of the congregation one by one, looking for some assurance, "Do you believe my son?"

It was to no avail. Ted, Mick, Tricky Trev, Jon-a-thong, Black Country Pete, The Proff, plain John Smith, Rocket Ron, N.R., Adswood, Charlie from Chorley, Cotty, Beats and Statto Dom were amongst the scores of my contemporaries, who whilst admiring my optimism thought in their heart of hearts that it was a step too far.

It was without question a massive ask to overturn a three goal deficit, but besides admittedly simple blind faith, I had detected a team spirit and battling mentality that I'd not seen since manager Stan Ternent's promotion winning team that welcomed in the new Millennium

Myself and Ralph Coates thought so anyway, which was good enough for me. That's not to say we weren't as shocked as the next person when our presentiment gained credibility.

From the off in the midst of a biting cold wind accompanied by lashing rain, Burnley took the game to Spurs, as indeed they had to.

The Clarets were by far the dominant team but it wasn't until Robbie Blake curled in a speciality free-kick to make it 1-0 did we dare to dream.

Tom Huddlestone, Luka Modric and Gareth Bale went close whilst the constant venomous booing of former Blackburn Rovers player David Bentley had the desired effect of unsettling him.

In the 73rd minute the roof nearly came off when Chris McCann stroked in the second goal from a Blake cross. But that was sensationally surpassed on the decibel scale when young prodigy Jay Rodriguez swept the ball home to make the score 4-4 on aggregate and force extra time. If only away goals had counted after ninety minutes, we would have been in the League Cup final for the first time in our history. Now all we had to do was keep or better the same score line in the next 30 minutes and we would be through.

"Now do ya believe?" …

There was a mass exodus to the toilets as both teams prepared themselves for two fifteen minute halves to decide an outcome.

I was as delirious as the rest of the scrimmage as we battled to get to the piss troughs, but even more so. My massive long shot on the correct score had paid off and I was collecting, as all football bets are paid out on the ninety minute result unless requested. Were my £134 winnings going to pay for a trip to Wembley?

"Now do ya believe, my children?" I shouted triumphantly across the expanse of the gents latrine, waving my betting slip wildly above my head.

Some of the doubters I had questioned before the game shouted back, "I believe Dave, I belieeeeve!"

I milked the moment for all it was worth. "Tell me again my children do you believe?"

More "I belieeeeeve!" pledges were undertaken resonating loudly amid fits of laughter. So many in fact that folk queuing up outside could be forgiven for thinking an instant pop up church service had taken place.

Spirits buoyed everyone eagerly made their way back to the Upper Longside to witness the next instalment of this epic thriller.

The noise now was on another level after Burnley's dismantling of Redknapp's side in normal time, they were now going for glory.

In fact Harry would later admit that with three minutes to go in an evenly matched half-hour of additional play, he was thinking that, "This could be the most embarrassing moment of my life!"

With good reason too, because if Burnley could hold out, they would go through on Pato's crucial away strike. The ruling on the right of passage being a complete anomaly as the vast majority of cup competitions worldwide are decided after ninety minutes by the away goal stipulation rather than resorting to a supplementary phase.

But it was to be Harry's lucky night as in those final three minutes of play Spurs undeservedly scored not once, but twice through Pavlyuchenko and Defoe to make the score 3-2 to Burnley on the night but 6-4 to Tottenham on aggregate. The lads had given everything, and were dead on their feet.

I felt violated! Sick to the very pit of my stomach that such a brave performance hadn't reaped its rightful reward.

Spurs had got out of jail and they knew it! Tears filled my eyes without actually falling as I clapped our boys off. Not only had we missed out on a great day at Wembley but also the chance of competing in Europe if winners. People that know me will be aware that I rate the league cup as Burnley's best opportunity to play in a European tournament and the reason I take the competition so seriously.

It was one of the most hurtful results of many bad ones over the years, but conversely it just might have turned out to be one of the best.

Deeply wounded by the injustice of our exit and a missed chance to play at the new Wembley stadium, it was the perfect motivational tool to 'kick on' and attempt to bolster our chances of getting there by the only available route remaining – via the play-offs!

Violent skirmishers followed outside Turf Moor with former Tottenham Hotspur captain Graham Roberts claiming to have been attacked by around 40 knife-wielding Burnley fans in their minibus his party had travelled up to the game in. The 49 year old alleged that they had kicked the door in attempting to punch them before the driver put his foot down and went down one way streets to escape the chasing mob.

The ex-Spurs hard man said that he was petrified during the incident. Burnley's football intelligent unit were heading the inquiry into the allegations.

In the hours and days following Burnley's stupendous Carling Cup run, the club was inundated with congratulatory e-mails from around the world. A flavour of the praise heaped upon the Clarets was printed in the next home league programme.

Out of the scores of tributes published, this particular accolade meant most to me,

> "To everyone involved, I would like to say you did yourselves and club proud. I've been following the Clarets through good and bad times since the early 70's and this game was one of those occasions when emotion transcends action: when you can't believe your eyes: when a dream almost comes true.
>
> We lost, but gained a heck of a lot as well. You were magnificent!"
>
> Anji Riley, Stockport.

That message of admiration encapsulated the thoughts of the majority that witnessed the game whether live or on TV. It was written from the heart.

How can I be so sure? Well, I knew Anji very well, and, as she stated, her loyalty had spanned four decades. Anji first caught my attention on the Longside terrace at Turf Moor during the 1980's. Along with her equally devoted husband Keith, they would wear matching knitted jumpers in Burnley's home and away colours in parallel horizontal striped sections, put together on their sewing machine.

Indeed that very night we had met for what was turning out to be a traditional half-time 'kiss for luck' in front of Keith which never failed to amuse him.

Also during January we had progressed steadily in the FA Cup too. After gaining draws at both Queens Park Rangers and West Bromwich Albion, Burnley beat both in the replays at Turf Moor, the West Brom 3-1 victory maybe being partly credited to myself and in particular 'Tricky Trev'.

You see, for most cup matches when we have to pay to get in, as our season tickets don't cover such games, we tend to migrate to the Bob Lord Stand opposite our upper Longside home in order to get closer to the action and the away dug out for a little friendly banter.

Even most West Brom fans had admitted that they were lucky to get a 2-2 result down at The Hawthorns so I suggested to Trev we let their manager Tony Mowbray and his assistant Mark Venus know how fortunate they were.

As both made their way towards us under the floodlights I called out, "Hey Tony, you shouldn't really be here tonight should you? I think you know that."

It was a statement made to unnerve him a little in a subtle way. Tony and Mark chose to ignore the comment. Then 'Tricky' who is more sledgehammer than subtle laid into them both big style!

Detailing how bad both were for every club they'd played for, he let rip without mercy in no uncertain terms making them feel about as welcome as foxes in a hen house.

I can still remember their shocked faces to this day as they scrambled for cover under their away team shelter, with Mowbray never to surface again in either half until the final whistle blew.

"Bloody hell Trev that was a bit harsh wasn't it, we're only supposed to wind them up a bit." "Ah bollocks to 'em, the truth always hurts," replied Trev.

Burnley's reward was yet another trip down to 'The Smoke', drawing Arsenal in the 5th round at the Emirates.

Another mighty 5,000 plus following ventured south on a Sunday afternoon to test the red leather seating that had been installed on their new ground. They witnessed a 3-0 defeat to a far more accomplished Gunners side than the one that had played at Burnley in the Carling Cup in December.

With no more major distractions we could now concentrate on the league as the age old saying goes. And so we did, losing just the once, 3-1 at Cardiff out of the last ten games to secure 5th spot and a play-off semi-final against Reading.

As the Royals had finished one place above us, they had the advantage of playing the first leg away.

In a feisty ninety minutes Reading had the better chances at Turf Moor, but Burnley won the game 1-0 from a penalty given away by defender Andre Bikey. So incensed was he by the subsequent decision to send him off that he tore off his skin tight shirt and threw it to the ground in a fit of petulant indignation to reveal a ripped, six pack torso.

It must have impressed the management team as we would later go on to sign him.

So we took this slender lead down to the Madejski Stadium on the following Tuesday for the 2nd leg.

The sold out away end was leaping to begin with, but two of the most stunning goals you're ever likely to witness at championship level turned the stand into a sea of delirium.

First Martin Paterson ran from the half-way line, took on three players before releasing a howitzer of a shot into the back of the net from 30 yards in the 51st minute.

Judging by the look of sheer disbelief on Pato's face immediately after the wonder goal, it must go down as the best of his career so far, as must Steve Thompson's superb strike just seven minutes later, which was in the unstoppable category.

It finished 2-0 on the night, 3-0 on aggregate. We'd made it to Wembley in the Play-Off Final and one of the most eagerly anticipated dates in the English football calendar.

The winner takes it all ....

The nail-biting, heart-stopping, stomach-churning grand finale gives many teams something to aim for, when previously only an elite few were involved with the chance of going up with ten games to play.

For me, the introduction of the Play-Off competition to determine an additional promotion candidate from each division is both the most innovative and lucrative concept the Football League has ever come up with.

Finally, it can be quite a money-spinner too, particularly so of course for the eventual winners.

With victory worth upwards of 60 million pounds for the 2009 showdown in terms of increased television rights, sponsorship revenue, prize money, gate receipts, merchandise sales and in the event of relegation additional parachute payments, it was little wonder that it carried the title of the 'world's richest match'. That figure quickly doubled in just four years to an estimated 120 million, whilst taking that step up in 2016 yields a club over a 100 million more than its 2009 equivalent. There was no time to waste with tickets to buy, accommodation to book and travel to organise.

Daughter Clarette and girlfriend Julie both wanted to be there for the big day and £50 seats were secured near the corner of the upper tier at the tunnel end.

In fact it was seat number 182 for me, just one digit short of our 1882 foundation year. Already a good omen then.

Trusted 'Tricky Trev' Slack offered his driving services for our big day, and along with his son Nick who like Clarette makes guest appearances at matches from time to time we all set off down the motorway to Watford in Hertfordshire. This would be our base for the night, leaving us with less than a ten mile journey to the stadium the following morning which we would make by train.

Trev. Dropped our party off at our pub accommodation in the Estcourt Tavern just a couple of hundred yards from the railway station while he and Nick journeyed on into town to a more salubrious chain hotel.

The Sunday dinnertime session was in full swing as we entered the saloon bar and the landlord's glazed eyes gave the impression that he was fully participating in it.

It wasn't the best of introductions for Clarette who had left the booking to me. But after introducing ourselves as his guests he seemed to gather himself together, and after a nonchalant wipe of his runny nose on an already green jersey sleeve he showed us to our room.

An immediate musty smell was present as we entered what was a basic arrangement with the painted walls more off-colour than off-white.

The windows looked like they'd last been cleaned before 'The Blitz' and the toilets were out in the passage.

Then Clarette let out a little shriek as she opened the wardrobe door.

"What is is Clarette? Is there a body in there?" I asked facetiously.

"Everything but a body dad! A big yellow rain jacket has just fallen on me and there's a pair of muddy wellies and a set of nasty looking hammers and saws."

I took a closer look and sure enough it seemed that the regular occupants of the cheap digs were either navvies or construction workers.

"Don't worry Clarette, that's only a handy tool kit if anything needs mending quickly in the room, "I tried to reassure her.

We set off for a night out in the town centre where we met other Burnley fans who were doing the same as we were. Meeting up with Trev and Nick a good time was had by all, and even Clarette who is usually a fairly moderate drinker knocked quite a few back claiming that it was to help her sleep. The poor girl must have pre-match tension I concluded.

Watford isn't a big town yet we still got lost, eventually finding our location after an hour, walking what should have been about three quarters of a mile.

So we settled down to try and sleep before the big day tomorrow. Clarette noticeably tossing and turning on a regular basis in her bed probably in anticipation of such an important event and her first trip to the home of football-Wembley Stadium.

The sixty million pound goal ...

We rose next morning, had a fry up, except for Clarette who is vegetarian, then made our way to Watford junction to catch the train south.

Clarette was scratching herself complaining that it must have been attributed to her accommodation.

"Dad, I didn't sleep a wink and it felt like there was something in bed with me".

I assured her that for £22 a night she wouldn't be entitled to any extras, and perhaps she may be allergic to the washing powder on the bedding.

Clarette's never been one for roughing it like her father, in fact her expensive 'Burberry' handbag was bigger than my overnighter. She must get it from her mother's side who was never a cheap night out on Bacardi and cokes!

Arriving at our destination we hit the main street for an early opener. As any fan that has visited Wembley for a domestic final will tell you, there are designated pubs for each set of supporters to avoid any confrontational issues.

All of Burnley's 36,000 ticket allocation had been sold so it was sure to be choc-a-bloc in the boozers.

Jules pointed one allocated to Burnley fans. It carried the same name as my rescued sheepskin coat, commonly referred to as 'The Bear'.

It was another omen and so we had to tick it. From there more good fortune followed as the Wetherspoons outlet J.J. Moons on the High Road had been given over to our followers.

Everything seemed to be coming together off the pitch, we just now needed it to go right for us on it.

The new Wembley, although both vastly over budget and way past its opening deadline date still represents a magnificent structure with its silver arch straggling the outside perimeter.

I turned to Clarette and took a deep breath, then to Jules to do the same and finally one enormous draw as I punched the air as referee Mike Dean signalled the kick-off. This was it. The 60 million pound game!

It was a typically stabilizing first ten minutes as each team got the measure of one another. But in the 13th minute that all changed when midfielder Wade Elliott went on one of his searing runs. The Blades defenders backed off and he laid the ball off to Chris McCann whose effort broke loose to his initial provider who curled the ball brilliantly into the top left-hand corner to spark a mass outpouring of joy at the tunnel-end. Was it another omen? 13 being my lucky number.

A great start, but was it too early? Burnley, as usual made it hard for themselves by missing a raft of chances to wrap it up. Martin Paterson clipped an effort inches wide, Steve Thompson nodded just past the past with both Joey Gudjonsson and Robbie Blake having shots cleared off the line. With Brian Jenson virtually untroubled all afternoon in the Burnley goal there is no doubt the best team won on the day. 5 minutes of added on time was played then the whistle blew.

Clarke Carlisle at centre half won almost every header at the back and deserved his man of the match accolade.

Graham Alexander – Mr Iron Man at 37 had missed only 26 minutes of action all season and it was particularly sweet for our regular penalty taker who had six failed attempts at promotion under his belt via the Play-Offs.

But the undisputed hero was without doubt super Wade Elliott, often underrated but rarely underestimated, his contribution was priceless. For a free transfer from Bournemouth four years ago that ain't bad.

Almost half the population of the town had turned out at Wembley and they were ready to party!

It's fair to say that Sheffield United did have a couple of legitimate appeals for penalties after thumping collisions in the area and their frustration boiled over with two of their substitutes being sent off. Jamie Ward for two deliberate hand-balls in five minutes and Lee Hendrie for foul and abusive language after the final whistle.

The tannoy system blasted out Queen's 'Don't Stop Me Now' which will be a song that will always be synonymous with that victory as I pulled off my top and did a 'dad dance' of full unbridled euphoria for the full three minutes thirty seconds duration.

Captain Steven Caldwell had hoisted the cup high above his head over fifteen minutes ago but I just wanted to take in the full enormity of the occasion.

Trev and Nick joined us and we made our way back to where it had all started that morning at The Bear.

Even after an all-singing all-dancing couple of hours celebrating, the traffic was still congested and because both sets of fans were heading in the same direction north, progress up the motorways was very slow. In fact after dropping Clarette off at Birmingham where she was living, by the time Trev dropped me off at our local The Offley Arms it was last orders at 10.50p.m. Nevertheless, so delighted was I with our promotion I pledged to buy every customer in there a drink. How much did that cost me? Answer – nothing. the place was pitifully empty!

Chairman Barry Kilby had made a truly magnificent promise to refund all season ticket holders their money back if Burnley got promoted to reward their loyalty. To their credit quite a number waived their right to the windfall but after absolutely hammering my credit cards to enable me to do the full 100% fixtures from start to finish I gratefully accepted the reimbursement.

STATS:

MONDAY 25TH MAY 2009	KICK OFF 3PM

MANAGERS

OWEN COYLE	KEVIN BLACKWELL

BURNLEY 1	SHEFFIELD UNITED 0
H.T. 1-0	

TEAMS

BURNLEY	**SHEFFIELD UNITED**
JENSEN	KENNY
ALEXANDER	WALKER
CARLISLE	MORGAN
CALDWELL	KILGALLON
KALVENES	NAUGHTON
DUFF	COTTERILL (WARD 59)
ELLIOTT	MONTGOMERY
McCANN (GUDJONSSON 27)	HOWARD (LUPOLI 82)
BLAKE (EAGLES 69)	QUINN (HENDRIE 85)
THOMPSON (RODRIGUEZ 73)	HALFORD
PATERSON	BEATTIE

REFEREE   MIKE DEAN   ATT. 80,518

SHOTS ON TARGET

3   3

SHOTS OFF TARGET

6   3

CORNERS

10   3

In the space of just 18 months the manager had transformed a team that had finished in the bottom half of the championship for the last six seasons to semi-finalists in the League Cup and a sensational promotion to the Premiership.

"Coyle is God!" screamed the placards in the crowd as far away as America. It seemed he could do no wrong, a match made in heaven as Burnley fans belted out his name, to the tune that I'd started at Leicester whilst Steve Davis was in charge for his one and only game.

"Der,der,der der...Owen Coy...le!

Der ,der der der...Owen Coy...le!"

In turn Owen Coyle showed his affection for the massed ranks by blowing them a kiss.

But in the not too distant future he would kiss us goodbye in extremely controversial circumstances.

41 When You Don't know Whether to Laugh, Cry – or Both

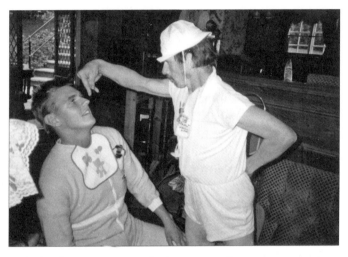

The Crafty Cowman casts his hypnotic spell on an unsuspecting volunteer.
Burl Outing in babywear Lichfield, Staffs.

A good life can be measured by how many laughs you have along the way. But sadness is the antithesis of joy that also has to be seriously confronted whenever it inevitably rears its ugly head. The following short anecdotes comprise a relatively equal mix of each.

Clubbing for beginners...

An unlikely pairing of blue comedian Bernard Manning and soul legend Major Lance once caused a full scale riot whilst the other's gig passed off without a problem ... but which were which?

Where to take a girl for an impressive first date is never an easy decision. Primarily you want to make sure it is a night she will never forget. This one certainly fell into that category, but unfortunately for all the wrong reasons!

Except for the really persistent trouble makers that would sooner thump someone than look at them, the concept of fighting to attain mutual admiration from your peers doesn't seem that 'cool' to the mainstream youth of today anymore.

I use the modern term 'cool' extremely loosely, but in past eras its definition of fashionably attractive seemed to reflect the degree of prestigious kudos a combatant gained from taking part in a bout of fisticuffs which would propel him up the respect league.

In those days you could get picked on for wearing a conflicting style of clothing or having the wrong accent, never mind sporting your club's colours.

The advent of the skinhead culture propagating the confrontational climate of territorial brutishness that existed between thirty and forty years ago throughout all aspects of social life.

That distinct historical period initially spawned playground scraps to determine the best fighters, or the 'Cock of the School' as it was known in Northern England. Most progressed to the next stage of gang leaders for being 'hard bastards', ultimately ascending to the title of 'top boy' for their endeavours.

Maintaining their position at the very peak of the pecking order necessitated regularly engaging in what amounted to little more than mindless gratuitous violence to achieve their aim. Such pugnacious acts earning them respect amongst their contemporaries and notoriety from their enemies.

Each conquest viewed as a badge of honour whether taking place in a street brawl, at a football match, or an altercation in a public bar or discotheque.

The look of outrage and sheer horror from the bystanders, along with the total disruption caused, only adding more oxygen to the fire of the fight and its bloody aftermath.

But what happens when the warped buzz of the shock factor is taken away and fear is replaced by mockery?

As I mentioned, 'It just doesn't seem cool anymore.'

Take this example for instance that really did occur, leaving those involved crimson faced with embarrassment rather than the liquid of the same colour streaming down their head.

Throughout the decades of the 1970's and 1980's most English towns and cities would have at least one notorious nightclub where an admission ticket would double up as a printed guarantee for a weekend ruck.

Ours just happened to be what was then part of the 'Top Rank' chain of complexes that operated nationwide. Located in Hanley, the largest of the six towns that form an amalgamation of Stoke-on-Trent, it played host to a number of top name performers.

I'd visited the venue on numerous occasions and each time a skirmish had broken out with one notable and perhaps somewhat surprising exception.

It was when I experienced the unashamedly, blatant, open racism of comedian Bernard Manning.

Admittedly it was probably not the best place to take a girl on her first date given his vitriolic spoutings.

I was with Lynn, who myself and neighbouring disco partner Pete Blaise had met a few weeks earlier and asked out along with her friend Hazel, who would go on to be Pete's wife of near on thirty five years.

His outrageous persecution of all other creeds and colours would have warranted a disturbance from any right-minded group, but there wasn't one dissenting voice amongst the audience as the overall majority were of the same bigoted ilk.

Major disturbance

Contrast that with the time legendary soul singing Major Lance was set to appear in concert.

The evening didn't go to plan at all. As the time for 'The Major' came and went, it initially only helped to crank up the atmosphere of anticipation for the swaying, singing crowd, and besides, it was generally accepted a little lateness was a prerogative for egotistical stars in those days.

But as the minutes turned to over an hour it became increasingly apparent that the sell-out crowd were getting even more restless and certainly more intoxicated.

Eventually, after an additional half hour had passed, a very nervous looking compère edged gingerly on to the stage as the now impatient gathering were demanding answers to his no-show with a rendition of a chorus from the old chant of: "Oh why are we waiting .... why are we waiting?"

Deeply apologetic the tuxedo suited host went on to timidly announce that, "Due to unforeseen circumstances I'm extremely sorry to have to inform you that Major Lance cannot make it tonight and tickets ..."

That's as far as his explanation got, the expression of regret being curtailed by a flying beer bottle that crashed on to the platform narrowly missing his leg. The messenger having to necessitate a swift exit through a side door which looked as though it had been precautionary left ajar in anticipation of just such a response from the baying masses.

It triggered a chain reaction and mayhem ensued as protective bouncers clashed with protesting punters. More glass receptacles reigned down, tables were overturned and chrome stools were hurled through the air as the mood degenerated into an angry full scale fracas.

The ballroom lights were fully turned on in a futile attempt at diffusing the escalating violence which was only finally brought to an end when a substantial influx of police charged into the premises with truncheons drawn to restore order and make a series of arrests.

From all accounts it represented the worst outbreak of disorder that anyone had ever seen at the place and according to regulars in the know, the local constabulary were becoming more and more concerned with the apparent regularity of such incidents. So much so, that the inference was that unless behaviour drastically improved, their alcohol licence could be revoked resulting in the club ceasing to trade.

Such an ultimatum needed immediately addressing by the senior management of the leisure organisation. We would have to wait another week to see their ideas implemented.

That we did on a return trip the following Saturday. All of us predicted that there would still be a fight, but would the new measures be able to deal with it effectively? The discipline had to get better - but what would they do?

We would find out half an hour before kicking-out time as two well-built youths began trading punches in the middle of the dance floor to finish their night with a flourish.

But within a few seconds of the disturbance breaking out, and even before the doormen could get involved, the melee had stopped soon after it had started, and it was all down to the new staff policy for dealing with such situations.

The method used to pacify the brawlers was more comical than radical and yet remarkably it worked. The whole operation centred around the skills of the resident disc jockey for which he was perfectly placed upon his elevated record deck.

The 'jock' would swiftly swing into action by mechanically deploying a large ceiling spotlight to brightly focus its main beam on to the perpetrators of the disruption to clearly single them out. As soon as that was in place, a slushy, extra loud rendition of Donny Osmond's 'Puppy Love' would be played on the turntable at full volume to the hilarity of the watching spectators that had gathered all around them.

Once it had dawned upon the budding 'Mike Tysons' that far from being portrayed as hard macho men, they were being ridiculed and laughed at, they would cease their shenanigans to go skulking back into the shadows totally humiliated. The quick thinking D.J.'s choice of accompanying music lyrics having the desired effect to nullify the confrontation. "The eye of the tiger" it certainly was not.

From that day on the same cringe worthy track would be activated, along with the powerfully trained lamp to promptly quell any sign of unrest.

And it succeeded, with only a bare minimum of trouble since, creating an altogether more friendly ambience which in turn attracted more custom.

I mean - be honest, would you want to be caught scrapping to the strain of:

"And they called it … puppy loooovve,

Oh I guess they'll never know, How a young heart really feels

And why I love her soooooo."

Not really a good advert for any self-respecting knuckle draggers street cred. is it?

Ashes to ashes…

Our annual village 'Burl outing' which is the equivalent of what is now commonly termed a 'Jolly boys outing' courtesy of the popular T.V. comedy series 'Only fools and horses' has now taken place each and every year since the founding of our organization in 1974. The aim of which is to get dressed up in a particular theme, have a laugh with the locals as we go from pub to pub, sometimes collecting for a particular charity.

But although continuity has been maintained, the excursions aren't the same since we lost our High Priest Jim Purcell in 2007. Jim was more survivor than scholar.

He would perform initiation ceremonies to new members and after they had pledged their allegiance by reciting an oath of loyalty, Jim would then seal the ritual with a full on kiss to the rookie's lips.

We had many funny moments with Jim who we used to look after with a few pints and food pushed his way as he rarely had much money after choosing to spend most nights in the village pub.

One of his many amusing moments came when we took a tour to the Isle of Man dressed in policemens' uniforms complete with plastic bobbies' helmets. As we walked around Douglas during the day a middle-aged foreign visitor to the island actually thought he was the real deal and asked him directions to the ferry port.

Jim in his mind obviously thought that the uniform must have bestowed some authority on him and so he rattled off some unintelligible instructions to this black chap who looked none the wiser for his enquiry.

On a positive note the genuine island constabulary congratulated us all during sundown adding that due to our silhouetted presence they had had the quietest Saturday night for years along the promenade.

Because Jim had been such a major part of our excursions a few of us got together to give him the send-off he would have loved.

The truly caring bloke that took Jim under his wing was pensioner Maurice Carter who helped him with the payment of bills and the general upkeep of his modest flat. Maurice had known Jim when he lived previously in the village of Woore just five miles from us over the Shropshire border,

Maurice grew to treat Jim as his son and in return Jim would assist him by carrying his shopping bags, and he was all in favour of my suggestion of laying his ashes to rest at a favourite spot. The problem being was that the local priest wanted £60 just to turn out and utter a few words.

"Well we can do just as good a job ourselves you know", I assured 'Mo' as I referred to him.

"Correct Ralph! I'll inform his brother who will drive up from Telford for the ceremony. You get it organized Ralph and I'll tell Gordon to bring the urn of ashes.

"Oh O.K. Mo, leave it with me", I agreed half wondering what I'd let myself in for.

I recruited Weedy and Shauno 'Burl', two of his previous minders into our farewell service and arrangements were made to meet at The Chetwode Arms, Pipe Gate just outside the football pitch where Jim had scored the winning goal representing Brazil in a large curly wig against Russia for whom I was captain going by the name of Bolockoff!

You really had to be there to witness an hilarious finale where Jim in disguise because he was a marked man from his previous prolific scoring exploits when we would ensure him scoring manufactured goals was due to be brought down in the penalty area in the last minute to secure a spot kick. As it happened that wasn't necessary as a determined Jim powered through the scything tackles to somehow slot the ball home himself. Priceless! The video of the game being passed round for years after.

But back to the plot, and it was such tales of many that were exchanged in the designated boozer on the evening of the ceremony.

As dusk descended we decided it was time to see Jim off. We all climbed over the gate to the farmer's field and headed for the centre of the marked out pitch.

The four of us gathered in a semi-circle and it was left to me to say a few words of condolence before I poured a measure of Jim's ashes into each of the assembled clasped hands.

"Here's to the crafty cowman" I shouted, relaying the name he had been given for his lack of darts prowess mimicking the "Crafty Cockney" moniker given to professional player Eric Bristow MBE who was then ranked World No. 1 a record six times.

With that we all simultaneously threw the ashes into the wind. Within seconds the sound of galloping hooves thundered towards us.

"Don't panic, stand your ground", I advised as a trio of horses one being a young foal were silhouetted against the night sky coming to a staggered halt just a few yards from us expelling a series of muffled snorts amidst neighing breath in the late evening chill.

Surrounded by a few tons of powerful horseflesh I suggested to the lads that it might just be time to go. I placed the remaining ashes fittingly into the centre circle before completing my abridged service.

"It's been great to know you Jim. See you in the other world!"

With the inquisitive beasts still intrusively looking on and now scraping their hooves into the grass we gingerly made our way back to the safety of the pub.

"Well done Ralph that was a truly appropriate tribute tonight. Jim would have been pleased with that you know", acknowledged Maurice with a tear in his eye.

"Yes, thanks Ralph, that's made me feel much better knowing that his final resting place is somewhere he would have wanted", added Jim's brother Gordon.

Taking a final casual glance back from where we had done the deed I was horrified to see the three wild horses chomping merrily away on Jim's ashes that I'd placed on the centre spot. The animals had obviously thought I was supplying them with some sort of horse feed!

After being the beneficiary of such kind sentiments I just couldn't bring myself to tell the others that Jim had just been eaten by the four legged mammals so I continued with the small talk whilst flicking my head around intermittently in disbelief at what I'd done.

I had fed Jim to the horses!

Yet after reflection I consoled myself that Jim who had been amongst livestock all his farming life would ironically be eventually returned to earth by some of the same breed of creatures he had so dutifully tended.

Or as the aforementioned reference to Del boy and Rodney Trotter might put it – a definite case of 'Only foals and horses'.

So close to meltdown on live TV.....

Over the years, simply by virtue of following my chosen football club unconditionally, I have been asked to appear on television programmes for related interviews, alongside the like of Alastair Campbell from the political world as well as a mix of other sporting celebrities.

They include the down to earth professional boxer Ricky 'The Hitman' Hatton M.B.E., a devout Manchester City supporter, amicable Burnley born, record-breaking England cricketer James Anderson who is also a Claret, and the grumpy looking, self-righteous Liverpool and Republic of Ireland footballer Mark Lawrenson who is now a regular radio and television match pundit.

And it was with the latter that I came very close to an unprecedented verbal set-to at a live broadcast to millions on the popular late Saturday morning, early Saturday afternoon edition of 'Football Focus' which is featured on the national B.B.C. 1 channel.

I'd already had a couple of 'scoops' with the lads in 'spoons' town centre bar The Brun Lea, before being cleared to enter the Turf Moor Stadium as scheduled by a B.B.C. representative via a call to my mobile phone earlier in the day before the game against West Ham United in February 2010.

As planned a security steward opened the big exit gate to let me in, where I saw a tall, dark haired smartly dressed bloke coming towards me.

Naturally assuming that he must be part of the production team I began to introduce myself.

"Football Focus?" I enquired, "My name's Dave Burnley".

"No, not quite", came the instant reply from a smiling face.

"I'm James Anderson, and I am waiting for them too"

Then it dawned upon me, I'd only failed to recognize probably one of the most famous dials from the current decade of sport.

In my defence I aren't, and never have been a cricket fan, or 'bat and ball' as I sometimes derogatory term the game, but even so I should have known the fast-paced bowling megastar known locally as the 'Burnley Express'.

Anyway, we were both soon greeted by the actual 'Beeb' staff and led to the lower tier of the Longside for the shoot.

Anchor man, the affable Dan Walker was the chap asking the questions who immediately positioned me next to Jimmy, who in turn was around half-a-dozen seats away from Mark Lawrenson or 'Lawro' as he was known to his intimate circle of friends. Then after a short countdown the cameras rolled.

James of course was first on recounting a few tales of his support as a young lad watching Burnley F.C. Then it was my turn to compose myself before a nationwide audience.

As is the norm. I hadn't been briefed about exactly what questions they were going to ask me, although I could make a calculated guess which happened to be proved right.

It was the usual in depth exploration concerning the circumstances of my name change from Beeston to Burnley, and that of christening my daughter Clarette in honour of the Clarets.

I began to routinely explain my amended surname by deed poll in1976 as a show of allegiance to my club who had just been relegated that year from the top tier of the Football League. It was a well rehearsed answer as it was predominantly the first question most interviewers asked and were interested in.

I then went on to discuss the reasoning behind choosing Clarette as my daughter's Christian name, adding that it was in honour of the Clarets with an additional letter 't' and 'e' on its singular to make it sound more feminine.

Just as I had finished my clarification, a rude interruption took place.

The condescending 'Lawro', who just happens unashamedly to be a fan of local rivals Preston North End, suddenly butted into the conversation with an unannounced quip, clearly within earshot.

"I bet she keeps that quiet when she's out on the town Saturday night", he chuckled.

That was totally uncalled for, and I certainly wasn't about to let him get away with tarnishing her title.

I let his chortling subside, before flashing my head around in his direction to administer a firm rebuke in a vexed but controlled tone.

"As it happens Clarette is very proud of her name, so much so that she has actually googled it to reveal that it is currently the only one of its kind in the United Kingdom ," I fired back staring him straight into his eyes.

Live T.V. or not, I was never going to just sit there and let someone denegrate my daughter's name with such a crass insinuation. Thankfully, I kept it together just enough to wipe his smug grin from a face that quickly diminished into a gawky like frown away from the gaze of the camera.

Dan Walker ever the diplomat, and now a host on the prestigious B.B.C. 'Breakfast' television programme , quickly moved the informal chat on to another subject with James Anderson looking on somewhat uneasily.

Then before you knew it the brief ten minute slot was over with all reputations intact- but only just!

Footnote....

Mark Lawrenson categorically proved that he is certainly not the 'know-all' he purports to be when he appeared on a special celebrity edition of the prime time television quiz show 'Pointless' just before the 2016 F.A. Cup Final between Crystal Palace and Manchester United.

The aim of the game is to guess the least popular answer given to a selection of questions that were asked to a 100 members of the public in a 100 seconds.

His poser was to name a country anywhere in the world beginning with either of the letters A,L, or S.

'Lawro' was seen to give it some thought before confidently announcing 'Alaska', which when I went to school was a detached state of the U.S.A.

You could see his team mate Dan Walker, the actual interviewer for my 'Football Focus' spot, physically cringe with embarrassment, whilst his fellow contestants did their best to stifle giggles over his assured stance.

Although it proved too good a chance to miss for football commentator Guy Mowbray who quipped, "That was a half-baked answer!," in reference of course to the culinary 'Baked Alaska' dessert dish.

The awkward silence being quickly broke up by the game show's host Alexander Armstrong.

Although, when asked his occupation the ever humble 'Lawro' introduced himself as a 'retired legend', maybe as an after thought he should have described this performance and his 'Football Focus' faux pas in player parlance as, "Having an absolute mare!"

'Chitty Chitty Bang Bang' to Swansea and back – just!...

Originally, I wasn't going to make the Swansea game a full blown weekender as my daughter Clarette's 21st birthday fell upon the Friday of the proposed departure date 27th August 2010.

Then circumstances changed when Clarette phoned to ask if we could swap the night I was due to take her out as some university girlfriends had booked a surprise, all expenses paid weekend in Manchester.

Having agreed to do so, I still needed convincing that the cost of the sojourn to deepest Wales was a warranted trip. The deciding factor being when I was informed that there was a beer festival on in the city for the August Bank Holiday.

Our nominated driver was to be the irrepressible 'Knock-Off' Nigel Standige from Walsden near Todmorden in West Yorkshire his residence at the time.

His moniker being derived from his over-eagerness to seek out a cheap deal in every transaction. This being perfectly demonstrated by his mode of transport choice that turned up over half-an-hour late at my work place for what was supposed to be an early 'dart' to beat the getaway traffic.

'Knock-Offs' jalopy was a P registration Ford Fiesta painted three tone in garish shades of red, grey and pink in a non-uniform design. The souped up exhaust was hanging off, and the passenger seat slid freely up and down its own base rails. Not forgetting the sweltering hot air that continuously blew up through the windscreen vents, amazingly according to K.O., to prevent the engine overheating! This, when it was a stifling 80° Fahrenheit outside.

"Where have ya had this scrapper from Nige? Trotters Independent Traders?" I asked, suitably perplexed by its decrepit condition.

"It'll get us there!" was K.O.'s totally unconvincing conclusion.

Because of the not only uncomfortable, but downright dangerous state of the passenger seat it was decided that for the sake of fairness the remaining three of us not driving, would take it in turns to occupy what amounted to little more than a 'crash dummy' testing launch.

'Jon-a-thong' Taylor from Macclesfield was nominated as the first guinea pig much to his utter dismay. Jonathon had acquired his 'thong' sobriquet due to his wholly inappropriate wardrobe of skimpy under garments that were totally unbecoming to a man of his advanced years in our company.

That left myself and the 'Weed' who made up the travelling quartet, endeavouring to hold back Jon's perch to prevent him flying into the windscreen upon braking.

Eventually after giving it some thought we placed a metal rod through a hole in one of its rails to restrict movement to a satisfactory minimum.

All windows were opened in an effort to disperse the constant waft of warm air that was flowing through the ventilation grill which only seemed to circulate it at head height. And with the exhaust pipe rattling up and down perpetually it was like riding in Chitty Chitty Bang Bang, though this one had no magical properties whatsoever!

After a torturous four and a half hour journey we managed to reach our seafront location in one piece, or maybe that should be many pieces.

Nigel had also taken it upon himself to book the accommodation, adding that on the internet it looked smart from the outside and it came with good recommendations on the website with a sea view.

Alarm bells started ringing when we were given rooms on the very top floor, which upon further inspection were denoted by particularly low ceiling joists where you could easily crack your head.

Furthermore, it transpired that although we had all paid exactly the same price for our digs three of us were allocated one room while Nigel had a designated place on his own.

Tentatively we opened our dwelling to reveal a trio of makeshift beds that looked like they must have been crowbarred into a twenty by six foot perimeter space. It was cosy to say the least and certainly left no room for sleep walking. A small wooden cabinet and a sink the size of a motorcycle crash helmet completed the furnishings with a toilet located one floor down from the outside passage.

Knock-Off's en suite residence was truly palatial by comparison with its king size bed facing a wide screen plasma T.V. , whilst we had to settle for a box shaped 'Bush' model from the nineteen eighties decade.

After the journey from hell we had endured we all protested vehemently to K.O. at the disparity of our lodgings. But Nigel pleaded his innocence claiming there had been no mention of three sharing when he booked it up. In a blatantly transparent effort to placate us he offered to knock a bit off our petrol charge. The guilt ridden landlord also refunded us £2 each.

We couldn't help but feel 'Knock-Off' Nigel had struck again! Getting the best deal for himself while we had to make do with the human equivalent of a rabbit hutch. But time was knocking on so we decided to bite the bullet and drown our sorrows at the nearby beer festival at the guildhall. And we must have done our share as the drink all but ran out early Saturday evening.

The game itself was dominated by Swansea for the opening twenty minutes playing some of the best short passing football I had seen for a good while. The Swans scored after just ten minutes, but Burnley eased their way back into the match until full back Tyrone Mears sought retribution for a bad foul on him that got the home player sent off, with himself quickly following. It finished 1-0 and even though it wasn't a convincing scoreline I was suitably impressed by their possession, retention of the ball and slick passing that I tipped them to go up, which they did that season before going on to establish themselves in the Premiership.

Our return journey on the Sunday also proved eventful just as we were pulling in to our designated afternoon beer stop on the outskirts of Worcester.

The exhaust which had been secured with string to keep it off the ground, and had lasted remarkably well so far, went over one pothole too many resulting in it rattling off down the road in protest.

It meant more running repairs with a mix and match amalgamation made up of both gaffer and duct tape tightly wrapped around the joint to affix it back on as an emergency measure.

'Knock Off' who was still blowing on his hands after foolishly picking up and retrieving the hot device from the gutter where it had come to rest was still adamant that his vehicle was a bargain, and I genuinely felt sorry for the deluded youth.

'Tricky Trev' and the Croston cat ...

On Saturday 26th February 2011 Burnley were scheduled to play Preston North End in a Championship fixture at their Deepdale ground.

With the Lilywhites, at that time, the only other league team in Lancashire, it had become a greatly anticipated local derby with a 5,500 away ticket allocation sold out. I had travelled up with Gin. 'The Veg' Mackriel from Wolverhampton and 'Tricky Trev' Slack from Stockport who had been picked up en route.

Our designated pre-match beer stop was to be the ancient town of Croston, just ten miles South West of Preston.

We duly pitched up just before 11am ready to do a tour of the historical settlement. As we parked up I noticed that pinned to a wooden telegraph pole nearby was a home-made computer generated poster. It was appealing for the whereabouts of a missing cat called 'Mog'. The feline was described as having a distinctive white blaze upon its face.

"Keep an eye out for that pussy Trev, they're bound to be offering a reward for a sighting" I reckoned. "I'm always on the lookout for wild pussies" countered Trev in his predictable innuendo speak.

Thinking no more about it, we entered our second pub of the day, The Lord Nelson, a fine establishment dating back to 1640.

It was here that we became aware of an extremely cautious puss that approached us gingerly for an introductory sniff. Looking like a dead ringer for 'Felix' the cartoon moggie featured in the tinned cat food television adverts, all three of us began to stroke it in turn.

"How long have you had the cat?" I asked the attentive landlady. "Oh no, it's not ours," she replied, adding "it just wanders in and out as it pleases."

Excusing herself for a moment, she walked into the nearby kitchen to get us some beer mats for our pints. Meanwhile, Tricky Trev had jumped out of his seat as if 2,000 volts had zapped through his body.

"That's the lost cat!" yelled Trev, his right index finger pointing at the animals rear as it nonchalantly strolled into the openly adjoining lounge bar area with its tail in the air shamelessly revealing its anus to all onlookers, as only cats can do.

Maybe they should have called it 'Ol' one eye' I observed accordingly.

"I'm going to check that picture, then phone the owner to tell them I've found their 'Mog' declared Trev sternly, sounding like Scottish detective 'Taggart' on a murder case.

"But Trev, I've only just ordered the drinks" I shouted after him. It was to no avail. Without further ado he began scuttling out of the front entrance towards the post on the car park where the notification printout was attached.

Just after Trev's hurried exit, the pub's tenant came back behind the bar to continue her conversation regarding the 'Croston cat'.

"Oh yes, it's been coming in to feed for the last twelve months or so. She thinks she owns the place she does".

My mind flashed back to the poster that I had read out. I remembered it stating the pet had only gone lost from February 10th 2011, just over two weeks ago, which obviously meant that this mouser could not be 'Mog' as it had been a regular visitor for over a year.

I relayed the information to Gin when she came back from the toilet. Her initial look of shock gave way to unrestrained laughter as the truth dawned that we had a clear case of mistaken identity on our hands.

Trev is led astray...

Trev, acting in totally good faith had hastily put two and two together and got five! I reached for my mobile phone to relay our new found information to him hoping to prevent a futile call but as I looked out of the large front window, I realised I was too late. Jogging across the pub car park was 'Tricky' who burst through the door with a satisfied flourish.

"I've rang the owner to tell him I've found his 'Mog' declared Trev assuredly. "But Trev...." He didn't give me time to finish. "Chuffed as mint balls he was, he'll be here any minute" he interjected.

"But Trev" I tried again unsuccessfully. "Here he is now" shouted Trev dashing to the entrance to beckon the bloke in enthusiastically.

Sure enough, bounding around the parked cars was a 'Peter Kay' the comedian lookalike with his Hawaiian shirt choice riding up high over a substantial midriff. The poor chap wearing a face of gleeful expectation entered the tap room like John Wayne confronting an outlaw in a cowboy western saloon bar.

"I've come for my 'Mog'!" he announced to a bewildered landlady, with an opened tin of Whiskas in his hand.

"I've heard you've found my cat" he added excitedly. "There it is, that's ya cat" interjected Trev confidently as the said animal emerged from its hiding place.

Wide eyed, I looked at Gin, Gin looked at me. We both knew what was coming next.

Peter Kay's double crouched down to get a better look before springing back up almost immediately in one movement. His demeanour changed from ebullient to earnest as he made a sad declaration. In fact I hadn't seen someone's face change so dramatically, within a split second, since I'd confronted Blackburn Rovers then Chairman Bill Fox after the Ewood Park riot in 1983 to enquire where our arrested fans were being held.

"That's not my bloody cat!" he scowled, forlornly pressing the lid down on his can of beef chunks in jelly. "It's nothing bloody like him" added P.K. as he glared at Tricky Trev before leaving in a hyperventilating huff.

Tricky shrugged his shoulders in disbelief as he reached for a first sip of his waiting pint of bitter.

"Some people eh? He never even said thank you, ignorant bastard!"

"But Trev,...." I opened up for the third time intending to offer the explanation that although unintentionally he had built the bloke's hopes up that he had finally found his long lost cat, only to be blown down in flames when reality had set in that it was a stray. A clear case of mistaken identi-kitty!

I aborted my clarification and simply erupted with laughter along with Trev and Gin before announcing, "You couldn't make it up Trev, you just could not make it up!".

It had to be the best pre-match entertainment I'd ever experienced. Epic!

We were still talking about our feline folly as we entered the vast expanse of the Bill Shankly Stand housing a capacity Claret's following. In keeping with the high profile of the game, Howard Webb was the appointed referee.

Preston took an early lead in their desperate attempt to play catch up on at least some of the twenty three teams above them.

Burnley's very own son Jay Rodriguez got a well taken equaliser before half-time and with time ticking away, Chelsea loanee Jack Cork threw himself full length to head in the winning goal within yards of the Burnley masses to start the party in the last minute.

Manager Eddie Howe commented that he had never seen or heard such vocal support. It was a great finish to a great day that will always be remembered for 'Tricky Trev and the Croston Cat'. The one that got away!

'The Bear' on the cross before its cremation.

'R.I.P 'The Bear'...

It is with great sadness that I have to announce the passing of 'The Bear'.

For the benefit of the uninitiated , 'The Bear' was my trusty sheepskin coat that had served me well since purchasing it for the grand sum of two pints of beer from my pal 'Weedy' way back in 1987.

Weedy himself had rescued it from a house clearance where it was found cowering in one corner unwanted and unloved. It was in a truly pitiful condition with badly scuffed sleeves, and bearing multi-lacerations to its arms and back. But after applying lashings of tender loving care I brought it back from the brink, stitching up its gaping wounds with a combination of safety pins and insulation tape to let it live again.

For over twenty five years it protected me from Britain's harsh winters making a timely appearance whenever the mercury dropped below five degrees Celsius. Even then it was laughed at, ridiculed and sometimes abused, yet we became an inseparable combination when battling the elements together.

But as with all life-forms nothing lasts forever, and after numerous outbreaks of mange which badly affected its former luxuriant coat I knew that it was time to say goodbye, as unfortunately 'The Bear' had become unfit for purpose.

Its outer layer was disintegrating before my eyes and supporters were asking for small pieces of it as token mementos which they could now easily pluck from any ripped hole, like picking cotton from a cotton plant.

That was particularly sad to see, and I was determined not to let it suffer any more. So with a heavy heart I decided to have 'the Bear' put down humanely and cremated accordingly.

'Teetotal Crog', Weedy's brother hammered together an impressive ten foot wooden cross to give it the send-off it surely deserved.

My duty was to now nail it to the cross before its last journey by Madeley pool in the centre of our village.

At last 'The Bear' looked at peace, as myself, Jules, Weedy and Shaun solemnly carried the carcass to its final resting place upon its wooden base.

I had chosen Bonfire Night 2012 for the commemoration with an accompanying bottle of Champagne to toast its passage to the 'Bear after-life' if indeed one existed. I would of course be dressed in funereal black for the occasion.

The pointed wooden stake was firmly planted into the surrounding grass alongside the water as fireworks exploded into the night sky.

Popping the Champagne, I poured the assembled congregation a drink before delivering my heartfelt eulogy to the sheepskin coat that had become my friend, in effect giving it the last rites.

Thanking the beast for its unwavering defence against the biting cold I held back a tear as I struck the match that would send it up in flames!

Just then Weedy pointed out that the new occupants at number eleven directly behind us were gathered together at a bedroom window with a wide-eyed look of incredulity on their faces. The single, middle-aged mother tightly gripping her young children's shoulders either side of her.

"They're probably thinking that we're some sort of obscure religious cult", I remarked, lighting a tattered sleeve to quickly ignite my decomposing shroud.

"To The Bear!", I raised my glass to the sky along with the others in our party.

"To the Bear!" they cried as one.

Now fully alight, and with the wood ablaze it made quite a spectacular site against the moonlit backdrop of the pond as we stood in a respectful silence looking on.

That quietude being rudely broken by a yelling voice striding towards us in a purposeful manner.

"What the bloody hell's going on here then?", demanded a clearly agitated youth.

"We're holding a private service if you don't mind!", I replied abruptly, annoyed at the young bloke's aggressive introduction.

"Who are you anyway?", I enquired.

"I'm a warden for the pool and I want to make sure you're not going to pollute the waterway".

"Well we're certainly not going to do that mate. After our ceremony is over we will clear all the debris away, and besides, we're ten foot away from the river bank".

"What are you doing anyway, I've never seen a bonfire like it?", asked the warden in a much more civil tongue. "In fact I had phone calls from worried residents claiming a dead animal had been sacrificed on a cross!", he added, now sniggering.

"Well you know, they aren't that far from the truth", I ruefully replied.

"Another one said that some weirdos were performing an extreme initiation ceremony", chuckled the lad.

"There ya go! I told ya Weedy. It'll be that new family who moved in this week on our street. They just won't understand our way of doing things around here".

Turning round to point their way I just about glimpsed them drawing the upstairs curtains probably going to bed thinking 'What the hell had they let themselves in for, relocating to an area full of nutters!'

The embers of our funeral pyre slowly burnt out, and after a couple of buckets of water were thrown over it, completely extinguished.

"There ya go mate – job done!", I addressed the officious pool warden for the last time, bidding him goodnight as I scraped the bits of remaining debris away with the aid of a small pan and brush with an accompanying metal bucket.

All that was left to do was one final rousing tribute to my second skin which I felt compelled to carry out at the top of my voice.

"The Bear is dead

Long live The Bear!

Hip Hip – Hooray!

Hip Hip – Hooray!

Hip Hip – Hooray!"

All those present joined in , and almost as an accolade a rocket firework despatched half a dozen intermittent loud explosions above our heads to close proceedings.

"That's for 'The Bear' that is! That's for 'The Bear'", I yelled out. And 'The Bear' was no more.

In Memoriam

Deric Roberts was yet another loyal supporter of many years, who along with his long-term partner Shirley, like myself, also chose to make weekends of any fixture resembling a long distance trip.

As such I would invariably bump into the couple before, during or after a match to engage them in their usual cheery line of chat.

Deric, whose Christian name is of a welsh derivation, sadly passed away in the April of 2008 from an aggressive form of stomach cancer after a battle bravely borne.

In Memoriam

In part one of 'Got to be there!' a group photograph featured our local Sunday football team Crown Villa F.C. at a trophy presentation. The majority of which also being part of our past village street gang the 'Madeley Mafia'.

It's my sad duty to report the death of a former member who appeared to the far right of the back row on the photo that opened chapter 4.

Friend, and all round 'good egg' Nicky Pitchford was suddenly taken from us on July 2nd 2011 aged only 56, a victim of a massive heart attack.

Nick 'pitch' came across as a quiet unassuming bloke who took life in his stride. He possessed a rare personal demeanour, so laid back that it was almost horizontal. A trait that gained him many friends.

Poignantly, the night before he died Nick had been out to commemorate the anniversary of his son Lee tragically passing away at a young age.

He leaves behind loving wife Sue and cherished son Scott.

Nick becomes the second bereavement of that squad picture with manager Freddie Webb who is featured at the bottom left of the front row collapsing whilst on a family break to Blackpool in 1986.

He is survived by his precious daughter Tricia who still lives in the village with her partner Steve and family.

42 Irony of Ironies: 2009-10

I point an accusing finger at referee Howard Webb who gave some very contentious decisions against Burnley in their 2-1 defeat at Sunderland in April 2010.

After 33 very long years the premiership computer had decreed that our first game back in the top flight of English football would take place at my nearest home town club of Stoke City F.C. It's a real irony, and for me it represented a true baptism of fire having lived in the area all my life!

First day nerves …

As the big day approached I was also preparing for the launch of my first book titled 'GOT TO BE THERE!' written to celebrate my personal attendance record of 35 years without missing a Burnley game home or away in any competitive fixture. With our promotion through the Play-Offs dovetailing perfectly with my feat, it was the most anticipated start to a campaign since Burnley last won the right to play the cream of English football clubs way back in the 1973-74 season.

My publisher Ant Dawber had sent a copy of my book to our local evening newspaper 'The Sentinel' for review. Just a week before the big kick-off a full page article with accompanying photographs of myself proudly wearing the club's excellent retro-strip from the 1959-60 First Division Championship winning campaign appeared on the inside back page. With Burnley adopting this replica shirt complete with the badge from the same era to celebrate 50 years since this achievement it seemed that we were fated to be here amongst the elite.

Because of the local publicity about my book and the fact that we were playing Stoke, a number of national newspapers and a Granada T.V. crew picked up on the coincidence of this first fixture. So I found myself conducting an interview with the said T.V. company outside my work premises at Manor Bakeries near Newcastle-Under- Lyme where I worked as a mixing bay operative for the busy Christmas production of over 10 million mince pies! Ideally, Granada wanted to interview myself with a Stoke fan to capture the sense of friendly rivalry that was bubbling up for this historic clash, but try as I might none were forthcoming. I must have asked a dozen or so to attend who were previously ever-willing to offer a considered outspoken comment, derogatory or otherwise in an instant, but it seemed once they knew the cameras were rolling they got a little bashful.

Of course they still had a lot to say for themselves when we met up in town for our regular lads night out on a Friday. Their rants and ramblings about how much better they were than Burnley at this new level became ever more tedious. They all knew that I would always fight my corner on Burnley's behalf so when the loud and boisterous debate eventually boiled down to

"Put your money where your mouth is!" I had to shake on it.

So besides the various side bets on the first game I had a £20 wager with rent-a-gob 'Snozer' Tunstall who as documented I had nicknamed 'Zippy' from the muppet character in the 'Rainbow' childrens television programme because of his similarly animated protestations.

Our bet, that Stoke wouldn't finish higher in the table than The Clarets.

The hectic build up continued on the day of the game Saturday the 15th.August 2009. As is traditional with this fixture I generally organise a venue for our supporters to meet at early doors to commemorate the occasion. For this one it was Knutton W.M.C. near to Newcastle, and only 5 miles from the Britannia Stadium. 'Ant' my publisher had brought along the first half-dozen proof copies of my soon to be released book. However I didn't get a chance to glance let alone read one as supporters' pressure led me to sell them to our gathered troops.

A few party games later as is our tradition followed before it was time for us to set off in convoy to the game.

We were to be the first of many teams that would suffer the after-effects of a Rory Delap exocet missile throw in that season. Executed from an approximate height of eight feet with arms raised to the full, it does stand to reason that a more powerful trajectory can be administered than from a ground level corner or free kick.

As a consequence of the damage wreaked by his powerful flings he is probably the only footballer in the entire history of the Premiership that has a transfer value of a couple of million for his throw-ins' alone!

It would be one of two set pieces that would confirm a 2-0 defeat in a game that although we retained a lot of possession we never got to hurt them. Even more galling was the way our emergency centre half Stephen Jordan firmly headed home from the long throw, with a strike that namesake Joe Jordan in his Leeds United heyday would have been proud of.

The temperature was hot but Burnley seemed to freeze almost as if the big stage they were being asked to appear on was just too much for them. This even though we were officially Stoke's 'bogey' team at the Britannia Stadium over the last decade with 5 wins 2 draws and just the single 1-0 defeat in the record books. We knew exactly what Stoke's strengths were but we simply didn't have the personel to deal with it.

I put it down to first day nerves but it was a less than auspicious start against a team that couldn't beat us home or away in their promotion year from the Championship in 2007-08.

So all that was left of the day was to meet up with the mix of both Burnley and Stoke fans at the designated after-match Dick Turpin pub to pay my monetary dues reluctantly to 'Zippy' with his typically antagonistic jibe of "The easiest win we've ever had in the 'Prem" ringing ominously in my ears!

Stunning home wins spoilt by away losses …

If that wasn't bad enough our next league fixture was against the might of Manchester United at Turf Moor. It would also be the official launch of my first book 'Got To Be There!' in the James Hargreaves stand reception area, or the former 'Longside' as it will be forever known.

I arrived early for my signing session which was well received, then it was on to the game for what we all knew would be an extremely stiff test.

With the ground packed to the rafters to see Premier League Football for the first time, as well as the reigning champions visiting, it created an electric atmosphere usually reserved for when Blackburn Rovers visit town.

The opening exchanges were at a predictably frenetic pace, then within twenty minutes a breakthrough was made. The ball was crossed into the penalty area where it bounced around until headed out up into the air, hovering temptingly for oncoming forward Robbie Blake. His volleyed strike almost bursting the net and giving goalkeeper Ben Foster no chance whatsoever. It was a magnificent connection that earned the little man hero status.

That standing being temporarily put on hold when he brought down Patrice Evra to concede a penalty just before half-time. But in another critical twist to the game the substantial body mass of the 'Beast' that is Brian Jensen guessed correctly to brilliantly save Michael Carrick's spot-kick down to his right hand side.

Burnley battled like demons to preserve their slender lead in the second half and after successfully surviving four minutes of injury time the glorious spoils were theirs for the first time since I had seen Brian O'Neil hit an equally spectacular thunderbolt from 30 yards in September 1968 to win by the same 1-0 scoreline in the 88th minute. Both victories were met by the same ecstatic acclaim that always accompany such David versus Goliath clashes.

Everton were next up once again at home, and the game followed a very similar script. This time Wembley hero Wade

Elliott executed a sublime chip to get the ground rocking to take another 1-0 lead. Then Tony Hibbert's spot of amateur dramatics gained 'The Toffees' a penalty when he dived unnecessarily. Justice seemed to have be done as Louis Saha put his penalty a yard wide. The Clarets hung on to record another precious three points which made an impressive seven in total, putting them at that same position in the league. What a difference a week makes eh?

Away from home we simply did not travel well at all, recording consecutive incremental losses of 3-0, 4-0 and 5-0 against Chelsea, Liverpool and Spurs respectively. Yet our home form was standing up as further triumphs were recorded over Sunderland 3-1 and Birmingham City 2-1.

A demoralizing 3-2 reverse at toxic rivals Blackburn Rovers proved a real setback as was even trying to get to the game for the 1p.m. start on the Sabbath.

Burnley fans, like Rovers, are only allowed to travel by designated buses or coaches to these fixtures such is the intense hatred between the two clubs. As it had been deemed too disruptive for a traditional Saturday football fixture, an early Sunday afternoon kick-off had been allocated. That all meant a Saturday night in the town to ensure an early dart next day resulting in a stay at 'plain John Smith's' Brierfield residence just three miles from the centre.

The following morning after joining a 500 yard queue of humanity we are herded on to the dated transportation which looked for all the world like it had come straight from the film set of the 'Last of the summer wine' T.V. comedy series. The near 100 conveyances are then sent to their destination of Ewood Park in convoys of ten with police cars and motorcycle outriders at both the front and back as an escort, whilst the Lancashire force's helicopter keeps a watching brief from the sky above.

After the match the same laborious procedure has to be followed back to Burnley's official club car park, and as if waiting for the crowd to clear for up to an hour isn't enough after such a painful defeat speed restrictions imposed by the constabulary add to the collective misery. That was still no excuse, although incensed, for Burnley fans wrecking their own town centre all through that night.

A 3-1 home defeat to Wigan Athletic would go on to be one of the defining results of the campaign. Even though we did win our next game at headquarters 2-0 against Hull City. That Halloween day's fixture on the last day of October 2009 would be the last time our defence kept a clean sheet all season!

Yet a gratifying 3-3 draw at Manchester City's Eastlands Stadium could have been oh so much better as Burnley conceded a 2-0 lead.

From thereon results deteriorated right up to Christmas with crucial defeats away to Portsmouth and Wolves, teams who would be involved in the relegation dogfight, being the hardest to stomach.

In fact so galling was the 2-0 loss at Pompey for the early afternoon televised game that our trio of 'Knock-Off' Nigel, Jon-a-thong and myself decided to get blitzed straight after the game instead of going back to our digs to get changed such was our rancour at the outcome.

With around ten hours of drinking time ahead we traversed the nearby Fratton Road, which in turn directly adjoins both the Kingston and London roads, a distance of around two miles.

Copious amounts of beer later after painstakingly dissecting each and every critical incident in the game with a fine toothcomb we had to conclude that given the lowly status of the opposition it just had to be the lowest point of the season so far.

Analysis over, and by now deeply intoxicated I released all my pent up frustration the only way I know how – on the dance floor.

Once I do decide to let off steam as people who know me will tell you I don't just throw a few quick nonsensical shapes then disappear into a dark corner with my pint. No siree, when I put my mind to it just like Forrest Gump 'kept on running', likewise I keep on dancing.

Having raved from two to four hours non-stop at a foam party as well as an open air rave at San Antonio, Ibiza and the Adriatic resort of Rovinj, Croatia respectively my bopping C.V. is up there with the best, and so I settled in to 'trip the light fantastic' big style.

Gyrating alone so as not to disrupt other participants I immersed myself wholeheartedly in the music to ease the pain of defeat until the floor clears leaving just me and one old sad looking transvestite wannabee bizarrely outfitted in a white vest, frock and boots!

Standing no more than 5 foot 5 inches tall, 'he' had made no attempt to cover his bald head or even dress convincingly enough to resemble the opposite sex, and the anchor tattoo on his forearm almost certainly denoted a former naval career.

Admiring his bottle and certainly nothing else, I too took off my tee shirt to reveal my white vest and began to have a playful bop with him to Elvis's ' Jailhouse Rock'. Although compliant, Joe as he called himself lacked any kind of rhythmic coordination which made our drunken strictly come dancing attempts look even more ludicrous.

Last orders, then drinking up time followed after a solid hour of prancing about in an absurd manner.

My companions had left me to it, either bored or embarrassed by my boorish behaviour or maybe both. But it had done the trick, I had danced away my despair for the day ably aided and abetted by Joe the sailor.

Thankfully the lads didn't capture the antics for 'You Tube!'

From hero to zero ...

Then came what I personally consider to be the defining fixture that would go a long way to determining our end of season fate – Bolton Wanderers at home on Boxing Day.

A near capacity, and what would be the best attendance of our Premiership stay at Turf Moor, had 2,357 away supporters in the 21,761 crowd, and it was they who let the Bolton hierarchy know in no uncertain terms which man they wanted to take over from present manager Gary Megson.

Megson himself had admitted that dressing room harmony was not all it might have been, and Trotters supporters remained sceptical of his motivation capabilities.

Owen Coyle had also made no secret of his affection for Wanderers, saying as much in his programme notes on the day, adding that winning the Play-Off final and scoring a goal at Wembley for them was his most terrific memory of that era, all under what would turn out to be a totally hypocritical highlighted headline of, "We will not waver."

Surprisingly, during the 1-1 draw the Bolton following were not shouting out the name of their own manager in charge but that of our very own Owen Coyle at regular intervals.

They had made their feelings crystal clear to watching chairman Phil Gartside as well as the Bolton board, and it would be the spark that lit the kindling to fan the flames of speculation.

Up until that day there had been no hint of conjecture linking the two clubs being made public. Now rumours were rife and my own theory is that the seeds of doubt about bossing Burnley Football Club were firmly planted in his head by Gartside during their inevitable meeting after the game.

Two goals in the last seven minutes was enough for Burnley to suffer a ninth away defeat in ten games just two days later at Everton's Goodison Park.

A welcome break from our struggling Premier League form took us to the fabled land of the concrete cows at Milton Keynes Dons in the 3rd round of the F.A. Cup.

As new grounds go stadium MK is one of the more impressive ones. A bowl like design built in the style of an American concourse on its interior, although it's a devil of a place to get to by limited public transport.

Burnley shaded the tie 2-1 but by now all eyes were on the reaction of O.C. after the match as mounting uncertainty from both the television and newspaper media had built this up as his last day in charge.

He strode purposefully part way down the far end of the pitch to give a high thumbs up sign, then he was gone.

Former Director of Communications at number 10 Downing Street Alastair Campbell asked me the question on everyone's lips as we were leaving the ground,

"What d,ya think Dave? Is he staying or going?"

I based my answer upon his mannerisms after the game when he acknowledged the travelling near two thousand faithful from afar.

"Well, he's given us the 'thumbs up' sign and not a wave so I reckon he's sticking with Burnley", I observed.

What I didn't know then was Coyle had ducked the post-match press conference leaving assistant Sandy Stewart to awkwardly answer the inevitable questions over his mentor's future.

Instead, Coyle took a taxi to Luton Airport to fly home to Scotland for a family reunion. The wily Phil Gartside following him over the border on Sunday, meeting up with him to discuss a move to his club Bolton. By Monday he had gone.

A £3.6 million compensation fee was paid, and the man who by many was regarded as god-like in stature for achieving promotion to the Premier League was with us no more, immediately inheriting the conflicting biblical title of 'Judas'.

His departure was met with incredulity both within the town and beyond. He had only signed a new deal to keep him at the club in the summer after interest from Celtic had been made public. Now he was leaving us for a team who were currently 18th in the Premier League table, four places below us!

It left a bitter taste, with Burnley now having to search mid-season for a suitable replacement, with ten senior players out of contract come summer adding to their difficulties.

In a statement after his move had been confirmed Coyle claimed that he was being held back by a lack of finances at the club. This from a man who had brought in debatably one of Burnley's worst ever signings with a heralding fanfare of "This player will go on to be one of the best in Europe!"

His full name being the mouthful that is Remco Jelmer van der Schaaf.

Reputedly the biggest wage earner by some margin at the club because of this grandiose personal tribute from his new manager he went on to make just one single league appearance.

That disastrous debut in the first game of the 2008-09 season at Sheffield Wednesday in a 4-1 defeat.

Also playing that day and signed in the same summer was 6ft 6inch Peruvian international goalkeeper Diego Penny who also had a nightmare as previously documented.

All I can say is that one of his country's native Andes llammas could have kept goal with equal affect such was his lack of presence.

They are just two examples of his bad judgement, so maybe the chairman and board of directors had every right to veto his proposed transfer bids.

An uninspiring managerial appointment …

But it had happened and we had to face up to the fact that we were slipping into a battle and we needed a strong managerial personality to fight our way out.

Instead, we got former full-back Brian Laws, previously in charge of relegation threatened Sheffield Wednesday, one division below in the championship.

Now you don't have to be Einstein to deduce that if the man couldn't do a salvage job with 'The Owls' he was hardly going to have an impact at this far more demanding level.

His first game should have been facing Stoke City at home but the winter weather put paid to that one, meaning that his initiation would be at Old Trafford against Manchester United.

Laws got full backing from the majority of the 3,000 plus travelling allocation that day, but it failed to galvanize the players as they succumbed to another heavy 3-0 defeat.

Three reverse results followed, 1-0 away to Reading in the F.A. Cup 4th round, with more narrow league losses to Bolton 1-0 and Chelsea 2-1.

The Bolton game on a cold Tuesday night in January giving the 4,654 travelling Burnley fans a first chance to vent their anger at the recently departed 'Judas' Coyle the new manager at the Reebok Stadium.

A regular barrage of abuse accompanying the many quickly painted home-made banners admonishing his name. It was a pity our players didn't display the same passion that evening turning in an insipid performance of no spirit.

For reasons, I found harder to comprehend than most Burnley fans, we signed Leon Cort during the January transfer window in an attempt to shore up the defence.

Remarkably we paid a staggering 1.5 million in the three and a half deal for a 30-year-old centre-half that was no more than fourth in the pecking order at Premier rivals Stoke City behind Ryan Shawcross, Robert Huth and Abdoulaye Faye.

The following Saturday he made his debut in that narrow defeat at home to Chelsea keeping his place until the end of a disappointing season.

Saturday February 6th brought about our first victory for our new managerial incumbent with a 2-1 home success against West Ham.

It would be temporary respite as four consecutive defeats 3-0 away to Fulham, 5-2 away to Aston Villa, 2-1 at home to Portsmouth and 3-1 on the road at Arsenal plunged us down to 19th position from which we would never recover.

The return fixture with the visit of Blackburn Rovers couldn't even offer a much needed and desperately wanted consolation of a long-awaited derby day win as the Clarets went down to the only goal of the game from a hotly disputed penalty.

Possibly the most farcical episode of the campaign came before that when we played Stoke City at home to counter the spectacularly long projectile throw-ins' of Rory Delap. The ruse to move in the advertising hoardings to within the minimum requirements from the pitch to restrict his run up might have worked if it had been done fully. However, a gap had been left just up from the halfway line which Delap effectively used to plonk the ball right on Tudgay's head for their goal well within the penalty area.

Then came the Easter crucifixion as an unstoppable Manchester City side visited Turf Moor over the Bank Holiday weekend. Burnley were nailed well and truly to the cross within the first seven short and shocking minutes. It was pitiful to observe as wave after wave of attacks breached our egg shell like defence. I can only compare it to a heavyweight boxer taking on a flyweight who is trying desperately to fend off a constant barrage of punches to no avail, with the team on the canvas lying totally dazed and confused in a prostrate position. A 5-0 half-time score being registered by our visitors.

Then the heavens opened, and with the incessant rain turning the playing surface into a marsh we were all hoping that referee Alan Wiley would deem the pitch unfit to continue, a decision that given City's commanding lead would have caused justifiable outrage.

However, the ongoing debate on the concourse was whether Burnley could prevent a record defeat in their 128-year history. This stood at 10-0 to Aston Villa in 1925, and to Sheffield United during the 1929 season by the same margin, each in the original Division One.

Fortunately, the sky blues slick pacey play was handicapped by the resultant quagmire on the turf, yet they still managed to notch another goal before my personal player of the season Steven Fletcher pulled one back recording a final and humiliating 6-1 result.

Even more hard to take was the sighting of our midfielder Kevin McDonald in the nearby 110 club where he was found drinking with his Scottish pals who had come down to watch him. For after being substituted at half-time he had opted to view the second half on the live television screening in the bar.

That showed an appalling lack of respect to the manager and players alike which would lead to him being substitute at best from thereon in until his inevitable departure.

Elation turns to deflation in just one week ...

Burnley now needed back to back wins on the road to stand any realistic chance of survival. A tall order indeed as they hadn't managed to win any games on their travels during the whole campaign and now it was approaching the second week in April.

Our first opponents were Hull City which also happened to coincide with my commemorative thirty-three-piece denim suit celebration. The April 10th date making it precisely 36 years since my last competitive match not attended at Newcastle United in 1974.

I was hoping to celebrate my personal achievement with a victory which would enable me to fully enjoy the weekend to the max.

But within three minutes I was in my Victor Meldrew " I don't belieeeeve it!" mode. Kevin Kilbane scoring yet another cheaply conceded goal that Burnley fans had sadly got all too accustomed to that season.

The defence was in total disarray and in more tatters than my thirty three-piece suit. I scoured the pitch looking for a reaction. It would come from the wise head of Graham Alexander who had echoed my thoughts in a pre-match interview I had given to the Sky T.V. sports reporter and fellow Claret Peter Robinson.

He had asked me the question,

"If you were Brian Laws what last message would you send the team out with as they left the K.C. Stadium dressing room?"

I answered his enquiry with a rallying call of some intent.

Clenching my fist for added emphasis, I stirred my emotions in preparation of the declaration.

"I'd tell them to go out there, fight for every ball from the 1st minute to the 90th, and show the determination to succeed for the fans, the shirt and most importantly themselves!"

They had already failed miserably to heed the introductory advice of my statement but to his immense credit "Grezza" as Graham is termed, turned the tide by berating, cajoling and bollocking them before leading by example to slam home two well taken penalties either side of a Martin Paterson and Wade Elliott goal resulting in a 4-1 victory.

Not only was it our first away win, it was also a first double and our highest score of the campaign.

It was a lifeline, but we still had to win at Sunderland the following Saturday to give ourselves a sporting chance of survival.

It constituted another weekend foray, so tickets for our transportation on the Megabus from Manchester were snapped up online for a fiver each way.

After a three hour journey, we located our Travelodge digs that just happened to be smack in the middle of what looked like 'disco-land'. In fact, myself and the Weed counted over a dozen late night bars within a 100 yard radius.

It was an observation not missed by our receptionist who apprehensively apologized for any inconvenience in advance as she explained that one of the partying venues going under the audacious name of 'Bill Bluebaker' was housed in premises directly under the hotel.

Still buzzing from the feel-good factor after celebrating our precious win at Hull into the early hours around the old town district I endeavoured to reassure her misgivings.

"Don't worry ya'self about it love we fully expect to be dancing the night away with them ourselves later on".

The ridiculing laugh of derision wasn't quite what we expected back, but of course she wasn't to know we were serial party animals!

At the game, it seemed that the Burnley players had given our drinking circuit a trial run as once again they gave their opponents far too much room in the penalty area to go 2-0 down. Our forward Steve Thompson on as a second half substitute netting nothing more than a consolation goal in a disheartening defeat, even though both their goals could have been quite easily been disallowed by referee Howard Webb.

Disconsolately leaving the Stadium of Light we were still determined to make a good session of it. Yet after stewing over the result, by the time one o'clock ticked by we decided to knock it on the head returning to our base earlier than planned as the consequences of the demoralizing result began to hit home with the beer seemingly getting stuck in my throat.

The Billy Bluebaker's disco was belting out the tunes as I tried to settle in my bed, so given my now melancholy state of mind I descended the stairs to lodge a formal complaint about the excessive noise at the reception desk where the same girl that had booked us in on Friday was still on duty.

"Can't ya do something about that flamin' racket next door? How's anyone supposed to get a night's sleep around here?", I demanded in a crotchety manner.

The startled meeter and greeter wasted no time in reminding me of our earlier conversation when I had booked in.

"But sir, you said that it wouldn't be a problem as you would be partying with them when I checked you and your friend in yesterday", she stated correctly.

"Well maybe I did, but that was before the match!",I countered tersely before taking the lift back to my room now resigned to my fate and probably my team's.

Its win or bust – and we bust! ...

Burnley's destiny was now 'win or bust' with just three matches remaining nothing but nine points would do.

The first of which took place on a Sunday for the sixth time this season as a consequence of their oppositions Europa League involvement. So far we had lost four of those contests and winning just the one, a prized 1-0 victory over Everton.

There would be no such repeat against their city neighbours as Burnley finally and painfully relinquished their right to the Premier League.

Liverpool administered the final coup de grâce in merciless manner racking up a heavy 4-0 thrashing.

And yep, an inevitable tear did make its way south down my cheek.

"Thirty three flamin' years it's took us to get here and we're down in one!", I raved almost incongruously as in all our heart of hearts we all knew that realistically this team wasn't capable of winning three games on the spin to stand a chance of preserving our status.

Therefore, Monday morning was a far more painful experience for myself and the tens of thousands of Clarets spread right across the globe as Burnley Football Club relinquished their right to play Premier League opposition on a regular basis.

'Relegation' – just how can one word potently hurt so much? I'll tell you why because it means demotion, a position of less authority, importance and ultimately respect.

It had been the seventh time that I'd gone through the grieving process of witnessing the team I love go down a division in the last forty years and each one had been a truly miserable experience.

Could we have stayed up? Of course we could! After our enforced change at managerial level the club was in 14th position with twenty precious points on the board. A point a game from the remaining fixtures wasn't an unreasonable target to maintain our status I don't think. The present squad had boxed above their weight to secure some tremendous victories and honourable draws, but they had also taken a mauling in too many games, particularly on their travels. Fundamentally that was because the nucleus of the team was of a championship standard and we hadn't made a major investment of any quality in the January transfer window which could have turned enough of those marginal defeats into vital points against our relegation contemporaries. In short, the sum of the whole had just not been good enough.

It was eleven months to the day that we had gained promotion in that fantastic Wembley final in May last year.

So, the premiership journey was over, but remarkably Burnley still had something to play for in their last two fixtures away at Birmingham and at home to Spurs. Up for grabs was an extremely prestigious additional place in the Europa league courtesy of the 'fair play' table.

After a typical end of season 2-1 defeat down at Brum Burnley went into their last fixture against Tottenham Hotspur with Fulham the only other team above them yet to qualify for Europe next season.

The Cottagers however were due to play Atletico Madrid in the final of the Europa League at Hamburg the following Wednesday. If they did overcome the Spanish side it would mean them defending their title, supposedly opening the door for Brian Law's side to head into the continent themselves with the first qualifying round stages scheduled for the beginning of July

As It happened, Fulham's hopes of glory were shattered with a Diego Forlan extra-time winner resulting in a score of 2-1 to the Madrid side.

Upon further examination of the criterion for inclusion it transpired that supporter behaviour was also taken into consideration. With a total of 93 fans arrested from both factions in the two clashes against Blackburn Rovers that season it is probably a safe bet that E.U.F.A would conclude that this conduct constituted anything but fair play.

In the last match of the campaign Burnley came from 2-0 down to amazingly win 4-2 against Tottenham Hotspur at home.

Did I enjoy the premiership adventure?

Only for the first two months I must say, when we did make a fist of it. After that we got ground down by some severe thrashings which felt like helplessly watching your very own child getting bullied by the bigger and older boys of the Premiership in the school playground unable to do anything about it.

There were too many preventable goals given away, not one registered from over a hundred corners taken by ourselves, with the team conceding at least once in their last 27 games creating a new league record.

It had been a chastening lesson of the quality chasm between the top two divisions.

Burnley had continued shopping at Poundland whilst the clear majority of our rivals had been regularly popping into Harrods for their purchases. That was the harsh reality between sinking or surviving, and we had sunk!

In Memoriam

The mood of depression plunged far deeper depths when Keith Riley informed me that his fun-loving partner Anji had passed away on the 20th May 2010.

Anji had died after suffering Atrial Fibrillation, a condition brought on from an irregular heartbeat. She was just 55. A good friend to Dozy, Martin, Brent, Joanne & Ginette.

Her eloquent letter featured by the football club in the previous season's next home game after the epic Tottenham cup tie was testimony to her love of the club.

Anji was buried wearing her husband's lucky Burnley shirt that made appearances at both Wembley Play-Off Finals, which of course the Clarets won.

In Memoriam

In remembrance too of devout Burnley fan Adam Donnelly who hanged himself wearing his club shirt after the rancorous 3-2 defeat at Blackburn Rovers. I would regularly bump into Adam at away games celebrating or drowning his sorrows at bars and clubs late into the night. He was only 23 years of age, and I can only hope that the derby result was not a deciding factor to his last act.

Gary Parkinson ....

Gary Parkinson suffered a very serious stroke in September 2010 at the age of only 42.

After months in hospital he was diagnosed with 'locked in' syndrome leaving him to communicate with little more than a blink of his eyes.

Gary's wife Deborah and their three children have now had their family home adapted to cater for his needs thanks to generous donations from not only his footballing friends, but many others. They include supporters from Burnley, Middlesbrough and Preston who represent the greater majority of clubs he served.

His last game for Burnley was against Watford in the final match of the 1996-1997 season. In this his 163rd appearance he scored Burnley's third goal in a 4-1 Division Two fixture at Turf Moor.

The defining photograph from our Wembley play-off success against Stockport County has to be the two goal scorers posing for the cameras at the end of the game suitably elated. His brother in arms that day David Eyres remains one of his loyalist friends, raising funds and keeping in regular touch to monitor Gary's progress.

I only spoke to Gary once and my dialogue consisted of just these five words that I had to say.

"Absolutely top draw strike Gary."

It wasn't however after the Wembley victory but in the Players' Bar at Grimsby Town. There, he scored his best goal in a Burnley shirt. A 35 yard thunderbolt that earned Burnley a 2-2 draw in the very last minute of an old Division One game in November 1994. It was a sensational hit that everyone in the room wanted to talk about hence my brief compliment that he duly thanked me for.

From all accounts his condition remains stable and the hope is that with his legion of friends and family offering their vital continued support he will one day answer the second question I was going to ask him after that screamer at Blundell Park.

"Did you mishit it Gary?"

Only kidding of course, but you know, I think he would have appreciated the humorous intent such was his laid back disposition.

I've witnessed Gary introduced to the crowd at half-time both at Middlesbrough and Burnley to a truly rapturous ovation, and he regularly attends Turf Moor to meet his old team mates, as well as watching the game.

Keep on in there Gary. We're all proud of you.

43 The In-Between years: 2010 – 2013

Brian Laws. An uninspiring managerial appointment.
Photo courtesy of Burnley Football Club

Eddie Howe. Good manager – wrong team.
Photo courtesy of Burnley Football Club

Had Burnley blown their one and only chance of tasting life in the Premiership? There were certainly plenty of examples of teams leaving that league never to return again, would we be another?

World Cup South Africa 2010

Against our better judgement over a few beers we decided to follow the England national team once more, over to South Africa for the 2010 World Cup Finals.

Hopes were high as they always seem to be before the knock-out stages when it matters, but it was a country neither of us had visited before and we also had an offer of accommodation around ten miles outside of Johannesburg at the comically named suburb of Radiocop.

This was with Anna who used to live in our village before she and her husband emigrated there. Anna being a good friend of Weedy's ma and pa Pat and John Read.

This wasn't going to be a cheap trip either, but after a couple of hours perusing our options at the Manchester branch of specialist travel agents Trailfinders we settled for a 'best value' flight that necessitated a five-day stopover in Ethiopia!

Now my only knowledge concerning this African nation came from the harrowing, biblical images of the starving tens of thousands of people living right on life's edge that were beamed into British homes in 1985 which galvanized Sir Bob Geldof into organizing Live Aid to raise emergency funds towards their desperate plight along with Midge Ure of Ultravox fame.

In one of the greatest humanitarian gestures in my lifetime on the 13th July of that same year Status Quo opened the concert at Wembley Stadium attended by a sell-out 72,000 people. Simultaneously a music based fundraising event took place at the John F Kennedy stadium in Pennsylvania, United States with an estimated 100,000 on site.

An approximate global audience of 1.9 billion across 150 nations watched the live broadcast.

So, what was Addis Ababa the capital going to be like on the 25th anniversary of the charitable phenomenon?

On Sunday June 6th, we got our answer as we touched down at 7.am. local time, and it didn't look at all bad if truth be told.

With the help of multi-investment, primarily it transpired from the Chinese, high rise modest buildings were springing up on the city's horizon and although there was still evidence of poverty in the shanty towns it had wholly improved since the famine of the mid-eighties. Upon further exploration, we found no less than fifteen premises selling beer down the one street just a hundred yards from our booked accommodation. At an average of about 25 pence equivalent in the local 'Birr' currency, and with most lagers and stouts a minimum 5.5% strength we developed a strong rapport with the patrons of the many bars who repeatedly referred to us as 'aid workers' totally convinced, no matter how many times we told them that we were here as tourists.

If the cost of living was cheap for us there it certainly wasn't in South Africa principally because of the poor exchange rate of just 10 rand to the pound, a figure that has doubled in subsequent years. To add insult to injury our £53.50p charge for what we were informed was a mandatory yellow fever inoculation certificate wasn't even asked for at passport control. At least that's one disease I shouldn't catch.

We caught a taxi to Anna's place and what an eye opener it was. Although well out of the city centre the gated complex protected by razor wire atop electrified fencing had an armed guard on a fortified entrance with every home fitted with an immediate response alarm. It was like being held in a prison camp!

Anna explained that all the security was necessary even though the houses on the estate were desirable but certainly not opulent. She even insisted upon driving us everywhere because of the dangers of being mugged, which even included regular visits to the nearby O' Hagons irish bar, little more than 500 yards away. It confirmed J'obourg as probably the most dangerous place to visit in the world.

For our first match against the U.S.A. we had arranged to meet up at a bar with a local Port Vale fan Darren Carter who had a couple of spare tickets at a cost price of about £50 each. Job done we booked our coach tickets at a local supermarket for the two hour, eighty-mile journey over to the former mining town of Rustenburg.

It had to be the most obscure place I had travelled to watch an England game with one road in and the same road out leading to chaotic congestion as we approached the Royal Bafokeng Stadium.

We got in, had time for a quick beer and took up our place on the open terracing of the 45,000-capacity ground.

Three quarters of the support was for England with a small enclave of Americans congregated to the paddock on our left side.

What a start England made with Stevie Gerrard, one of the holy trinity the team's hopes for the tournament were built upon along with Frank Lampard and Wayne Rooney, scoring after only four minutes to begin what we thought would now become an elementary rout.

Not so! The yanks clawed their way tenaciously into the game equalizing just before half-time when an ordinary shot squirmed under the body of goalkeeper Robert Green. And that's the way it stayed. It was terrible keeping, in an awful game and yet the hapless custodian would keep his place in the next match against Algeria in Cape Town after getting a vote of confidence from head coach Fabio Capello.

A Kuala Airlines plane flew us to the coastal city for a reasonable £75 each one way. We booked our digs at the airport information desk and were picked up at the railway station by Charlie the proprietor of the bed and breakfast place.

A night in the multi-bar district around Long street followed.

We always designated one day a 'tourism day' so the nearby attraction of Table Mountain looked particularly appealing against a cloudless blue sky.

A wait of over an hour and a half ensued as it seemed every other tourist in the city had the same idea to scale the famous flat topped peak.

It was as good a time as any to text my contact Kev. Lewis from Leek who we were meeting up along with his wife Tracy for a drink. It transpired that he was also in the same queue too and was just about to get the cable car lift to the top. And although never having met before by giving physical descriptions we finally deduced who each other were.

Kev had played professionally for Stoke City, Man United and latterly Telford United and classified himself as the last of 'The Busby Babes', the group term given to manager Matt. Busby's young prodigies at Old Trafford.

We arranged to meet up in a balcony bar overlooking the Atlantic Ocean before England's next game against Algeria at the impressive purpose built 70,000 capacity Green Point stadium which cost a staggering 4.5 billion rand.

Still having no tickets for the match three hours before kick-off I wrote out a cardboard sign stating plainly, 'Two tickets wanted'. A constant stream of fans was passing by until Otto a Hungarian chap stopped to say that two of his friends had cried off and he was prepared to sell their £90 individual tickets for £50 each. We snatched his hand off at the offer arranging to meet him on Level 6 in the stand.

We caught up with Kev Lewis and his party at the Waterfront, a huge harbour side complex of bars, restaurants and fast food outlets. There, he came up with a double proposition too good to miss.

Not only did he invite us both to a house party that his good friend Garry France ex-Burnley player of the 1960's era was hosting that night, Kev and Tracy asked if we fancied taking their place at a four-bedroomed coastal villa they had already paid for en- route to Port Elizabeth where England would be playing their final qualifying game against tiny Slovenia who they needed to beat for guaranteed qualification into the last sixteen knock-out stages.

Both offers were of course accepted instantly by myself and Weedy. Our attempt to tender some amount of monetary recompense for their generous gesture was met with repeatedly resolute refusal so our grateful thanks had to suffice.

Saying our goodbyes until later that night we made our way to our seats high in the stands. My particular location being on an aisle seat directly opposite the few hundred chanting mob of the Algerians who credit to them sung all through the ninety minutes, even though their intrusive flag waving towards my face had to be pointed out in no uncertain terms.

England turned in the worst performance that I have witnessed since any of the 1988 European Championships in Germany. They were woeful, misplacing so many passes, having no game plan it seemed and creating few chances which were inevitably scorned. Entertainment value nil!

0-0 it finished, and so bad was it that I found myself apologising to our ticket source Otto for such a wretched display.

We caught a bus to Garry's party where we also met George Eastham, a Cape Town resident of many years, and the former Stoke City player was one of the main protagonists who got the maximum wage abolished in the early 1960's.

Because of which top footballers now bring home obscene amounts of money and that was the allegation I dared to level at George.

In fairness, he didn't go on the defensive agreeing that today's players were being vastly overpaid, and citing the fact that in those days' footballers pay wasn't that attractive even compared to the ordinary working man's annual income.

Then the television cameras rolled for a documentary based upon their time playing for Cape Town City centred around the league and cup double winning side of 1976.

Next day we caught a bus out to the Wilderness Dunes the luxurious beachside location that had been bestowed upon us. We revelled in the extravagance of it all, but because it was set out on its own and almost every resident had a car we were forced to hitch into the few intermediate towns nearby.

We both decided that a few more days here easily beat watching England further on in Port Elizabeth so we watched the wearisome 1-0 victory by walking the three kilometres into the centre of Wilderness Town.

Then came the shocking debacle against the old enemy Germany in Bloemfontein as England had only finished second in the group.

Draping my union flag over the outside verandas me and Weedy watched the game on the big screen in a pub astounded at what we saw. A shocking performance followed which was a mix of humiliation and controversy ending in a 4-1 score line to the Germans.

Of course, it will be remembered for Frank Lampard's superb lofted goal that never was. Although feet over the goal line behind keeper Manuel Never, Uruguayan referee Jorge Laronda and his officials amazingly waved play on. It would have brought England back into the game at 2-2, but there was no disguising yet another bitterly disappointing exit as they suffered their heaviest ever defeat at a major championship.

I'd spent a lot of money once again watching second rate showings from a national side of losers managed by a bloody Italian.

Surely it just couldn't get any worse? But it surely would and surely did.

A postcard from a small island ...

"Selamat tengah haridaripada Singapore!", – or "Good day from Singapore" for those not conversant with the Malay language.

Go back ten years and Burnley's pre-season would be preparation for the first of three consecutive trips to the Isle of Man tournament. Now I found myself taking out a loan to cover the immense cost of a visit to the far east. Even then it was via India to save a couple of hundred quid on the direct air fare.

I finally docked in Singapore on the Tuesday morning of the game after an arduous six-day journey that Phileas Fogg would have turned down.

The first leg of my odyssey by the most economical route taking me from Heathrow to Mumbai, formerly Bombay when I last visited in 1985. My next flight not being until another fifteen hours so it was time to catch up on a bit of kip in the airports appropriately titled 'snooze room'.

It's quite an innovative idea as the passenger has a choice of over sixty sturdy sun lounger type seats to choose from, although the distinctive scurrying of tiny paws confirmed a mouse infestation, meaning that to prevent rodents pilfering it was advisable to sleep with your baggage off the wooden floor.

My overnight six-hour flight taking me directly to Singapore by Kingfisher Airlines yep, the same company that serves up the beer of the same name in Britain's curry houses. Changi airport being the most impressive I'd been to.

But this wasn't to be my final destination, oh no, the Lion City as it is often referred has a national anthem called 'Onward Singapore', and that mirrored my travel plans.

You see I had visited the world's only island city-state just four years ago on the way back from 'nam'. No not Birming 'nam' but Vietnam, so I knew just how expensive it was to exist here as a traveller.

Therefore, my plan was to take a seven-hour train ride to Kuala Lumpur in Malaysia where the cost of living was reportedly half that of Singapore.

I got to lay on my first bed a full sixty-four hours after departing my village home, and boy did I sleep well that night.

Burnley were due to play the might of Gombak United, Home United and the island's Asian games team no less, in what was being billed as the Asian Cup.

That meant a twelve-hour overnight train ride from Kuala Lumpur arriving on the Tuesday of the first scheduled match to secure digs in a district called Gelong. The Ritz it certainly wasn't with the 'Lonely Planet' traveller's guide describing my chosen location thus:

"Nowhere else in Singapore are food, religion culture and sleaze more at ease with each other than in Gelong!"

O.K. its's a notorious red light district in a rougher area of town, but it is one of the cheaper options, and besides my army of cockroaches carry away any crumbs that find their way to the floor for no additional charge.

The first two friendlies both took place at the Tampines Rover Stadium whose team were currently top of the national 'S' League. After bedding in for the first twenty minutes Burnley cruised to a comfortable 5-0 victory. The second game against Home United who were 3rd in the same division proved for more physical, but Burnley maintained their discipline to record a second 5-0 win.

Tickets were selling well for what would now constitute the final against the Singapore Asian games XI in the Jalan Besar National Stadium on Saturday which doubles as the headquarters of the Singapore F.A.

Although up to five thousand fans were expected I wasn't expecting any crowd problems as an absolute zero tolerance to any kind of anti-social behaviour is stringently adopted by the police. There was certainly no chance of me binge drinking as an average equivalent of £6 a pint in Singapore dollars seems to be the going price which severely restricts any celebrations. In fact I found myself regularly visiting the off-licence type of grocery supermarkets where surprisingly the stronger the can of beer the cheaper it seems to be resulting in a few 'tinnies' from anywhere between 8% and 14% alcoholic volume being sunk, all wrapped up in a brown paper bag.

Besides myself there were two other diehards who had made the tour from England. Long standing Yorkshireman Ian Beattie or plain 'Beats' to his mates and 'Roger the mad Jock' former head of security at the Earls Court Exhibition Centre. The remaining thirty or so Burnley Fans had travelled from other parts of Asia and even as far as Australia to be here.

It was also the first time that I had come across the man who had organized the tour to the far east, Co-chairman of Burnley Football Club and points packed scrabble hand, John Banaszkiewicz , a self-made businessman originally from the nearby town of Nelson who had made his money in the international freight industry.

Initially John gave me that deep-set frown look, a little bewildered by my circuitous route to get here. But he eventually did warm to me, so much so that before the final John asked journalist Royston Sim from the Straits Times daily newspaper to run a story on my trek which appeared under the match report the following day.

In a game played in 90 percent humidity with the temperature a stifling 80F by 8.p.m. it was an understandably slow paced tempo with no goals and few chances recorded at half-time in an even contest amidst it must be said quite a vibrant atmosphere.

Five minutes into the second half a perfectly executed free-kick from just outside the penalty area forced a breakthrough.

It came from the boot of the player most of the locals had turned up to see, a certain Chris Eagles.

Fast forward six years and you would find him residing in Accrington Stanley's team squad in Division Two such was his steep decline from the Premiership.

That thought must have been a million miles away as his only goal would be enough to win The Asian Cup.

It had been a great trip. The whole party of playing personnel worked hard in difficult conditions and that team spirit clearly evident under our previous managerial incumbent seemed to be definitely re-emerging.

What I won't miss are the extortionate beer price and some of the bizarre local food specialities. I wouldn't recommend either the frog leg porridge or live frog in the clay pot as it gives you a terrible bout of the hiccups!

Formula for success is not quite right ...

The newly sponsored N Power Championship was our home for the 2010-11 campaign and although current manager Brian Laws had only managed to win three league games since his appointment in mid-January he was once again entrusted with the task of providing an immediate return to the Premiership.

Prospects initially looked good after two opening home games against Notts Forest 1-0 and Leicester City 3-0 with a creditable 1-1 draw in between them propelling Burnley up to 3rd in the league. It would be the highest they got, and after a demoralizing 2-0 home defeat to his old club Scunthorpe at the end of December who went on to be relegated, Mr Laws was relieved of his duties as the Clarets slipped to 9th. Stuart Gray becoming caretaker manager until the acquisition of the up and coming fresh faced ambitious persona that was Eddie Howe. He had done a good job at his previous club

Bournemouth with limited resources which ticked all the boxes for Burnley's board of directors it seemed.

Taking over the reins on the 16th January 2010, once again as his predecessor, early results were impressive winning six out of nine league fixtures to climb up to 7th in the table. Although the next four out of five were lost, a late rally kept Burnley in with a chance of play-off contention right up to the last away trip at Leeds United, where a 1-0 reverse ultimately extinguished all hope of that bonus promotion route with a final 8th ranking.

For their next consecutive season in the second tier both potent goalscorers Jay Rodriguez and Charlie Austin would net over 15 goals apiece but a very disappointing 13th placement would be the end product of a period when too many home defeats were recorded to sustain any kind of tangible challenge.

There were highlights away from home however with a battling 2-1 win at West Ham, our first victory at Upton Park since Colin Waldron scored the only goal in an old division one fixture in 1973.

I'd had my usual £6 wager on this one at the William Hill branch outside Euston station. This turned out especially sweet as the counter assistant just happened to be a 'Boiled Ham' fan as I term them. He was a little too cocksure for my liking as are the vast majority that follow the 'World Cup winning' Hammers.

As I placed my bet the conversation went like this.

"Could I have the odds for this forecast please mate?", I asked Rod whose christian name was lettered upon his plastic company badge pinned to his shirt.

Rod's reply was indignant to say the least.

"Six quid on Burnley to beat West Ham 2-1 on our manor. You're 'aving a giraffe (laugh) aren't ya?".

"I reckon you can almost pick your own odds on that one. We're flying at the moment", he added.

"Maybe so, but we've regained some much needed confidence coming back from 2-0 down to win at Hull, followed by a 4-0 demolition job on Ipswich at home last Tuesday putting ourselves in fine fettle also", I countered.

"Yeh , whatever. I can't go 'cos I've got to work today but I don't expect to see you back after the game put it that way," he chuckled annoyingly.

"We'll see!", I stated firmly before leaving 'Rodders' to wind up the next unfortunate customer.

And so it came to pass that after matching the Hammers' 4-5-1 formation and it must be said riding our luck a little bit we developed a strategy to go on and win the game by that exact score line after defending for our lives.

I went to collect my £90 winnings before catching my homeward train, and made a point of waiting to be served by a suitably cheesed off Rod.

"Oh no! Not you again! 'Ow did you manage that then? After we took the lead as well."

I cast him a disparaging glance after his earlier disrespectful assumptions, before counting my money and leaving him with a final throwaway line that Del Boy would have been proud of.

"Who dares wins Rodney – who dares wins!"

After a 3-0 Boxing Day win at home to Doncaster Rovers we were up to 9th, but the real damage would be done with five sequential away fixtures that might make Michael Palin wince given their distances. Southampton, Reading, Watford, Cardiff and Ipswich secured us just the one point in the Welsh capital. An equally long trip to Portsmouth was our next road trip where a stunning hat-trick from substitute Charlie Austin helped secure a 5-1 victory with all his goals coming in the last 16 minutes.

These were my two stand out games in an uninspiring nine months of inconsistency.

The 2012-13 crusade would bring a certain Owen 'Judas' Coyle to the scene of his crimes against Burnley humanity in our first home game.

Now I will always give full credit to Mr. Coyle for guiding us to the Premiership in what really was a remarkable 2008-09 season. But at the same time hold him morally responsible for our swift demise after his absconsion to visitors and near neighbours Bolton Wanderers, for what can only be regarded as purely selfish reasons.

Even the usually composed co-chairman John Banaszkiewicz dispensed with his usual etiquette in a clear 'Let's give it 'em' gesture on the pitch minutes before kick off.

There was also a divine biblical message from above for devout catholic Mr. Coyle as a light aircraft flew overhead trailing a banner declaring;

"YOU REAP WHAT YOU SOW", alongside his self-inflicted 'Judas' tag, just as the game was about to start. Burnley winning the contest 2-0 in front of a hyped-up attendance of 18,407, which immediately positioned us in 2nd spot.

But the champagne start had lost its sparkle after three defeats on the spin against Middlesbrough, Huddersfield and Brighton & H.A. which placed us into a 22nd relegation slot.

The early door transfer window had shut and with injuries to both Danny Ings and Martin Paterson, Charlie Austin was left to plough a lone furrow up front. Our need for a replacement striker had seemingly gone unnoticed by manager Eddie Howe. Yet we were still scoring plenty of goals with Charlie Austin on fire banging in 14 goals in just 8 games, but we were also conceding at an alarming rate. Charlie's hat-trick against Sheffield Wednesday at home only good for a 3-3 draw on a Tuesday night in October, and three goals at Crystal Palace on the following Saturday were still not enough to gain any reward in a 4-3 reversal.

Eddie Howe leaves – but who next?

He left by mutual agreement in the same month citing 'personal reasons' for his departure.

Now who were we going to have in charge to manage the club?

Speculation mounted in the coming weeks as club stalwart and youth team coach Terry Pashley became the temporary caretaker manager.

My contact Jordan Croisdale from Barrowford had teased me with the line, "I know something you don't know" in one of his regular phone calls.

"Go on Jord, hit me with it!" I humoured him.

"Well, my dad's friend's, step-sister, who goes out with her best mate's brother, heard off his nephew that he had seen Ian Holloway at the Pendle Inn on his team's darts night."

"Cosmic Jord, cosmic", I replied before bringing the conversation to an abrupt halt. But Burnley being such a small town, rumours would be added to as the stories developed with a propensity to exaggerate any hearsay.

My own reliable source was keeping me up to speed however with regular updates, and one Saturday morning my mobile rang with the caller asking rather mysteriously,

"What do ya know about Sean Dyche?"

"Well, I know he was a hard bastard centre-back wherever he played at Chesterfield, Bristol City, Luton Town, Millwall, Watford and Northampton Town because we've played against him many times in the lower divisions. Oh, and of course he's just been unfairly booted out at Watford in the summer. Why d'ya ask?" I replied somewhat hesitantly almost anticipating the next quote.

"He's going to be our new manager. His presentation with a flip chart was easily the most impressive of the strong candidates. But keep it under your hat till it's announced. Byeee".

"Bloody hell! He's only done a year in management, is he going to be another stop gap appointment?" I mused, fairly unimpressed by the disclosure that what amounted to little more than a rookie manager was being tasked with the immense challenge of returning us to the top tier once again.

In his first match in charge against Wolves at home I have to say his enthusiasm was boundless. He clapped, encouraged, gestured and praised in equal measure throughout every one of the ninety minutes of play. Punching the air in a victory salute at the end of a 2-0 win instantly won over myself and the watching fans.

"If he's been doing that in every game that he has managed, it is little wonder that he possesses a voice which sounds like he's been gargling with gravel!" I remarked to Trev.

"He'll do for me!", endorsed 'Tricky'.

After beating Wolves Burnley occupied 13th spot, by the end of the season they would only improve that position by two places. We were still conceding too many goals albeit at a vastly reduced rate, and only one man was scoring them and he was Charlie Austin. Netting 28 times in all competitions represented a 41.8% ratio of the 67 total with next nearest Martin Paterson hitting 7.

Maybe, just maybe with some reinforcements in defence the 2013-14 challenge could be a serious one, particularly as Lee Grant our goalkeeper seemed to have at last realized his potential.

As it happened none of this key trio of players would be with the club come the first game of this new era. Sean Dyche's assignment would become infinitely more difficult this time around, but there was no hiding place now as this would be HIS team!

44 Premier Placement Against All The Odds 2013-14

It's time to call for super-heroes.

It's the start of a new season when each and every supporter hopes that this just might be their team's year.

Expectation levels rise even more if quality acquisitions are signed up.

Conversely, if your top players disappear before the fresh campaign kicks in, so do your hopes and aspirations.

James Alexander Gordon

The 2013-14 football season was fast approaching. Yet this time around it just would not have the same ring to it as the classified results were read out either by the B.B.C. world service, Radio 2 and 5 Live radio programmes at the traditional time of 5p.m. on a Saturday afternoon.

Legendary announcer James Alexander Gordon or 'Jag' to his worldwide legion of followers was retiring from the coveted role after over forty years on the grounds of ill health.

One of the most recognizable voices on the airwaves, his much imitated rise and fall intonation instantly informing the listener of a game's outcome before it had been proclaimed elevated him to an iconic level.

Throat cancer had forced him to have his larynx removed and so James naturally deduced that as a consequence his spoken words would not be strong enough to effectively carry out his duties.

Sadly, quite soon after the initial diagnosis James passed away on the 18th August 2013 at the age of 78, and a national institution was no more.

Having been brought up with the lilting tones of the great man throughout four decades of concerted support for my club, like millions of others it truly felt like I had lost a friend, such were his presenting skills.

Prospects don't look good …

For their pre-season friendlies Burnley played just the one game at Turf Moor, which was an impressive enough 4-1 win against the Dutch side Sparta Rotterdam.

There were four matches on the road however, at Morecambe, Carlisle and Tranmere on the mainland, which were supplemented by a visit to Cork City in the Republic of Ireland.

Myself and 'The Weed' decided to turn the latter into a week long hitchhiking trip taking in visits to Shannon, where we landed, then on to Limerick, Clonmel and Waterford, before arriving in our beautiful destination city of Cork. Besides saving a handy amount of euros in transportation costs it was also the best way of getting to know the locals first hand.

We had both journeyed to the Emerald Isle before on numerous occasions and I wanted to reaffirm my long held belief that the Southern Irish, politics and religion apart, were the most welcoming, convivial and accommodating race on the planet. Their obliging demeanour would be put to the test however, as a cash-strapped economy had spiralled the country into a deep decline over the last five years or so, requiring a massive bail out of millions of euros from the European Union to keep them afloat.

There again, the high cost of living, and particularly drinking in our case, wasn't such an overwhelming hardship to the nation's unemployed as we found to our amazement.

From all accounts, and having received confirmation from various drivers that had stopped to give us a lift, the going rate for being out of work was around 180 euros a week, with additional benefits available on top of that. This generous standard pay-out for a single person equated to over double the allowance pound sterling in the UK. All things considered, that was a pretty sturdy safety net as general expenditure on everyday necessities worked out no more than 25% higher than Great Britain.

Of course our staple liquid diet of vitamin 'B' meant greater hardship, as a pint of beer was equivalent to between four and five pounds a throw.

It was the only downside to a glorious week of almost unbroken sunshine that had been the best spell of good weather the Irish had enjoyed for many years.

We only played the one game but the 3-0 score line certainly didn't flatter us, albeit against a majority second string eleven due to the Irish team's mid-season league commitments.

Although non-competitive matches can never replicate the first class encounters, I was suitably impressed to praise their positive attitude in my opening column for the Lancashire Telegraph newspaper which read,

"In the pre-season fixtures Sean Dyche's squad has looked refreshingly sharper, more physically adept and full of confidence in front of goal. Although the Clarets have a tough start, if they can carry those vital qualities into their Championship fixtures they can be a match for anyone."

At the time it may have been nothing more than an optimistic rallying call, but by the end it would turn into a hugely prophetic statement.

As we prepared to embark on a new campaign the stark facts were that attendances were dwindling, parachute payments were due to end, and we had lost our two top scorers as well as our experienced goalkeeper Lee Grant.

Both Martin Paterson and the aforementioned custodian, who incidentally had somewhat surprisingly taken the 'Player of the Season' award from four supporters clubs had rewarded their belief by deciding to try his luck at what he obviously must have thought were a much better promotion prospect in Derby County. 'Pato', like Grant was at the end of his contract and as a free agent plumped for our divisional neighbours from the adjoining county of West Yorkshire at Huddersfield.

But the dagger to the heart transaction that cut all Burnley fans to the quick was the transfer of hit man Charlie Austin to the mega-rich conglomerate that is Queen Park Rangers.

Immediate comparisons flashed back to the 1972-1973 old 2nd Division season when Dave Thomas jumped ship to the West London club two months into the season after an internal disciplinary suspension. Then, Burnley went on to pip the Hoops by a point to win the league and promotion to the top level of the football pyramid.

To say expectations were low wouldn't begin to reflect the enveloping mood of despondency that descended upon our gathering as we met up in our usual Wetherspoons watering hole in the Brun Lea for our first Championship League match of the season.

I'd barely got through the door when regular drinker Craig greeted me with the news that,

"They've made Burnley one of the favourites to go down at the bookies Derv. Have you heard?"

"Well if I hadn't Craig, I have now haven't I?" I replied somewhat prickly, rankled by even more bad news.

My next enquiry came from Alan 'Beeky' Beecroft a Clarets fan of over 50 years standing.

"What d'ya think Derv? Asked Al in the same colloquial pronunciation of my Christian name.

I didn't need to enquire "About what?" as recent events had overtaken us.

"Well, I'll be honest with you Al. I think we're now in for a real struggle. In fact in the tiebreaker question that me and Trev write down to determine Burnley's final position, I've put us in a 16th place finish".

This was a deciding answer if our predictions for teams finishing at the top and bottom of each division ended up equal, in our annual challenge that gained the winner a prize of free beer all through the day of their choice.

"D'ya know what I think?" Beeky fired back, "I don't reckon we'll be out of the bottom three all season!" was his somewhat dramatic assertion.

That really was a worst case scenario outlook, and yet throughout the afternoon I was meeting others that couldn't rule it out.

A reasonable start is made ...

The match itself was a 12.15 kick off to accommodate television scheduling to commemorate the 125th anniversary of the Football League's formation. So this premeditated arranged fixture with Bolton Wanderers was one of a few that pitted together original members from the inaugural 1888 competition.

Life without 'Charlie' got off to a satisfactory start with a 1-1 draw against what looked a handy Bolton side that had been immediately reinstated as one of the favourites to attain promotion.

It just happened to be the identical opening fixture to last season, but with much less added spice in the absence of fallen hero Owen Coyle being shown the door in the interim from the very same Reebok hierarchy that so actively pursued him for his services.

In fact, for those sages who reason that it is a persons previous behavioural actions in present life which actually determines their future fate, the defecting ex-Burnley manager who left the club so abruptly gives great credence to the devout Hindu and Buddhist religious belief in the power of Karma.

He had gone from bossing two of the oldest established clubs in the country with a rich successful history and heritage before taking the helm at Wigan Athletic in 2013 where he was also shown the door to – well let's see if I can paint you a picture.

If you would just allow me to adjust my Stetson cowboy hat for a moment and adopt a deep Texan drawl as the news came through in December 2014 that,

"Owen 'Columba', (Yes that middle name very similar to the American T.V. detective really is his) Coyle has accepted gainful employment stateside as Head Coach for M.L.S. Houston Dynamo soccer club.

Y' all give him your full support y' all!"

Yes, Houston we do have a problem! The Dynamo's steeped tradition going right back to their foundation in the year..... er....2005, "Doh!!," as Homer Simpson might exclaim. A proud ancestry there then!

Which made me conclude that if we couldn't understand his deep Scottish brogue delivered with machine gun rapidity at pre and post-match interviews, as the cockneys would say in their own equally obscure rhyming slang, "The septic tanks' (yanks) would have 'Bob Hope!" (no hope).

It has to be said that the pitiful 'Trotters' of Bolton had been architects of their own downfall. Reportedly almost £200 million in debt at the turn of 2016, relegated to the third tier of English league football and narrowly avoiding a winding-up administration order that would have incurred a 12 point deduction penalty. Former player Dean Holdsworth fronting a consortium to take over the club which has probably kept them from the brink of oblivion , by amongst other things selling off the club car park.

Nobody should feel sorry, for them, yet everyone should care. For in the Seventies, just like ourselves in the Eighties when financial troubles were accumulating, their fans, including legendary former player Nat Lofthouse shook collection tins for money in an effort to help keep the club afloat.

And to think our very own 'Columba Coyle' quoted that one of the major reasons for defecting no more than just twenty miles south was because he reckoned, quote;

"Bolton were ten years ahead of Burnley".

Oh dear! He seems to have got that one wrong too. Quite amazingly given his Burnley connection after the culmination of the 2015-16 campaign rivals Blackburn Rovers installed him as their new boss, thus completing a managerial quadruple of clubs from the old Lancashire county incorporating Burnley, Bolton and Wigan before being relieved of his Ewood park duties in February 2017. Beware Accrington Stanley you could be next on his 'to do' list!

So continuing, our apprehension was temporarily put on hold, particularly after three consecutive victories over York City away 4-0 in the League Cup 1st round and a couple of Championship wins over Sheffield Wednesday away 2-1 and Yeovil Town at home 2-0.

Suddenly we were up to fourth in the table, but soon back down to ninth after a bad day at Brighton. Balls were misplaced, distribution poor and few chances created as the defence came apart at the seams. Kevin Long responsible for an under hit back-pass to the goalkeeper Tommy Heaton who was forced to bring down their intercepting forward Will Buckley.

Amazingly, only a yellow card being brandished as the referee on the linesman's advice deemed that club captain Jason Shackell was behind the goalie so technically he wasn't the last man, preventing a sending off. Shackell may have been, but he was a long way from the incident to do anything about averting a goal once Heaton had been rounded.

He was left in no doubt what the Brighton fans thought about this decision which must have preyed on his mind as the comically named Darren Sheldrake, all the way from the neighbouring county of Surrey I might add, decided to take their advice and dismiss our keeper in the second half for what has to be the most ridiculous second booking that I've witnessed.

Heaton was effectively banished for taking avoiding action as the same player, Buckley, attempted to illegally prise the ball out of his grasp, having lobbed the ball over his head to catch it again. So the errant ref. chose to sack the juggler! As commentator David Coleman would say "Quite remarkable!"

Onwards and upwards....

But if most people came to the conclusion, and the vast majority did think that this was the inevitable beginning of the end, they were in for a very rude awakening.

Burnley defiantly stormed back by winning their next nine out of ten league games. The only spoilers preventing that perfect 10 were arch-rivals Blackburn Rovers who we played at Turf Moor. Their substitute Lee Williamson made what turned out to be no more than a cameo appearance after seeing a straight red card for hauling down forward Danny Ings who would otherwise have had a clear run at goal and maybe the winner. That single cheating act denoted just how desperate Rovers had become to preserving their long unbeaten run against us.

Another defining moment came in our next away game at Elland Road, Leeds, where a 2-1 win lifted Burnley back up to second spot. They would never be out of the top three from that day on.

On a cold Tuesday night in Doncaster goals from right back Kieran Trippier and big Sam Vokes sealed a 2-0 victory to put us top of the league for the first time since August 2006.

The most accomplished performance of the campaign so far came next as dynamic duo Vokes and Ings, who I'd termed the 'Vokings' provided the goals in a hard fought 2-1 win over Reading to take their combined tally to nineteen already.

My next weekend excursion took me away to East Anglia and a real graveyard of a ground for Burnley in deepest Suffolk.

The last time I had seen us win at Ipswich also happened to by my first visit to Portman Road way back in January 1970 and we had played them many times since then.

Frank Casper scored the only goal that day, and it would be left to Scott Arfield to replicate that 1-0 score line. To commemorate the feat I partied long and hard into the early hours in the town centre Revolution music bar. Even though the overwhelming majority were probably a generation younger it didn't matter a jot after such a momentous result.

It now constituted our best start to a season since the nineteenth century. In fact, during that 1897-98 campaign Burnley lost only once in their first 25 matches on the way to winning the Division Two championship.

Manager Sean Dyche who I have now given the nickname 'Dynamo' after the young British magician, deservedly wins his second consecutive 'Manager of the Month' award for September after achieving this fantastic feat.

This was a massive statement of intent given the doom-mongers predictions, myself admittedly included. Burnley supporters were walking on air and daring to dream that they just might be on to something special here, and maybe even a repeat success of that 19th century era.

We had now won all four league games in October with just a 2-0 home reverse to West Ham in the League cup 4th round the only blemish.

November was not quite so productive as we draw three on the bounce against Millwall away, AFC Bournemouth at home and Notts Forest at the City Ground, before losing 2-1 at Huddersfield, yet remained in 2nd position.

In December we stay unbeaten up to Christmas with the 2-1 home success over Blackpool sealing our top spot at least up until then.

It is a psychological boost as the team that is on the summit at this time of year generally, according to past statistics, wins their prize of promotion.

Christmas with none of the trimmings....

With the festive period getting ever closer, I contemplated just how I was going to attend, what was from the outset, always going to be my trickiest trip of the season.

When I had scanned the fixture list way back in July the Boxing Day visit to Middlesbrough, Teesside had immediately set the alarm bells ringing.

Like most people, I do prefer to spend Christmas Day at home with family and friends in the traditional manner with a few beers before getting stuck into a plump bird on the dinner table, something I'd spent many a weekend doing in my formative years I must confess. However, this cosy arrangement was becoming less and less of an option as the weeks went by.

For the vast majority of the country the public transport system grinds to a halt soon after 9pm on Christmas Eve as workers wind down for the start of the big holiday. That means the last trains hit the buffers on December 24th not returning to a normal service until three days later on the 27th.

As a non-driver that becomes a major issue, unless any of the southern based supporters are intending to travel up early morning. After exhaustive enquiries none were, and I'd even asked to share a car with local Stokies who were also badly drawn to play at Newcastle United in their Premier League fixture. But it seemed that those who were making the journey had opted for the free coaches that Stoke had provided for them all season to encourage their away support.

There was also the unpredictable British weather to factor into the operation which could change on a daily basis. Indeed, over the five previous decades I had generally been forced to contend with sub-zero snow and ice conditions around this time of year, but with the relatively new phenomenon of worldwide climate change, the biggest threat to travelling now came from ferocious gale force winds combined with the worst flooding in living memory.

Left with little alternative to categorically ensure my presence at the Riverside Stadium, I induced 'Weedy' into making it a Christmas to remember with three nights in the north east of England at different locations for each.

The Weed didn't need that much persuasion given that his Christmas Day now invariably consists of dinner at his 'foodie' brother 'Crogs' house at Nantwich, where with the aid of his Antiguan missus Veronica, they cook up a sumptuous main course of anything from a five bird roast to a haunch of venison. Yes sir, there were no austerity measures in place for teetotal 'Crogger'.

Although Weed enjoys the priviledge of good food himself, he is more of a 'pecker' than a 'packer' preferring to leave ample space for a few drinks, insisting that he finds it hard to do both comfortably.

Having assured him that there was no chance of compromising a good festive drinking session on my proposed itinerary, he set about booking up the trip on the internet as up until press I don't possess a personal computer.

So on Christmas Eve morning we wished everyone an early 'Merry Christmas' as we caught the budget Megabus from Manchester to our first port of call at Sunderland, a local service from the same station taking us to our dinnertime refreshment stop in the old mining town of Peterlee, before an onward journey to our first overnight stay at Durham Travelodge.

As is the general trend now, the city's pubs were very quiet with even the local Yates's chain bar deciding to close it's doors at 10.30pm through lack of trade. A sad reflection on what was in the Seventies and Eighties regarded as a top night out.

The countdown to the big day at midnight passing away almost unnoticed in the busiest place visited on the night at The Water House, one of the two Wetherspoons outlets in the centre.

Next day the freezing cold certainly helped to ease our hangovers as we walked the three miles to a decent hitching point for our next destination Darlington,fifteen miles south.

As we stuck our thumbs out along with our lettered, cardboard place name sign, I commented to Weedy that, "I bet ya, there's no more than a dozen people in the whole country hitchhiking a lift out of necessity on a major road today".

Weedy contested my guess in his usual dry, humourless way,

"I'd say there's a lot more than that Ralph," he deliberated, before predictably adding, "I think more like thirteen."

"Ha, bloody ha Weedy, your witty repartee knows no bounds, does it?" I replied sarcastically.

Then something truly funny happened. Rattling along, exhaust billowing a cloud of thick black smoke was an unshaven stocky bloke clad only in a grubby vest on his upper torso, driving his low loader pick-up truck with his substantial belly wedged tight against the steering wheel. Next to him was a wild haired, equally large woman dragging on a fag with her two young kids alongside her.

"Don't give us much chance with this one Weed", I commented as it approached, but there's room at the back so I'll give it a go."

As the off-white vehicle spluttered closer towards us, we adopted our hitching stance only to receive an aggressive double salute of both a one and two finger combination from the pair of adult occupants.

I was absolutely flabbergasted by such a response from little more than a skip on wheels as I turned wide eyed to Weedy.

"Did you see that Weed? We've just been bloody 'dissed' by a bunch of flamin' gypos! Well, that's just about as low as you can get, on Christmas Day too. Not very Christian of them was it?"

We instantly both collapsed in a heap holding on to each other's shoulders for support as we laughed out loud uncontrollably. Now we really did feel at the bottom of the food chain!

It was one of those 'you couldn't make it up' moments that could only happen by placing yourself in such a vulnerable position.

After an hour a car did eventually pull up and we were invited in. Its single occupant was named Lee , a former 'squaddie' turned adventure trainer. He was making his way down the A167 en route to his mother's home at Hartlepool for his Christmas Dinner. Although he should have turned off halfway towards our goal, he insisted on dropping us off just a couple of miles outside 'Darlo'. What a top bloke.

So our traditional Christmas Day drinking session was amongst the throngs of other people's friends and relatives in the four pubs we came across. That left us with one more custom to observe. The great British Christmas dinner of course!

Upon arrival at our second Travelodge of the tour another mile outside the town, we were now both ready for our festive blowout.

There wasn't a cooker or microwave, but that was of no consequence to us. All we required was a kettle.

After a preparation time of a mere 5 minutes our homemade six course feast was ready to serve as the enclosed menu testifies.

Darlington Travelodge, Yarm Road

Christmas Day Menu 2013

APERITIF: 12 YEAR MATURED GLENFIDDICH SCOTCH WHISKY

(Served in a plastic bathroom mouthwash tumbler)
From a half bottle of the spirit we had brought with us.

ENTRÉE: SOUP OF THE DAY

(A minestrone cup-a-soup with croutons).

MAIN COURSE: FILLET DE POULET EN CROUTE

STEAMED NOODLES WITH AN ESSENCE OF CHICKEN FILLET
IN A LIGHT MUSHROOM SAUCE.

(A chicken and mushroom pot noodle)

DESSERT: ARCTIC ROLL GLENFIDDICH

(A Cadbury's mini-roll left upon the outside window sill
overnight and smothered in our Glenfiddich whisky)

PETIT FOURS: CRACKERS AND CHEESE

(Half a packet of Jacobs crackers and a chunk of cheese
obtained from our Christmas hamper).

COFFEE AND MINTS: (A sachet of Travelodge Nescafé with a
couple of Mentos chewy dragees)

Total cost for this sumptuous six course menu

Just one English pound!

Jon-a-thong' Taylor picked us up on the Boxing Day morning, driving us to the small market town of Yarm, just six miles from Middlesbrough where we partook of some liquid refreshment in the pubs.

Jon had kindly offered to pick us up en-route from Burnley where he was staying at his mother's residence.

Ex – Middlesbrough and England footballer Gary Pallister was cheerfully chatting to a coach load of Burnley fans in the Black Bull boozer and we all set off for the game in good spirits.

Boro have always been a hard team to beat at their Riverside Stadium and today wasn't going to be the day, as Republic of Ireland goalkeeper Shay Given produced a couple of international class saves to preserve a single goal victory for the home side.

A battling 0-0 draw at Wigan saw 2013 out with Burnley sitting a handy third in the Sky Bet Championship.

Huddersfield were defeated 3-2 at Turf Moor on New Years Day before an end to end 4-3 defeat down at Southampton in the 3rd round of the F.A.Cup.

Down to Yeovil with the blue rinse brigade...

Then came our trip to new boys Yeovil Town. Grounds that I haven't visited with Burnley don't come around too often these days, but the intriguingly named Huish Park in Somerset was one I hadn't been to as it was the first time we had played them, after the Glovers had gained promotion from League One when defeating Brentford 2-1 in the Play-Off Final at Wembley the previous season.

This called for something special to celebrate the occasion and it would definitely have to be a weekender.

Just by chance when flicking through my local Evening Sentinel newspaper I glanced an advert for a 'West Country cosy break' run by GB Tours on the Wirral, Merseyside.

It was a Friday to Monday trip with three nights bed, breakfast and evening meal for £99 per person. The hotel being based in the Somerset town of Street just 12 miles north of Yeovil. Not only did the dates coincide with our visit for the match, an excursion to the cathedral city of Wells was thrown in on the Sunday morning. All were virgin pub copping territory for me so I relayed my discovery to the lads to see if they were up for it.

Unsurprisingly, 'Weedy' jumped at the chance of a bargain piss up in Somerset for a long weekend. 'Knock off' Nigel also liked the sound of it, he too being a seasoned 'alecan', but plain John Smith needed more convincing.

"A mid-winter break with incontinent pensioners! It might be yours Dave, but that's not my idea of a good time", commented Smithy on my proposal.

"It's not supposed to be a 'pulling' trip 'Smythe', using my denigratory term for his surname to denote my contempt at such a slur.

"The bottom line is 'Smythe', that it's a great deal, and fits in perfectly with our match against the 'Mangledwurzels'. Besides , there's a fancy dress do on the Sunday night and I know you like dressing up, and remember, cider be good for 'ee!"

He laughed and made his mind up to go, but not before uttering a final derogatory quip.

"Fancy dress dance! It'll be more like a whist drive."

Anyway we were on board, and I have to say that we did get quite a few quizzical looks, from it has to be said mostly elderly couples as we commandeered the back seat of the coach that was going to take us to our destination in deepest Somerset.

Because of the bad reputation that had been acquired by some football supporters in the past, I thought it best to have a cursory word with the lads advising them against disclosing our primary reason for taking the excursion so as not to unduly worry what was almost a full coach of sedate senior citizens.

But as discreet as we had been discussing the forthcoming game and related footy topics, I suppose it was always going to be somewhat inevitable that snippets of our chat would be picked up by a casual eavesdropper sooner or later.

This one was younger than the majority, probably mid-fifties and sitting right in front of us with her partner.

Turning around to address us she posed the question in a polite, almost timid tone.

"Sorry to interrupt fellas, but I couldn't help overhearing you talk. Are you football fans down here for a match?"

Just as I was about to point an accusing finger at 'Knock Off' for being too loud, I readied myself to offer a complete denial to avoid complaints from the bulk of the Darby and Joan club that had now swivelled their heads around to await an answer.

Smithy however beat me to it by piping up with one of his typically confrontational outbursts purposely announced to rankle everyone within earshot, which included most of the party and the driver.

"Yes! We are Burnley fans going to Yeovil to rape, pillage and riot before drinking all the town's pubs' dry!" he blasted out defiantly staring straight at the enquirer, poker faced like some Erik The Red Viking leader.

There was a hushed silence as blue rinse after blue rinse tutted before telling their husband's to turn back round facing front, away from the self-confessed plebs.

"Well done 'Smythe', I'm surprised you didn't tell 'em' we all had highly contagious leprosy as well!!," I berated him sternly for blowing our cover.

"They'll be alright once it's sunk in," Smithy reasoned unconvincingly.

"Alright? Alright? We'll be about as bloody popular as mods at a Hells Angels convention.

Carol, the woman who had originally asked the question did make light of it however as I endeavoured to reassure her we weren't football hooligans.

Few mixed with us as we ate our evening meal after sampling a few beers around Street town centre.

Next day relations had thawed a little as we set off for Yeovil, whilst the rest of the group keenly awaited their inclusive day trip to the Georgian city of Bath. The driver wished us well and we even got a few waves from some couples we had mingled with at the Wessex Hotel base who gave the impression that they were ready to blow the whole of their winter fuel allowance on an all out shopping spree.

Yeovil's only a small town, but in the past had been many a victor against higher opposition in the F.A. Cup when they had been a non-league outfit.

The West Country men battled hard in their compact stadium, but it would be the seventeen hundred or so Burnley fans who celebrated with a 2-1 win.

I was now happy the game had gone ahead after the horrendous floods on the Somerset levels as local rivers burst their banks.

We celebrated at a local pub to begin with before catching a cab into town where we met a couple of Knock Off's pals Bob and Neil for a few beers then headed back to our digs totally content.

Batmans's double trouble with his 'Robin'...

There was still the free trip to the beautiful cathedral city of Wells on the Sunday morning where we decided to stay for an afternoon drinking session before catching a service bus back.

We swerved the scheduled tea dance much to the apparent chagrin of 'plain John Smith' who insisted he had perfected his fox trot after watching the D.V.D . box set compilation of 'Strictly Come Dancing' for the past week.

But by now we had sufficiently ingratiated ourselves with our new found companions, and when the news circulated that me and the 'Weed' were going as Batman and Robin to the fancy dress party that night a substantial number vowed to be there to witness what we had rehearsed as a dramatic entrance through the double doors in classic Del Boy and Rodney Trotter fashion from one of their 'Only Fools And Horses' Christmas specials.

That plan didn't quite come to fruition as Weedy who was supposed to be my sidekick 'Robin' got waylaid in a pub with 'Smithy' and 'Knock Off' as it started pouring down with rain. I had gone ahead to prepare myself, with the Weed promising to follow ten minutes later.

He didn't , so after a three quarters of an hour wait I made the decision to go down to the hotel by myself so as not to disappoint the ones that had pledged to stay up a while longer to see us in our superhero outfits.

Now that wasn't going to be plain sailing, as since the last time I had worn the outfit about two years ago my waistline had expanded a good couple of inches. The result of which stretched the hundred percent polyester jumpsuit over-tightly around my nether regions as the fabric searched for room in every crevice. My arse cheeks sprang out like Kim Kardashian's rear quarters and the pronounced bulge in the meat and two veg department went supersize due its upward tension.

I edged towards the long dressing mirror to survey my body realignment. Reflecting back to me was an image bordering on obscene. In fact the last time I had seen anything resembling such a manifestation was when

Jamaican sprint runner Linford Christie wore skin tight lycra shorts to streamline his physique against wind drag.

My parts stuck out like the proverbial sore thumb, but now had been transformed into anything but thumb size through its spandex like tightness.

"I can't go down like this. If any of the older biddies have got a condition I could trigger a seizure," I whispered to myself.

Now that would have made the front page of some periodicals I'd wager.

No matter how much I tried to adjust my package by doing a bit of nip and tucking, it soon became apparent that beyond taking the drastic step of chopping them off completely it just wasn't going to happen.

In a final desperate attempt to disguise my newly acquired Errol Flynn appendage I resorted to adding a long twist of shiny blue tinsel and the remnants of a party popper to my costume, each salvaged from the bottom of my holdall bag as leftovers from our Christmas trip to the north east just a month previous.

But where was the cod-piece when you needed one!

The metal foil decoration being wrapped around the daffodil yellow thick waistband to hang over my own baubles as a part of modesty screen at least, with the coloured paper streamers draped over my bat ear to hopefully avert wandering eyes upward.

It still looked well dodgy, but now time was ticking on and I had to have the resolution to either crack on or buck out!

Thinking that it might be dimly lit in the reception area that preceded the ballroom, something that I was desperately short of I might add, I resolved to fulfil my promise as maybe I was making far too much of my sartorial dilemma and no one would give it a second glance anyway.

Wrong!! As the lift doors opened adjacent to the hotel bar, for a moment it was as if Batman had acquired Superman's super breath power to freeze the clearly astonished gathering of something numbering a dozen or so women who were smartly turned out in an even mix of formal frocks and dresses.

It was no more than a ten yard walk to the drinks servery but it felt like fifty, as darting eyes glanced me up and down before focusing their gaze on one central focal point.

Some of the group giggled nervously, others whispered short messages in ears with a cupped hand. I was just glad that their husbands weren't there.

"Anyone seen Robin?", I asked flippantly in an attempt to divert attention from my crown jewels.

Just then Carol, the passenger that rumbled us on the coach coming down, piped up,

"Quick take a picture. My son's a massive Batman fan!" Yes, I bet he is, I thought to myself, 'massive' being the operative word in this case.

She then proceeded to pass her camera to one of the throng before squeezing my waist so tight it left a mark.

Others took up the opportunity with even one excitable grandma videoing the moment. As is the norm. for their generation most retired to bed soon after 11p.m. just as Knock Off, Smithy and Weedy came through the door.

"Oh well done Robin! The Penguin and The Joker have just burnt down Gotham City and The Riddler has just slipped Catwoman a crippler while you've been pissing it up against the wall! Whe've ya bin?. Everyone's gone to bed," I stormed angrily.

I was annoyed more for the guests than myself as Batman without Robin was like Laurel without Hardy, even though I'd made the most of the night.

It wasn't long before Weedy realizing the error of his ways decided to rush upstairs to get into his costume for the last hour or so even though only about ten people had remained behind.

Meanwhile Smithy and K.O. looked on aghast at my particular outfit before bursting out laughing.

"It looks like you've come straight from a porn movie Dave. Either that or you need to put a cricket box down there!" observed Smithy.

"Bloody hell Ralph is that all your own, or have you put a pair of football socks in ya pants?", added Knock off.

The night finished with a karaoke session dominated by myself and K.O. where he tamely tried to pass off himself as The Cadbury's Milk Tray man from the late sixties onwards T.V. advert. Although he had made an effort wearing black trousers and jumper like the actor he was a good six stone heavier, giving the impression he had already eaten the chocolates tucked under his arm!

We set back home on the Monday having now made good friends with most of the coach passengers, with my Batman appearance seemingly the talk of the trip. From time to time I bump into some of them around town with Carol still insisting seeing me in that outfit made her day.

Yes, I'm sure it did!

With 'Rocky' after our first win over Rovers in near on 35 years!
Rocky's scarf says it all.

Dream derby day....

But for dyed in the wool Burnley fans one day stands out like an illuminated night-time beacon atop, Pendle Hill.

Sunday March 9th 2014 will live long in the memory as the calendar day when Burnley FC beat deadly arch-rivals Blackburn Rovers for the first time in near on thirty five years.

It may have only been contested on twelve occasions during that period but believe me each failure to achieve victory had festered like a weeping sore.

However the vast gap that had once existed with the massive injection of millions of pounds by their now deceased former chairman, steel magnate Jack Walker, had now diminished.

Before the game I felt that there was definitely 'something in the air' about this one and it seemed that 4,640 others of the same persuasion thought likewise and believed it was going to be our day.

Uncharacteristically perhaps largely due to the enormity of the occasion, our lads misplaced far too many passes and hoofed the ball skyward with repeated regularity for the first 70 minutes. This put our defence under increasing pressure leading to us conceding the first goal from a Jordan Rhodes shot that would normally have been closed down far more efficiently.

That malaise surfaced once more when a David Jones mistake let in Rovers goal scorer Rhodes who could only hit a post. That incident and the game-changing double substitutions that introduced Ross Wallace returning from an extensive injury lay off, and our only real money signing of the season Ashley Barnes to the fray went on to prove the turning point. Both were instrumental in the two quick second half goals within six minutes that won us the game 2-1 when Blackburn's nemesis centre half and captain Jason Shackell, who had scored the previous season at Ewood Park, and hot shot Danny Ings sealed the contest which for three quarters of the clash had looked an unlikely outcome.

It transpired that shed loads of lucky charms had been dusted down with all sorts of superstitions also adhered to before the game. Solely because of this historical result they would go on to be used for the remainder of the campaign.

House parties went on long into the night resulting in mass absenteeism the following day by those currently in a job. For others, they celebrated in the most natural way known to man leading to all local hospital staff being put on standby for a predicted baby boom mid-November!

That is how important that single result was. It just seemed to encapsulate the sheer ecstasy of the fans. Whether they had been at the game or watched it live at home or down the pub on Sky TV, the joy was in equal measure to them all.

After the event certain local individuals had the temerity to suggest that the long awaited victory must have meant more to Burnley fans from the east Lancashire region than myself.

The only way I can reply to that ill-advised assumption is to say since our last triumph at Ewood Park in the league on Saturday April 14th 1979 that I of course attended, I have had to wait no less than thirty four years, ten months and twenty three days for a repeat. Or to put it another more mathematical way 12,748 days, or 305,952 hours or even 18,357,120 minutes.

Does that answer your question Zippy and Bungle? You know who you are!

Burnley carried on apace, unbeaten up until the 2-0 home win over Doncaster Rovers where a Sam Vokes penalty and one from Danny Ings made the 'Vokings' the first Burnley striking partnership to score at least 20 league goals each since Willie Irvine and Andy Lochhead back in the 1964/65 season.

Then came Leicester City, who as champions elect ended the Clarets 16 game undefeated league run at Turf Moor with a 2-0 victory, and the first home reverse in 23 matches dating back over a calendar year.

It proved disastrous for Sam Vokes whose season was cruelly ended by a serious injury to the anterior cruciate ligament in his left knee within five minutes of the game.

That meant five key players in Ings, Trippier, Vokes, Marney and Stanislas were all missing through either injury or suspension when Burnley faced Watford in their next match at Vicarage Road. A late quality finish from Scott Arfield rescuing a hard earned point.

Two away wins at Barnsley and Blackpool were sandwiched between an unjust 1-0 home defeat to Middlesbrough which put any celebrations on hold until the Easter Monday game against play-off chasing Wigan Athletic at Turf Moor.

Ashley Barnes finished off a sensational team passing move for his first home goal for Burnley after being signed in the January transfer window from Brighton. It was Sean Dyche's first acquisition that cost a fee since his managerial appointment at Turf Moor back in October 2012 and fatefully would become the perfect replacement for the unlucky Sam Vokes. A stunning Michael Kightly free-kick confirmed Burnley's return back to the top tier of English football inside the opening 45 minutes.

And that's the way it stayed with goalkeeper Tom Heaton – the man behind the meanest defence in the division , with to date just 35 goals conceded in 44 games, - keeping the team's 20th clean sheet in all competitions.

The final whistle was blown by referee Keith Stroud and the celebrations started with a pitch invasion from the masses on the lower tier.

I certainly wasn't going to miss out so after male bonding jubilant hugs to Smithy, Dom and Jon who sit either side of us, myself and Tricky Trev decided we wanted a piece of the action too, so descended the stairs.

The stewards patrolling the exit doors to the ground level asked where we were going?

"just nipping to the toilet mate", I replied unconvincingly.

"No you're not you're trying to get on to the pitch aren't you?" he enquired.

"Too right son!" I fired back as both myself and Trev dodged his advances to run around him.

By now, both bare chested with exhuberance, we vaulted the perimeter wall to join the throng of humanity on the turf.

Dancing, singing, hand shakes and kisses followed and I'm not sure to which gender, but I just didn't care. We had done it once again against the odds for the second time in five years we were Premier League!

A first ever double against the Ipswich Tractor Boys was sealed 1-0 at Turf Moor in the penultimate game of the season before the grand finali at Reading finished in a 2-2 draw which also ended any hope of a play-off place for The Royals.

That led to a large proportion of Burnley fans taunting their supporters regarding them missing out which was totally out of order given the congratulatory greetings Reading F.C. had displayed in and around the away entrance for ourselves as in the central page photograph to this chapter.

What a nine months it had been. The same gestation period as a baby in the womb with all the trials, tribulations and worry that naturally brings until that magical moment of actual birth.

Well this was more a re-birth against all the odds. The pre-season doubts, anxiety, unease, disquiet, fretfulness, nervousness, agitation, misgivings and even fear, all replaced with one single word; ECSTASY!

Co-chairman and good friend John Banaszkiewicz had invited myself and driver for the day Ginette 'The Veg' Mackriel into the directors lounge to join in the promotion celebrations, if indeed we did clinch it that day. But I wasn't going home tonight, oh no, every promotion deserves a party. So upon congratulating chairperson Mike Garlick, a hundred percent claret who always gives me a warm welcome, after a few beers and several glasses of champagne courtesy of Sky Sports T.V. I prepared to continue the festivities in the town with the supporters.

But there was still one man I hadn't thanked yet as he had been continually surrounded by dozens of well wishers all expressing their personal thanks and good wishes to himself. That man was manager Sean Dyche who had achieved this miraculous feat. Sean was surrounded by a crowd but still called me over and we embraced like long lost brothers.

I had met Sean once before after we had played Nottingham Forest at home in the Capital One cup 3rd round, a game we won 2-1. Before the game J.B. the co-chairman had rang my mobile to invite me into the directors lounge for a chat. Knowing he hadn't been too well recently I naturally assumed John wanted to have a private word to update his condition.

And initially thats what it seemed like as he offered me a drink and a plate for the after-match buffet. Having complied with his bidding, within minutes he had ushered me into the boardroom. There, waiting for me was an iced cake with 60 lettered upon it which I later found out was made at good friend and Burnley F.C. stalwart Barrie Oliver's Bakery. Although my sixtieth birthday wasn't due until next month someone had tipped John the wink and he had generously decided to honour my personal milestone.

Mike Garlick, former chairman Barry Kirby who himself was fighting prostate cancer were in attendance, along with a few players who were good enough to stay a while. An impromptu gift of a claret and blue bedecked garden gnome was presented to me by Barry's fun-loving wife Sonia which still takes pride of place on my bedroom window sill. I accepted the applause, made a little thank you speech and was about to set off on the 75 mile journey back home as I had to be up at 5a.m. next morning in order to cycle the eight miles to work at the cake factory when manager Sean Dyche came in.

We were left alone to chat at the small corner bar, and as you don't generally ever get a chance to have an in depth discussion with your team's boss I sort of went into overdrive a little giving my opinion on the season so far and hopes for the future of Burnley F.C. which must have gone on for a full ten minutes or so.

To his credit Sean had listened intently, and had even managed to squeeze in the odd comment in reply when from out of nowhere he asked me a question.

"Tell me Dave, how did you come to miss that one match at Newcastle in 1974?"

Which could only mean he had either read my first book himself, or more probably someone had told him.

Astonished by his apparent interest I went on to tell him the tale of woe from that fraught day in full considerable detail.

But I ask you, how many football managers would concern themselves with enquiring about an aspect of a supporters life?

What a 'top man', and that was my greeting to him as he took time out from the massed gathering to call me over after the Wigan victory that clinched promotion.

We both smiled large grins, shook hands firmly and instantaneously hugged each other in celebration, just stopping short of a quick peck on the cheek.

He knew how much this meant to me and had thoughtfully ushered me over to acknowledge the moment.

As I said what a top man!

It topped off one of the best seasons of my Burnley supporting life.

Footnote

It would be a perfectly fitting end to the season as Burnley Football Club commemorated 100 years since winning the F.A. cup for the only time in their history.

A single goal from Bert Freeman being enough to overcome Liverpool at the old Crystal Palace ground. It was the first time a reigning monarch had presented the famous trophy. Captain Tommy Boyle being the proud recipient from King George V.

An invite to tour Germany followed in the region that was then Austria-Hungary. Burnley playing their final game against an Austrian XI on June 1st 1914. In little over two months the bloodiest conflict ever to be chronicled would break out from the same district Burnley had just left when Franz Ferdinand the archduke of Austria-Hungary was assassinated in Sarajevo. In early August war was finally declared by Austria on Serbia the former Yugoslavia, the home country of the killer.

On a lighter note the 1st scheduled airline flight took place between St.Petersburg and Tampa, both locations in the U.S.A.

The 1st steamboat passed through the Panama Canal.

Charlie Chaplin debuts 'The Tramp' at the cinema.

Sunloch wins the 76th Grand National.

RMS Aquitania, 45,647 tons, the then largest ocean liner sets sail on her maiden voyage from Liverpool, England to New York City.

Paramount pictures is formed, and the first full colour film of 'World, Flesh & Devil' ' was shown in London.

If you wanted to either celebrate or indeed drown your sorrows a pint of beer was just three pence, although you would have to take into account Britain's last Liberal Prime Minister Lloyd George who introduced 'emergency war measures' to both halve the volume of beer brewed and its strength and slash pub opening hours by up to two thirds. What a bastard!

45 It's Better – But Ultimately Another Premier Exit: 2014-15

Danny Ings kisses disabled fan Joseph Skinner after scoring at Turf Moor. He later gave the wheelchair-bound youngster his boots as a memento

What a player – what a man!
Danny Ings makes a fan's day. He would later finance a local
disabled sporting project.

To be a member of what is widely regarded as one, if not THE most prestigious leagues in world football and the exclusive cachet that brings is every fans dream. That is why when your team is not a guest at the top table it feels like for the second time in five years you have been asked to leave a Michael Roux restaurant to dine at McDonalds.

Our first Premiership game doesn't go without a hitch ...

From Austria to Accrington, Preston to Blackpool, with a flavour of both Spanish and Italian football flair thrown in. This constituted Burnley's pre-season friendlies as they prepared themselves for their teak tough opening Premier League fixture against the bookies' favourites Chelsea at Turf Moor.

Myself and regular Burnley F.C. tourist 'Weedy' had decided to make a trip of this only European game scheduled, by doing a land circumnavigation to our destination hitchhiking through Slovakia, Hungary and Slovenia.

This we did for over a week in some of the toughest places encountered in Europe for obtaining a lift. So much so that after travelling little more than five miles on a Saturday over the Slovenian border with Hungary we were forced to hitch a ride to the nearest town twenty miles up country that had a train link. Catching the express next morning from Maribor to our base camp village of Leibnitz, then hiring a bike to cycle the 15 miles into the Austrian hills for our game against F.C. Grossklein of the regional Styrian Championship.

An 8-0 thrashing was duly dished out to our hospitable hosts within a small ground that colourfully distinguished itself by a large field of tall sunflowers at one end with a big hospitality tent at the other.

On our return three games against our Lancashire neighbours followed before the double-header against Spanish side Celta Vigo and the Italian Serie A team Hallas Verona.

Although these latter two matches against foreign opposition were relatively more competitive, both chose to use it as a squad rotation exercise, and so nullifying any robust competitive challenge.

So, with the self-named 'Special One' bringing his multi-million-pound squad up from Stamford Bridge I was questioning once again whether we had given ourselves a stiff enough test in the preliminaries.

The 'David versus Goliath' clash had been chosen as a match for a live Sky T.V. transmission to take place on a Monday night in mid-August.

Anticipation for this one had been building since the fixture announcements in June, and as the rest of the division had already played their first game I had accepted 'Lawman's' cheeky wager of a pint of beer at odds of 100/1 that Burnley would be top of the prem, in the newspapers come Tuesday morning. That would have kept me in ale for weeks, and when Scotty Airfield opened the scoring for us in the 14th minute with a thunderous shot I later heard that his son Martin had texted his dad to remind him of his rash flutter to keep him on edge.

However, that moment would be the pinnacle of our performance as a star-studded Chelsea raised their game a couple of gears before easing to a 3-1 final result.

It was a sobering night and a definite 'welcome to the Premiership' moment.

A case of déja vu at Swansea ...

Our first away game of the new campaign took us to Swansea for the August Bank Holiday weekend. The Liberty Stadium being a place we were hopeful of picking up our first points.

We designated it another mini-break match and so the self-same quartet that had made that arduously fraught journey in 'Knock-Off's' death trap Ford Fiesta were teaming up again exactly four years to the day of that ill-fated excursion. Only this time I put myself in charge of overnight bookings after K. O's, yet to be confirmed Guinness Book of Records bid to squeeze three fully grown adults into the smallest bedroom possible on the last trip!

Accordingly, Nigel's newer motor dropped us off at our Port Talbot destination for 7 p.m. in a Travelodge accommodation of which at least you can be sure of its uniform regulatory standard.

That is where the sense of déja'vu began to kick in as we quickly got changed and ordered a taxi to the guildhall beer festival, the very same location visited previous to our last meeting in the Championship.

Although the beer didn't run out this time, Burnley's luck did the following day as once again they succumbed to defeat by a solitary goal.

After the game, we stopped off at Neath, a rough and ready town halfway between Swansea and Port Talbot before ending our night at the latter.

Ross-On-Wye was the refreshment stop on the way home Sunday afternoon where we debated whether Burnley could register a first league win in our next game at home to Man. United.

Before that we exited the Capital One Cup 2nd round losing 1-0 at home to Sheffield Wednesday but showing little appetite for this much-maligned competition where most top tier teams play a weakened side to avoid injuries to their key players.

Talking of much maligned, next up as stated that team they all love to hate 'Manu'. This was a Sunday afternoon fixture where to their credit Burnley really gave it a go but couldn't get that breakthrough goal, although ex-red David Jones did hit the bar with a curling free kick. Final score 0-0.

Soon after a representative From Barclays bank, the sponsors of the Premier League got in touch. It transpired that I had been nominated to represent the club as part of their 'True spirit of the game' campaign which they were about to roll out.

I was invited to a training session to meet manager Sean Dyche and the players at their Gawthorpe Hall headquarters where photographs were taken and an interview with the Sun newspaper took place.

We had just drawn away at Crystal Palace yet could quite easily have won our first game as midfielder Scott Airfield had his penalty saved by the Eagles goalkeeper Julian Speroni in added-on time. There would have been no way back, but Scott had gone for placement not power and that's what found me discussing the science of the theory of velocity against reaction to a penalty kick with Sean as the cameras rolled.

That theory states that the goal size, distance from the ball and reaction times of the goalie put the odds overwhelmingly in a shooter's favour. With an average ball kicked in a penalty travelling at 70 m.p.h. it all means it will take the sphere less than half a second to reach the net giving the custodian around 700 milliseconds to look which way the ball is going, decide which way to jump and finally move his body in that direction.

Sean, knowing we were being filmed, although looking somewhat perplexed by my supposition, nodded his head in agreement. Noticeably, our next penalties were definitely struck with more venom and were netted accordingly. Anything to help of course!

As it stood we now hadn't even scored a goal in our last four games and that would stretch to six with another goal less draw at home to Sunderland, and in what would be our worst performance and thrashing of the season a 4-0 reverse at West Bromwich, once again on a Sunday. A result that put us where the majority of pundits tipped us to be at the end of the season – rock bottom of the league in 20th spot.

A sensational Ross Wallace speciality free-kick saw us at last score two goals on the road at Leicester with his added-on time equaliser. But then two home games were lost by the same 3-1 score line to West Ham and Everton respectively with the majority of the goals being worryingly conceded from headers.

A 3-0 loss at Arsenal followed before at last we collected our first win of the Premier League season with a 1-0 home win over Hull City on Saturday November 8th 2014.

That seemed to inspire some renewed confidence as did the next fixture away at my home town club of Stoke City for the following reason.

Since the Britannia Stadium became the Potters new home in 1997 Burnley had taken more points from there than any other club recording 5 wins, 2 draws and 2 defeats in their last 9 visits in Division One, The Championship and just the one in the Premiership.

The impressive run continuing with two incisive strikes from Danny Ings in as many minutes establishing a nice cushion within the first fifteen minutes of the game. Stoke pulled back a goal just before half-time to pile on the pressure in the second half which resembled a re-enactment of the Alamo as Burnley survived a relentless bombardment to claim their second successive win and offer some hope.

Clarke Carlisle suffers a meltdown ...

It was the last Premier league fixture before Christmas when Burnley travelled down to play Tottenham Hotspur on Saturday 20th December 2014.

We occupied the safe seat of 17th in the table on the back of a 1-0 home win against Southampton the previous week.

A real sucker punch caught us out for their opening goal scored by home grown local prodigy Harry Kane. He took a quick free kick catching the Burnley defence unaware. This was cleverly ignored by the offside Christian Erikson allowing Nacer Chadli to run on and provide a cross for the unchallenged Kane, who had run 40 yards from taking the set-piece, to head home easily past goalkeeper Tom Heaton.

In fairness, our response was spectacular, as within six minutes Ashley Barnes unleashed an Exocet missile of a shot into the top corner of the net from the edge of the penalty area.

It would go on to be my goal of the season, but I must confess to doing a double take at the scorer, as I simply didn't think 'Barnsey' had that in his locker.

An equally sensational long shot from Spurs man Erik Lamela won them the game 2-1 but no one attending could have been sure of the result until the final whistle.

So, it was back to Euston for a couple of pints in the nearby Bree Louise and Doric Arch pubs to discuss something that would be a recurring topic of conversation as the season progressed. That of another narrow defeat.

I half-read my match day programme in between intermittent snoozes on my London Midland train back to Stoke-On-Trent until a text alert on my mobile phone caught my eye.

It was a message from regular supporter Pete Horsfield from Knaresborough, North Yorkshire who had travelled north from Kings Cross. It simply said "I am sat next to Clarke Carlisle".

Now Clarke was our former captain who had put in a superb man-of-the-match performance in the 2009-10 Play-Off final at Wembley in a 1-0 victory against Sheffield United that assured our place in the top flight last time before an immediate return to the championship.

"Tell him he was the top man when we beat the Blades Pete, but don't bore him to death!"

I'd added that last comment because Pete does have a tendency to ramble on a bit, but what I didn't realise at the time how very close Carlisle would come to the last word of my sentence.

At 7.30 a.m. on the A64 road near to York Clarke Carlisle was struck by a lorry the following Monday morning.

At the time the cause of the accident was unknown.

I'd only met Clarke once over in America on a pre-season tour. Fans were invited to a bar after the game in the town of Cory to meet the players.

He was sitting by himself somewhat aloof from the rest of the squad in an open makeshift V.I.P area sectioned off by nothing more than a length of nylon tape.

Taking a chance to talk football, I first congratulated him on his marvellous performance at Wembley in the 1-0 championship play-off final victory over Sheffield United in 2009, before moving on to ask what he thought of our prospects for the upcoming season.

A dead pan expression looked back at me, his big brown eyes were glazed and distant as they looked right through my head. It couldn't have been alcohol induced as we hadn't been there long enough from the game finishing, and besides he was drinking a cordial. No, it was as if this demeanour was part of his make up almost like there was something else that was permanently occupying his mind.

He then went on to reply to my question in a robotic, seemingly well-rehearsed rhetoric more associated with public speaking than a bar room chat.

It was the unusual appraisal of commitment and hope that most footballers give as a stock encouragement to the enquiring supporter, but it was the way it was delivered which caught my eye.

Very reminiscent of local lad and former Stoke player Garth Crookes whose accent transgressed from a Potteries vernacular to Queens English once he secured regular employment as a television football pundit.

The 35-year-old centre back had played 153 times for Burnley amongst over five hundred appearances for nine clubs in total.

He had gained 10 grade A G.C.S. Es' at school and became known as "Britain's Brainiest Footballer' after winning a nationwide competition, followed by invitations to appear on television programmes 'Question Time' and 'Countdown'.

Offers to commentate for Sky Sport and I.T.V. were taken up and I remember watching many of his Europa League commentaries on a Thursday night where a more measured analytic dialogue was expressed.

Clarke wrote a book called 'A Footballers Life', a warts and all account of his early road to self-destruction. That frank admission should have helped him, but it didn't.

The Epitome of a tall, dark and handsome muscular man he was married to wife Gemma, had three children and was sufficiently well regarded to be appointed chairman of the Professional Footballers' Association in 2010, as well as an ambassador for anti-discrimination group KICK IT OUT.

New Year – new hope quickly extinguished …

A stirring 2-2 draw at Manchester City's Etihad Stadium brought the curtain down on 2014 with Burnley now precariously sitting just one place off the bottom of the league.

So, it was a trip to Newcastle United on New Year's Day in the pipeline and I suppose if there is anywhere in the country that you would choose for a great New Year's Eve party this part of the north east of England would be high on the list. Trains, coaches and hotels were booked and drinking partner 'Weedy' jumped on board for another heavy duty 'bish-bash-bosh!'

The Geordies didn't disappoint with a lively atmosphere giving way to a spectacular firework display at the stroke of midnight from the Tyne bridge. That's where we bumped into Dublin Claret 'Golden Graham' and his son Calum who had decided to do the same as us and celebrate the night in style.

Our hotel was around four miles out of the city but on this occasion, we were in no fit state to walk it, so settled for a cab.

Next day we located a bus stop that we hoped would take us both into the city on a freezing cold morning. But upon enquiring we were told that even though it was a match day with over 50,000 fans expected there was ridiculously no public transport laid on.

That left us with little alternative but to hitch it. We were still chuntering to each other about the lack of any service for non-drivers at such a busy event when after a hand numbing half-hour, a car pulled into the bus lane to transport us to the centre.

We had only managed to have a short chat with the middle-aged male behind the steering wheel given the short length of the journey, but he did tell us that he would be soon parking his car up before going to a local town to join in their traditional New Years' Day pub crawl, which for some reason seemed to tickle Weed as he began to chuckle to himself. He then dropped us off on the edge of the city centre and I exited the passenger seat after wishing him the compliments of the season with a grateful hand shake.

Weedy however proceeded to take his 'Happy New Year' greeting to a higher level. Clambering ungainly out of the rear of the vehicle, instead of a simple hand wave farewell, he inexplicably stretched his stick insect like body over to the surprised driver. Weedy then clutched his hand inside both of his and with his pancake arse popped up in the air delivered a thank you speech normally reserved for a lifelong friend who is about to emigrate to a far-off land.

"Thank you, thank you very much, great meeting you. Hope you have a great time, which I'm sure you will…. Ha,ha! Bye, bye now, bye bye."

With that Weed extracted himself from his motor and the startled Geordie drove off.

I doubled up in a fit of laughter.

"What the fuck was that all about Weed? I don't know why you didn't just finish off with giving him a blow job for good measure! He's only taken us four miles down the road, not four hundred miles across the Gobi Desert. What's a matter with ya? That was well over the top."

"It's called appreciation Ralph, something you wouldn't understand," he fired back scornfully.

"I'd better get you a drink," I offered as we made our way to our first port of call still shaking my grinning head at the impromptu comedy sketch.

This match itself was an absolute cracker and the 3-3 result represented a hard-earned point particularly as Burnley had to employ all three of their substitutes in Kevin Long, Michael Kightly and Steven Reid before half-time.

After a 1-1 draw at home to Tottenham in the 3rd round of the F.A. Cup hopes were high of progressing to the next stage when goals from Ross Wallace and Marvin Sordell gave us a handy two nil lead. The latter's exquisite volley from a penny precise through ball from Kieran Trippier would constitute his one and only competitive score.

Yet neither strikes would be enough on the night as Spurs stormed back to win 4-2.

A second two goal lead was extinguished in our next game at home to Crystal Palace which ended in a 3-2 defeat.

Then followed a demoralising 2-0 reverse at fellow strugglers Sunderland as Burnley were undone by two crosses from the flanks. Even more galling was that in his programme notes Manager Gus Poyet had written that even he would struggle to score in his own side as his wingers were not supplying not near enough balls in to the forwards.

The match that really hit home that we were going down came next when for the third time in four games Burnley surrendered a two-goal advantage, succumbing to a 2-2 draw with West Bromwich Albion at home, another club in the relegation mix.

I was incandescent with rage at us once again not being able to close the contest down, and I was ready to explode as I entered the 110 Catholic Club for my post-match pint.

Knock-Off Nigel and his good pal Brian from Todmorden just happened to be in my path towards the bar.

"That's it! We're doomed, it's back to the Championship for us!", I bellowed into their faces.

Somewhat taken aback by my lack of confidence in our survival each responded vehemently to my statement of resignation by firing back simultaneously.

"Call yourself a Burnley Fan? We're only just into February. What's up with ya?" bawled Knock-Off.

"Well I've heard it all now! Dave Burnley throwing in the towel already!", added Brian.

"Listen to me. I will never surrender and I am as loyal as the next man you should know that, but a team that throws away a two-goal upper hand in three out of four fixtures is a team that doesn't deserve to stay up at any level of Football! Once is perhaps unfortunate, twice is careless but three times is unforgivable!", I contested.

Derisory put-downs followed, but by the second week in May it gave me absolutely no pleasure at all to have been proved correct.

A Wednesday night defeat at Old Trafford was equally hard to take in our next game as Burnley dominated the first half yet still went in 2-1 down after a superb team move led to Danny Ings scoring. It would be slack marking at the back post to concede a couple of headers which would inflict a final 3-1 result.

Then it was down to the capital to face Chelsea, a game no one had given us a chance of getting a result. But we did in a fractious 1-1 draw with full back Ben Mee heading the all-important equaliser.

The warrior in chief that day being Ashley Barnes who was fortunate to stay on the pitch with first a studs-up lunge on Branislav Ivanović near the touchline followed by a more than robust challenge on Nemanja Matic which got the Chelsea player sent off for retaliation.

A tremendous strike from George Boyd would earn him the goal of the season from our supporter's clubs and net Burnley a 1-0 home win once again against the current League Champions Man. City, but it was no more than a temporary reprieve.

Burnley go down on the day they win away ...

That all defining moment when most Burnley fans began to realise that their time might soon be up, and safety slipping away from them, came in the crucial bottom of the table clash at home to Leicester City.

Having won their last three Premier League games The Foxes had effectively swapped places with Burnley who were now bottom of the table, yet still only two points behind both them and Hull City, who hovered just above the drop zone.

On the day, The Sun newspaper featured a striking mocked up picture on the front of its 'Goals' centre page pull out which perfectly encapsulated the tense situation.

It featured manager Sean Dyche chucking a pair of dice along a casino table in a game of craps with the other seven managers still involved in the relegation fight anxiously looking on either side of him with the headline.

"Last throw of the Dyche."

A tight game in keeping with the importance of the result followed with Burnley being only denied by the brilliance of goalkeeper Kasper Schmeichel making two saves in particular that his father Peter would have been proud of.

Then came 'THAT' moment. Just before the hour mark, Paul Konchesky clipped Matt Taylor who was making his first appearance at Turf Moor since coming back from his archilles injury picked up in August.

He won a spot-kick and instantly grabbed the ball despite Danny Ings slamming home Burnley's penalty against Aston Villa. Although in that same Sun supplement he had actually stated that having taken high pressure penalties in the past during a ten-year Premiership spell with Bolton, Portsmouth and West Ham if the same situation arose he would be quite happy to do it again.

Which is exactly what he did with a game changing outcome.

As he ran up to take the kick his standing foot slipped first before connecting, sending what has to be said a decently struck shot onto the wrong side of the post with Schmeichel diving the wrong way.

Within a minute, an Albrighton cross inadvertently forced a good save off goalkeeper Tom Heaton which defender Michael Duff's interception diverted towards him, only for Leicester's Jamie Vardy to tap in the rebound.

It felt about as devastating as it could be, and Burnley went on to snatch defeat from the jaws of victory in that sixty second window of opportunity.

Adding to the gloom was the statistic that we had now only scored one Premier League goal in the last eight games against opposing clubs and lost three on the spin by a one nil result. An identical full time deficit in the next fixture away to West Ham only adding to my view that a proven scorer alongside Dany Ings wasn't an option, but an absolute necessity in order to survive the relegation trap door way back in the January transfer window.

But the game that put us out wouldn't be against the team we would be playing but other results elsewhere.

A gutsy 1-0 swing in our direction followed at Hull City as I went to join the gathered masses watching the results come in on the televisions dotted about the concourse to see how the stragglers we were chasing had got on.

It was left to fanatical fan Dave Timberlake from Nottinghamshire to deliver the news I was dreading to hear.

"We're down Dave. Villa have beaten West Ham 1-0, Leicester have done Southampton 2-0 and Sunderland have won away at Everton somehow."

"What! They've all bloody won as well?

Bastards!!", I added, after our hard-fought victory had been rendered valueless.

I took a gulp of air, bit my lip till it bled and stormed out angered at what seemed the unlikelihood of all our relegation rivals winning as well as ourselves.

That night myself, Weedy and Knock-Off Nigel circumnavigated the nearby town of Beverley in a zombie-like state looking for elusive pubs that I hadn't yet visited.

And almost as if it was fated to compound an already miserable day our trio eventually reached our first alehouse that we had targeted a good two miles out from the railway station only to find it closed and boarded up.

So, by the time we had ordered a taxi on a busy Saturday night to our next pub a good hour of the proposed session of drowning our sorrows had been wasted.

With the evening tarnished by both the results elsewhere and our poor sense of timing to drink in the now defunct furthermost boozer we all agreed to just drink where it took us and that's what we did catching the last train back to Hull for a steady night.

Sunday morning came with the newspapers highlighting Burnley's demise and it wouldn't be too long before on the back of that home defeat Hull City would be joining us along with the long-time doomed Queens Park Rangers.

I immediately declared a week of mourning via my twitter account on my mobile phone. In reality, that week would last all through the summer months.

We'd gone down again after just one attempt, as we had from the Premier in 2009-10, as we had from Division One (now championship) in 1994-95, and as we had from the other Division Two (now Championship) in 1982-83.

It clearly seemed that Burnley found that initial consolidation campaign following promotion a regularly troublesome hurdle to overcome, leaving some fans querying whether it was worth the effort of going up in the first place.

Of course, for the football club the riches were there for all to see, and from the board's understandable point of view when it came to the choice of splashing out such a vast amount on one player or a brand new state of the art training complex there could only be one outcome.

But as supporters we still felt short changed. The team was probably just a couple of players shy to stay in the division. An attacking, goal scoring midfielder and an out and out striker with a proven record would have kept us up. Jutkiewicz and Marvin Sordell made over forty appearances between them in all competitions either from the start or as was the general case as substitutes, yet neither could muster one Premier League goal between them, try as they might. The lack of fire power being the single most reason we went down. Just 28 goals in 38 games was easily the lowest strike rate in the division and I'm afraid to say ultimately told its own story.

The club had approached Troy Deeney, a player manager Sean Dyche knew very well from his time at Watford. Their reported ten million plus asking price was considered too much. Yet the following season with Watford promoted to the top tier on the back of skipper Deeney's goals, and going a long way to maintaining their status the year after with his reported scoring contribution that substantial fee would have been paid back within an eighteen-month period if we had only dared to take a punt on him.

At the end of the day that conjecture boiled down to if's, buts and maybes; and as the mock reply to such debatable suggestions goes,

"If my auntie had bollocks she would have been my uncle!"

So, we had to accept our second downgrade in five years from England's elite league and prepare once more to throw ourselves into the choppy vortex of the Championship, but boy did it hurt!

Mind over matter reversed

The term 'mind over matter' is used to describe a situation in which someone is able to control a physical condition or problem by using the mind to overcome those circumstances. But what happens when the opposite occurs and the phrase can be reversed to read 'Matter over mind' to describe all the implications that state of agitation brings with it?

Burnley supporter and previous right hand man to former Prime Minister Tony Blair , Alastair Campbell, has always fronted up about his personal issues with mental health and his descent into abject depression.

Indeed, during 2017 he has been at the forefront of a highlighted campaign to further educate the general public on mental health awareness by bringing the illness out into the open. Amongst the many books he has written is his first novel titled, 'All In The Mind' which chronicles the agonies and insecurities of mental trauma delving deep into the co-dependency between patient and doctor in both a comedy and tragedy of ordinary lives.

No matter what your political views are, it cannot be denied that he has successfully attained an elevated position of power throughout his career, even with the handicap of despondency that has blighted parts of his life.

Which only goes to show that this state of mind balance is a precarious abyss that we can all fall into. An affliction which is no respecter of wealth or stature as detailed in the following pages, which once again is Burnley F.C. related to a large extent.

Clarke Carlisle…

Thinking back to my one and only brief meeting with the man in the States, even I could tell his behaviour was just off kilter in a social sense, so maybe the clues were there for all to see if you delved deep enough.

Everything to live for, yet evidently not enough for someone blighted by the dual diagnosis of a mental health and addiction problem.

I'm pleased to say that having heard Clarke on Radio Five in May 2017 in an interview with Adrian Chiles promoting his social foundation to combat mental health it would seem he is now in a far better place.

With an undiminished intellect he talked both eloquently and intelligently about his upcoming project.

But he did make one quote which might give an indication to people with a hair-trigger response behaving as they do with the slightest provocation when he said,

"The short answer to my suicide attempt was a seemingly innocuous final straw that broke the camel's back".

Analysing that statement, it would infer that Clarke had tortured himself to the point of no return.

Similar comparisons can be made to another ex-claret Paul Gascoigne, who also seems to experience some kind of short-circuiting to his brain's nerve centre which combined with his alcohol dependency kicks off all sorts of wholly irrational thoughts and behaviour. Unfortunately that case is ongoing.

Then there was the shock tragic news of the suicide of Wales national team manager Gary Speed who was found hanged at his home on November 27th 2011 aged just 42.

Another professional at the peak of his managerial career, yet once again haunted by inescapable demons.

And the latest casualty of this uncompromising illness is troubled England star Aaron Lennon who suffered his complete breakdown in early May of 2017.

Having been grieving since his grandad's recent death Aaron was detained by police who feared for his welfare after being seen walking down a busy dual carriageway barefoot.

The winger was taken to Salford Royal Hospital and sectioned under the Mental Health Act. His reported £75,000-a-week wage at Everton not mattering one jot in a life that can be indiscriminately cruel to any one of us.

I myself, have been close to 'flipping' during the dark years of following my football club proving that it is what matters most to an individual that can sometimes tip them over the edge, or conversely, as Clarke Carlisle stated, "An innocuous final straw that broke the camel's back".

The rise and fall of 'Gazza'...

After Gazza's amateur dramatics during the World Cup, the prankster became almost untouchable in the public's eyes. No matter how crude or outrageous he behaved the everlasting image of him blubbering like a baby in that semi-final would override all else.

He wanted to please people and be liked, and wherever he went the clown prince was expected to perform much like a comedian taking to the stage. However Gazza's stage commanded a worldwide audience in May 1991 when Spurs faced Nottingham Forest in the F.A. Cup Final at Wembley Stadium.

Paul Gascoigne the footballer, had featured strongly throughout the games leading up to the final culminating with a stunning free kick goal past David Seaman of Arsenal in the semi that television commentator David Coleman eulogized over with these memorable words.

"It's a free kick to Tottenham, Gascoigne to take it and it looks like he's going to have a go………….. I say – brilliant! That is schoolboys' own stuff!"

In the pre-match introduction to Lady Diana, Gazza was so confident of his national appeal that he gave her a gentle kiss which just seemed to add to his plainly evident hyperactive demeanour. But it would be on the pitch where he blew up like a bottle of pop. Once referee Roger Milford had whistled the game under way Gazza was on a mission. Like a pedigree bull released from his holding pen to track down the matador he unleashed his pent up aggression with two wild tackles within a short space of time, both of which would have warranted red cards on any other day. First Gary Parker was left reeling by an ill-judged challenge that went unpunished, but the irresponsible full length lunge on Gary Charles in quick succession could easily have been a career ending injury for the Forest man. Instead, through his own recklessness Paul Gascoigne was stretchered off with shredded knee ligaments such was the force of his contact on the victim.

It was particularly ironic as he'd only recently brought out a coaching video advising kids how to tackle correctly to avoid injury! But that was typical Paul Gascoigne – impetuous, insecure, incautious and on that day some would say insane!

So the proud Geordie had to watch the rest of the game from a hospital bed alone with his thoughts of what might have been. Tottenham went on to win the game 2-1 after extra-time and soon after the final the squad went to visit him with the prized trophy. According to his good friend and Spurs team mate Paul Stewart he once again burst into tears and he was one of the first to console him with the words,

"We wouldn't have won it without you Gazza" which led to warm embraces all round.

Both Paul Stewart and Paul Gascoigne would go on to play for Burnley in the latter stages of their career. Unfortunately, each would prove equally ineffective.

Since Gazza retired from football he has made almost as many headlines as when he was playing. The vast majority of which have revolved around his many drinking exploits.

Although variously described as the former Newcastle, Spurs and Lazio footballer he did , thanks to Stan Ternent, wear our famous claret and blue shirt for three starts and the same number of substitute appearances. In my eyes that makes him ex-Burnley too.

Perhaps that, and the fact my alcohol intake puts me in the heavy drinking category is the reason why I have a great deal of empathy if not sympathy for 'Gaz lad'.

My rationale for this is that he has had every chance to reform himself with expensive treatments at specialized institutions on many occasions, a privilege most ordinary folk don't have.

As I wrote in Part One of my autobiography in Chapter 9, 'That mourning after feeling:' my solution to control my excessive drinking was to compromise thus –

"As a mere supporter, pub copping has turned out to be a sort of personal, working class equivalent of a structural rehabilitation clinic or a 'drying-out' centre into which today's pampered professional footballers all too readily admit themselves. The difference was that instead of facing complete abstinence from the 'sauce' I had successfully established a much more controlled form of drinking.

The simple act of writing down details of every different pub or bar I visited gave me both a focus and a target to pursue."

Gazza has none of these incentives in his life in any form. Maybe he should take up 'pub copping?'

In the interim, at the beginning of February 2013 Paul Gascoigne flew out with a minder to the £6,000-a-week Meadows Rehabilitation Centre located in Phoenix, Arizona, U.S.A.

The emergency rehab to address his drink problems was organized and paid for by a consortium of his friends which included Radio 2 D.J. Chris Evans, ex-England team mate Gary Lineker, Britains Got Talent judge Piers Morgan and former England cricketer Ronnie Irani.

This all came about after mobile phone footage from one of the 600 strong audience at a charity function where 'Gazza' made an appearance was handed to the media for public consumption.

It showed him shaking uncontrollably, sobbing, slurring his speech and swearing at the gathered assembly.

The widely held view is that the only person that can steer them away from their dependency is themselves. As stated, I still believe that it is an addiction that can be controlled, and I can only hope that Gazza one day proves that he has the strength of character to do just that. To achieve that goal would surpass any of those he has scored on the football pitch at any level.

In Memoriam

In early February 2015, I learnt of the death of former London based claret Paul Burrows. Paul was 65 and had only recently moved north to be nearer to his beloved football club after selling up down south.

A member of the London supporters branch Paul came across as a man with his own agenda, but still enjoying a smoke and a big drink with seasoned 'beer monsters' like 'Woody, Paddy and Firmo; along the way.

Perhaps one of his most regular supping partners was Mike Benyon who is now Bedfordshire based. He and Paul could always be found propped up against the bar on neighbouring stools before each match in the corner of Burnley's best real ale pub, The Bridge Bier House, located on Bank Parade just off the town's main thoroughfare.

'Benny' as he is amicably and somewhat predictably known remains a stalwart from the same era attending the vast majority of matches home and away despite his mobility becoming increasingly more painful and restrictive due to an undermining condition.

His pal Paul represents yet another established face that will be missed on match days.

In Memoriam

2015 was a bad year off the pitch as I lost two close work colleagues from my first job as an invoice clerk at Castle House, the regional headquarters of the Silverdale Co-operative Society.

In the June of this year Stuart Allen who had been the assistant manager at my works died after a long-protracted debilitating illness that had sadly confined him to a nursing home for the past few years. He was 76 years old.

As documented in part one Stuart dealt with my many requests for time off to follow my club with due consideration and sensitivity.

In the December of 2015 Stuart's right-hand man in the banking department John Lockett passed away also in the care of a rest home. Blighted by increasingly progressive neurological complications like his former boss Stuart he was always pleased to see his friends visiting, none more so than his loyal soul mate Sylvia who attended to his many needs most days of the week. It was a sad farewell at only 63 years of age.

Both, had a dry sense of humour that totally belied their responsible positions in the 'House' and will be sadly missed.

46 Up as Champions and Staying Up: 2015-17

Dynamo Dyche, The Magician, takes us up for the 2nd time in three years.
Photo courtesy of Burnley Football Club

After two big bites of the Premiership cherry it really did feel as if our chance had gone to play the elite. To his immense credit manager Sean Dyche embraced what looked like an unlikely challenge of an immediate return to the top tier.

Devastated ...

The Monday following our relegation confirmation just happened to be our designated once monthly pub-meet with my former Kippo's work mates. However, I was still raw from Burnley's demotion, and certainly in no mood to combat the open antagonism that would inevitably materialize from some of those present when discussing our demise. Therefore, I wrote a short note to explain my absence to pass on to those assembled.

On paper our opening three league fixtures for the 2015/16 Championship season looked a tricky proposition having been draw away at Leeds United in the opener, followed by a visit from an always physically competitive Birmingham City then travelling to Portman Road, Ipswich, not one of our happier hunting grounds.

And that is how it turned out. A 1-1 and a 2-2 draw in the first two games and a 2-0 reverse to the Suffolk club left us 17th in the table. Add to that a 1-0 1st round Capital League Cup defeat at one of my local clubs in Port Vale and any optimistic thoughts of an immediate return to the Premiership were slowly fading.

Although a rousing triple of league wins over Bristol City, Sheffield Wednesday and MK Dons propelled us up the table to 5th there was one piece of the jigsaw short in my mind to make a concerted push for a promotion or play-off place. We needed a leader of men.

With an absolute master stroke of intuition Sean brought regular bad boy liability Joey Barton into the side to perfectly fulfil that role.

His full debut at Rotherham on a Friday night helping Burnley gain a 2-1 win, which would inspire a run of nine games undefeated until a disappointing 2-0 home loss to Preston North End.

Bolton Wanderers were then routinely beaten 2-0 at home before a classy Matt Taylor goal earned a point at Nottingham Forest to maintain 5th spot. But there was much better to come and next up were traditional rivals Blackburn.

In the Blackburn Rovers away fixture on Saturday the 24th of October Burnley fans witnessed a truly seminal moment when Scotty Arfield fired in a superb shot to score the only goal of the game. His instant reaction being to sprint 100 yards down the pitch to the massed ranks of the claret support with Michael Duff clutching his hand as he bolted off!

Scott and the other ten players from his team knowing just how much the final result meant to their followers embraced as joyously on the pitch as we did in the Darwen End, and from that day on it felt as if an unbreakable bond existed between that crop of players and their devotees.

There were still tough trips ahead where the squad's never-say-die attitude would be severely tested. Cardiff City in the welsh capital being one such stern examination of their resources.

2-0 down with five minutes to play should have been enough to secure the points for the home side but a late show gained a precious draw to epitomize manager Sean Dyche's 'Relentless' buzzword to describe the dogged, unremitting 100% effort of the players.

Questions were asked however after three defeats during the month of December, when six goals were conceded without reply. The 2-0 home defeat to Lancashire rivals Preston North End was hard to take and whilst the 1-0 loss at Middlesbrough felt like a six-pointer the weary 3-0 thrashing at Hull City on Boxing Day knocked the supporters back on their haunches.

On Christmas Day, the players were given some allotted time to spend with their families. Whether it was an extra mince pie, a large portion of Christmas pudding or even a couple of brandies we will never know but if there was a time for a proverbial 'rocket up the backside' this was it, as a definite malaise set in after the 70th minute of this game when the real damage was done. What made matters worse was myself, Weedy, Knock-Off Nigel and plain John Smiths three day Christmas sacrifice in a becalmed Hull city centre hotel. Our festive dinner consisting of a paper plate of food made up of a sorry slice of pink pork pie, a cocktail sausage on a stick, a silver skin pickle about the size of a marble, a curled-up couple of ham and egg mayonnaise sandwiches with a liberal sprinkling of cheesy Wotsits and Chipsticks that were of a soft crunchless consistency. Probably worth about 50 pence all-in, but a nice gesture all the same from The Sandringham pub near Hull Paragon rail station. The premises itself just about as far removed from the Queen's Norfolk retreat of the same name as it could be. Whatever was said after the Hull game certainly seemed to do the trick as it would be the last league game they would finish on a losing side that season.

New year… new hope…

After the turn of the year a 2-1 3rd round F.A. Cup win at Middlesbrough went some way to avenging the league defeat less than a month earlier. The following fixture being a hard to get to Tuesday night game at the pseudo football club masquerading as Milton Keynes Dons, an ill-fated reincarnation of Wimbledon F.C., the genuine reformed outfit who they now compete against in League One after the latter's sensational rise through the non-league pyramid.

Although I'd pre-booked on the train to get down early for this match, since then a former work colleague that I'd been visiting in a care home had tragically passed away. That necessitated a ticket switch in order to pay my respects. With a terrible infrequent bus service to the isolated stadium a £10 taxi fare conveyed me from the rail station.

It would all be worth it however as Burnley blew away M.K. 5-0 in what would be the most comprehensive victory of the campaign. It was the night that I thought to myself 'You know we could just have something going for us here,' such was our complete clinical dominance of the Dons.

Brentford away on a Friday night had to be one of the stand out performances given the quality of all of our goals in the 3-1 win. Another previous deserter, Jason Shackell returned to Turf Moor on a Monday night with his Derby County team mates, but along with his colleagues left with his tail well and truly between his legs after being on the receiving end of 4-1 thrashing. To top off his miserable night he was an unwilling contributor to two of our goals through conceding a penalty and a massive deflection past his own keeper.

Arsenal then dispatched us from the F.A. Cup with a narrow 2-1 win at the end of January down in London which left the team to concentrate on the job in hand. A successful February culminating in a hard fought 2-1 win at Bolton's Macron Stadium placed the Clarets top of the league for the first time that season.

The priceless double over Blackburn Rovers was banked on Saturday 5th March when an Andre Gray penalty settled the fiery contest.

But the most dramatically deciding moments came in the last minute of two crucial games in April. Brighton away and Middlesbrough at home would only return us a point from each, but both were pivotal in denying our closest challengers in the promotion race all three. At Brighton after Michael Keane had clearly headed the ball over the goal line in the last few minutes without it being given, from a carbon copy cross he did exactly the same but this time his header rippled the back of the net for a 2-2 equalizer.

That 'Champagne moment' equalizer from Michael Keane
against Middlesbrough.
Photo courtesy of Burnley Football Club

The second of what were rightly termed 'Champagne moments' came on a Tuesday night at Turf Moor when the same defender shinned in a last minute deserved leveller which led to one of the most enraptured goal celebrations I've ever seen from a group of players as substitutes and squad players progressively added to the mound of humanity that had submerged Keano.

The Saturday before I had celebrated my 42 years without missing a Burnley competitive game at Birmingham City. Knock-Off Nigel and ex-villager and good mate Clive Pritchard had joined me for the annual boozy commemoration. The 2-1 victory being one of the most hard earned of them all against a physically imposing, aggressive Brummie side.

Preston were beaten away on another memorable Friday night when an early Joey Barton goal was enough to send five and a half thousand Burnley fans delirious going into the weekend.

That meant promotion back to the Prem. could be achieved with a win over Q.P.R. at home in our penultimate fixture. Appropriately the hero of the day being Sam Vokes who headed a David Jones free-kick into the back of the net, this after missing the run-in to promotion two years ago after suffering a cruciate knee ligament injury.

Magical scenes followed as Burnley became the first team since Newcastle United six years ago to bounce back to the top flight with automatic promotion. Another promotion meant another party and the town bounced to the chant of "The Clarets are going up – again!"

That just left one more hurdle to jump in the race for the Championship title. The team in our way being already doomed to relegation Charlton at their Valley ground.

This one warranted a weekender too, so four of us booked accommodation at nearby Sidcup to soak up the preliminaries before the main event next day.

And what day it was! Burnley's sold out allocation in the South stand were joining in with the home fans vociferous protests against the club's Belgian owners. After at least matching their opponents in the early exchanges the 'Addicks' as they are uniquely nicknamed were slowly worn down by a determined Burnley side. 3-0 the final score line triggering the traditional pitch invasion from myself and a few hundred supporters who had breached the line of stewards. We all knew we had done it!

Burnley were Champions! Fierce rivals Middlesbrough drew 1-1 with 3rd place Brighton & Hove Albion to claim the runner-up spot.

Charlton fans continued with their protests on the pitch whilst shaking the hands of Burnley fans in congratulation. Three quarters of an hour later the playing surface was cleared and the victorious team along with chairman Mike Garlick a number of directors and backroom staff and of course the architect of our success manager Sean Dyche went over to accept the acclaim from their adoring proud supporters.

But there was one small item missing – the league trophy! It wouldn't be making an appearance either as the hierarchy of the Football league in their infinite wisdom had decided that because of the planned protestations from the locals it would be too risky to present it on the day. Indeed, we would have to wait for the official parade through the town on the following Monday to view our silverware.

All that was left was to carry on our celebrations through the night which we all did, finishing up in Catford – I think.

Now we had the summer to reflect upon our brilliant achievement of three promotions to the Premiership in seven years and consider whether or not this would be third time lucky and we would stay up.

2016-17 season

Third Time Lucky?

The seemingly bottomless pot of money membership of the Premier League provides goes up year on year. Every team is not only desperate to get there but more importantly to stay there. The magical 40 points mark is always the aim of newly promoted clubs, but of course that is easier said than done, and first you have to get there.

We share a nation's tears on two fronts…

Pre-season friendlies were announced and once again it was to be in Switzerland for our first game, a warm up against Stade Nyonnaise 15 miles north of Geneva.

Myself and regular travelling companion 'Weedy' didn't fancy the exorbitant cost of living in the alpine banking capital of Europe, and so we thought outside the box.

As the EUFA Euro 2016 Final was taking place on the 10th of July at the Stade de France in Paris, what an opportunity to mix with the locals in a French city en route to our destination to soak up the atmosphere of the occasion, with our game not until Friday 15th.

We chose Lyon as our base, expecting one massive party when, not if France disposed of a poor looking Portuguese side that had limped into the final.

On a sunny Sunday morning, we flew in from Luton, dumped our bags, and hit the city, Lyon was like most places in the host nation inundated with fans of both sexes waving their tricolour flags. There wasn't a seat to be had at the extensive fan zone to view the big screen and every bar each side of the river Rhône was packed to the rafters. So much so that we could only view the match on a television from outside the venues.

All the euphoria, all the anticipation led to despair as somehow Portugal who had lost their star man Christiano Ronaldo to an early injury, won the game 1-0 when Swansea flop Eder netted in extra time.

So, it was commiserations not celebrations for the rest of the evening, and reflections of Euro 2004 when Portugal lost to massive outsiders Greece at the Estádio da Luz in Lisbon by the same 1-0 score line. It seemed then, like tonight, we were the only two still ready to party!

The following days we spent hitching to Geneva. In order to stay out of costly Switzerland for as long as possible, the day before the scheduled fixture in the town of Nyon we purposely chose to stay at a small French border town going under the name of St. Julien.

Noticing that there seemed a lot of long haired characters about and almost all of the limited hotels were full we decided to explore the location further to see what was taking place. Following our ears in the direction of loud music coming from an open space I figured that if we could locate the source, we should find a bar serving beer.

And we did! Not only had we found some ale but remarkably stumbled upon what was termed a 'Guitare-en-scene' heavy metal and rock concert featuring Twisted Sister, Europe, Carlos Santana and my own favourite band Status Quo over four nights. Today was Thursday and the ageing rockers Twisted Sister were headlining with Quo on Saturday. The price of admission being a staggering 70 euros for tonight alone, which was way out of our price bracket. Just as we were walking away I had noticed a bloke outside the main gates just standing around with two pieces of A4 size paper in his hand. Guessing they were some kind of generated E-ticket I pointed at them and asked 'Combien?' He wouldn't take anything for them, and so through his generosity we entered the field. The gig itself was good, but the live news relayed by lead singer Daniel 'Dee' Snider wasn't, as he stopped to announce the atrocities that had just taken place in Nice, southern France that same night. It would lead to 84 people being killed in the Bastille Day atrocity when a terrorist truck driver drove through celebrating crowds for 2 kilometres.

Instantaneously Snider broke into a second defiant rendition of one of their top songs 'We're Not Gonna Take It' with all the gathered thousands of fans joining in accordingly copying the angry vocalist's one finger salute gesture.

Both of us woke next morning still numbed by the barbarity of the paramilitary killings that had struck in the country we were travelling through, with the so called Islamic State claiming responsibility for the despicable act.

Next day at the match, Burnley beat the Swiss team 3-1. We flew back on the Sunday suitably well out of pocket after paying up to £10 an equivalent pint in Geneva old town on the Saturday night.

A win at Glasgow Rangers by the same 3-1 margin preceded the second stellar opposition at home to Real Sociedad of Spain, an Andre Gray goal earning a 1-1 draw.

So, to the long-awaited season proper and an opening fixture to Swansea City at Turf Moor seemed on paper a decent change of some reward. But there was none as a late goal unfairly sent all the points back to South Wales.

It was the worst possible start, but what came next would surely be the result of Burnley's season. Liverpool had switched their home fixture with our consent as Anfield was still undergoing a construction extension to their capacity. The reds had a remarkable 81% possession rate during the game, a Premiership record, and yet lost 2-0 to two exquisite strikes from front man Andre Gray and Sam Vokes. Watford 2-0 and Everton 2-1 were both dispatched at The Turf in the following weeks leading up to the end of October but ominously we had lost all our games away and next up was a trip to Old Trafford.

Man. U meltdown...

I'd arranged to meet a pal I'd met on a raucous holiday to Tunisia way back in 1981. Although over 35 years ago myself and Stevie Russell from Didsbury have kept in touch. He is a 'red', but thankfully one of the more knowledgeable and tolerable ones. He took me around a number of new bars that had emerged in this place to be hip district before I bid him a fond farewell and caught the tram to the ground.

Up to press I had not responded to any of the chit chat along the way inferring that given Burnley's poor away form, this should be a walkover, although it had quietly festered in my subconscious mind as I was once again appalled at their sheer arrogance. So far, I had chosen to ignore the frankly insulting assumption preferring to walk on and get amongst my own clan in the stadium, until a chance meeting popped the cork of my bottled-up irritation.

As I turned off for the away end down the rightfully honoured Sir Matt Busby Way a lone Burnley fan passing in the opposite direction stopped me to ask the question,

"How d'ya think we will do today Dave?"

Coming to a halt adjacent to a mobile snack bar I gave him my considered opinion.

"We've got absolutely nothing to fear as long as we don't try and defend for ninety minutes. They were totally exposed at Chelsea last week as an ordinary side after their 4-0 thrashing."

By now I had alerted the chip van crowd who were munching the usual selection of footie fodder from their polystyrene trays. They turned around to a man giving me the evil eye of discord after my comment which only acted as an accelerant to my developing demeanour of disapproval. Finishing with a flourish the smoking tinder of antipathy deep inside me burst into flame with this parting reposte to the gathered onlookers.

"Besides, this lot are now a perfect match. The most arrogant manager in the country, with the most arrogant fans! They deserve each other!"

The Burnley fan looked on open-mouthed as I pointed a finger at the by now angry assemblage behind him. He made a quick getaway as a combination of pie, burger and peas were propelled my way. With that point made in a totally unpremeditated way I casually joined the rear of the visiting supporters queue giving them some more food for thought to go with their chips!

I stood up at the back out of the way of the stewards to compose myself after my outburst and the match kicked off to the usual 75,000 plus capacity.

Once again, we were up against it from the off, but this time Sean Dyche had bravely decided to play the previously suspended Andre Gray up front with big Sam Vokes.

It gave United's defence another body to cover and eased the pressure on our midfielders, although including blocks our goalkeeper Tom Heaton had a staggering 37 shots towards him. He made eleven saves including an outrageous star jump effort from a venomous Zlatan Ibrahimovic's close-range volley equalling the record he himself set against Southampton just under two weeks previous. Indeed, after the first ten Premier League matches Tom had made 57 saves which was 21 more than bottom club Sunderland's Jordan Pickford had stopped in a distant second position. That particular statistic illustrated the intense level of pressure our defence had been put under and it would be relentless. By the end of the season our custodian had produced more saves than any other in the division and that outstanding stop against Brahimovic won him the best save of the campaign in a B.B.C. Match of the Day award, and also won us a valuable point with a blank out.

Another 4-0 mauling at West Brom. on a monsoon of a Monday night would be our worst performance and biggest thrashing of the season, and almost a carbon copy of when we played them last time in the Prem. losing by the same score.

Then came my one and only home game at Stoke City. I'd have to say neither team played well but the home side scored two slick, well worked goals. The proposed celebration party at Arnie and Ginge's pad being cancelled due to the disheartening outcome meaning around twenty local clarets just melted into the night suitably cheesed off.

Crystal Palace and Bournemouth were also beaten at headquarters but two trips to London in five days saw us go down 1-0 and 2-1 to west Ham and Spurs respectively putting us in a precarious 16th position.

However, our strong home form would continue apace with two crucial victories against what look like early relegation contenders in Middlesbrough and Sunderland.

So, with back to back 'six pointer' wins against two north east teams it really was a case of 'Happy New Year' for all Burnley followers as they made their way to the eagerly awaited Bank Holiday Monday fixture at the Etihad Stadium home of Manchester City.

But it wouldn't be a happy start to 2017 as what seemed like a very disjointed team went down 2-1 to the sky blues. This after the home side had Fernandinho sent off in the first half. Surely, we could now step it up to get some reward from the game. Yet we laboured as if there was no man advantage, and when the 'crown jewels' of Sergio Aguero and David Silva stepped off the bench as able reinforcements the match swung City's way largely due to this twosome's influence. A two-goal lead being established through an injection of pace that we had no answer to. Although Michael Keane did pull one back leading to a condensed flurry of chances for the leveller it never came. They proved that even with ten men they were still too good for us. In terms of our league position there was little damage done as we dropped just the one place to a moderate 12th slot, although City had now inflicted a double against us by the same 2-1 score.

Joey Barton had waited 601 days for his Premier League return at home to Southampton, yet it was as if he had never been away.

Coming on as a 72nd minute substitute with the game still finely poised at 0-0, Burnley were awarded a free-kick 25 yards out. Barton claimed the ball before drilling it through Saint's wall, with a slight deflection, sending goalkeeper Fraser Forster the wrong way. Even at 34, it showed he still had the Midas touch making it a staggering 25 league games without defeat for him in a Burnley shirt.

Lincoln green…

No matter how successful a campaign your team has, invariably there is at least one odd blip along the way. A perfect example being Burnley's 3-0 demolition on Boxing Day at Hull City as recorded the previous season, which then led to an unbeaten 23 game league run to secure top spot in the Championship.

But if that amounted to a mere hiccup then the mystifying F.A. Cup defeat to National League side Lincoln City was more a convulsion!

This, after is seemed that fate had dealt The Clarets a good hand. Both the last two F.A. Cup draws had taken place on a cold Monday evening, and on each occasion, it just happened to coincide with my former 'Kipps's' bakery colleagues, monthly get together which also just happened to include 'Stokie' protagonists Gaz 'Zippy' Tunstall and Phil 'Bungle' Law.

Purposely, before entering out chosen bar venue The Hopwater Cellar at Newcastle-Under-Lyme, I would appear outside the window of the premises in full view of my waiting companions.

Looking back at me with considerable disdain as I clasped my small transistor radio to my ear were Zippy and Bungle. Stoke had already gone out to Wolves at home in the 3rd round 2-0 which immediately ended their interest in the competition.

Now it was up to the new England manager Gareth Southgate to pick out the home balls in the see-through canister. First out was number 12. I knew that was our numerical shout from the order of those chosen from the previous round.

"Good call Gareth!", I mouthed to our lads inside. "We've got a home draw" I added mutely.

"Will play," …it was left to former professional footballer and wind-up merchant Robbie Savage to pull out the away team "… Lincoln City."

My fist pump in the cool night air was met with full on laughter from retired employee Dave Porter, another Stoke fan but with a much less belligerent attitude than Zippy and Bungle who had made a premeditated effort to look totally unconcerned by turning their backs on me.

All the assembled knew that it was a perfect chance for us to progress to the last eight of what is regarded by supporters if not clubs, as still the most prestigious domestic trophy in world football.

For many home cup matches myself and Trev like to migrate to the Bob Lord Stand directly opposite the Longside to get a closer perspective of the action and a clear view of activities in each of the two neighbouring managers' dugouts.

In the ground, I was due to meet New Zealander Ben Jackson who had been in touch to conduct an interview for a sports related journal he was putting together. Little did he know that he would be an unlikely witness to a football fairytale that day. Although, credit where it's due he had purchased a claret and blue scarf to ingratiate himself with the home crowd.

So the long awaited whistle got this tie underway blown by referee Graham Scott with a naturally boisterous 3,210 away following singing their hearts out for what we were hoping would be their 'Cup Final'.

Such improbable surnames in the Lincoln line up consisted of Farman, Waterfall, Habergham, Woodyard, Muldoon and Raggett, but the real stand out character went under the more common family name of Rhead. Matt Rhead played as their spearhead and was a 6ft. 3in., 17 stone juggernaut of a man who only four years previous was a regular in the local Stoke-on-Trent pub side Butchers Arms, Forsbrook, a tiny hamlet that you drive through on the A521 en route to the Alton Towers theme park. A welder by trade at the massive J.C.B. digger plant at Uttoxeter he played at a higher level for Kidsgrove Athletic and Nantwich Town before jacking his job in to pursue a career at Mansfield Town then Lincoln City of the National League which is a feeder division for promotion to the Football League.

Yet here was the epitome of what a Sunday league player might look like getting the better of his diminutive by comparison man-marker Joy Barton. It would prove to be the completely wrong choice for such a task as Rhead used his sizeable weight advantage to outdo firebrand Barton at every opportunity both in the air and on the deck. So frustrated was he by his lack of effectiveness the exasperated scouser could quite easily have been sent off on three occasions all within one crazy minute.

Barton was the instigator as Rhead was made to take an unquestionable premeditated, cowardly, backward stamp to his right foot. Quickly followed by a clearly simulated dive from the 'Bartman' after he dramatically and comically threw himself to the turf when forcing contact with his head against Rhead's outstretched pointing hand. And if that wasn't shocking enough J.B. had also forcefully pushed the palm of his hand into the face of Lincoln's number 11 Terry Hawkridge. All three of the despicable actions from the ever more desperate out of control scouser could have resulted in a red card. Only a yellow was brandished. In that mad short passage of play in the eyes of many Burnley fans he had gone from yesterday's hero to today's zero!

Sean Raggett's cheaply conceded 89th minute winning header wrote minnows, Lincoln City into the record books as the first non-league team to reach the quarter-finals since 1914.

The Imps had played in their green shirts on the day whilst Burnley just played green. There was no getting away from it, both the club and their fans had suffered the most chastening experience since the third round F.A. Cup knockout at the hands of then, Southern League, Wimbledon in January 1975. At the time Burnley occupied 7th position in the top tier before going down and out by the same 1-0 score line.

After that debacle, in his report for the Burnley Express newspaper Peter Higgs wrote:

"Hang your heads in shame after this defeat Burnley. The match they said was a 'free pass' into the next round of the F.A. Cup provided arguably the most humiliating result in the history of Burnley Football Club!"

Although not made public, those sentiments must have gone through the head of all those closely associated with the club, us supporters included.

There could be no excuses, Burnley's starting eleven were valued at 50 million plus in today's market and should have more than enough about them to do the job required.

Forty-two years previous it could be argued that the Wimbledon Wombles' only goal came vastly against the run of play with their goalkeeper Dickie Guy stopping everything that was thrown at him. By comparison Lincoln custodian Paul Farman had a relatively quiet afternoon.

Before the game Burnley became the first professional English football club to invite their older generation supporters onto the pitch as player mascots. They said it was their way of giving something back to the community. Maybe they should have taken it a step further and put them in the starting eleven!

From thereon in I just knew that only one English city would get the most verbal and written mentions in the media throughout the next few days. That city was of course Lincoln.

Each time I turned on the T.V. that name would be highlighted on both the main news channels and all the football programmes. Every newspaper had them on the back page with some on their front headline.

I went into forced hibernation until Wednesday of the following week vowing to reintroduce my embargo on the nobbly biscuits that carry their name, after relaxing the ban when the Imps slipped out of the football league once again.

If we had accumulated ten points less than our current thirty it would have been an even worse scenario, so now we just had to concentrate on one objective – survival in the Premier League.

Arsenal away turned out to be as much as a case of daylight robbery as it was at home. Back then the only goal that the visitors scored to win the game could have been ruled out for three reasons. The allotted added-on time had ticked well over into the next minute for no apparent stoppage during that passage of play, the two players both looked offside on the goal line as they received the ball, and Laurent Koscielny certainly looked to handle it in as the ball cruelly crossed the line.

Down at The Emirates Burnley having drawn level in the 92nd minute must surely have thought they had done enough but an inept linesman missed a clear offside to the build-up of a dubious penalty that Sanchez converted to take, no rob, another three points. A point I vehemently made to Mick Cunningham the regular Gooner at Stoke railway station who genuinely looked embarrassed by both unsatisfactory conclusions.

Burnley were the day's biggest spenders on the last day of the transfer deadline shelling out a combined £18 million on Robbie Brady and Ashley Westwood. Meanwhile a controversial 87th minute Sam Vokes winner strikes his arm but is decided by the referee that contact was accidental and Burnley take three more precious points against Leicester City.

In the next home game a stunning Robbie Brady free kick immediately pays back a large lump of his substantial incoming fee to gain a 1-1 draw against champions elect Chelsea to put us on 30 points.

Then it was time for revenge against Stoke City where a sharply taken goal from Georgie Boyd was enough for the maximum return, after it has to be said the Potters had fluffed the better chances.

But for me the best all round team performance came with our first, yes only away victory down at Crystal Palace as late as the 29th April 2017.

Two goals from Andre Gray and Ashley Barnes without reply setting off final whistle celebrations akin to winning the Championship. A home point against West Bromwich Albion taking us to the magic forty-point mark, and virtual guaranteed safety for at least another season.

Burnley should have taken a few more points in their last two league matches against A.F.C. Bournemouth away and West Ham at home, but somewhat carelessly lost them both.

It was all incidental in the end as the north-east coast trio of Hull City, Sunderland and our newly formed rivals Middlesbrough went down to the second tier.

Add to that a last game relegation to the third strata of English football by acidic neighbours Blackburn Rovers which signalled a rash of impromptu parties in town, and a complete reversal of each club's standing in 1995, I have to ask the question;

"Has there ever been a better time to be a Burnley fan?"

Well, after safely securing a second consecutive season in the Premiership how are we rewarded? Badly, I'd have to say, with our first five away fixtures all against teams that finished in the top seven during the previous 2016-17 campaign.

An opening game against the champions Chelsea being followed by a trip to the temporary Wembley home of runners-up Tottenham Hotspur. Fourth placed Liverpool provide the next hurdle before a trip just across Stanley Park to Everton who took seventh spot. The titanium tough quintuple ending with a clash against third placed Man. City at the Etihad Stadium.

Phew! That will be a mega-test of our capabilities given the poor return of points on the road last time out.

It is to be hoped that the ten home wins Burnley took at Turf Moor can be replicated to give us another sporting chance of survival. If not our away form just has to improve.

But all players and managers want to challenge themselves to attain what they are capable of, none more so than the closely-knit unit at Turf Moor.

However, manager Sean Dyche's C.V. gets progressively more impressive as time goes by and other clubs are sniffing a good catch. Although he seems a perfect fit at Burnley other outside factors will determine whether he goes down in local folklore as one of the club's great managers or stays to contest the title for the club's greatest boss. For me, given the less than level financial playing field he's well on the way to the latter.

Of course, for my part, I will endeavour to maintain my personal attendance record of getting to every Burnley game home and away. I will also continue to celebrate my feat if achieved by wearing my less than traditional 33-piece denim suit for the first away game after that one missed on April 10th 1974 at Newcastle United. And would you believe that as things stand the Premiership computer has decreed that commemoration will take place at one of my local clubs' Stoke City at The Bet 365 Stadium on Saturday 21st April 2018 to mark 44 years without missing any competitive Burnley game. Bring it on!!

A Commendation

Let's hear it for the board ...

There's very few supporters that seem to have a good word to say about the men who are probably the most powerful members of any football club.

They are the individuals who ultimately make the final group decision on such important issues of buying or selling players, hiring or firing managers and negotiating deals for everything from footballers to caterers' contracts. They are the Chairman and Board of Directors.

Well I'm going against the grain on this occasion to heap praise upon those most unlikely to receive the full recognition they deserve here at Burnley Football Club.

Not only have they invested their hard-earned money into the day to day running of the business, their combined acumen has seen them mastermind not one, not two but three unlikely promotions to the Premier League within a short seven-year period. That is something I could never imagine twenty years ago as we floundered in the third tier of the football pyramid.

Okay, we've also been relegated twice from the top table within twelve months but that should not diminish the massive achievement of getting to that level so prolifically

So here is my tribute to those men in suits.

With more than 13 years as the figurehead Chairman behind him Barry C. Kilby oversaw his last game in that all-important position when Burnley played Bristol City in the last championship fixture of the 2011-12 season.

His devotion and loyalty towards the football club falls into that all too rarely bestowed classification of 'true love'. A genuine sentiment he probably only shares with his fun-loving wife Sonia along with his immediate family and relations.

Having played in Burnley's 'A' team as a teenager-alongside the likes of Martin Dobson, Steve Kindon and Mick Docherty, Barry's success had ultimately come to fruition as a businessman rather than a footballer.

He became chairman in the December of 1998 and after selling his Euro print enterprise which incidentally won the lucrative contract to produce the Sun newspaper bingo cards which are still played to this day, Barry decided that he could afford to help the club he had represented in the Sixties.

His initial injection of £3 million gained him a majority shareholding as Burnley proceeded to pay for the cost of the new-build James Hargreaves stand that will eternally be known as The Longside to the thousands that regularly occupied the famous terrace that it replaced.

In the 2001-02 season Burnley, had missed out on a Play-Off position by just a single goal but what followed almost skint the club once more.

The new-found stability brought about by his investment almost evaporated overnight after the collapse of I.T.V Digital who had pledged to pump hundreds of thousands into Football League clubs in return for television rights. Around £4 million of expected cashflow being the final projected estimate of the overall contract value to Burnley Football Club. But Barry steered the good ship Burnley out of choppy waters and navigated their first passage ever into the Premier League ocean in 2009.

Not a lot of fans herald their chairman with such vigorous heartfelt appreciation but on this last day the chant of," There's only one Barry Kilby!" echoed around all three sides of the home support as he stood up to receive a deserved acclaim of this massive contribution to the welfare of his home town club.

Barry would still be on the board of directors while he fought a more personnel well documented battle with the demonic disease that is cancer.

I'm extremely pleased to report that up to press, and over four years later Barry is in remission, and with former Co-Chairman John Banaszkiewicz having to also take a step down to be a director due to a heavy workload of family and business commitments, he has took on the mantle of Vice Chairman as support to new incumbent Mike Garlick.

Having met all three I would have to conclude that without any bias they are all dyed in the wool Clarets fans each of which share one aim – to do their damndest to ensure Burnley Football Club achieve and maintain the position of being one of the top teams in English football.

It's a far cry from when I asked the equally loyal but consistently cantankerous Bob Lord for his autograph as I returned from Carlisle rail station after a league match in the 1970's.

"Would ya mind signing my programme please Mr Lord?", was my somewhat tentative enquiry to a larger than life character who looked suitably peeved after our 2-1 defeat.

"What d'ya want that for?", replied an agitated Bob as he motioned towards the train carriage grumpily,

"Because you're our Chairman Mr Lord," I answered to his condescending tone.

With that he reluctantly scribbled his name on the front page before scuttling off unimpressed by my written request.

The difference between that era of exclusivity and the present are markedly stark by comparison. Of course the boardroom remains a sanctuary for its members, but you're just as likely to see a whole cross-section of ordinary friends and supporters on their invitation list within the adjoining bars and hospitality sections.

There you'll regularly find another director who it must be said I have seen at more pre-season trips abroad than any other over the last four decades. He is Clive Holt who is originally from down south but like myself adopted the club and fell in love with it when he moved north.

Funding each trip himself Clive has travelled the world following Burnley and for that he deserves immense credit.

Then there's Brendan Flood, perhaps the most enthusiastic director of them all. The property developer originally joined in 2006 and was appointed Head of Operations but left in January of 2013 citing personal reasons.

An ebullient character who himself brought out a book after Burnley's initial promotion to the Premiership titled 'Big club, small town and me! In it he documents growing up watching Burnley of course, but also reveals that at one stage the now departed Colonel Gaddafi who was Libya's leader for so many years wanted to invest in the club after admiring their football in the Sixties.

The remaining two relatively recent additions to the team are Brian Nelson and Terry Crabb who I haven't conversed with, but once again each are keen Burnley fans. With Brendan Flood re-joining in 2014 making a directorate of five.

Don't get me wrong I've been as vociferous as anyone in campaigns to oust chairman when I believed we should have been performing better in the dark days of the Seventies and Eighties, but equally where credit is due our hierarchy should take their fair share of the accolades. So, a full set of genuinely radical supporters on your board. I bet not many clubs could say the same.

The full-time round up…

So that was the past fifty years plus of my footballing life in two parts, but what of the future?

Well, we have to start with easily the biggest under-achieving football nation in the entire world given their resources and vast pool of potential talent – and that of course, although it hurts me to say it ….is England.

A team that promises so much, yet yields so little time after time, but will still get 80,000 plus to support them even after all their abject failings for a World Cup qualifier against the minnows of Malta in October 2016, and even similar attendances for subsequent friendly matches.

REMARKABLE!

There is probably little hope of England winning any silverware in my lifetime, that after waiting over half a century since they last did so. A victory that kick-started not only myself but hundreds of thousands into attending live matches more frequently.

Following the ignominy of their latest cringeworthy exit at the hands of tiny Iceland in the 2016 European Championships the unconvincing and generally unintelligible Roy Hodgson paid the ultimate price for his lack of tactical nous by being relieved of his managerial duties.

INSCRUTABLE!

But he wasn't the first and he wouldn't be the last of inadequate managerial appointments set on by a Football Association that wouldn't know a good boss if he poked them in the eye. An incongruous outfit on a par with the closed shop mentality that was F.I.F.A. until its recent dismantling. Until these powers that be have a root and branch clear out within their ranks I don't expect anything to change both on and off the pitch!

DEPLORABLE!

Unbelievably seven of their nominations have been shown the door over the last four decades alone through the actions of nobody but themselves.

Let's start with Don Revie 1974-1977 who thought it a good idea to sell his story to a national newspaper for £20,000, claiming that he was handing in his resignation for a position with the United Arab Emirates, well before he had given the F.A. any notification about his plans. His parting quote being,

"Nearly everyone in the country wants me out, so I am giving them what they want".

He received a ten-year ban from English football for this misdemeanour which was later lifted on appeal.

CULPABLE!

Even Sir Bobby Robson who had the longest reign of those banished from 1982 – 1990 committed the equivalent of a football own goal by controversially announcing that he would be 'jumping ship' to Dutch club PSV Eindhoven as soon as the 1990 World Cup tournament was over, even though England by his guidance had come within a penalty shoot-out of reaching the final.

REGRETTABLE!

Then there was old 'Turnip Head' Graham Taylor 1990 – 1993 whose reputation was left to vegetate after a revealing Channel 4 fly-on-the –wall documentary which showed him making a series of nonsensical touchline exclamations including the eternally comical "Do I not like that!" retort as he agonisingly witnessed his charges exit Euro 92 qualification by way of those other root vegetables the Swedes. (Although that game proved to be Graham Taylor's eventual downfall the high regard that he was held surfaced after his death from a heart attack on January 12th 2017 when tributes to the man poured in. He was 72.)

LAUGHABLE!

El-Tel followed from 1994-1996 and of course restored a degree of misplaced national pride by getting us to the semi-finals of Euro 96 on home soil before bowing out on penalties predictably to the Germans. Terry Venables was your stereotypical wheeler-dealer cockney geezer type and he left to deal with five court cases pending that required his attention in true Arthur Daley style.

Glenn 'God' Hoddle bestowed his David Icke views to the nation by first shamelessly consulting faith healer Eileen Drewery about his football practices, then contemptibly suggested that disabled people were being punished for their sins in a former life. His tenure from 1996-1999 being terminated in the February of that year. Amazingly this heartless being, is being touted to once again reclaim his former role.

DESPICABLE!

Not forgetting the Viking pork sword that was Sven-Goran Eriksson who ruled our country not his, from 2001-2006 and rogered fellow Swede Ulrika Jonsson whilst living with Nancy Dell'Olio.

Then came the newspaper expose in 2006 when our Sven told a fake Sheikh reporter that he would be happy to become Aston Villa manager as part of a suggested takeover.

INSATIABLE!

Tommy Cooper lookalike Fabio Capello took over from 2008 – 2012 as the desperate F.A. once again went continental. Fabio, whose name would be a perfect fit for a male stripper criticised the F.A. on Italian television after they had taken away John Terry's captaincy in a race row – against his wishes. Two days later he walked after talks with former chairman David Bernstein. Capello was also criticised for devising his own index ranking of players performances.

LAMENTABLE!

And of course the F.A.'s ineptitude didn't end there as 'Big' Sam Allardyce was promoted to the position he had always craved. A previous accusation of being involved in unscrupulous dealings that in fairness he was acquitted of, should certainly have at least been flagged up before his appointment as a warning to his future conduct.

So just who would make a good England manager after the abject failure of so many over the last fifty years?

Ron Greenwood C.B.E. was born at Worsthorne just a couple of miles outside Burnley and managed the national football team from 1977 until 1982. Having been in charge of 55 games his record read won 33, drawn 12 and lost just 10 giving a more than decent winning return of just 60%.

Well call me biased if you want, but I'm quite sure that a good percentage of neutral supporters would echo my call for another two present managers with Burnley connections, both having worked wonders to maintain their membership of the Premier league thus far. Having got to know both fairly well, here are my views.

Our former manager Eddie Howe has become one of the most-wanted men in English football. He has achieved wonders with the 'Cherries' , not only taking them up, but keeping them there for a third consecutive season at least. He retains an acute tactical awareness.

Talk of him taking the Three Lions job may be premature, but each time the vacancy arises his name will always crop up.

Then of course there is our very own Sean Dyche. With two promotions to the top tier within three seasons under his belt and this time staying there, his c.v. makes impressive reading.

Both are english first and foremost, which should be an automatic prerequisite to applying for the appointment of national team manager, and each are young enough to apply a winning mentality along with an innovative strategy towards team selection. I predict that either one, or both as a dual management partnership will be at the head of affairs within the next decade, and then England fans can really 'dare to dream'.

As for myself, you can be sure that I will endeavour to carry on supporting my team through hell or high water. Even if my current personal attendance record of just the one failure to get there in 48 years for whatever reason does come to an end in the future I will, if able, carry on regardless.

And if I do manage to maintain both my health and ongoing run, you can be sure that a further collection of football related japes, scrapes, tales and stories will be collected in Part Three to recollect that last quarter of a century of support.

That will take me up to around the year 2042 when I would be approaching the ripe old age of 89. However given my chosen lifestyle which has no doubt taken a heavy toll on my body that would seem highly unlikely.

But fear not! A contingency plan is in place to employ a literal 'ghost' writer upon my eventual demise to complete the trilogy. After 'Got To Be There!' & 'Still There!' I have suggested it might go under the title of 'Not There Any More!'

Until that day, I leave you with a final rallying call to inspire your loyalty.

Whoever your chosen team, be it Burnley, Bury, Bognor Regis or all those in between, remember, if you only make one pledge make it this.

Whatever happens to your club, it is yours for life. Through all the dizzy highs and all the rubbish lows, throughout your best dream or worst nightmare seasons, always, but always.....

"Keep The Faith!"

Dave Burnley August 2017

Past Players/associates with Burnley Football Club

Unfortunately there simply isn't the space to write eulogies on each and every member associated with Burnley Football Club that has passed on, or it would turn into a book of condolence. As for the cases that I have written about it is generally because I have had personal contact with them to varying degrees.

This in no way diminished the significance of their departure as this season by season order of remembrance denotes from the beginning of Part Two.

SEASON	NAME	POSITION
1986-87	Reg. Attwell	Half-Back
1987-88	Peter Kippax	Winger
1988-89	George Waterfield	Full-Back
1989-90	Jimmy Strong	Goalkeeper
1996-97	Tommy Lawton	Centre Forward
1997-98	Keith Newton	Full-Back
1998-99	Harold Mather	Full-Back
1999-2000	Walter Joyce	Half-Back
2001-02	George Bray	Half-Back, Trainer & Kit Man
2001-02	Billy O'Rourke	Goalkeeper
2002-03	Jackie Chew	Winger
2003-04	Billy Morris	Inside-Forward
2006-07	Jimmy Holland	Trainer
2006-07	Brian Miller	Centre/Wing-half, Coach, Chief Scout, Trainer, Manager
2007-08	Albert Maddox	Secretary
	John Jackson	Chairman
	Doctor Ivan	Club Doctor
	Les Shannon	Inside-Forward

SEASON	NAME	POSITION
	Mark Kendall	Goalkeeper
2008-09	Ray Deakin	Centre-Full-Back
2009-10	Billy Ingham	Midfield
	Adam Blacklaw	Goalkeeper
	Tommy Cummings	Centre Half
	Jack Hixon	North East Scout
2010-11	John Benson	Manager 1984-85
	Billy Gray	Winger
	Ralph Coates	Midfield/Forward
	Gordon Haigh	Inside-Forward
2011-12	Jimmy Adamson	Wing Half/Manager 1970-76
2012-13	John Bond	Manager 1983-84
	John Connelly	Winger
	Harry Thomson	Goalkeeper
2013-14	Ronnie Fenton	Inside-Forward
	Harold Rudman	Full-Back
	Paul Comstive	Midfield
	Arthur Bellamy	Inside-Forward/ Midfield
	Gordon Harris	Inside-Forward/ Wing-Half
2014-15	Joe Brown	Wing-Half/Manager 1976/77
	Dave Walker	Wing-Half
	Ian Towers	Winger
2015-16	Brian Hall	Midfield
	Ray Pointer	Centre Forward
	Frank Teasdale	Chairman
	Ian Britton	Midfield/Winger
2016-17	Gerry Gow	Midfield
	Peter Noble	Full-Back/Midfield Forward

To all the above, and any others associated with the club that my have been inadvertently omitted, full credit for getting Burnley F.C. to where they once were, and where they are today.

Sponsors Memories

A massive thank you goes out to all who helped back the publication of this book.

In return I asked my major sponsors for their all-time memory watching Burnley.

Mine was, and remains, the bitter-sweet moment referee George Courtney blew the final whistle to signal the end of the 'Orient game' in 1987 that I personally believe preserved our very existence.

Here are some of the other contributors' 'I was there!' moments.

Mike Garlick, Hertfordshire

There have been many, but one of my proudest moments as chairman was to see the players come away with a point after repelling all raiders at Old Trafford in October 2016's Premier League Fixture.

John Banaszkiewicz, Blackheath London

No contest! March 2014 and we were once again playing our local rivals Blackburn Rovers at Ewood Park. We came from behind to beat them for the first time in just short of 35 years. I was on the away end surrounded by Burnley fans and got completely soaked with beer when our winning goal went in. A great way to celebrate our famous victory.

Alastair Campbell

It has to be Paul Fletcher's bicycle kick strike at Leeds United in March 1974. With his back to goal he smashed the ball home for Burnley's second in a 4-1 demolition. Although it silenced the near 40,000 crowd 'Fletch' has never stopped talking about it since!

Dr Phil Ratcliffe. Highfield, Southampton, Hampshire

Yes!! Simply 4.54p.m. at Wembley Stadium on the 25th May 2009.Our 1-0 victory over Sheffield United in the Championship Play-Off Final.

Andrew & David Smith, Waterfoot, Rowtenstall, Lancs

Scunthorpe at Glanford Park in our promotion year to the old Division one (Championship). Glen Little's goal led to wild celebrations in the centre circle with father and son both amazed and delighted.

Pete Toner, Fulwood, Preston, Lancs

Being a Blackburn Claret it just had to be winning at Ewood Park 2-1 on Sunday 9th March. After almost 35 years up in smoke, now it's time for a period of Claret dominance.

'Tricky' Trev Slack, Heald Green, Stockport, Greater Manchester

September 11th 1965 Burnley 3 Manchester United 0.

The very first game I travelled to on my own at the age of 13 on a Bostock's coach from Macclesfield full of opposition fans. I knew from there on that Turf Moor would be where I would spend my Saturdays.

Dermott O'Neill Maida Vale, London February 12th 1994

Johnny Francis's 2-0 clincher against Cardiff City at Turf Moor in Division Two. Afterwards, an essential pub game of invisible bowls with invisible curling brushes. Johnny entered, and just gazed in amazement.

Mark Griffiths, Winsford, Cheshire

The final whistle at Wembley in the 1-0 victory over Sheffield United to win promotion to the Premier League. So much sheer joy in that moment, the memory will live with me until the day I die.

Dr Stephen Hodgson, Anderton, Near Chorley, Lancs

September 27th 1978 Anglo-Scottish Cup 2nd leg at Celtic Park 2-1 to Burnley.

My decision to travel after the riot at Turf Moor wasn't made until the day of the game. A feeling of apprehension until back on the train south, but goals from Brennan and Kindon made it feel like the biggest adventure in 50 years of support.

Gina & Graham Exton, Duddon, Tarporley, Cheshire

At Hull City November 2011. Losing 2-0 and in despair of a fifth consecutive defeat looming. With 12 minute to go, David Edgar, of all people gets us two in four minutes and Jay Rod nets the winner after three minutes of added time.

Brian Speak, Maidstone, Kent

January 19th 1952. Tommy Cummings scoring probably the best ever goal at Turf Moor in our 2-1 win against Newcastle United.

Bryan (The Poacher), Nantwich, Cheshire

The 'Orient game', 9th May 1987. The rebirth of my beloved Clarets. After that great escape everything else was a bonus.

Keith Riley, Stockport, Greater Manchester

Charlton away last game of the 2015-16 season, as the feeling built up through the game that this was it…and then the final whistle. Champions!

S.SGT Liam Walsh, Kathmandu, Nepal

May 29th 1988. The Sherpa Van Trophy Final v Wolves. As an eight year old kid the moment I entered the terrace to a packed Wembley Stadium was something I will never forget.

Nigel 'Knock-Off' Standige, Burnley, Lancs

First memory Everton (H) 1974. First tears Wimbledon (H) F.A.C.1975. Most tears Orient (H) 1987. All promotions but best title win has to be away at Charlton 2016 to clinch the Championship before partying hard with the author!

'Plain' John Smith, Haslingden, Nr. Accrington, Lancs.

Sheffield United V Burnley January 2nd 1993, F.A. Cup 3rd round at Bramhall Lane. Adrian 'Inchy' Heath putting us 2-0 up in front of an 8,000 plus following only to be pegged back 2-2. What a great game and atmosphere.

And Finally... If you see this man please return him
to the address inscribed upon his chest.

Postage paid of course!
First class stamp inked on left shoulder blade.